T0360428

International Economic Integration and Domestic Performance

World Scientific Studies in International Economics
(ISSN: 1793-3641)

The complete list of the published volumes in the series can be found at
http://www.worldscientific.com/series/wssie

58 World Scientific
Studies in
International
Economics

International Economic Integration and Domestic Performance

Mary E Lovely

Syracuse University, USA

World Scientific

NEW JERSEY · LONDON · SINGAPORE · BEIJING · SHANGHAI · HONG KONG · TAIPEI · CHENNAI · TOKYO

Published by

World Scientific Publishing Co. Pte. Ltd.
5 Toh Tuck Link, Singapore 596224
USA office: 27 Warren Street, Suite 401-402, Hackensack, NJ 07601
UK office: 57 Shelton Street, Covent Garden, London WC2H 9HE

British Library Cataloguing-in-Publication Data
A catalogue record for this book is available from the British Library.

World Scientific Studies in International Economics
INTERNATIONAL ECONOMIC INTEGRATION AND DOMESTIC PERFORMANCE

ISBN 978-981-3141-08-7

Desk Editor: Jiang Yulin

Typeset by Stallion Press
Email: enquiries@stallionpress.com

Printed in Singapore

About the Author

Mary E. Lovely is Melvin A. Eggers Economics Faculty Scholar and Professor of Economics at Syracuse University's Maxwell School of Citizenship and Public Affairs, where she serves as chair of the International Relations Program. Dr. Lovely is also a Senior Associate of the Moynihan Institute for Global Affairs and a Research Network Fellow of CES*ifo*, Munich Germany. She was coeditor of *China Economic Review* from 2010–2014. Dr. Lovely's current research programs investigate links between trade liberalization in China and labor market performance in China and in the United States, the role of foreign ownership and processing trade in the pollution intensity of Chinese industries, and the link between wages and access to domestic and foreign markets. Her recent papers focus on innovation in the Chinese solar equipment industry, North Korean export patterns, China and the Trans-Pacific Partnership, and the influence of market access on the geographic dispersion of manufacturing wages. Her work has been published in the *Review of Economics & Statistics*, the *Journal of International Economics*, the *Journal of Development Economics*, *World Economy*, *Regional Science and Urban Economics*, and the *Journal of Public Economics*, among other journals. Her courses for Syracuse University focus on international economics and global markets. She earned a Ph.D. in Economics from the University of Michigan and an MCRP degree from Harvard University.

Preface and Acknowledgements

I am indebted to the co-authors of the articles in this volume for their professional contributions and personal good will. I thank and acknowledge the following publishers (listed in alphabetic order) for permission to reprint the articles contained in this book: Elsevier (Articles 3, 4, 5, 6, 7, 8, 9, 10, 14); MIT Press (Article 11); Oxford University Press (Article 13); Sage (Article 1); Wiley-Blackwell (Articles 2, 12). I am grateful to Robert Stern for the invitation to contribute to this series. Bob offered encouragement and support generously and it was an honor to have known him.

The Maxwell School of Citizenship and Public Affairs at Syracuse University has been my professional home since I received my Ph.D. from the University of Michigan, Ann Arbor. I thank the Economics Department for creating an environment in which research is encouraged and valued. In particular, I thank Douglas Holtz-Eakin, Jan Ondrich, and Stuart Rosenthal for their generosity as colleagues and co-authors. I gratefully acknowledge the Eggers Family for their support of the Melvin A. Eggers Faculty Scholars in Economics. Eggers Scholar support allowed me to access datasets, conferences and colleagues, especially those from East Asia, which I would otherwise not been able to access.

Over the years I have learned much from colleagues in the International Trade and Development Group. I thank, in particular, Devashish Mitra who is a dedicated researcher, insightful critic, and caring friend. I had the good fortune of sharing the early years of building the Trade and Development Group at Maxwell with committed and talented colleagues, including Douglas Nelson, J. David Richardson, and Theresa Greaney. David Popp, from the Department of Public Administration and International Affairs, and Judy Dean, of Brandeis University, graciously allowed me to join them in work on environmental topics. I continue to be delighted by the accomplishments of the doctoral students I have had the privilege of working with, including Xuepeng Liu, Cong S. Pham, Shalini Sharma, Puman Ouyang, and Fariha Kamal.

Lastly, I acknowledge the endless patience and encouragement of John M. Yinger, who made it all possible.

Mary E. Lovely
Syracuse, New York, USA
June, 2016

Contents

The Power of Mobility

Growing up in the smallest state in the United States, Rhode Island, my early life was shaped by the power of mobile capital to influence local employment and wages. As a teen, I watched older family members struggle to find new jobs as factory after factory closed, leaving them with unwanted skills and poor health from years of breathing in fibers and fumes. I watched the Blackstone River flow by in ever-changing colors, depending on the dyes used on any given day in the upstream mills, until the pollution followed the jobs to places less restrictive and more profitable.

With my father serving as a local councilman, I also witnessed the limited effectiveness of local government attempts to counterbalance the power of capital's mobility. The center of our city emptied out, despite the construction of a downtown pedestrian mall. Oil price shocks, the lure of non-union locations in the American south, and import competition from Japan combined to overwhelm the advantages of New England's skilled work force. The region's textile, leather, and costume jewelry clusters slowly vanished. In the 1980s, higher unemployment, slower wage growth, and depressed housing prices were commonplace in the blue-collar cities and towns surrounding Brown University, an institution founded, in part, by wealth acquired through international trade.

Mobility rewards those who possess it and some of those I knew as a child profited handsomely from larger markets, lower labor costs, and emerging opportunities in the service sector. Hasbro, a toy company derived from a local textile remnant business, evolved to become the third largest toy company in the world. It remains headquartered in Pawtucket, Rhode Island, but toys are no longer made there. The owners and managers of many smaller companies profited from expansion into international markets, through increased specialization and entry into global supply chains, and by delivering professional services to those investing outside the local area. Younger people, like myself, completed college and entered professions, often leaving their hometowns behind to find rewarding careers as doctors, teachers, programmers, engineers, and business executives.

The papers in this volume explore the power of international markets and factor mobility to influence government policy, firm location choice, wages, and the environment. The first section considers the welfare effects and optimal design of retail sales taxes when consumers can avoid taxation by crossing jurisdictional boundaries. The second section highlights the role of scale economies in the design of industrial policies and as a determinant of firm location. The third section explores the influence of environmental policy on foreign investor's location decisions and the role of trade and technology in promoting environmental regulation. The final section considers the determinants of wage differences, the attraction of low wages for foreign investors, and misallocations of labor in an emerging economy, China. The collection, taken as a whole, highlights the power of factor mobility to determine the location of economic activity, domestic tax burdens, and the welfare implications of domestic policy alternatives.

Part I: Sales Taxation and Cross-border Evasion

Many local governments rely on taxes that may be evaded or avoided by mobile consumers or households. Because such activity results in lost revenue, governments tend to portray such activity as socially inefficient. The case for welfare loss is compounded by the possibility of wasteful expenditure of resources used for evasion or avoidance.

The two papers in this sector focus on local commodity taxation. They present simple analyses that offer insights that apply to a wider array of taxes. The first chapter shows how households' attempts to avoid taxation can be considered in tax design. It provides modified versions of the inverse elasticity rule, proportionate shrinkage rule, and covariance interpretation of the optimal tax conditions modified for the case of costly noncompliance. The second paper (Chapter 2) in this section argues that more enforcement is not always welfare improving. Indeed, the analysis shows that the welfare effect of evasion depends on how well designed the tax system is and how effective enforcement resources are in deterring costly noncompliance.

Part II: Scale Economies, Policy, Firm Location, and Trade Patterns

It is easy to be inspired by the beautiful modeling of Wilfred Ethier (1982), who offers an illuminating analysis of the gains from specialization and trade in producer inputs. The Ethier model provides a useful way to conceptualize industry-level returns to variety in producer inputs and, thus, the benefits of global value chains. Various versions of this model, with an emphasis on scale economies and imperfect competition, provide the foundation for the papers in Part II of this volume.

The first paper (Chapter 3) evolved from my doctoral dissertation. It explores the ways in which a capital subsidy can be used to mimic targeted industrial policy, which may be inconsistent with WTO obligations, when productivity in one sector depends on the size of the national industry. The analysis shows that the desirability of capital subsidies depends on how reliant the economy is on foreign investment and how sensitive foreign investors are to factor price changes. If capital is highly mobile, the analysis shows that capital subsidies can do much of the work of targeted industrial policies and can raise welfare in a small economy, even if much of the capital is foreign owned.

The analysis in Chapter 4 emphasizes both increasing returns to scale and imperfect competition in the design of optimal policy. External economies of scale may be justification for subsidization of an activity but such a policy's full welfare impact depends on how it interacts with the distortion caused by deviations from marginal cost pricing. In this paper, Douglas Holtz-Eakin and I show that generally two instruments are needed for first-best outcomes and that optimal policy may require both subsidies and taxes on the target industry. We conclude that subsidies to externality generating sectors may do more harm than good and that information on market structure as well as technology is needed to intervene productively.

With little empirical evidence on how government policy influences manufacturing productivity, Douglas Holtz-Eakin and I incorporate public infrastructure into a model that features both firm-level scale economies and industry-level external returns to variety. The analysis, reproduced as Chapter 5, shows that theoretically the effect of public capital on manufacturing output is indeterminate when competition is imperfect. We assemble a state-level panel dataset to estimate the effect of public infrastructure on both manufacturing output and variety. We find that public capital has no significant effect on output per firm but a positive and significant effect on manufacturing variety, as measured by the number of establishments. This study provides one of the first attempts to use an equilibrium model to analyze public capital.

Chapter 6 looks at how policies in other countries, in this case the level of difficulty faced by exporters seeking market access, influences the spatial pattern of domestic firms. Stuart S. Rosenthal, Shalini Sharma and

I hypothesize that the benefits of information sharing for firms engaged in exporting to difficult locations will result in spatial clustering of their headquarters. We test this hypothesis by applying differencing methods to disaggregate industry data for the United States. Our results suggest that when information on foreign markets is more difficult to obtain, exporter headquarter activity is more agglomerated.

Scale economies influence trade patterns as well as optimal policies, firm productivity and firm location. In Chapter 7, Judith M. Dean, Jesse Mora and I explore the intricate patterns of trade between China and two of its most important partners, the United States and Japan. Analyzing detailed trade data from China Customs, we find extensive two-way trade, deep vertical specialization, and a prominent role for foreign-invested enterprises in China's relationship with both the U.S. and Japan. These features of trade flows are consistent with a prominent role for scale economies in shaping bilateral commercial relations.

The final paper in this section, Chapter 8 revisits the evidence in favor of a home-market effect on bilateral trade patterns, as developed and supported empirically by Hanson and Xiang (2004). The home-market prediction is that production in industries with high transport costs and high product differentiation will be more concentrated in large countries. Using the trade flows studied by Hanson and Xiang, as well as alternative settings, we investigate the relationship between relevant industry characteristics and the strength of the home-market effect. We find that support in the data for the predicted relationships is not robust to standard variations in gravity model estimation techniques nor to alternative groupings of countries and regions.

Part III: Environmental Policy in the Open Economy

The literature on trade and the environment is large, as befits a topic of great importance for the welfare of all peoples. My contributions have centered on the role of mobile capital and global markets in supporting or undermining local efforts to improve environmental outcomes.

The papers presented in this section illustrate two different strands of inquiry. Chapter 9, co-authored with Judith M. Dean and Hua Wang, investigates the extent to which variation in local environmental stringency influences the location of multinational production. We collect data on foreign investment flows into China, including information on the province into which the capital flowed and the industry of the new enterprise. These data allow us to do something that was largely absent from the empirical literature at the time — look for differences in the responsiveness to environmental controls based on the pollution intensity of the investor's activity. We are also able to observe whether the investment was made by investors from Macao, Taiwan, and Hong Kong or from other sources. We leverage these details to test whether investors from these locations differ in their attraction to weak standards than investors from higher income countries.

The second paper in this section, Chapter 10, views the relationship between environmental policy and international markets from the opposite direction. Instead of taking policy as given, David Popp and I ask whether better access to international abatement technology is associated with a higher likelihood of adopting coal-fired power plant regulation. The genesis of the paper was a preliminary analysis of where coal-fired power plants used abatement technology. We quickly realized that abatement equipment is installed when it is required and that the real variation in adoption comes from cross-country variation in regulation. This observation led us to create a database that catalogs SO_2 and NO_X regulations in all countries that have coal-fired power plants. We combine these data with a patent-based measure of the technology frontier to ask whether technology innovation by early adopters influences the timing of new regulation in non-innovating countries.

We find that international economic integration eases access to environmentally friendly technologies and leads to earlier adoption, all else equal, of power-plant regulation in non-innovating countries. Our analysis is noteworthy for its treatment of how regulation adoption is associated with domestic protection and international market power. Our results suggest that domestic trade protection allows the costs of regulation to be shifted to domestic consumers, while market power due to country size allows large countries to shift costs onto foreign consumers. We also find that other political economy factors, such as the quality of domestic coal and election years, are important determinants of when regulation are adopted.

Part IV: International Economic Integration and Wages

The impact of international economic integration on domestic wages has emerged as a flashpoint for political forces favoring the reinstatement of barriers to trade and migration. The papers in this section offer a number of vantage points on how globalization influences wages using the experience of China. China offers a useful laboratory both because of its size and because of the rapid pace at which it has integrated with the world economy.

Development of information technologies and decreasing logistical costs promote the growth of global value chains, defined as the fragmentation of the production process across multiple locations. China has been the recipient of much of the direct investment flowing to developing countries over the last 25 years within these value chains and its labor markets have been transformed by the impact of this inflow.

The first two papers in this section examine the attraction of low wages for foreign investors. The analysis in Chapter 11 addresses a major technical difficulty in the literature, the positive correlation of local wages and beneficial local amenities, which can lead to the erroneous inference that low wages are not an attraction for foreign investors. Xuepeng Liu, Jan Ondrich and I address this issue by using a control function in our estimation of conditional logit models of location choice, allowing us to account for unobserved location-specific attributes that may be correlated with the local wage. Examining the decisions of 2,884 firms investing in China between 1993 and 1996, we find that the location of labor-intensive investment is highly sensitive to provincial wage differences and that this sensitivity declines as the skill intensity of the industry increases. We also find that a failure to control for local amenities correlated with local wages leads to a substantial downward bias in the estimated wage elasticities. These results confirm the importance of local wages in the formation of global value chains.

The second paper in this section, Chapter 12, extends our examination of the behavior of foreign investors. Instead of considering only how the skill intensity of an activity affects the choice of production location, we recognize that investors are also influenced by their ability to pass cost differences along to final customers. We again use a control-function approach within a conditional logit model, this time to test whether firms in industries facing highly elastic final demand conditions are more sensitive to provincial variations in wages than are other industries. We find strong evidence that final-market demand conditions play a role in the movement of manufacturing activities to low-wage locations, with firms operating in highly competitive markets more sensitive to wage costs. This insight suggests a role for policies that address consumers as well as those that target investors or host governments alone.

The third paper in this section, Chapter 13, turns to differences in labor productivity between the state sector and the private sector in China. Many analysts have noted that state-owned enterprises tend to be less productive than their private-sector peers, both in their use of capital and in their use of labor. Using balance sheet data from all major manufacturing firms in China, Fariha Kamal and I focus on differences in the marginal revenue product of labor across firms within each industry, distinguished by ownership status. We find that labor productivity varies systematically within industries by ownership type and that non-state firms face implicit labor taxation relative to state-owned enterprises. We also find that, in keeping with ongoing reforms of the state sector, ownership differentials fall over time, with gaps between non-state enterprises and state-owned enterprises falling by about half over time between 1998–2002 and 2002–2005.

The final paper in the volume, Chapter 14, considers how global markets shape spatial variation in wages within China. Reform of China's planned economy unleashed massive movements of workers across sectors, regions, and enterprises leading to both higher wages and increased income inequality. Key policy determinants of this transformation include restructuring of urban enterprises and massive public-sector layoffs beginning in 1995, the gradual erosion of constraints on rural-to-urban migration, and adoption of the 2004 Labor Law, which remade employer-employee relations and expanded employment flexibility.

Fariha Kamal, Pumon Ouyang, and I view spatial wage variation through the lens of the "new economic geography," which emphasizes the relation between access to supplier and consumer markets and the wages firms can pay in any given production location. Using information on the wages and characteristics of individual workers located in cities across China, we find that wages are higher in locations with better access to domestic and international markets. We also find that this sensitivity increased between 1995 and 2002, in keeping with the development of more flexible wage setting and labor allocations over the time period.

Taken together, the papers in this volume offer new perspectives on how international economic integration influences domestic economic performance. In particular, the research offers new evidence on the design and effectiveness of policy, where firms locate their headquarters and overseas production, how innovation affects the adoption of environmental regulations, and the performance of domestic labor markets. In all these areas, often only weak support exists for strongly held beliefs about the harm or benefit of greater openness. The papers here suggest that the effect of deeper international integration is shaped by domestic institutions, industry characteristics, and firm performance.

References

Ethier, W. J., 1982. "National and International Returns to Scale in the Modern Theory of International Trade," *American Economic Review* 72: 388–405.

Hanson, G. H. and Xiong, C., 2004. "The Home Market Effect and Bilateral Trade Patterns," *American Economic Review* 94: 1108–1129.

PART I
SALES TAXATION AND CROSS-BORDER EVASION

Because noncompliance has efficiency and equity implications, it should be a concern in the design of the commodity tax structure. This article derives the optimal commodity tax conditions and modifications to their standard interpretation when consumers engage in costly border crossing to evade local taxes. It presents a model of costly noncompliance behavior and a modified version of Roy's theorem describing the effect on indirect utility of a tax change when cross-border shopping occurs. This modified Roy's theorem permits the inverse elasticity rule, proportionate shrinkage rule, and covariance interpretation of the optimal tax conditions to be adapted to the case of costly noncompliance.

OPTIMAL COMMODITY TAXATION
WITH COSTLY NONCOMPLIANCE

MARY E. LOVELY
Syracuse University

Because noncompliance has efficiency and equity implications, it should be a concern in the design of the commodity tax structure. Despite an extensive literature on optimal commodity taxation, however, no revision has been made of standard interpretations of the optimal tax structure accounting for the possibility that consumers engage in costly noncompliance.[1] As noted by Mirrlees (1986), an "aspect of public policy omitted from the basic models is the evasion and enforcement of government policies" (p. 1199). This article derives the optimal commodity tax conditions and modifications to their standard interpretation when consumers engage in costly border crossing to evade local commodity taxes.

The possibility of commodity tax evasion arises primarily from the heterogeneity of local commodity tax rates, which enable households to reduce their tax burden by crossing the border into a lower-taxing jurisdiction. Because most American states that levy a general sales

AUTHOR'S NOTE: The author thanks, without implication, Paul Courant, Roger Gordon, Douglas Holtz-Eakin, Michael Wasylenko, David Wildasin, and John Yinger for helpful comments.

PUBLIC FINANCE QUARTERLY, Vol. 23 No. 1, January 1995 115-130
© 1995 Sage Publications, Inc.

tax also levy a use tax, which in practice is a sales tax on purchases by residents made in other jurisdictions, this border-crossing behavior is a form of tax evasion. States have a limited ability to enforce the use tax, given restrictions on their power to force businesses to collect it.[2] Empirical evidence supports the belief that U.S. consumers do engage in border crossing in response to interjurisdiction tax differentials.[3]

Interjurisdictional differentials also exist in the European Community, which in its progress toward a "Europe without frontiers" faces an increase in cross-border shopping. Many of these cross-border purchases are legal, as there is currently no limit on the amount a traveler may import for personal use.[4] Nonetheless, these purchases are a form of noncompliance (i.e., tax avoidance), and they influence both the equity and the efficiency of member states' commodity taxation. Difference in value-added tax rates within the EC are large enough to encourage cross-border shopping. As of January 1, 1993, standard value-added tax rates range from 15% in Germany, Spain, and Luxembourg to 25% in Denmark. Moreover, rates on a variety of goods such as children's clothes, alcohol, and tobacco vary more widely.[5]

Commodity tax compliance is a concern in optimal tax design because it affects the excess burden of taxation as well as the distribution of the tax burden. Noncompliance is an efficiency issue because of its effect on tax rates and because it is costly. First, to the extent that noncompliance reduces commodity tax revenue, governments with a revenue requirement are forced to raise tax rates in response, which may raise the excess burden of taxation.[6] Second, border crossing uses real resources, which are a waste from society's viewpoint.[7] Indeed, it is precisely because border crossing is costly that commodity tax differentials can persist when borders are open. These wasted resources constitute another source of deadweight loss. In addition to these efficiency concerns, noncompliance affects the equity of a given tax structure to the extent that it alters the distribution of the tax burden by income group.[8]

The second section of this article describes a model of a regional economy in which local tax rates differ. This section also describes the household's problem and characterizes the household's choices as to the quantity and location of purchases. The third section presents the government's problem and develops a modified version of Roy's theorem to describe the conditions for optimal taxation. We turn next to the case of identical consumers and derive an inverse elasticity rule and a proportionate shrinkage rule accounting for costly noncompliance. Finally, through the use of Diamond's (1975) covariance interpretation, we extend the optimal tax characterization to the case of heterogeneous consumers.

A MODEL OF BORDER CROSSING

Consider a small mixed economy operating within a larger economic unit. Among the class of all possible indirect tax schemes, the government uses only a linear commodity tax. Moreover, consumers and firms always participate on opposite sides of each market in which they transact, and all commodity taxation takes place on this set of transactions. An implication of this assumption is that if intermediate goods in production and resource transactions among consumers exist, they are not taxed.

All agents in the economy behave competitively. Firms choose net output to maximize profits using technologies that do not involve externalities. There are no profits as all firms use technology exhibiting constant returns to scale. All goods are traded and given free trade between jurisdictions, producer prices of traded goods are the same everywhere. The taxing jurisdiction is economically small, implying that changes in commodity tax rates do not affect producer prices of traded goods.[9] Firms are legally responsible for tax collections and reporting, and firms within the taxing jurisdiction act in complete compliance with the tax law.[10]

The household's choice of net consumption is denoted by the vector C^h, where net sales of factor services appear as negative elements. In the absence of lump-sum income, purchases of goods by the household must be offset by sales of factor services to firms. There are $J+1$ commodities in the economy with labor, the only factor service, denoted commodity 0 and the remaining J commodities consumer goods.[11] Labor is not subject to taxation, and it serves as numeraire with $p_o = 1$. The price vector faced by the household for transactions within the taxation jurisdiction is $p+t^d$ where p is the vector of producer prices and t^d is the corresponding vector of home taxes.

Tax evasion may be the product of consumer or firm decision making.[12] We focus here on the consumer and build the model on the presumption that a consumer's decision to evade taxes is motivated by economic factors alone. In particular, consumers receive no disutility from behaving illegally by evading the commodity tax. Consumers are depicted here as choosing between purchases within the home jurisdiction and purchases outside the jurisdiction, with their behavior influenced by commodity tax rates (which determine the benefits of evasion) and by the costs of noncompliance (which determine the costs of evasion).

The household is able to make purchases of traded goods outside or inside the jurisdiction. The consumption vector, C^h, is the sum of the vector of net purchases made in the home jurisdiction, C^{dh}, and the vector of net purchases made in the neighboring (foreign) jurisdiction, C^{fh}.[13] Because producer prices are the same everywhere, p is the price received by firms for transactions occurring outside the border of the home jurisdiction. Firms in the neighboring jurisdiction do not collect the tax for the home jurisdiction. Rather, they collect taxes at the neighboring rates, given by the vector t^f. We assume that some elements of t^f are strictly less than the corresponding elements in t^d. Thus the household can evade commodity taxation by making purchases across the border.

Because the home jurisdiction is small, it is assumed that the neighboring jurisdiction does not change its tax rates in response to revenue-neutral tax changes by the home government. Moreover, it is assumed that the home jurisdiction has no significant opportunity for tax exporting and thus is not concerned with the behavior of residents of the neighboring jurisdiction.[14] These assumptions simplify the analysis by removing the need to model foreign as well as home behavior. Whereas tax competition issues involving the behavior of foreign governments or residents arise in many settings, we do not address such competition here where the taxing jurisdiction is perceived to be economically small by its neighbors.

We assume that the government funds some activity through commodity taxation without a source of lump-sum revenue. The commodity tax revenue requirement is denoted G and is measured in terms of the numeraire, labor. We assume that border crossing uses resources, also expressed in terms of labor. These resources may be thought of as untaxed transportation costs. Transport costs are assumed to be an increasing, differentiable, and quasi-convex function of the quantity of foreign purchases and are denoted $R^h(C^f)$.[15]

The household's problem[16] with costly evasion is

$$\text{Max } U^h[I - \sum_{k=1}^{j}(p_k(C_k^{dh}+C_k^{fh}) + t_k^d C_k^{dh} + t_k^f C_k^{fh}) - R^h(C^f), C_1^{dh}+C_1^{fh},\ldots,C_J^{dh}+C_J^{fh}]$$

subject to $C_k^{dh} \geq 0; \quad k=1,\ldots,J$
$ C_k^{fh} \geq 0; \quad k=1,\ldots,J$

where I indicates lump-sum income in terms of labor and where the budget constraint has been used to solve for C_o^h.[17] $U(\bullet)$ is a twice differentiable, strictly quasi-concave utility function. Letting U_j^h be $\partial U^h/\partial C_j^h$, the Kuhn-Tucker conditions for the household's problem are[18]

$$U_j^h - U_o^h(p_j + t_j^d) \leq 0, \quad C_j^{dh} \geq 0, \quad C_j^{dh}(U_j^h - U_o^h(p_j + t_j^d)) = 0$$

$$U_j^h - U_o^h(p_j + t_j^f + R_j^h) \leq 0, \quad C_j^{fh} \geq 0, \quad C_j^{fh}(U_j^h - U_o^h(p_j + t_j^f + R_j^h)) = 0 \tag{1}$$

where $R_j^h \equiv \partial R^h(C^f)/\partial C_j^f$. By setting the wage at unity, U_o^h is a measure of the marginal utility of income.

By the quasi-concavity of U, the quasi-convexity of $R(C^f)$ and nonsatiation, the Arrow-Enthoven sufficiency conditions for a maximum are satisfied. Three types of goods can be distinguished. The first type includes those purchased only domestically, for which $t_j^d - t_j^f \leq R_j^h(\overline{C}^{fh})$ where $\overline{C}^{fh}$ is the chosen vector of foreign purchases. The second type of good is purchased in both locations, with $t_j^d - t_j^f = R_j^h(\overline{C}^{fh})$. The third type of good is purchased only across the border, with $t_j^d - t_j^f \geq R_j^h(\overline{C}^{fh})$. Because the resource cost of noncompliance affects the consumption bundle, it affects the level of utility achieved by the household as well as the level of expenditure. If we let α be the vector of parameters of the resource function, we can express indirect utility for household h as $V^h(p,t^d,t^f,I;\alpha)$ and the expenditure function as E^h $(p,t^d,t^f,U;\alpha)$.

OPTIMAL COMMODITY TAX STRUCTURE

The government's problem is to choose the vector t^d to maximize a Bergson-Samuelson social welfare function, subject to its revenue requirement of G.[19] Labor sales by households to firms are not taxed, so t_o equals zero. There are J taxable commodities and H households. The optimal tax problem with costly noncompliance may be stated as

$$\text{Max}_{t^d} \ W[V^1(p,t^d,t^f,I;\alpha), \ldots, V^H(p,t^d,t^f,I;\alpha)]$$

$$\text{subject to} \quad G \leq \sum_h \sum_j t_j^d C_j^{dh}$$

where the summation over j runs from 0 to J and the summation over h runs from 1 to H. I assume that a solution exists and that the Lagrangian conditions are necessary.[20]

Assigning a multiplier of μ to the government budget constraint, the first-order conditions for a maximum with respect to the kth tax rate are[21]

$$\sum_h \frac{\partial W}{\partial V^h} \frac{\partial V^h}{\partial t_k^d} + \mu \left\{ \sum_h C_k^{dh} + \sum_h \sum_j t_j^d \frac{\partial C_j^{dh}}{\partial t_k} \right\} = 0, \quad k = 1, 2, \ldots, J. \quad (2)$$

To simplify these conditions, we note that the change in household h's indirect utility resulting from a change in t_k can be written

$$\frac{\partial V^h}{\partial t_k} = \sum_j U_j^h \left\{ \frac{\partial C_j^{dh}}{\partial t_k} + \frac{\partial C_j^{fh}}{\partial t_k} \right\}, \quad (3)$$

where $U_j^h = \partial U^h / \partial C_j$. Without tax evasion, this expression involves no distinction of goods based on location of purchase and can be simplified using Roy's theorem. With tax evasion, modification of this method is needed as some portion of consumption escapes taxation and thus an increase in t_k by one unit will not cost C_k^h in terms of the numeraire.

The modified application of Roy's theorem is derived by differentiating the consumer's budget constraint with respect to t_k^d:

$$0 = C_k^{dh} + \sum_j \left\{ (p_j + t_j^f)\frac{\partial C_j^{dh}}{\partial t_k^d} + (p_j + t_j^f)\frac{\partial C_j^{fh}}{\partial t_k^d} + R_j^h \frac{\partial C_j^{fh}}{\partial t_k^d} \right\}. \tag{4}$$

Using the first-order conditions for the consumer's problem, given by (1), this expression can be written as[22]

$$-\lambda^h C_k^{dh} = \sum_j U_j^h \left\{ \frac{\partial C_j^{dh}}{\partial t_k} + \frac{\partial C_j^{fh}}{\partial t_k} \right\}. \tag{5}$$

Thus the appropriate form of Roy's theorem is

$$\frac{\partial V^h}{\partial t_k^d} = -\lambda^h C_k^{dh}, \tag{6}$$

which describes the effect on indirect utility of a change in the home region consumer price when some portion of consumption may not be subject to taxation. Although the consumer may adjust consumption and the location of purchases in response to a marginal tax increase, these adjustments have no first-order effect on utility.

Because the characterizations of the optimal tax structure that follow rely on this application of Roy's theorem, it is useful to consider the role of resource costs as a source of deadweight loss. Samuelson (1986) notes that taxes that can be fully evaded should be avoided as the resulting distortions are incurred without compensating revenue.[23] Yet expression (6), which measures the effect on consumer's welfare of a tax increase, does not explicitly include the marginal effect of the tax on resource costs (waste). The reason for this exclusion, of course, is attributable to the consumer's optimization. Adjustments to purchasing locations in response to the tax have only a second-order effect on welfare. These resource costs, however, have influenced the value of both λ and C_k^d. Moreover, whereas resource costs do not explicitly figure into marginal loss expressions, they do appear in total deadweight loss calculations.[24]

Letting $\beta^h = (\partial W/\partial V^h)\lambda^h$, the social marginal utility of income for household h, the optimal tax structure meets the conditions

$$\sum_h \beta^h C_k^{dh} = \mu \left\{ \sum_h C_k^{dh} + \sum_h \sum_j t_j \frac{\partial C_j^{dh}}{\partial t_k} \right\} \quad k = 1, 2, \ldots, J. \tag{7}$$

These conditions differ from the standard case in that they involve domestically purchased quantities and the responsiveness of domestic quantities to tax changes. We emphasize, however, that these quantities and responsiveness measures depend on foreign as well as home fiscal characteristics. For example, if, for some good m, $t_m^d < t_m^f$, no foreign purchases of m will be made even if t_m^d is slightly raised. However, a higher t_m^d can affect all domestic demands through the usual adjustment of consumption and also through the effect of these adjustments on resource costs, $R(C^f)$. To gain further insight into the optimal tax structure with noncompliance, we turn now to consideration of the standard optimal tax interpretations.

A RAMSEY RULE WITH COSTLY NONCOMPLIANCE

To simplify the specifications used previously, we assume that all households are identical and have identical costs of noncompliance and that the objective of the government is to maximize the utility of a representative household. In this case, the conditions for an optimal tax structure are

$$\lambda C_k^d = \mu \left\{ C_k^d + \sum_j t_j \frac{\partial C_j^d}{\partial t_k} \right\} \quad k = 1, 2, \ldots, J. \tag{8}$$

From these conditions, we obtain a modified "Ramsey rule" if an additional assumption is made.[25] This assumption, the analog to the standard case, is that there are no cross-price effects except in connection with the numeraire, or $\partial C_j^d / \partial t_k = 0$ if $j \neq k$. Besides the well-known restrictions this assumption places on preferences, with noncompliance this assumption also restricts the nature of the resource function. In particular, it implies that consumption adjustments involving good k and the numeraire do not influence C_j^d through their effect on R_j. There will be no such influences if R_j depends only on C_j and not on the full bundle of foreign purchases, C^f. This assumption about the resource cost function is obviously quite restrictive, as are the conditions necessary to derive an inverse elasticity rule in the standard case.

With these cross-price restrictions, the optimal tax structure becomes

$$\frac{\mu - \lambda}{\mu} \frac{1}{\xi_{\ast kk}^d} = \frac{t_k^d}{q_k^d}, \quad k = 1, 2, \ldots, J \tag{9}$$

where

$$\xi_{\ast kk}^d \equiv -\frac{\partial C_k^d}{\partial t_k} \frac{q_k^d}{C_k^d}.$$

The distinction from the standard inverse elasticity rule is clear: Tax rates are lower for those goods with large elasticities for domestic demands, ceteris paribus, where the nature of noncompliance costs influences these elasticities. Beyond the usual cases, such goods may be those with slowly rising costs for noncompliance—that is, those goods that are "cheap" at the margin to purchase across the border.

A PROPORTIONATE SHRINKAGE RULE

In the absence of noncompliance, it has been shown that the optimal tax structure involves an equal proportionate movement along the compensated demand curve for all goods.[26] The proportionate shrinkage rule is more appealing on theoretical grounds than is the Ramsey rule as it requires no special restrictions on the preferences of the representative household. With evasion, however, this shrinkage interpretation is complicated, as is the Ramsey rule, by the ability of consumers to escape taxation on a share of their consumption. A proportionate shrinkage rule with costly noncompliance can be derived, however, by exploiting the logic underlying the modified version of Roy's theorem presented previously. In deriving the rule, we need not place special restrictions on preferences or on the resource cost function, which were necessary for the modified Ramsey rule.

With identical households, the optimal tax conditions are given by (8). Let $\tilde{C}_j^d$ be the compensated demand for good j. The Envelope theorem can be used to show that

$$\frac{\partial E(p, t^d, t^f, U; \alpha)}{\partial t_j^d} = \tilde{C}_j^d(p, t^d, t^f, U; \alpha)$$

where we have assumed that the expenditure function is continuously differentiable. The Slutsky relationship is then

$$\frac{\partial C_j^d}{\partial t_k^d} = \frac{\partial \tilde{C}_j^d}{\partial t_k^d} - \frac{\partial C_j^d}{\partial I} C_k^d.$$

Using this relationship, the optimal tax conditions can be written as

$$\lambda C_k^d = \mu \left\{ C_k^d + \sum_j t_j \left[\frac{\partial \tilde{C}_j^d}{\partial t_k^d} - \frac{\partial C_j^d}{\partial I} C_k^d \right] \right\} \quad k = 1,2,\ldots,J. \tag{10}$$

Rearranging, we obtain

$$\left[\frac{\lambda - \mu + \mu \sum_j t_j \frac{\partial C_j^d}{\partial I}}{\mu} \right] C_k^d = \sum_j t_j \frac{\partial \tilde{C}_j^d}{\partial t_k^d} \quad k = 1,2,\ldots,J. \tag{11}$$

Noting that by the properties of the expenditure function and Young's theorem,

$$\frac{\partial \tilde{C}_j^d}{\partial t_k^d} = \frac{\partial^2 E}{\partial t_j^d \partial t_k^d} = \frac{\partial^2 E}{\partial t_k^d \partial t_j^d} = \frac{\partial \tilde{C}_k^d}{\partial t_j^d}.$$

Introducing θ as the coefficient of C_k^d in (11), the optimal tax conditions become

$$\theta C_k^d = \sum_j t_j S_{kj}^d \quad k = 1,2,\ldots,J, \tag{12}$$

where S_{kj}^d are the Slutsky terms for domestic demands. These compensated elasticities depend not only on preferences but also on the nature of resource costs.

The modified proportionate shrinkage rule can be interpreted by noting that for small taxes the right side of (12) is the change in the domestic demand for good k that would result if the consumer were compensated to stay on the same indifference curve. Because θ is independent of k, the optimal tax structure involves an equal proportionate shrinkage in the compensated domestic demand for all goods, where this compensated elasticity depends not only on preferences but also on the costliness of substituting foreign purchases for domestic purchases.

A COVARIANCE INTERPRETATION

We can extend the proportionate shrinkage rule to the case of heterogeneous households, albeit with added complexity. This extension is based on Diamond's (1975) covariance interpretation of optimal taxation in which the government also is able to offer a head subsidy of equal value to all households. Diamond uses the first-order conditions for the head subsidy to interpret the optimal tax structure. We now apply this procedure to the case of costly noncompliance.

With the household subsidy, the government's problem becomes

$$\text{Max} \ W[V^1(p,t^d,t^f,I;\alpha), \ldots, V^H(p,t^d,t^f,I;\alpha)]$$
$$t^d,I$$
$$\text{subject to} \quad G + HI \le \sum_h \sum_j t_j C_j^{dh}$$

where I is the per-household subsidy and H is the number of households. The form of the first-order conditions with respect to tax rates are unchanged by the presence of the household subsidy. The first-order condition for the household subsidy is

$$\sum_h \beta^h + \mu \left\{ \sum_h \sum_j t_j \frac{\partial C_j^{dh}}{\partial I^h} - H \right\} = 0. \tag{13}$$

We now define

$$\gamma^h = \beta^h + \mu \left\{ \sum_h \sum_j t_j \frac{\partial C_j^{dh}}{\partial I^h} \right\}$$

as the full social marginal utility of income for household h, consisting of the direct increase in social utility, β^h, plus the social marginal utility of increased tax revenue when I^h is raised.

Using this definition and the Slutsky relationships, the optimal tax conditions (7) become

$$\sum_h \gamma^h C_k^{dh} = \mu \left\{ \sum_h C_k^{dh} + \sum_h \sum_j t_j S_{kj}^{dh} \right\} \quad k = 1, 2, \ldots, J.$$ (14)

The first-order condition for the head subsidy indicates that

$$\mu = \sum_h \gamma^h / H \equiv \bar{\gamma},$$

which allows μ to be interpreted as the average full social marginal utility of income. Note further that

$$\sum_h (\gamma^h - \bar{\gamma}) = 0; \quad \bar{C}_k^d \sum_h (\gamma^h - \bar{\gamma}) = 0; \quad \sum_h (\gamma^h - \bar{\gamma}) \bar{C}_k^d = 0,$$

where $\bar{C}_k^d$ is the average quantity of good k purchased in the taxing jurisdiction. Using these expressions, the optimal tax conditions become

$$\frac{\sum_h \sum_j t_j S_{kj}^{dh}}{C_k^d} = \frac{\sum_h (\gamma^h - \bar{\gamma})(C_k^{dh} - \bar{C}_k^d)}{\bar{\gamma} C_k^d} \quad k = 1, 2, \ldots, J.$$ (15)

This expression indicates that the aggregate percentage change in the compensated demand for domestically purchased good k should be proportional to the covariance between the full social marginal utility of income and consumption of domestic good k purchases. Roughly, it suggests that the shrinkage in demand of domestic purchases should be smaller the more consistently deserving households make relatively large domestic purchases.

This covariance result adds to our understanding of the optimal tax structure to the extent that resource costs and the composition of consumption vary systematically by income. Consider, for example, a good for which the marginal resource costs of noncompliance are large so that a relatively high tax rate is needed to induce cross-border purchases. If the demand for this good is highly income elastic, wealthier households will make larger than average purchases at home and the covariance between "deservingness" and domestic purchases will be negative. The optimal shrinkage of such a good would, therefore, be large. By contrast, if households show little variation by income group for these goods (because of a low income elasticity), there will be a minimal covariance between deservingness and domestic purchases. In such a situation, there should be little shrinkage in domestic purchases.

CONCLUSION

Optimal tax rules for a small economy in which households engage in costly border crossing can be characterized in terms of the response to home taxes of the domestically purchased component of consumption. The responsiveness to home taxes of resources wasted through noncompliance does not appear directly in the optimal tax conditions, as these adjustments have only a second-order effect on a household's welfare. Noncompliance costs do play an important role in optimal tax design, however, as they influence the uncompensated and compensated elasticities of demand used to characterize the optimal tax structure.

NOTES

1. The optimal commodity tax structure was first treated systematically by Ramsey (1927), with the classic modern treatment provided by Diamond and Mirrlees (1971). Extensions to the theory have been made to include public goods, externalities, international trade, public utility pricing, and the presence of an optimal direct tax. Sandmo (1976) provides a survey of these extensions.

2. A firm is not required to collect the use tax unless the firm has a certain presence within the state, as defined by the courts. Due and Mikesell (1983) describe the use tax and restrictions on a state's ability to collect it.

3. This evidence is reviewed by Fox (1986) and Walsh and Jones (1988).

4. Prior to January 1, 1993, the value of a traveler's imports for personal use was restricted to $660. See "Country-Hopping Shopping" (1992, 78-9).

5. See "Country-Hopping Shopping" (1992, 78-9).

6. Although it is tempting to conclude that evasion must reduce government revenue, it need not. Consider the case of a jurisdiction that taxes shoes only, with a low tax rate (compared to the neighboring jurisdiction) on right shoes and a prohibitive tax rate on left shoes. The ability to evade taxes on left shoes may increase purchases of right and left shoes, thereby raising domestic government revenue.

7. Yitzhaki (1987) considers a third source of excess burden, that arising from the uncertainty produced by government efforts to enforce tax laws. Additional welfare considerations arise when additional distortions are present. For example, Trandel (1992) considers a model of spatial competition in which evasion can reduce the welfare loss created by a seller's market power.

8. Scotchmer (1992) shows that, in the case of income tax evasion, noncompliance and enforcement bias the tax structure toward regressivity.

9. Nontraded goods can be easily incorporated into the present framework if they are produced using a linear production technology, which ensures that these producer prices also do not change in response to commodity tax changes.

10. Due and Mikesell (1983) suggest that tax collected but not reported is not more than 3% of the tax due in U.S. states with minimal audit procedures and not more than 0.5% in states with good audit programs.

11. I choose to assume that households supply one factor, which is untaxed, because most factor transactions are not subject to commodity tax laws. Moreover, I assume that household location is fixed; households do not respond to changes in commodity tax rates by moving to another jurisdiction.

12. Papers by Allingham and Sandmo (1972) and Srinivasan (1973) prompted a substantial literature on tax evasion, much of it concerning income tax evasion. Marelli (1984) and Virmani (1989) consider indirect tax evasion by firms and its implications for production inefficiency.

13. Units purchased in the neighboring jurisdiction but for which the indirect tax is paid voluntarily may be considered part of C^d. If nontraded goods exist, the elements of C^f corresponding to nontraded goods are zeros.

14. In a model in which evasion uses resources, Mintz and Tulkens (1986) characterize the outcome of commodity tax competition between two large, autonomous, neighboring states. They analyze optimal policy using an origin-based commodity tax levied on one of two private goods to finance a local public good.

15. The quasi-convexity of $R(C^f)$ reflects economies to "mixed bundles" for transport purposes.

16. For the two-good case, the consumer's problem is similar to that in Mintz and Tulkens (1986), who explore in detail the characteristics of three types of equilibria when regions are not small.

17. An additional constraint, assumed to hold at the optimal choice of C^d and C^f, is that the quantity of labor sold, C_o, does not exceed the total time endowment. Nonsatiation is also assumed.

18. The Kuhn-Tucker conditions are necessary because the constraint qualification is met by the assumed properties of $R(\bullet)$.

19. We assume that the government does not engage in cross-border inspections or in punishment of border crossers. In fact, such inspection is very rarely performed by U.S. states and is often precluded between nations by trade agreements. If we were to consider enforcement in the present model, it would be optimal to set the fine for border crossing at the highest level possible and to reduce enforcement to its lowest level, as enforcement is costly to the government but fines are not. When there is the possibility of falsely accusing the innocent, the optimal fine may not be the maximum fine, as argued by Pestieau, Possen, and Slutsky (1992) for the case of income tax evasion.

20. The possibility for multiple solutions to the first-order conditions is well documented. See Atkinson and Stiglitz (1980) and the references cited therein.

21. The multiplier is defined as the marginal social value of tax revenue and thus will be positive for an optimizing government.

22. This result relies on the assumption that a marginal tax change will alter the purchasing location of only those who are indifferent as to the location of their next purchase. For those who purchase good k only in the neighboring jurisdiction and who are not indifferent as to the location of the next purchase, $U_j < \lambda(p_j + t_j^d)$, and we assume $\partial C_j^d / \partial t_k = 0$. For those who purchase good k only in the home jurisdiction and who are not indifferent as to the location of the next purchase, $U_j < \lambda(p_j + t_j^f + R_j)$, and we assume $\partial C_j^f / \partial t_k = 0$.

23. Samuelson (1986) does not formally address evasion, however, nor does he discuss the possibility that evasion is incomplete.

24. Lovely (1994) includes an expression for the welfare loss from costly commodity tax noncompliance with a given (perhaps optimal) tax structure.

25. See Atkinson and Stiglitz (1980) for a statement of the Ramsey tax problem.

26. Diamond and Mirrlees (1971) attribute the proportionate shrinkage rule to a memorandum for the U.S. Treasury in 1951 published as Samuelson (1986). Mirrlees (1975) notes that the interpretation is an approximation when tax rates are arbitrarily large and derives an analogous condition for an economy with two classes of consumers.

REFERENCES

Allingham, M., and A. Sandmo. 1972. Income tax evasion: A theoretical analysis. *Journal of Public Economics* 1:323-38.

Atkinson, A. B., and J. E. Stiglitz. 1980. *Lectures on public economics*. London: McGraw-Hill.

Country-hopping shopping. 1992. *The Economist*, 26 December, 78-9.

Diamond, P. A. 1975. A many person Ramsey tax rule. *Journal of Public Economics* 4:335-42.

Diamond, P. A., and J. A. Mirrlees. 1971. Optimal taxation and public product. II: Tax rules. *American Economic Review* 61:261-78.

Due, J. F., and J. L. Mikesell. 1983. *Sales taxation: State and local structure and administration*. Baltimore, MD: Johns Hopkins University Press.

Fox, W. F. 1986. Tax structure and the location of economic activity along state borders. *National Tax Journal* 39:387-401.

Lovely, M. E. 1994. Crossing the border: Does commodity tax evasion reduce welfare and can enforcement improve it? *Canadian Journal of Economics* 27:157-74.

Marelli, M. 1984. On indirect tax evasion. *Journal of Public Economics* 25:181-96.

Mintz, J., and H. Tulkens. 1986. Commodity tax competition between member states of a federation: Equilibrium and efficiency. *Journal of Public Economics* 29:133-72.

Mirrlees, J. A. 1975. Optimal commodity taxation in a two-class economy. *Journal of Public Economics* 4:27-33.

————. 1986. The theory of optimal taxation. In *Handbook of mathematical economics*. Vol. 3, edited by K. J. Arrow and M. D. Intriligator, 1197-249. Amsterdam: Elsevier Science.

Pestieau, P., U. M. Possen, and S. M. Slutsky. 1992. The penalty for tax evasion when there are audit errors and taxes are set optimally. Unpublished manuscript, Liege University.

Ramsey, F. P. 1927. A contribution to the theory of taxation. *Economic Journal* 37:47-61.

Samuelson, P. A. 1986. Theory of optimal taxation. *Journal of Public Economics* 30:137-43.

Sandmo, A. 1976. Optimal taxation: An introduction to the literature. *Journal of Public Economics* 6:37-54.

130   PUBLIC FINANCE QUARTERLY

Scotchmer, S. 1992. The regressive bias in tax enforcement. *Public Finance/Finances Publiques* 47 (Suppl.): 366-71.

Srinivasan, T. N. 1973. Tax evasion: A model. *Journal of Public Economics* 2:339-46.

Trandel, G. A. 1992. Evading the use tax on cross-border sales: Pricing and welfare effects. *Journal of Public Economics* 49:313-31.

Virmani, A. 1989. Indirect tax evasion and production efficiency. *Journal of Public Economics* 39:223-37.

Walsh, M. J., and J. D. Jones. 1988. More evidence on the "border tax" effect: The case of West Virginia, 1979-84. *National Tax Journal* 41:261-5.

Yitzhaki, S. 1987. On the excess burden of tax evasion. *Public Finance Quarterly* 15:123-37.

Mary E. Lovely is an assistant professor of economics in the Maxwell School of Citizenship and Public Affairs at Syracuse University. Her recent work in public economics appears in the Canadian Journal of Economics *and in the* National Tax Journal. *She also conducts research in international economics and is chair of the International Public Finance Committee of the National Tax Association.*

Crossing the border: does commodity tax evasion reduce welfare and can enforcement improve it?

MARY E. LOVELY   Syracuse University

Abstract. This paper compares discrete equilibria in which consumers do and do not evade commodity taxes by making cross-border purchases. When the government faces a revenue requirement, the comparison shows that border crossing reduces welfare if resources wasted by evasion exceed the benefit of consumption changes, where these changes reflect lower prices across the border and induced changes in domestic tax rates. Enforcement reduces welfare if administrative and uncertainty costs outweigh the benefits of consumption changes and the reduction in resource costs. The analysis shows that the welfare effect of evasion depends on how well designed the tax system is and how effective enforcement resources are in deterring border crossing.

Traverser la frontière: est-ce que éviter la taxe sur les biens réduit le niveau de bien-être et est-ce qu'une application vigoureuse des lois peut améliorer la situation? Ce mémoire compare des situations d'équilibre: les cas où les consommateurs évitent ou n'évitent pas la taxe sur les biens en faisant ou en ne faisant pas leurs achats outre-frontières. Quand le gouvernement fait face à des besoins de revenus, la comparaison montre que l'achat outre-frontières réduit le niveau de bien-être si les ressources perdues par évasion fiscale dépassent les avantages dérivés des changements dans la consommation, ces changements reflétant l'impact des prix moins élevés outre-frontières et les changements induits dans le niveau des taxes au plan domestique. Une application vigoureuse des lois réduit le niveau de bien-être si les coûts administratifs et les coûts entraînés par l'incertitude sont plus grands que les avantages attribuables aux changements dans la consommation et à la réduction dans les coûts des ressources. L'analyse montre que les effets de bien-être de l'évasion fiscale dépendent du design plus ou moins bon du système fiscal et de l'efficacité de l'application vigoureuse de la loi pour décourager l'achat outre-frontières.

I. INTRODUCTION

When commodity tax rates differ between neighbouring jurisdictions, residents

I thank Douglas Holtz-Eakin, Greg Trandel, John Yinger and participants in seminars at Syracuse University and Union College for helpful comments.

158   Mary E. Lovely

of the higher-tax jurisdiction may evade taxes by making purchases across the border and failing to remit taxes voluntarily to the domestic fisc. Although it is generally agreed that tax evasion causes welfare loss, there are few formal analyses of the excess burden of tax evasion.[1] This paper develops a model of consumer border crossing induced by commodity tax differentials and examines the efficiency consequences for an economically small jurisdiction of such tax evasion and efforts to reduce it.

Border crossing occurs both nationally, between counties, states, or provinces, and internationally. The analysis here is applicable to jurisdictions that do little strategic commodity tax exporting. These situations include intra- or interstate border crossing in the United States where a relatively small jurisdiction, such as a single city or county, levies tax rates higher than those of a neighbour. Similarly, the analysis can be applied to provincial value-added tax evasion by Canadians who cross into the United States for same-day shopping trips. An important fiscal concern for these jurisdictions is whether this border crossing is harmful and, if so, whether enforcement effects are helpful.

Despite the overwhelmingly negative view of tax evasion, the welfare effect of tax evasion is generally analytically indeterminate. This ambiguity arises from the second-best nature of the assessment – evasion typically occurs when tax distortions exist and thus when the price changes caused by evasion are potentially welfare improving. In this paper I derive a sufficient condition for identifying situations in which evasion unambiguously reduces welfare. Using an economy without border crossing as a benchmark, I characterize conditions under which this benchmark economy has higher welfare than an economy characterized by costly evasion opportunities, given that the government has a commodity tax revenue requirement. When taxes are not optimally set, these conditions involve the net benefits of consumption changes and the value of resources wasted through evasion. When taxes are set optimally to meet the revenue requirement, I show that evasion cannot improve welfare.

When evasion reduces welfare, the key policy concern is whether the collection of taxes from border crossers will improve welfare. Enforcement may increase tax revenues and permit adjustment of tax rates, but itself is costly. Moreover, enforcement requires detection of border crossers and evasion penalties, thus subjecting taxpayers to risk. When do the direct and indirect costs of enforcement outweigh the benefits of tax rate adjustments? In answer to this question I provide a sufficient condition for enforcement to be welfare reducing, thereby establishing a threshold that specific enforcement programs must pass if they are potentially beneficial.

The analytical method used throughout the paper is the comparison of discrete equilibria. This method is widely used for normative analysis in international economics[2] and is highlighted by Dixit (1985) in his discussion of tax policy for

---

1 See Yitzhaki (1987) and the literature discussed below. See also Deardorff and Stolper (1990), who argue that smuggling (trade tax evasion) is welfare improving in the African context.
2 The method is typically used to show gains from trade, as for example in Dixit and Norman (1980).

open economies. Comparisons of discrete equilibria are integral to most tax reforms, since reform typically involves non-marginal tax changes. Similarly, most statements concerning the welfare effects of evasion explicitly or implicitly involve discrete comparisons – the distinction between some and no evasion is typically not a marginal one. By using discrete comparisons, it is possible to identify for policy makers the magnitudes – consumption changes, resources wasted by evasion, enforcement activity costs – about which they should be concerned and seek to estimate.

The paper proceeds in sections. The next provides a brief survey of normative analyses of border crossing to evade commodity taxes. The following section presents the model of consumer commodity tax evasion. The fourth section compares a benchmark no-evasion equilibrium with an equilibrium characterized by border crossing and contains a sufficient condition for evasion to be welfare diminishing. The fifth section assesses the desirability of engaging in costly enforcement activity. The last section summarizes the results.

II. NORMATIVE ANALYSES OF COMMODITY TAX EVASION

In the international context, much of the literature on commodity tax evasion addresses the welfare effects of smuggling (trade tax evasion). The smuggling literature builds from the seminal contribution of Bhagwati and Hansen (1973), who analyze the welfare effects of smuggling for a small country. They find that in general the welfare effects of smuggling are indeterminate. This ambiguity obtains because smuggling involves real costs in excess of legal trade that may lower welfare despite the circumvention of distortionary government policies. Kemp (1976) considers smuggling with a probability of detection and fines. He defines conditions, including lump-sum redistribution of tariff and fine revenue and costless evasion, under which smuggling has no effect on welfare. Sheikh (1974), in a model in which smuggling uses real domestic resources, and Pitt (1981), in a model in which legal trade camouflages illegal trade, find that smuggling may or may not reduce welfare. In these models the ambiguity again arises from the opposing effects of distortion and resource waste. More recently, Thursby, Jensen, and Thursby (1991) examine how market structure and enforcement affect smuggling and welfare. They find that smuggling improves welfare if the distortion reduction outweighs smuggling costs and that this welfare effect is directly related to the degree of competition. Increased enforcement in this model potentially reduces welfare. The present analysis shares with the smuggling literature a focus on resource costs and distortion reduction and the search for conditions under which the welfare effect of evasion is determinate.

The literature on domestic commodity tax evasion addresses evasion both by firms and by consumers. Marelli (1984) and Virmani (1989) consider indirect tax evasion by firms and its implication for production efficiency. Trandel (1992) uses a spatial model of competition to analyse the welfare effects of border crossing by consumers. With one taxed good and a revenue target, his analysis shows that

160   Mary E. Lovely

border crossing may be welfare improving even though a higher tax rate is needed, if it reduces sellers' market power. Mintz and Tulkens (1986) also focus on border crossing by consumers. Their model of consumer behaviour is similar to that used in the present analysis in that purchasing patterns depend on taxes and transportation costs. Only one good is taxed, however, and their purpose is to characterize the outcome of tax competition.

Kaplow (1990) differs from these papers by introducing enforcement into a model of consumer commodity tax evasion. The main concern of the analysis is the relationship between optimal taxation and optimal enforcement. With costly evasion, Kaplow finds that the effect on welfare of an increase in enforcement depends on the cost of enforcement, its effect on consumption distortion and its effect on resources spent in evading. Thus, the analysis shares with the present paper an emphasis on the welfare of enforcement, but the two models and methods are quite different. Kaplow's model posits two private goods, one taxed, and one public good, the supply of which is endogenously determined. There is no uncertainty in the model, since consumers know in advance if they will be detected evading. He considers marginal changes and provides conditions for interior solutions. In contrast, the present model allows for many goods; and the probability of detection, when taxes are enforced, is endogenous. Discrete rather than marginal analysis is used, so that the welfare effect of evasion can be assessed and the welfare consequences of enforcement activity highlighted. The revenue requirement, and hence the level of public goods, is exogenous, rather than endogenous as in Kaplow.

III. A MODEL OF BORDER CROSSING

Consider a small mixed economy, operating within a larger economic unit. Among the class of all possible indirect tax schemes, the government uses only a linear commodity tax. Moreover, consumers and firms always participate on opposite sides of each market in which they transact, and all commodity taxation takes place on this set of transactions. An implication of this assumption is that if intermediate goods in production and resource transactions among consumers exist, they are not taxed.

All agents in the economy behave competitively. Firms choose net output to maximize profits using technologies that do not involve externalities. There are no profits, since all firms use technology exhibiting constant returns to scale. All goods are traded, and given free trade between jurisdictions, producer prices of traded goods are the same everywhere. The taxing jurisdiction is economically small, implying that changes in commodity tax rates do not affect producer prices of traded goods.[3] Firms are legally responsible for tax collections and reporting,

---

3 Non-traded goods can be easily incorporated into the present framework if they are produced using a linear production technology, which ensures that these producer prices also do not change in response to commodity tax changes.

and firms within the taxing jurisdiction act in complete compliance with the tax law.[4]

All consumers are assumed to be identical, and thus the consumption sector is treated as one consumer maximizing a utility function subject to a budget constraint. The consumer's choice of net consumption is denoted by the vector, C, where net sales of factor services appear as negative elements. In the absence of lump-sum income, purchases of goods by the consumer must be offset by sales of factor services to firms. There are $J+1$ commodities in the economy, with labour, the only factor service, denoted commodity 0 and the remaining J commodities consumer goods.[5] Labour is not subject to taxation and it serves as numeraire with $p_0 = 1$. The price vector faced by the consumer for transactions within the taxation jurisdiction is $p + t$, where p is the vector of producer prices and t is the corresponding vector of taxes.

The consumer is able to make purchases of traded goods outside or inside the jurisdiction. The consumption vector, C, is the sum of the vector of net purchases made in the home jurisdiction, C^d, and the vector of net purchases made in the neighbouring (foreign) jurisdiction, C^f.[6] Because producer prices are the same everywhere, p is the price received by firms for transactions occurring outside the border of the home jurisdiction. Moreover, firms in the neighbouring jurisdiction do not collect the tax for the home jurisdiction. Thus, the consumer can evade commodity taxation by making purchases across the border.

Because the home jurisdiction is small, it is assumed that the neighbouring jurisdiction does not respond to revenue-neutral tax changes by the home government. Moreover, it is assumed that the home tax base is unaffected by the behaviour of residents of the neighbouring jurisdiction.[7] These assumptions simplify the analysis by removing the need to model foreign as well as home behaviour. While tax competition issues involving the behaviour of foreign governments or residents arise in many settings, it can be argued that the main concerns of the tax competition literature do not arise in situations where the taxing jurisdiction is perceived to be economically small by its neighbours. For example, there has been no discussion in the United States of responding via tax policy to Canadian efforts to collect provincial value-added taxes from Canadian citizens. Nor is it believed that

---

4 Due and Mikesell (1983) suggest that tax collected but not reported is not more than 3 per cent of the tax due in U.S. states with minimal audit procedures and not more than 0.5 per cent in states with good audit programs.

5 I choose to assume that households supply one factor, which is untaxed, because most factor transactions are not subject to commodity tax laws. Moreover, I assume that household location is fixed; households do not respond to changes in commodity tax rates by moving to another jurisdiction.

6 Units purchased in the neighbouring jurisdiction but for which the indirect tax is paid voluntarily may be considered part of C^d. If non-traded goods exist, the elements of C^f corresponding to non-traded goods are zeros.

7 In a model in which evasion uses resources, Mintz and Tulkens (1986) characterize the outcome of commodity tax competition between two large, autonomous, neighbouring states. They analyse optimal policy using an origin-based commodity tax levied on one of two private goods to finance a local public good.

162   Mary E. Lovely

revenue-neutral changes in provincial VAT rates will induce significant northward flows of shoppers.

IV. WHEN DOES COSTLY BORDER CROSSING REDUCE WELFARE?

We consider first the case in which the government does not deter border crossing to evade commodity taxes. We assume that the government funds some activity through commodity taxation without a source of lump-sum revenue. The commodity tax revenue requirement is denoted $\bar{G}$ and is measured in terms of the numeraire, labour. We assume that border crossing uses resources, also expressed in terms of labour. These resources may be thought of as untaxed transportation costs. Transport costs are assumed to be an increasing, differentiable, and quasi-convex function of the quantity of foreign purchases and are denoted $R(C^f)$.[8]

The consumer's problem[9] with costly evasion is

$$\underset{C^d, C^f}{\text{Max}} \; U \left[I - \sum_{k=1}^{J}(p_k(C_k^d + C_k^f) + t_k C_k^d) - R(C^f), \; C_1^d + C_1^f, \; \ldots, \; C_J^d + C_J^f \right] \quad (1)$$

$$C_k^d \geqq 0 \qquad k = 1, \ldots, J$$

s.t.

$$C_k^f \geqq 0 \qquad k = 1, \ldots, J,$$

where I indicates lump-sum income in terms of labour, and where the budget constraint has been used to solve for C_0.[10] $U(\bullet)$ is a twice differentiable, strictly quasi-concave utility function. Letting U_j be $\partial U / \partial C_j$ the Kuhn-Tucker conditions for the household's problem are[11]

$$U_j - U_0(p_j + t_j) \leqq 0, \qquad C_j^d \geqq 0, \qquad C_j^d(U_j - U_0(p_j + t_j)) = 0$$

$$U_j - U_0(p_j + R_j) \leqq 0, \qquad C_j^f \geqq 0, \qquad C_j^f(U_j - U_0(p_j + R_j)) = 0,$$

where $R_j \equiv \partial R(C^f) / \partial C_j^f$.

By the quasi-concavity of U, the quasi-convexity of $R(C^f)$ and non-satiation, the Arrow-Enthoven sufficiency conditions for a maximum are satisfied. Three types of goods can be distinguished. The first type includes those only purchased domestically, for which $t_j \leqq R_j(\bar{C}^f)$, where $\bar{C}^f$ is the chosen vector of foreign purchases. The second type of good is purchased in both locations, with $t_j =$

---

8 The quasi-convexity of $R(C^f)$ reflects economies to 'mixed bundles' for transport purposes.

9 For the two-good case, the consumer's problem is the same as it is in Mintz and Tulkens (1986), who explore in detail the characteristics of three types of equilibria when regions are not small.

10 An additional constraint, assumed to hold at the optimal choice of C^d and C^f, is that the quantity of labour sold, C^0, does not exceed the total time endowment. Non-satiation is also assumed.

11 The Kuhn-Tucker conditions are necessary because the constraint qualification is met by the assumed properties of $R(\bullet)$.

$R_j(\bar{C}^f)$. The third type of good is purchased only across the border, with $t_j \geqq R_j(\bar{C}^f)$.

The welfare effect of this form of costly evasion is indeterminate. First, because the government must raise sufficient revenue to cover public expenditure, $\bar{G}$, evasion may require an increase in some subset of taxes, thereby raising the excess burden.[12] Second, the consumer uses real resources in the process of border crossing, which is waste from society's viewpoint. Third, holding tax rates fixed, evasion may result in relative consumer prices that differ from those obtaining in the absence of evasion, perhaps raising welfare.[13]

Although the welfare effect of evasion is generally indeterminate, we can identify circumstances in which evasion diminishes welfare. To make this identification precise, we derive a sufficient condition for costly evasion to be welfare worsening through the comparison of two alternative equilibria. The costly evasion case, denoted E, is as described by the consumer's problem (1). The no-evasion case, denoted N, is a situation in which no evasion occurs and the standard consumer's choice problem prevails. We allow tax rates to differ between the two equilibria, so as to hold tax revenue at $\bar{G}$.

The no-evasion case is a benchmark against which we measure the efficiency loss attributable to evasion. This benchmark reflects the (perhaps) idealized base case implicit in many public statements concerning evasion. This benchmark equilibrium represents a situation in which border-crossing incentives are absent, even though the domestic government does not use resources to prevent it. It may represent, for example, a previous period in which evasion was prohibitively costly to the consumer, before this cost was reduced by neighbouring country behaviour (e.g., by building shopping malls on the foreign side of the border). Because this benchmark is an equilibrium in which evasion is costlessly absent, efficiency losses measured thereby are worst-case measurements.

To compare this no-evasion benchmark, case N, with the evasion case, E, we consider the Hicksian equivalent variation in consumer surplus caused by costly evasion, holding public expenditures fixed. This measure is denoted HEV ($N \rightarrow E; \bar{G}$), and it indicates the amount of additional income necessary to compensate the consumer for the move from N to E.[14] Omitting from the expenditure function the parameter p, which does not change, define

---

12 Although it is tempting to conclude that evasion must reduce government revenue, it need not do so. Consider the case of a jurisdiction that taxes shoes only, with a low (compared with the neighbouring jurisdiction) tax rate on right shoes and a prohibitive tax rate on left shoes. The ability to evade taxes on left shoes may increase purchases of right and left shoes thereby raising domestic government revenue.

13 The effect of evasion on relative prices implies that evasion has an indeterminate effect on welfare provided some goods are not available across the border (i.e., non-tradables), even if evasion is costless, tax rates are fixed and a lump-sum instrument exists. If all goods are tradable under these circumstances, no revenue is raised by the commodity tax, and in the absence of other distortions the first-best outcome can be achieved through evasion. In contrast to commodity tax evasion, smuggling induced by domestic tariffs always raises welfare when no real resources are used, no other distortions exist, and lump-sum fiscal instruments are available. Tariffs, by definition, do not apply to non-traded goods.

14 Tresch (1981, ch. 4) describes HEV and its properties.

164   Mary E. Lovely

$$M(t^E, U; E) \equiv \min pC + t^E C^d + R(C^f), \qquad \text{s.t. } u(C) \geqq U,$$

where the E indicates that costly evasion possibilities exist. Note that t is the vector of domestic tax rates, and vector products are inner products. Further, define

$$M(t^N, U; N) \equiv \min pC + t^N C \qquad \text{s.t. } u(C) \geqq U,$$

where the N indicates that no evasion possibilities exist. Now we may define

$$\text{HEV } (N \rightarrow E; \bar{G}) = M(t^E, U^E; E) - M(t^N, U^E; N). \tag{2}$$

As discussed by Mayshar (1990) in the context of a revenue-neutral tax reform, HEV > 0 implies $U^N > U^E$.

To derive a sufficient condition for HEV $(N \rightarrow E; \bar{G}) > 0$, we add and subtract from HEV the expenditure needed to purchase at the no-evasion consumer prices the bundle chosen when evasion is possible. The bundle chosen with evasion is denoted $C(t^E, I^E; E)$. This procedure yields

$$[M(t^E, U^E; E) - (p + t^N)C(t^E, I^E; E)]$$
$$+ [(p + t^N)C(t^E, I^E; E) - M(t^N, U^E; E)]. \tag{3}$$

The second term in square brackets is non-negative because the bundle $C(t^E, I^E; E)$ provides U^E, while $M(t^N, U^E; N)$ is the minimum expenditure needed to obtain U^E when all purchases are taxed. Therefore, a sufficient condition for HEV $(N \rightarrow E; \bar{G}) > 0$ is

$$[M(t^E, U^E; E) - (p + t^N)C(t^E, I^E; E)] > 0. \tag{4}$$

Using the definition of $M(t^E, U^E; E)$, the sufficient condition (4) becomes

$$t^E C^d(t^E, I^E; E) - t^N C(t^E, I^E; E) + R(C^f(t^E, I^E; E)) > 0. \tag{5}$$

The tax vectors, t^E and t^N, must raise the same level of actual commodity tax revenue, $\bar{G}$, in equilibrium. Therefore, t^E and t^N must be set so that

$$t^N C(t^N, I^N; N) = t^E C^d(t^E, I^E; E), \tag{6}$$

where lump-sum income is zero in both equilibria, so $I^E = I^N = 0$.

Substituting the relationship (6) into (5) yields the sufficient condition for $U^N > U^E$:

$$t^N[C(t^N, I^N; N) - C(t^E, I^E; E)] + R(C^f(t^E, I^E; E)) > 0. \tag{7}$$

The first term is a measure of the net benefit of the consumption differences between the two equilibria, weighted by the tax rates from the no-evasion equilibrium. Note that this term is a comparison of the actual consumption bundles chosen under each situation, N and E. It can be interpreted using the logic employed by Ohyama (1972) in an examination of policy changes in open, distorted economies and interpreted by Dixit (1985). Considering one element of the vector product of the first term of (7), suppose $t_k^N[C_k(t^N, I^N; N) - C_k(t^E, I^E; E)] > 0$ for some taxed good k. As $t_k^N > 0$, this condition implies that consumption of good k is larger when no border crossing occurs than when it does. Because $t_k^N > 0$, the consumer price, reflecting good k's marginal value in consumption, exceeds the shadow price of obtaining a unit of good k and, thus, there is some benefit to increasing its consumption. The first term of (7) is the sum of all such consumption differences, weighted by the respective tax wedges, over all commodities. If this weighted sum is positive, border-crossing opportunities reduce home welfare even when they are costless.

The condition (7) is the sum of these net benefits plus the resources expended by the consumer through border crossing. These resource costs are positive for any positive quantity of foreign purchases and are waste from the viewpoint of the home region. Even if evasion results in a positive net benefit from consumption changes, the no-evasion equilibrium may still be preferred if this consumption gain is outweighed by the resource cost of evastion.[15]

If t^N is chosen optimally for the no-evasion equilibrium, the first term in (7) must be non-negative and evasion must reduce welfare. To see this, we define the optimal tax vector t_0^N as the vector for which

$$(p + t_0^N)C(t_0^N, I) \geqq (p + t_0^N)C(t^N, I), \tag{8}$$

for any other tax vector t^N that raises actual revenue of $\bar{G}$. Condition (8) states that the equilibrium characterized by optimal taxes, t_0^N, is revealed preferred to any

15 An alternative to treating $\bar{G}$ as fixed is to assume that tax revenue is redistributed to the consumer in a lump-sum manner rather than used to finance public expenditure. This analytical approach is of interest because it matches the approach of the Pigou-Harberger-Browning (PHB) tradition in marginal-cost-of-public-funds calculations. As characterized by Ballard and Fullerton (1992), the PHB approach may be depicted as a lump-sum rebate financed by a distortionary tax; that is, as treating the tax revenue as lump-sum income. In keeping with the PHB tradition, we may analyse the welfare effect of tax evasion by treating the resulting revenue changes as changes in lump-sum income. When evasion is costly, this alternative approach produces a sufficient condition for evasion to be welfare diminishing of the form

$$M(t, U^E; E) - (p + t)C(t, I^E; E) - [I^E - I^N] > 0,$$

where tax rates are the same in both equilibria but lump-sum incomes vary with actual tax revenue. An interesting special case arises when the consumer is indifferent as to the location of her next purchase of any good. In this case, $t_k = R_k$ for all k. If the resource function is homogeneous of degree one or less, then

$$R(C^f) \geqq \sum_k R_k C_k^f, \text{ and } M(t, U^E; E) \geqq \sum_k (p_k + t_k)C_k(t, I^E; E).$$

In this case, because consumer prices are the same in both equilibria, evasion has only an income effect on consumption. A finding that evasion results in lower tax revenues, $I^N - I^E > 0$, is sufficient to show that evasion diminishes welfare.

166   Mary E. Lovely

other equilibrium characterized by an equal-revenue tax vector. The consumer's budget constraint implies

$$(p + t_0^N)C(t_0^N, I) = (p + t^N)C(t^N, I).$$ (9)

Combining (9) with (8) yields

$$(p + t^N)C(t^N, I) - (p + t_0^N)C(t^N, I) = [t^N - t_0^N]C(t^N, I) \geqq 0.$$ (10)

The vectors t^N and t_0^N raise the same revenue, so $t_0^N C(t_0^N, I) = t^N C(t^N, I)$. Combining this equal-revenue characteristic with (10) yields

$$t_0^N [C(t_0^N, I) - C(t^N, I)] \geqq 0.$$ (11)

The condition (11) states that realization of any equal-revenue tax vector other than t_0^N cannot result in positive consumption benefits. Thus, if taxes are optimally set, the first term of (7) must be non-negative. Because resource costs $R(C^f)$ are non-negative, costly evasion cannot improve welfare when there is a revenue requirement and taxes are optimal.[16]

V. WILL ENFORCEMENT IMPROVE WELFARE?

When significant revenue losses are believed to occur as the result of border crossing, attempts to collect revenue on cross-border purchases result. In Canada, losses of provincial tax revenue by Canadians shopping in the United States has prompted an offer by the federal government to collect provincial taxes on all goods at the border.[17] In the United States, where interference with interstate commerce is prohibited, states have entered into interstate agreements designed to enhance their ability to collect taxes on out-of-state purchases.[18]

Whether tax enforcement efforts occur at the border or through interstate agreements the consumer purchasing across the border faces only a change of having her purchases detected. We assume that the probability that a consumer's purchases are detected depends on the level of resources devoted to enforcement, denoted S for 'surveillance,' and the bundle of goods purchased across the border, C^f. The probability of detection, $\pi(C^f, S)$, is assumed to be increasing in C^f and S, differentiable, and convex.[19] If detected, the consumer pays an exogenously set tax

16 There is a link between this result and Bhagwati and Hansen's (1973) analysis of smuggling in the presence of an exogenously set production target. In both cases, the distortion-reducing aspect of evasion works counter to the desired policy and makes target attainment, production or revenue, more costly than necessary.

17 Under the proposal, Canadian federal officers would collect provincial taxes only if the provinces broadened their taxes to apply to all goods covered by the federal goods and services tax (Farnsworth 1992).

18 The first successful interstate agreement was introduced by New York and New Jersey in 1986. The program provides audit incentives for firms to collect voluntarily both states' commodity taxes. A number of regional use-tax compacts have been signed since then. See Duncan (1988).

19 Previous treatments of tax evasion that treat the probability of detection as endogenous include Srinivasan (1973) and Yitzhaki (1989) for the case of income tax evasion and Kemp (1976), Sheikh (1974), and Thursby, Jensen, and Thursby (1991) for the case of smuggling.

plus penality on each undeclared purchase. The tax-plus-penalty rates are denoted by the vector F.[20]

With enforcement, the consumer is subject to the risk of detection and penalty. The usual approach to the consumer's problem under uncertainty is to consider the maximization of expected utility. When the consumer has many choices, as in the present case where C^f is a J-dimensional vector, the expected utility approach becomes intractable. Consequently, an alternative approach is used here, first-order certainty equivalence around the expected value of consumption. This approach is a direct application of the method used by Thalmann (1992) to examine factor taxes and evasion in general equilibrium. The appendix shows that the choice of consumption under uncertainty can be replaced by a program without uncertainty.

This program without uncertainty treats the expected fine as a mark-up over the producer price of goods purchased across the border. The problem is

$$\max_{C^d, C^f} U\left[I - \sum_{k=1}^{J}(p_k C_k + t_k C_k^d + \pi(C^f, S)F_k C_k^f) - R(C^f),\right.$$

$$\left. C_1^d + C_1^f, \ldots, C_J^d + C_J^f\right], \qquad (12)$$

$$C_k^d \geqq 0 \qquad k = 1, \ldots, J$$

s.t.

$$C_k^f \geqq 0 \qquad k = 1, \ldots, J.$$

As before, resource costs depend on the quantity of foreign purchases. Given our assumptions about the properties of $U(\bullet)$, $R(C^f)$ and $\pi(C^f, S)$, the Kuhn-Tucker conditions are necessary and sufficient. These conditions are

$$U_j - U_0(p_j + t_j) \leqq 0, \qquad C_j^d \geqq 0, \qquad C_j^d(U_j - U_0(p_j + t_j)) = 0$$

$$U_j - U_0(p_j + R_j + \phi_j) \leqq 0, \qquad C_j^f \geqq 0, \qquad C_j^f(U_j - U_0(p_j + R_j + \phi_j)) = 0,$$

where ϕ_j is the effect on the expected total fine from an additional purchase of j across the border. As before, there are three types of goods: those purchased only domestically, for which $t_j \leqq R_j + \phi_j$; those purchased in both locations and for which $t_j = R_j + \phi_j$; and those purchased only abroad and for which $t_j \geqq R_j + \phi_j$.

20 The optimal trade-off between the probability and the size of fines has been studied by Polinsky and Shavell (1979, 1984) and Kaplow (1989). In these papers, it is socially desirable for some individuals to engage in the externality generating activity. Consequently, fines serve to deter undesirable activity by some but not all individuals. In contrast, for the case of commodity tax evasion, evasion is never socially desirable, because border crossing is not needed to minimize excess burden when taxes can be chosen optimally to do so. Thus, because enforcement is costly but increasing fines is not, it is optimal in the present model to set fines at their upper bound. Why punishment may not be set at its upper bound is explored by Pestieau, Possen, and Slutsky (1992), who consider the maximization of ex-post social welfare when individuals evade income taxes and there are audit errors.

168   Mary E. Lovely

The first concern that arises in comparing an equilibrium with enforcement to one without is that the consumer faces uncertainty when taxes are enforced and none otherwise. The uncertainty introduced into the economy by enforcement is itself a source of excess burden, which Yitzhaki (1987) calls the 'excess burden of tax evasion.' We define this aspect of excess burden as the amount the consumer would be willing to pay to avoid the risk of detection and fine, holding average tax rates fixed.

In characterizing the consumer's choice, we were able to treat the expected fine as a simple mark-up because of certainty equivalence, as shown in the appendix. For normative purposes we must recognize that the consumer is subject to uncertainty in that the consumer must provide more labour than expected, if detected evading, or less labour if not detected. Graphically, we can represent the utility loss due to this uncertainty by figure 1.[21] Holding other consumption choice variables at the levels implied by the solution to (12), let C_0 (the negative of) labour supply, vary. Utility declines as labour supply increases. Point A indicates the labour supply corresponding to undetected evasion, point B to detected evasion. The labour supply necessary to fund the chosen consumption bundle at the expected value of evasion penalties lies between A and B, at D. Expected utility is a combination of the utility levels associated with A and B, and is denoted by U^S. The utility loss due to the uncertainty of detection is KL. LM is the additional labour supply the consumer could supply with no uncertainty while holding utility at the level occurring with uncertainty. The value of this labour supply reflects the consumer's willingness to pay to avoid the tax gamble and thus is our measure of the excess burden arising from the uncertainty introduced by enforcement. If the consumer is risk averse, this willingness to pay is positive.

In addition to this uncertainty cost, enforcement leads to changes in consumption, resources wasted through evasion, and tax rates. We account for these changes by comparing the expenditure needed to achieve U^S, the utility level expected with enforcement, when taxes are enforced and when they are not. The Hicksian equivalent variation measure of moving from costly evasion, E, to costly evasion with enforcement, S, is

$$\text{HEV} (E \longrightarrow S; \bar{F}, \bar{G}) = M(t^S, U^S; S) - M(t^E, U^S; E). \tag{13}$$

The parameters $\bar{F}$ and $\bar{G}$ indicate that the penalty rates and revenue requirement are taken as given. $\text{HEV} (E \longrightarrow S; \bar{F}, \bar{G}) > 0$ if $U^E > U^S$; that is, if the utility level available without enforcement exceeds the expected utility available with enforcement. If consumers are risk averse or risk neutral, $U^E > U^S$ is sufficient to conclude that enforcement reduces welfare.

As above, to derive a sufficient condition for $U^E > U^S$ we add to and subtract from (13) the value of the 'S' bundle at prices obtaining when there is no enforcement. This value is

$$pC(t^S, I^S; S) + t^E C^d(t^S, I^S; S) + R(t^S, I^S; S).$$

21 Figure 1 is suggested by Yitzhaki's (1987) graphical treatment of income tax evasion.

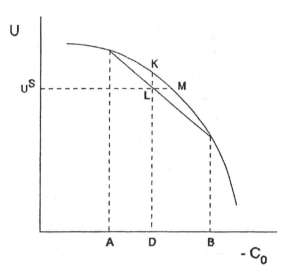

FIGURE 1 Utility loss from probabilistic enforcement

The bundle $C(t^S, I^S; S)$ provides U^S but the minimum expenditure needed to obtain U^S in the absence of enforcement is $M(t^E, U^S; E)$. Thus, a sufficient condition for $U^E > U^S$ is

$$M(t^S, U^S; S) - pC(t^S, I^S; S) - t^E C^d(t^S, I^S; S) - R(t^S, I^S; S) > 0. \quad (14)$$

By definition,

$$M(t^S, U^S; S) = pC(t^S, I^S; S) + t^S C^d(t^S, I^S; S) + R(t^S, I^S; S) + \phi(t^S, I^S; S),$$

where $\phi(t^S, I^S; S) = \pi(C^f(t^S, I^S; S), S) FC^f(t^S, I^S; S)$. Thus, (14) can be written as

$$t^S C^d(t^S, I^S; S) - t^E C^d(t^S, I^S; S) + \phi(t^S, I^S; S) > 0. \quad (15)$$

The tax vectors t^S and t^E must raise $\bar{G}$ so,[22]

$$t^E C^d(t^E, I^E; E) = t^S C^d(t^S, I^S; S) + \phi(t^S, I^S; S) - S. \quad (16)$$

Using (16) in (15), and noting that $C = C^d + C^f$, the sufficient condition for $U^E > U^S$ becomes

$$t^E[C(t^E, I^E; E) - C(t^S, I^S; S)] - t^E[C^f(t^E, I^E; E)$$
$$- C^f(t^S, I^S; S)] + S > 0. \quad (17)$$

22 As shown in the appendix, the demand functions arising from the consumer's problem characterized by no uncertainty and the expected value of penalties are the same, to a first-order approximation, as those arising from expected utility maximization. Thus, the revenue on the right-hand side of (16) is the same as expected government revenue, to a first-order approximation.

170   Mary E. Lovely

The first term is the net benefit of the difference between the 'E' and 'S' consumption bundles. It may be positive or negative. The second term is a measure of the change in wasted resources. Consider the kth element of this vector product. The tax rate t_k must be greater than or equal to the marginal resource cost R_k if any cross-border purchases of k are made. If enforcement reduces cross-border purchases of k, the marginal societal value of this reduction does not exceed $t_k^E(C_k^f(t^E, I^E) - C_k^f(t^S, I^S))$. This value is subtracted from the sum in (17) as it reflects the waste that is avoided by enforcement. The last term in (17) is S, the value of resources used in enforcement. It adds to the sum because S is saved if no enforcement activities occur.

The discrete comparison considered here identifies the behavioural and administrative changes that must be considered in assessing whether enforcement makes economic sense. Condition (17) potentially allows policy makers to eliminate from consideration enforcement programs that will not raise welfare. To use this condition in practice, estimates of overall consumption changes and of the level of foreign purchases are needed. These estimates require, among other things, that the revenue authority estimate simultaneously the revenue consequences of enforcement and thus the tax rates reduction made possible. While making such estimations is undoubtedly difficult, failure to do so may lead to the implementation of enforcement programs that do not enhance efficiency.

VI. CONCLUSIONS

We have presented comparisons of discrete equilibria involving evasion of commodity taxes through border crossing. The first comparison provides a sufficient condition for border crossing to reduce welfare from the level achievable in the absence of evasion opportunities. Because the government must raise a certain level of revenue through the commodity tax, consumers are linked not only through the waste created by their individual border crossing but also through the change in tax rates induced by evasion. Border crossing worsens welfare if resources wasted by evasion exceed the net benefit of consumption changes, where the consumption differences reflect both lower prices available through border crossing and the induced changes in domestic commodity taxes. When taxes are optimally set to meet the revenue requirement, however, the excess burden of taxation is at a minimum and we show that border crossing cannot improve welfare.

The second comparison assesses the ability of a program of costly probabilistic enforcement and penalties to improve welfare. Using a certainty equivalence approach, we derive a sufficient condition for undeterred evasion to be preferred to evasion with enforcement. This condition requires the sum of the value of enforcement costs and the net benefits of consumption differences to outweigh the resource cost of undeterred evasion.

An implication of our analysis is that the efficiency consequences of evasion depend on the design of the tax system. If the tax system is well designed, it is unlikely that evasion improves welfare, in the sense that it is unlikely that the distortion reduction provided by evasion outweighs the resource cost once evasion-induced tax changes are taken into account. Even if the tax system is well designed, however, it may not be wise to use resources to enforce taxes by detecting and penalizing border crossers. Enforcement subjects consumers to uncertainty and is costly. Clearly, the wisdom of enforcement activity depends on the power of these expenditures to reduce border crossing, and hence resource waste, and to allow tax-rate, and hence, distortion, reductions. Given the likely difficulty and expense of border checks, as indicated by the European Community's decision to eliminate them, careful assessment of proposed enforcement plans is warranted.

APPENDIX: CERTAINTY EQUIVALENCE

This appendix shows how the choice of the quantity and location of goods purchases under uncertainty can be represented as the solution to (12). In that representation, the stochastic value of consumption, inclusive of penalties, is replaced by the expected value of consumption. The demonstration here is a direct application of the demonstration by Thalmann (1992), who analyses factor tax evasion.

Define the value of consumption as

$$V = \sum_{k=0}^{J} [p_k C_k + t_k C_k^d] \qquad \text{with probability } 1 - \pi(C^f, S)$$

$$\sum_{k=0}^{J} [p_k C_k + t_k C_k^d + F_k C_k^f] \qquad \text{with probability } \pi(C^f, S).$$

Variables are defined in the text. The expected value of consumption is

$$E(V) = \sum_{k=0}^{J} [p_k C_k + t_k C_k^d + \pi(C^f, S) F_k C_k^f],$$

where $\pi(C^f, S)F_k$ is the expected tax-plus-penalty rate. Therefore

$$V = \sum_{k=0}^{J} [p_k C_k + t_k C_k^d + (\pi F_k - e) C_k^f],$$

with

$$e = e_1 = \pi F_k \qquad \text{with probability } 1 - \pi(C^f, S)$$

$$e = e_2 = \pi F_k - F_k \qquad \text{with probability } \pi(C^f, S)$$

where $E(e) = 0$. The representative consumer maximizes expected utility with respect to C^d and C^f:

$$\sum_{e=e_1,e_2} U \left[I - \sum_{k=1}^{J} (p_k C_k + t_k C_k^d + (\pi F_k - \mu e) C_k^f, C_1^d + C_1^f, \ldots, C_J^d + C_J^f \right]$$

$$\times \text{Prob} (e, C^f).$$

172   Mary E. Lovely

If $\mu = 1$, the problem is maximization under uncertainty; if $\mu = 0$ the problem is maximization under certainty. The two problems are solved by the same demand functions, to the first order in e. This property can be shown by letting the optimum if $\mu = 0$ be denoted $\bar{C}^d$ and $\bar{C}^f$ and computing the marginal changes in utility from raising consumption if $\mu = 1$. If these marginal changes are zero, then $\bar{C}^d$ *and* $\bar{C}^f$ maximize expected utility.

Let

$$V(C^d, C^f, e) \equiv U\left[I - \sum_{k=1}^{J} p_k C_k + t_k C_k^d + (\pi F_k - \mu e)C_k^f, \right.$$

$$\left. C_1^d + C_1^f, \ldots, C_J^f + C_J^f\right],$$

and let $P(\ \ )$ indicate probabilities. Then,

$$\frac{\partial}{\partial C_k^j} E(U) = \sum_e \left[\frac{d}{dC_k^j} V(\bar{C}^d, \bar{C}^f, e)P(e, \bar{C}^f)\right.$$

$$\left. + V(\bar{C}^d, \bar{C}^f, e)\frac{\partial}{\partial C_k^j} P(e, \bar{C}^f)\right] \qquad j = d, f$$

$$= \sum_e \left[\frac{\partial V(\bar{C}^d, \bar{C}^f, e)}{\partial C_k^j} P(e, \bar{C}^f) + \frac{\partial V(\bar{C}^d, \bar{C}^f, e)}{\partial e}\frac{\partial e}{\partial C_k^j} P(e, \bar{C}^f)\right.$$

$$\left. + V(\bar{C}^d, \bar{C}^f, 0)\frac{\partial}{\partial C_k^j} P(e, \bar{C}^f)\right] \qquad j = d, f,$$

where $e = e_1, e_2$.

Using first-order Taylor approximations,

$$V(\bar{C}^d, \bar{C}^f, e) \approx V(\bar{C}^d, \bar{C}^f, 0) + e\frac{\partial V(\bar{C}^d, \bar{C}^f, 0)}{\partial e}$$

$$\frac{\partial V(\bar{C}^d, \bar{C}^f, e)}{\partial C_k^j} \approx \frac{\partial V(\bar{C}^d, \bar{C}^f, 0)}{\partial C_k^j} + e\frac{\partial V(\bar{C}^d, \bar{C}^f, 0)}{\partial C_k^j \partial e} \qquad j = d, f$$

$$\frac{\partial V(\bar{C}^d, \bar{C}^f, e)}{\partial e} \approx \frac{\partial \nu(\bar{C}^d, \bar{C}^f, 0)}{\partial e} + e\frac{\partial V(\bar{C}^d, \bar{C}^f, 0)}{\partial e^2}.$$

Because $\bar{C}^d, \bar{C}^f$ maximizes utility when $\mu = 0$, $\partial V(\bar{C}^d, \bar{C}^f, 0)/\partial C_k^j = 0$. Hence,

$$\frac{\partial}{\partial C_k^j} E(U) = \frac{\partial^2 V(\bar{C}^d, \bar{C}^f, 0)}{\partial C_k^j \partial e} \sum_e eP(e, \bar{C}^f) + \frac{\partial V(\bar{C}^d, \bar{C}^f, 0)}{\partial e}$$

$$* \sum_e \left[\frac{\partial e}{\partial C_k^j} P(e, \bar{C}^f) + e\frac{\partial}{\partial C_k^j} P(e, \bar{C}^f)\right]$$

$$+ \frac{\partial^2 V(\bar{C}^d, \bar{C}^f, 0)}{\partial e^2} \sum_e eP(e, \bar{C}^f)\frac{\partial e}{\partial C_k^j}$$

$$+ V(\bar{C}^d, \bar{C}^f, 0) \sum_e \frac{\partial}{\partial C_k^j} P(e, \bar{C}^f) \qquad j = d, f.$$

All sums over e are zero. The first sum is zero because $E(e) = 0$, the second because $E(e)$ is a constant, and the fourth because probabilities always sum to one. The third is

$$e_1 P(e_1, \bar{C}^f) \frac{\partial e_1}{\partial C_k} + e_2 P(e_2, \bar{C}^f) \frac{\partial e_2}{\partial C}$$

$$= e_1 P(e_1, \bar{C}^f) \left[\frac{\partial e_1}{\partial C_k^j} - \frac{\partial e_2}{\partial C_k^j} \right] = 0 \qquad j = d, f.$$

This demonstration justifies the use of the expected consumption value in the max-imization problem (12). Thalmann (1992) uses this certainty equivalent approach to perform comparative-statics exercises involving factor tax evasion that are in-tractable in the expected utility formulation.

REFERENCES

Ballard, C.L., and D. Fullerton (1992) 'Distortionary taxes and the provision of public goods.' *Journal of Economic Perspectives* 6, 117–31
Bhagwati, J., and B. Hansen (1973) 'A theoretical analysis of smuggling.' *Quarterly Journal of Economics* 81, 172–87
Deardorff, A., and W. Stolper (1990) 'Effects of smuggling under African conditions: a factual, institutional and analytic discussion.' *Weltwirtschaftliches Archiv* 126, 116–41
Dixit, A. (1985) 'Tax policy in open economies.' In *Handbook of Public Economics*, vol. I, ed. A.J. Auerbach and M. Feldstein (Amsterdam: North-Holland)
Dixit, A.K., and V. Norman (1980) *Theory of International Trade* (Cambridge: Cambridge University Press)
Due, J.F., and J.L. Mikesell (1983) *Sales Taxation: State and Local Structure and Admin-istration* (Baltimore: Johns Hopkins University Press)
Duncan, H.T. (1969) 'Interstate cooperative efforts to enforce sales and use taxes.' *Pro-ceedings of the Eighty-First Conference of the National Tax Association – Tax Institute of America*, 93–8
Farnsworth, C.H. (1992) 'Canada is discouraging shopping in the U.S.,' *New York Times*, 13 February 1992, A10
Kaplow, L. (1989) 'The optimal penalty and magnitude of fines for acts that are definitely undesirable.' NBER Working Paper No. 3008, Cambridge, MA
— (1990) 'Optimal taxation with costly enforcement and evasion.' *Journal of Public Economics* 43, 221–36
Kemp, M. (1976) 'Smuggling and optimal commercial policy.' *Journal of Public Eco-nomics* 5, 381–84
Marrelli, M. (1984) 'On indirect tax evasion.' *Journal of Public Economics* 25, 181–96
Mayshar, J. (1990) 'On measures of excess burden and their application.' *Journal of Public Economics* 43, 263–89
Mintz, J., and H. Tulkens (1986) 'Commodity tax competition between member state of a federation: equilibrium and efficiency.' *Journal of Public Economics* 29, 133–72
Ohyama, M. (1972) 'Trade and welfare in general equilibrium.' *Keio Economic Studies* 9, 37–73

174   Mary E. Lovely

Pestieau, P., U.M. Possen, and S.M. Slutsky (1992) 'The penalty for tax evasion when there are audit errors and taxes are set optimally.' Manuscript, May

Pitt, M. (1981) 'Smuggling and price disparity.' *Journal of International Economics* 11, 447–58

Polinsky, A.M., and S. Shavell (1979) 'The optimal tradeoff between the probability and magnitude of fines.' *American Economic Review* 69, 880–91

Sheikh, M. (1974) 'Smuggling, production and welfare.' *Journal of International Economics* 4, 355–64

Srinivasan, T. (1973) 'Tax evasion: a model.' *Journal of Public Economics* 2, 339–46

Thalmann, P. (1992) 'Factor taxes and evasion in general equilibrium.' *Regional Science and Urban Economics* 22, 259–83

Thursby, M., R. Jensen, and J. Thursby (1991) 'Smuggling, camouflaging, and market structure.' *Quarterly Journal of Economics* 106, 789–814

Trandel, G.A. (1992) 'Evading the use tax on cross-border sales: Pricing and welfare effects.' *Journal of Public Economics* 49, 313–31

Tresch, R.W. (1981) *Public Finance: A Normative Theory* (Plano, TX: Business Publications)

Virmani, A. (1989) 'Indirect tax evasion and production efficiency.' *Journal of Public Economics* 39, 223–37

Yitzhaki, S. (1987) 'On the excess burden of tax evasion.' *Public Finance Quarterly* 15, 123–37

PART II

SCALE ECONOMIES, POLICY, FIRM LOCATION, AND TRADE PATTERNS

Playing by the new subsidy rules: capital subsidies as substitutes for sectoral subsidies

Mary E. Lovely*

Department of Economics, Syracuse University, Syracuse, NY 13244-1090, USA

Abstract

In a small, open economy characterized by an increasing-returns sector and foreign-owned capital, a sector-specific instrument generally is needed to achieve the optimum. A capital subsidy alone can be used for decentralization, however, when the optimal production plan is specialization in the externality-generating activity. The effect of a capital subsidy on home income and its distribution depends on the pattern of production and the share of domestic capital that is foreign owned. In a diversified economy, a subsidy benefits capital owners, harms labor and raises national income only if foreign capital ownership is sufficiently small. In a specialized economy, a subsidy may raise national income even if all domestic capital is foreign owned and, if it does, both labor and capital owners gain. Thus, a capital subsidy may be an attractive replacement for sector-specific subsidies proscribed by international agreements.

Keywords: Factor subsidies; Capital mobility; Increasing returns

JEL classification: F12

1. Introduction

The Uruguay Round of the GATT has sharply restricted the use of subsidy policies targeted toward particular sectors.[1] The new subsidy rules, however, leave

---

*Corresponding author: Tel.: 315-443-9048; Fax: 315-443-9085; e-mail: melovely@maxwell.syr.edu.
[1]Under the Agreement on Subsidies and Countervailing Measures, subsidies that are specific to a particular industry may be actionable, in the sense of being subject to the consultation and dispute settlement procedures of the World Trade Organization, and may be subject to countervailing duties. For more details on the Agreement see Schott (1994) and Baldwin (1995).

0022-1996/97/$17.00 © 1997 Elsevier Science B.V. All rights reserved
PII S0022-1996(96)01474-2

464   *M.E. Lovely / Journal of International Economics 43 (1997) 463-482*

considerable room for targeting, particularly in the form of general factor subsidies. Such subsidies may be appealing on several grounds. First, sector-specific subsidies may be first-best policy in the presence of beneficial spillovers, and in their absence, general factor subsidies may be used to shift resources toward sectors that are believed to raise factor productivity. Second, factor subsidies may be used to alter the income distribution. With increasing income inequality in many countries, and with many traditional border instruments for redistribution restricted by the new trade agreement, policymakers may look more intensely at factor subsidies as a method for raising real incomes of local factors, particularly labor, by attracting footloose factors to their jurisdictions.

This paper investigates the extent to which a general capital subsidy can substitute for sector-specific policies by shifting production toward a spillover-producing sector and by raising domestic income. We consider a small, open economy that may produce two final goods using labor and capital. Production of the manufactured good is assumed to be capital intensive and experiences increasing returns from variety in the intermediates sector.[2] Labor is inter-jurisdictionally immobile and represents the non-tradable productive base of a local economy. Capital is internationally mobile and represents locationally footloose productive factors. We allow for the possibility that the home country faces an upward sloping capital supply curve.

Subsidizing a sector generating returns to variety may be optimal if domestic policy has a non-negligible effect on the number of intermediates producers (see Markusen, 1989; Francois, 1992; Holtz-Eakin and Lovely, 1996). With targeted subsidies restricted as unfair trade practices, however, can general factor subsidies substitute for sector-specific policies by raising home income in the presence of increasing returns and foreign capital? We show that generally optimal policy requires a sector-specific instrument, but that a capital subsidy alone can be used when the optimal production plan is specialization in the spillover-generating sector. We investigate the introduction of a small capital subsidy to a market economy and show that when the economy is diversified the impact of the subsidy on home income depends on the extent of foreign ownership of domestic capital. A capital subsidy cannot raise home income when foreign capital ownership is sufficiently large as then the income increase produced by a larger externality-generating sector is transferred to foreigners through factor-price movements. When the economy is specialized, a capital subsidy may raise home income even if all domestic capital is foreign-owned. Moreover, if a capital subsidy raises home income, both factors benefit. Thus, a capital subsidy may be an attractive replacement for sector-specific subsidies.

---

[2]This model is based on Ethier-type models of trade in intermediates. A similar analysis would derive from the use of models involving differentiated consumer goods, as in Dixit and Norman (1980). Markusen (1990) and Francois (1994) exploit the structural similarities between these two types of models.

M.E. Lovely / Journal of International Economics 43 (1997) 463–482 465

The next section summarizes the model of increasing returns to variety. In the third section, we portray the social optimum and characterize the policies needed to support it as a competitive equilibrium. In the fourth section, we consider the ability of a small capital subsidy to raise home income and its distributional consequences in the context of two stable equilibria: diversification and specialization in manufacturing. We conclude with an assessment of the attraction of capital subsidies when sector-specific policies are proscribed.

2. A model of increasing returns to variety

The model is adapted from Ethier (1982) and emphasizes returns from increased variety of intermediate inputs. A small, open economy consumes two internationally-traded final goods, grain (G) and finished manufactures (M) taking the relative price, P_M/P_G, as given. Grain is supplied by perfect competitors using capital and labor in a constant-returns-to-scale technology. Capital and labor may also be used, again in a constant-returns-to-scale technology, to produce factor bundles (f), which serve as inputs into the production of intermediates. In the final stage, intermediates are costlessly assembled into the finished manufactured good. Manufacturing is capital intensive relative to grain production and there are no factor-intensity reversals.[3]

Factors are intersectorally mobile. Labor is internationally immobile and capital is internationally mobile. The home country faces a supply curve for capital that may slope upward if foreign capital owners demand a premium as home capital comprises an increasing portion of their investment portfolios. The supply price of capital is $r^*(K^*)$, and the elasticity of r^* with respect to the domestically-located, foreign-owned capital stock, K^*, is denoted by $1/\phi(K^*) \geq 0$. If the home country is a price taker for capital, $\phi = \infty$. For exposition, we assume that the home country imports capital, implying that changes in the total stock occur through changes in K^*.

Supplies of capital and labor and the technology for producing grain and factor bundles define a transformation function for the economy: $f = T(G, K^*)$, which, for a given K^*, may be represented by a familiar strictly concave-to-the-origin production possibilities frontier, with $T_G < 0$ and $T_{GG} < 0$.[4] If both grain and intermediates are produced, the opportunity cost of factor bundles in terms of grain is given by

$$P_f(G, K^*) \equiv \frac{-1}{T_G(G, K^*)}. \tag{1}$$

---

[3]Wong (1990) shows that if all sectors have CES technologies, factor intensity reversals cannot occur.
[4]$T_G = \partial T/\partial G$ and other derivatives are defined analogously.

Holding G constant, a capital inflow raises the maximum amount of f that can be produced, implying $T_K > 0$.

The production technology for assembling the manufactured good, M, is given by

$$M = \left[\sum_{i=1}^{n} x_i^{\beta} \right]^{(1/\beta)}, \tag{2}$$

where x_i is the input of intermediate i. Intermediate varieties are imperfect substitutes; β measures the degree of differentiation of inputs, $(0 < \beta < 1)$. The production technology exhibits constant returns to scale for a given number of intermediate varieties and increasing returns with higher degrees of specialization, as measured by the number of intermediates producers, n. These economies are external to the finished manufactures industry and each competitive firm assembling finished manufactures takes n as given.

Intermediates are not traded, perhaps due to the existence of barriers to trade in producer inputs, as in Markusen (1991).[5] Alternatively, the lack of trade may reflect prohibitive transport costs, as when close proximity is required between the intermediates producer and final-goods assembly. Such a formulation is consistent with the notion of localization economies identified in the urban literature (see Sullivan, 1993).

As in Ethier (1982) and Markusen (1989), we assume that all intermediates have identical homothetic cost functions, implying that in equilibrium any produced variety will be produced in the common quantity, x. Given this symmetry, (2) collapses to

$$M = n^{\alpha} x. \tag{3}$$

where $\alpha = 1/\beta > 1$.[6] The cost of producing the quantity x of a given variety of intermediate input is $C_x = (ax + b)P_f$, where a and b are marginal and fixed cost, respectively, indicating increasing returns to scale at the firm level. The total number of factor bundles, f, needed to produce n varieties of intermediates is $f = n(ax + b)$.

3. Optimal policy for income-maximization

Can a capital subsidy be used to raise home income? We address this question by first characterizing optimal policy without policy constraints, thereby defining conditions under which a capital subsidy is a first-best policy. Because we are

---

[5]Grossman and Helpman (Grossman and Helpman, 1991; Chapter 6), in a model in which R and D activity is needed to develop new varieties of differentiated producer goods, also implement the notion of smallness by confining spillover generation to a sector that produces nontradable goods.
[6]As noted by Markusen (1990), this reduced form is consistent with a number of alternative specifications of external scale effects.

M.E. Lovely / Journal of International Economics 43 (1997) 463–482 467

interested in situations in which scale economies are relevant, we consider only those first-best allocations that involve an active manufacturing sector.

3.1. First-best resource allocation

If lump-sum instruments are available for redistribution, domestic welfare depends upon aggregate consumption of grain and finished manufactures, $U = U(C_G, C_M)$. Because we assume free trade in consumption goods, domestic consumers equate the marginal rate of substitution in consumption with the world relative final-goods price ratio. Hence, the first-best allocation maximizes the value of domestic production at world prices.

The planning problem is to choose G, x, and K^* to maximize national income,

$$P_M n^\alpha x + G - r^* K^*, \tag{4}$$

subject to $n = f/(ax + b)$, $f = T(G, K^*)$ and $r^* = r^*(K^*)$. Optimal values are characterized by the first-order conditions[7]

$$\frac{\alpha P_M n^{\alpha-1} x}{ax + b} T_G + 1 \le 0; \text{ if} <, G = 0 \tag{5}$$

$$\alpha P_M n^\alpha xa = P_M n^\alpha (ax + b), \tag{6}$$

and

$$\frac{\alpha P_M n^{\alpha-1} x}{ax + b} T_K = r^* + \frac{\partial r^*}{\partial K^*}, \tag{7}$$

where we have allowed for the possibility that the optimum entails specializing in manufactures.

Using (6) the optimal (defined by a tilde) scale of production for each variety is

$$\tilde{x} = \frac{b}{(\alpha - 1)a}, \tag{8}$$

which depends on the ratio of fixed to marginal costs, the latter of which are weighted by $\alpha - 1$, the rate at which the economy realizes the external economy. If the optimum is a diversified production plan, the optimal diversity of components can be defined using $\tilde{x}$ and (5) as:

---

[7]The conditions for income maximization with nontraded intermediates have been derived by Markusen (1989) and by Holtz-Eakin and Lovely (1996) for the case of internationally immobile capital. Grossman and Helpman (1991) show that subsidization is also required for optimality when new intermediates varieties arise through R and D activity. When a country is large enough to influence world prices, welfare maximization requires the weighing of scale effects arising from subsidization against the resulting term-of-trade effects. As Francois (1992) notes, when these term-of-trade effects are large, subsidization of the traditional sector may be indicated.

$$\tilde{n} = \frac{f(\tilde{G}, \tilde{K}^*)}{a\tilde{x} + b} = \left[\frac{P_f(\tilde{G}, \tilde{K}^*)a}{P_M} \right]^{\frac{1}{\alpha - 1}}. \tag{9}$$

The optimal domestic capital stock equates the value marginal product of capital in manufacturing to the marginal cost of capital. For a given G, (7) implicitly defines the optimal capital inflow:

$$P_f(\tilde{G}, \tilde{K}^*)T_K(\tilde{G}, \tilde{K}^*) = r^* \left[\frac{\phi(\tilde{K}^*) + 1}{\phi(\tilde{K}^*)} \right]. \tag{10}$$

Eqs. (9,10) constitute a system of two equations that implicitly defines $\tilde{G}$ and $\tilde{K}$. If the optimum is consistent with specialization in manufactures, expression (5) is an inequality and $\tilde{G} = 0$. Eq. (8) continues to describe $\tilde{x}$ while Eq. (10) describes the optimal capital inflow. The optimal production plan will be a specialized one if, using (5), the shadow price of domestic grain production (expressed as the value of manufactures foregone) exceeds the shadow price of importing the same good (which is unity). Such a situation will arise when there is no value of K^* for which the value marginal product of capital in a diversified economy is equal to the marginal cost of capital.

3.2. Decentralizing the optimum without policy constraints

Can the government induce the market economy to achieve the first-best allocation when it is unconstrained in its use of policy instruments? Decentralization may require two independent instruments. First, an instrument may be needed to raise the number of intermediates produced by the market, as shown by Markusen (1989) in a model with immobile capital.[8] In light of this, we allow for a subsidy to factor-bundle purchases by intermediates producers, with the *ad valorem* subsidy denoted by s_f. A second instrument may be needed in recognition of the influence of K^* on the cost of capital. This instrument is a tax on domestic capital earnings, regardless of the residence of the capital owner (source-based taxation), at the rate t_k.[9]

Because intermediate varieties are imperfect substitutes, each producer experiences some market power. We assume there is free entry into the industry and

---

[8] It can be shown that the laissez-faire equilibrium will be characterized by an insufficient variety of intermediates if, in the neighborhood of the equilibrium, the production possibility frontier for G and f, given K, is concave to the origin. The PPF will be locally bowed out if the "intersectoral effect", given by the elasticity of the opportunity cost of factor bundles, exceeds the "scale effect", given by $\alpha - 1$, in the terminology of Ethier (1982).

[9] The need for two instruments when there is a goods market and a capital market distortion is well established in the context of a large country facing variable terms of trade (Kemp, 1966). Jones (1967) and Brecher (1983) examine the policy problem when either the trade or capital tax/subsidy is arbitrarily set to zero.

M.E. Lovely / Journal of International Economics 43 (1997) 463–482   469

that the number of firms is large enough so that each firm behaves as a monopolistic competitor. Within this framework, the elasticity of substitution between any pair of intermediate varieties is approximated by $1/(1-\beta)$, which is also the price elasticity of demand. Each intermediates producer takes the price of factor bundles in terms of grain, P_f, as given.

Producers equate marginal cost and marginal revenue, setting a price of

$$P_x = \frac{P_f(1-s_f)a}{\beta}, \tag{11}$$

which reflects constant mark-uppricing. Free entry implies zero profits in equilibrium and that the common value of x will be

$$x^e = \frac{b}{(\alpha-1)a}. \tag{12}$$

where the superscript "e" denotes an equilibrium value. A comparison of x^e and $\tilde{x}$ confirms that the competitive and optimal scale of production coincide. The price of finished manufactures is the international trading price, P_M. Free entry generates zero profits in assembly of intermediates into final goods, implying $P_M M = P_x nx$. Using the technology for M, given by (3), the price of manufactures generates a demand price for intermediates of

$$P_x = P_M n^{\alpha-1}. \tag{13}$$

Using (11) in (13), the variety achieved by the competitive equilibrium is

$$n^e = \left[\frac{P_f(G^e, K^{*e})(1-s_f)a}{\beta P_M}\right]^{\frac{1}{\alpha-1}}. \tag{14}$$

Perfect capital mobility implies that capital owners locate their capital so that the after-tax domestic return equals the required rental rate:

$$r(1-t_K) = r^*(K^*), \tag{15}$$

where $r = r(P_M, K^*)$ and is the domestic rental rate obtaining in the market equilibrium. With no distortions in the market for factors, the value marginal product of capital in factor bundles equals the domestic rental rate, r. Therefore, using (15), the competitive equilibrium is characterized by

$$P_f(G^e, K^{*e})T_K(G^e, K^{*e})(1-t_K) = r^*(K^{*e}). \tag{16}$$

We consider first decentralization of an optimal plan in which both grain and manufactures are produced in positive quantities. Comparing (14) and (16) with the planning conditions (9) and (10) indicates that the number of firms will be optimal if intermediates are priced at marginal cost and if marginal cost reflects the social marginal cost of capital. The competitive equilibrium will achieve the

470   *M.E. Lovely / Journal of International Economics 43 (1997) 463–482*

income-maximizing resource allocation if the factor-bundles subsidy and the capital income tax is set so that

$$s_f = 1 - \beta > 0, \quad t_K = \frac{1}{1 + \phi(\tilde{K}^*)} > 0. \tag{17}$$

These two instruments permit the simultaneous adjustment of the allocation of resources to the manufacturing sector and of the private cost of capital.

Although s_f and t_K are not the only instruments that may be used to achieve the first best, when the optimal production plan is diversified any successful intervention must contain a sector-specific instrument. Combined with a capital tax, a variety of sector-specific tools, such as a subsidy to finished manufactures, a subsidy to factor-bundle purchases, or a combination of an output subsidy and a lump-sum tax on intermediates producers can be used to decentralize the optimum.[10] Non-sector-specific policies cannot both allocate labor and capital between grain and manufactures and maintain K^* at the optimal level. In particular, general factor subsidies cannot play this role. A capital subsidy shifts production toward the capital-intensive sector, thereby achieving the desired expansion of the manufacturing sector. Such a subsidy, however, is simply a negative capital tax and, thus, is not independent of the instrument needed to ensure an optimal capital inflow. A general labor subsidy, in contrast, is independent of the capital tax but has no effect on resource allocation; rather, it is simply shifted to labor which is in fixed supply.

If the optimal production plan is specialization in manufactures, and if the competitive equilibrium is specialized, there is no misallocation of resources between grain and manufacturing because all resources are devoted to manufacturing. The task for welfare-improving intervention, therefore, is to ensure that the market achieves the optimal capital inflow. Intervention that raises the local capital stock raises production of factor bundles, and hence the number of local intermediates varieties.

To express capital-market equilibrium with specialization, we recognize that P_f is not given by the slope of the production frontier for G and f, but instead use (11) and (13) to obtain an expression for P_f. Noting that the value marginal product of capital in factor bundles equals the rental rate, using the new expression for P_f, and noting that $n = f/(ax + b)$, the capital-market equilibrium condition becomes:

$$\frac{\beta P_M}{a(1 - s_f)} \left[\frac{f(0, K^*)(\alpha - 1)}{\alpha b} \right]^{\alpha - 1} T_K(0, K^*)(1 - t_K) = r^*(K^*), \tag{18}$$

which is an expression in K^* characterizing the market outcome. The analogous planning condition is, using (3) and the solution for $\tilde{x}$ (given by Eq. (8)),

---

[10]See Holtz-Eakin and Lovely (1996) for an analysis of these policies with a fixed capital supply.

M.E. Lovely / Journal of International Economics 43 (1997) 463–482   471

$$\frac{P_M}{a}\left[\frac{f(0,\tilde{K}^*)(\alpha-1)}{\alpha b}\right]^{\alpha-1} T_K(0,\tilde{K}^*) = r^*(\tilde{K}^*)\left[\frac{\phi(\tilde{K}^*)+1}{\phi(\tilde{K}^*)}\right]. \tag{19}$$

A comparison of (18) and (19) reveals that the market K^* will equal the planner's choice when

$$\beta\frac{(1-t_K)}{(1-s_f)} = \frac{\phi(\tilde{K}^*)}{\phi(\tilde{K}^*)+1}. \tag{20}$$

Because there is only one distortion in the market economy in the neighborhood of the optimum, only one instrument is needed to achieve the optimum. Either a capital tax/subsidy or a factor-bundles tax/subsidy could alter the domestically-located capital stock and equate the social marginal value and the marginal cost of capital. In particular, if the capital supply curve is horizontal ($\phi=\infty$) the optimal allocation can be achieved with any combination of s_f and t_K such that $(1-s_f)/(1-t_K)=\beta$, including no specific subsidy ($s_f=0$) and a capital subsidy of $\alpha-1$.

4. Playing by the new subsidy rules

If sector-specific policies and tariffs are proscribed by international agreement, government action is limited to the use of general factor taxes or subsidies. A general capital subsidy may be an attractive policy because it promotes expansion of the increasing-returns sector. With foreign ownership of domestic capital, however, the effect of this expansion on national income depends on the domestic share of additional income created through factor reallocation. Because it is capital income that flows to foreign residents, national income implications are tied to the subsidy's effect on wages and the return to capital.

These distributional effects can be traced out by examining the comparative-statics properties of the economy. As is well known in the literature on variable returns to scale, however, perverse comparative-static results are possible when one or more sectors is subject to increasing returns to scale, as in the present case.[11]

One way to determine the signs of comparative-statics results, as first suggested by Mayer (1974), is to consider only stable production equilibria.[12] Ide and Takayama (1991) have shown that a production equilibrium is Marshallian stable

---

[11]See Wong (1995) for a full discussion of perverse comparative-statics results and production stability.

[12]The justification for such a procedure is Samuelson's (Samuelson, 1947) correspondence principle, which suggests that there is no need to consider perverse comparative statics results because unstable production equilibria are almost never observed.

472   *M.E. Lovely / Journal of International Economics 43 (1997) 463–482*

if and only if output responses to prices are normal (i.e. the relative supply of good 1 to good 2 rises when the relative price of good 1 to good 2 rises). In the analysis to follow, we restrict ourselves to consideration of stable production equilibria. A second stability issue arises with regard to the international capital market.[13] First, there is a possibility of multiple international equilibria. Secondly, not all of these equilibria will be Marshallian stable. In particular, stability is of concern when the home economy is diversified because then the local demand curve for capital is upward sloping, as is the supply curve for capital. We therefore restrict our attention to two stable international equilibria, each with an active home manufacturing sector. In the first equilibrium we consider, which we assume has an initial capital stock consistent with diversified production, we also assume that $1/\phi$ is large enough to ensure that the supply curve of foreign capital is more steeply sloped than the demand curve (i.e that the capital market equilibrium is stable). The second equilibrium considered has an initial capital stock consistent with specialized production in manufactures. Such an equilibrium is stable, regardless of the value of $1/\phi$, when the capital stock is large thereby ensuring that the marginal product of capital falls when the local capital stock rises. In analyzing this case, we assume that the capital stock meets this condition. For each case, we derive the effect of a capital subsidy on factor prices and use these solutions to evaluate the subsidy's distributional and national income consequences.

We find that in a diversified economy, a capital subsidy has a magnified effect on the return to capital and lowers the wage. Thus, it transfers income from immobile labor to capital owners. The effect of this transfer on national income depends on the share of domestic capital owned by domestic residents. Unless this share is sufficiently large, national income will be diminished by a capital subsidy. In contrast, a subsidy offered in a specialized economy raises the return to capital by proportionately less than the subsidy and raises the wage. If the subsidy raises the after-subsidy-financing return to labor, it also raises national income, regardless of the extent of foreign capital ownership. If labor's net return falls, a subsidy nonetheless will raise national income if foreign ownership is sufficiently small.

---

[13]International capital-market stability is formally treated in an appendix available from the author on request. The analysis uses a Marshallian quantity-adjustment rule: if the domestic return to capital exceeds the supply price of foreign-owned capital, additional capital flows to the domestic economy. Only capital-market stability is analyzed because the supply price of capital is the only external price over which the home economy may have influence. The home may be large only in the market for its own debt. Multiple capital-market equilibria may exist. In particular, if the supply curve is flat, three capital-market equilibria may exist. The diversified equilibrium is unstable while the two specialized equilibria are stable. Although there may be a stable equilibrium consistent with specialization in grain, we do not analyze the effect of a capital subsidy in this case because a small subsidy cannot raise national income. The only distortion in the economy is the average cost pricing of foreign capital and a capital tax rather than subsidy would be needed to correct this.

4.1. A capital subsidy in a diversified economy

The government is assumed to offer a small *ad valorem* capital subsidy, s_K. The effect of this subsidy on factor prices and outputs can be derived in two steps. First, we totally differentiate the constant-returns-to-scale portion of the system (which may be termed the "virtual system," as in Wong, 1995). This differentiation treats P_f as an exogenous variable and proceeds by total differentiation of the familiar price-equals-cost and full-employment equations for factor bundles and grain. Appendix A contains these solutions, where the proportionate change in the subsidy is measured as $\hat{S}_K = d(1 + s_K)/(1 + s_K)$. The full-employment conditions have been modified to permit capital mobility, using the condition for equilibrium in the local capital market: $r(1 + s_K) = r^*(K^*)$. Differentiating and rearranging this condition leads to an expression for the capital inflow, $\hat{K}^* = \phi(\hat{r} + \hat{S}_K)$.

An expression for $\hat{P}_f$ can be derived by noting that with mark-up pricing, an increase in P_f is passed through to the intermediates sector: $\hat{P}_x = \hat{P}_f$. A fixed external price of manufactures, however, implies that an increase in P_x can only be sustained by an increase in the average productivity of intermediates arising from greater variety. This relationship can be seen by differentiating the condition for zero profits in finished manufactures, noting that the scale of production, x, is not affected by factor subsidies: $\hat{M} = \hat{P}_x + \hat{n}$. Increases in manufacturing output, however, must conform to the production technology (3), implying that $\hat{M} = \alpha \hat{n}$. With x unaffected by factor subsidies, an increase in resources devoted to factor bundles translates directly into an increase in the number of varieties, $\hat{n} = \hat{f}$. Thus, combining these results,

$$\hat{P}_f = (\alpha - 1)\hat{f}, \tag{21}$$

which provides the elasticity of the derived demand curve for factor bundles, reflecting the rate at which the economy realizes returns to variety.[14] Combining (21) and the expression for the change in factor-bundle production from Appendix A yields

$$\hat{P}_f = \frac{(\alpha - 1)\phi\lambda_{LG}}{\lambda D_1} \hat{S}_K, \tag{22}$$

where $D_1 = 1 - (\alpha - 1)\eta_{Pf}$, $\eta_{Pf} = (A_f + \phi\theta_{LG}\lambda_{LG})/\lambda\theta$, A_f is a positive constant

---

[14] Eq. (21) indicates that the demand curve for factor bundles is upward sloping. This upward-sloping demand curve raises concern about local production stability. Our assumption that the price–output response is normal ensures production stability: the slope of the factor-bundle demand curve must then be flatter than the factor-bundle supply curve. See Wong (1995) for a discussion in the more general context of external economies of scale.

defined in Appendix A, the λ_{ij} are factor shares, and the θ_{ij} are value shares. λ and θ are determinants of the matrices of factor shares and value shares, respectively, and both are positive by the factor-intensity assumption. D_1 is positive because we have assumed the final-goods price–output effect is normal, as required for production stability and as shown in Appendix B.

The capital subsidy leads to an increase in the price of factor bundles because of the capital inflow.[15] If the price of factor-bundles is held fixed, then by the Rybczynski theorem a capital inflow leads to increased production of f and less of G. Because x is constant, there is an equi-proportionate increase in the number of intermediate varieties. Scale economies in final manufacturing imply that with a normal price–output response the increase in derived demand for factor bundles exceeds the supply increase and the price of factor bundles must rise.

The concomitant expansion of f production can be obtained from Eq. (21) and the expression for the change in factor bundles in Appendix A,

$$\hat{f} = \hat{n} = \frac{\phi \lambda_{LG}}{\lambda D_1} \hat{S}_K > 0, \tag{23}$$

indicating that a subsidy raises the number of intermediates producers when capital is mobile.

We now express the effect of a subsidy on the wage, w, and the rental, r, inclusive of the subsidy, using Eq. (21) and factor price expressions from Appendix A:

$$\hat{w} = -\frac{\theta_{KG}}{\theta \lambda} \frac{(\alpha - 1)\phi \lambda_{LG}}{D_1} \hat{S}_K < 0 \tag{24}$$

$$\hat{r} + \hat{S}_K = \left[\frac{\theta_{LG}}{\theta \lambda} \frac{(\alpha - 1)\phi \lambda_{LG}}{D_1} + 1 \right] \hat{S}_K > 0. \tag{25}$$

A capital subsidy lowers the wage and raises the return to capital, with these effects larger the flatter the capital supply curve and the greater the magnitude of the increasing returns.

We have shown that the subsidy produces distributional conflict in that real wages decline while the return to inframarginal capital rises above the amount necessary to keep it located in the domestic economy. We turn now to assess the subsidy's effect on national income to see if labor's loss could be compensated by domestic capital owners.

If the equilibrium is diversified, national income is $NI = P_M \, M + G - r^* K^*$. Totally differentiating NI with respect to the capital subsidy, expressed in percentage changes, yields

---

[15]Differentiation of (23) with respect to ϕ shows that this price effect is larger the more elastic the capital stock, for then the productivity effect of the subsidy is larger.

$$\frac{\hat{NI}}{\hat{S}_K} = \frac{P_M M}{NI} \frac{\hat{M}}{\hat{S}_K} + \frac{G}{NI} \frac{\hat{G}}{\hat{S}_K} - \left[1 + \frac{1}{\phi}\right] \frac{r^* K^*}{NI} \frac{\hat{K}^*}{\hat{S}_K}. \tag{26}$$

To simplify this expression, note that $\hat{M} = \alpha \hat{n} = \alpha \hat{f}$. Additionally, zero profits in manufactures implies $P_M M = P_x nx$ and using the expressions for P_x and x given by (11) and (12), $P_x nx = P_f f$. With these substitutions and adding and subtracting $P_f \hat{f} / \hat{S}_K$, the national income effect is

$$\frac{\hat{NI}}{\hat{S}_K} = \frac{(\alpha - 1)P_f f}{NI} \frac{\hat{f}}{\hat{S}_K} - \frac{1}{\phi} \frac{r^* K^*}{NI} \frac{\hat{K}^*}{\hat{S}_K} + \frac{P_f f}{NI} \frac{\hat{f}}{\hat{S}_K} + \frac{G}{NI} \frac{\hat{G}}{\hat{S}_K} - \frac{r^* K^*}{NI} \frac{\hat{K}^*}{\hat{S}_K}. \tag{27}$$

The last three terms on the right-hand side of (27) cancel because cost minimization and perfect capital mobility ensure that $P_f \, df/dK^* + dG/dK^* = r^*$. What remains is

$$\frac{\hat{NI}}{\hat{S}_K} = \frac{(\alpha - 1)P_f f}{NI} \frac{\hat{f}}{\hat{S}_K} - \frac{1}{\phi} \frac{r^* K^*}{NI} \frac{\hat{K}^*}{\hat{S}_K}. \tag{28}$$

An expression for $\hat{f}/\hat{S}_K$ is given by (23). An expression for $\hat{K}^*/\hat{S}_K$ can be derived using the capital mobility condition, $\hat{K}^* = \phi(\hat{r} + \hat{S}_K)$, and Eq. (25). Substituting these into (28),

$$\frac{\hat{NI}}{\hat{S}_K} = \frac{(\alpha - 1)P_f f}{NI} \frac{\phi \lambda_{LG}}{\lambda D_1} - \frac{r^* K^*}{NI} \left[\frac{(\alpha - 1)\phi \lambda_{LG} \theta_{LG}}{\theta \lambda D_1} + 1 \right]. \tag{29}$$

Because $\theta = \theta_{LG} - \theta_{Lf}$, substitution and rearranging yields

$$\frac{\hat{NI}}{\hat{S}_K} = \frac{(P_f f - r^* K^*)}{NI} \frac{(\alpha - 1)\phi \lambda_{LG} \theta_{LG}}{\theta \lambda D_1} - \frac{P_f f}{NI} \frac{(\alpha - 1)\phi \lambda_{LG} \theta_{Lf}}{\theta \lambda D_1} - \frac{r^* K^*}{NI}. \tag{30}$$

A capital subsidy raises national income only if the first term on the right-hand side is positive and large enough to outweigh the remaining negative terms. Thus, a necessary but not sufficient condition for national income to rise is $P_f f > r^* K^*$, that revenue from factor-bundles production exceeds rental payments to foreign capital owners. Unless this condition is met, implying that the value of the induced increase in factor bundles production exceeds the higher net-of-subsidy payments to foreign capital also induced, the subsidy cannot raise national income.

Insight into this condition can be gained by considering two extreme circumstances. First, suppose the initial capital stock is almost entirely owned by domestic residents. In this case, K^* is almost zero and inspection of (28) shows that $\hat{NI}$ must be positive. The inflow of capital raises gross national product by raising output in the manufacturing sector. Even though the return to capital rises by more than the subsidy ($\hat{r} + \hat{S}_K > \hat{S}_K$), transferring the real-income gain from expanding manufactures to capital owners, gross domestic product also rises since the capital stock is locally owned.

Alternatively, if the domestic capital stock is entirely foreign owned, national income must fall in response to a capital subsidy. As shown above, the return to domestic labor declines and is further reduced by the burden of subsidy financing. The increase in the value of production created by the capital inflow is completely transferred to foreign capital owners with a concomitant effect on wages that reduces labor's real income beyond the subsidy payment.

In sum, a capital subsidy offered in the context of a diversified economy with external economies of scale produces distributional conflict. It raises national income only if foreign-owned capital is a sufficiently small portion of the total capital stock. Although the subsidy offsets the underproduction of manufactures caused by monopoly pricing of intermediates, the social surplus generated by a capital subsidy flows entirely to capital owners. To the extent these owners are not domestic residents, this transfer reduces national income.

4.2. A capital subsidy in a specialized economy

We will now see that a capital subsidy has a qualitatively different effect in a specialized economy. The effect of a small *ad valorem* capital subsidy, s_K, in the specialized equilibrium can be derived by combining results from total differentiation of the virtual system, provided in Appendix A, and the derived demand for factor bundles, Eq. (21). The change in P_f is

$$\hat{P}_f = \frac{(\alpha - 1)}{D_2} \epsilon_{Pf} \hat{S}_K, \tag{31}$$

where $D_2 = 1 - (\alpha - 1)\epsilon_{Pf}$ and ϵ_{Pf} is a positive constant defined in Appendix A. $D_2 > 0$ by our assumption of a positive final-goods price–output response, as necessary for a stable production equilibrium and as shown in Appendix B. The associated increase in factor-bundles production is

$$\hat{f} = \frac{\phi \sigma_f \theta_{Kf}}{\gamma D_2} \hat{S}_K, \tag{32}$$

where σ_f is the elasticity of factor substitution in factor bundles and γ is a positive constant defined in Appendix A. The flatter the capital supply curve, the larger the capital inflow and the increase in n induced by the capital subsidy, and the larger the increase in P_f.

Using (31) and the factor-price expressions in Appendix A, changes in factor returns are

$$\hat{w} = \frac{\phi \theta_{Kf}(1 + (\alpha - 1)\sigma_f)}{\gamma D_2} \hat{S}_K \tag{33}$$

M.E. Lovely / Journal of International Economics 43 (1997) 463–482 477

$$\hat{r} + \hat{S}_K = \frac{\sigma_f}{\gamma D_2} \hat{S}_K. \tag{34}$$

These solutions indicate that in a specialized economy, a capital subsidy raises both the wage and the subsidy-inclusive return to capital owners, given $D_2 > 0$. Using (34), it can be easily shown that $\hat{r} + \hat{S}_K < \hat{S}_K$; that is, in contrast to the diversified economy, the subsidy-inclusive return to capital rises by proportionally less than the subsidy.

Although both the wage and the return to capital rise, a subsidy must be financed; thus, we investigate the wage net of subsidy financing. Assuming that labor bears the full burden of subsidy financing, labor's real income from each unit of labor is the wage minus his or her share of capital subsidy financing. The change in net-of-subsidy-funding earnings per unit of manufacturing labor, $\hat{Y}_L$, is:

$$\hat{Y}_L = \hat{w} - \frac{\theta_{Kf}}{\theta_{Lf}} \hat{S}_K. \tag{35}$$

Substituting in the solution for $\hat{w}$ (Eq. (33)), and rearranging yields

$$\hat{Y}_L = \frac{(\phi(\alpha - 1) - 1)\sigma_f \theta_{Kf}}{\theta_{Lf} \gamma D_2}. \tag{36}$$

This expression is positive if $\alpha - 1 > 1/\phi$. This condition is a simple cost-benefit test for an incremental capital inflow to benefit immobile factors. The marginal increase in aggregate income (GNP) of an incremental capital inflow is αr while the marginal increase in capital income is $(1 + 1/\phi)r^*$. Since capital market equilibrium ensures $r = r^*$, the marginal benefit to labor exceeds the marginal cost only if $\alpha - 1 > 1/\phi$.

While an increase in the net wage guarantees an increase in national income, since both capital and labor gain, it is not necessary. With specialization, national income is $NI = P_M M - r^* K^*$. Totally differentiating NI and using percentage changes,

$$\frac{\hat{NI}}{\hat{S}_K} = \frac{(\alpha - 1)P_f f}{NI} \frac{\hat{f}}{\hat{S}_K} - \frac{1}{\phi} \frac{r^* K^*}{NI} \frac{\hat{K}^*}{\hat{S}_K} + \frac{P_f f}{NI} \frac{\hat{f}}{\hat{S}_K} - \frac{r^* K^*}{NI} \frac{\hat{K}^*}{\hat{S}_K}, \tag{37}$$

where we have used $P_M M \hat{M} = \alpha P_f f \hat{f}$. Because $P_f \, df/dK^* = r$ and $r = r^*$, the last two terms on the right-hand side of (37) cancel. Using (32) and (34) and the capital mobility condition,

$$\frac{\hat{NI}}{\hat{S}_K} = \frac{(\alpha - 1)P_f f}{NI} \frac{\phi \sigma_f \theta_{Kf}}{\gamma D_2} - \frac{r^* K^*}{NI} \frac{\sigma_f}{\gamma D_2}. \tag{38}$$

Further insight into this result can be gained by noting that

478   *M.E. Lovely / Journal of International Economics 43 (1997) 463–482*

$$\frac{P_f f}{rK}\frac{rK}{NI} = \frac{\lambda_{Kf}}{\theta_{Kf}}\frac{rK}{NI} = \frac{1}{\theta_K f}\frac{rK}{NI},$$ (39)

where $\lambda_{Kf} = 1$ due to specialization and K is the total capital stock. Using (39) in (38),

$$\frac{\hat{NI}}{\hat{S}_K} = \frac{(\alpha - 1)\phi rK - r^*K^*}{NI}\frac{\sigma_f}{\gamma D_2}.$$ (40)

Because $rK \geq r^*K^*$, a sufficient condition for the change in national income to be positive is $\alpha - 1 > 1/\phi$. This condition ensures that the rate at which the economy realizes scale economies because of the capital inflow $(\alpha - 1)$ exceeds the rate at which the inflow raises the cost of capital $(1/\phi)$. This is the case we have noted above in which net labor income increases and thus national income rises even if all capital is foreign owned. However, if this condition is not met but foreign ownership is sufficiently small, (40) is positive. A subsidy will raise national income when losses from a lower net wage are outweighed by gains to domestic capital owners.

5. Conclusion

Desiring to capture external economies, but restrained by international agreements proscribing sector-specific remedies, policymakers may consider the use of general factor taxes and subsidies. When resources are misallocated across sectors and when a country's excess demand for capital influences the foreign supply price, a sector-specific instrument as well as a capital tax/subsidy is needed to decentralize the optimum. A capital subsidy alone can be used for decentralization, however, when the optimal production plan is specialization in the externality-generating activity.

The effect of a capital subsidy on home income and its distribution depends on the pattern of production. In a diversified economy, a subsidy benefits capital owners, harms labor and raises national income only if foreign capital ownership is sufficiently small. In a specialized economy, a subsidy may benefit both labor and capital and, if it does, national income increases even if all domestic capital is foreign owned. When the subsidy reduces labor's income net of subsidy financing, national income nonetheless may rise if a sufficiently large share of domestic capital is domestically owned.

These results underscore the importance of capital mobility and increasing returns to the ability of policymakers to help immobile factors with general factor subsidies. Without capital mobility, a general capital subsidy merely transfers resources from taxpayers to capital owners, with no effect on resource allocation. To capture increasing returns, sector-specific policies must be used. When capital

M.E. Lovely / Journal of International Economics 43 (1997) 463–482 479

is mobile, however, a general capital subsidy raises output in the spillover-producing sector and, under the circumstances we have identified, raises national income and, in the specialized economy, the real income of immobile labor. With international capital mobility, therefore, there may be compelling efficiency and equity reasons for adhering to the letter but not the spirit of the new subsidy rules.

Acknowledgments

I thank, without implication, Zhiqi Chen, Douglas Holtz-Eakin, Douglas Nelson, J. David Richardson, John D. Wilson, John Yinger and two anonymous referees for helpful comments.

Appendix A

Selected Results from Total Differentiation of the Virtual System

Diversified equilibrium

The conditions for a stable, diversified equilibrium include the familiar price-equals-cost and full-employment equations. Total differentiation of this system, letting $\hat{S}_K = d(1 + s_K)/(1 + s_K)$, $\hat{K} = \phi(\hat{r} + \hat{S}_K)$, and treating $\hat{P}_f$ as exogenous, yields expressions for factor price and output changes as functions of $\hat{P}_f$ and $\hat{S}_K$. From the price–cost equations,

$$\hat{w} = -\frac{\theta_{KG}}{\theta} \hat{P}_f; \qquad \hat{r} = \frac{\theta_{LG}}{\theta} \hat{P}_f, \tag{A1}$$

where the θ_{ij} are value shares, w and r are the wage and rental rate, respectively, P_f is the relative price of factor bundles in terms of grain, and a "$\wedge$" indicates a percentage change.[16] $\theta = \theta_{Kf} - \theta_{KG}$ is a measure of relative factor intensity and is positive by our assumption that intermediates production is capital intensive relative to grain. In addition to goods-market equilibrium, factor markets must also

---

[16]The value share for labor in f production is defined as $A_{LF}w/P_f$ while the share of labor in f production is defined as $A_{Lf}f/L$, and similarly for the other terms. A concise derivation of the four-equation system is given in Caves et al. (1990), Supplement 7.

clear. Using the expressions for factor prices, the full-employment equations, and letting σ_j denote the elasticity of factor substitution in industry j,

$$\hat{f} = \frac{(A_f + \phi\theta_{LG}\lambda_{LG})}{\lambda\theta}\,\hat{P}_f + \frac{\phi\lambda_{LG}}{\lambda}\,\hat{S}_K \equiv \eta_{Pf}\hat{P}_f + \frac{\phi\lambda_{LG}}{\lambda}\,\hat{S}_K, \tag{A2}$$

where $A_f = \sigma_f(\lambda_{LG}\lambda_{Kf}\theta_{Lf} + \lambda_{KG}\lambda_{Lf}\theta_{Kf}) + \sigma_G\lambda_{LG}\lambda_{KG}$, the λ_{ij} are factor shares, and $\lambda = \lambda_{Kf} - \lambda_{Lf}$.

Specialized equilibrium

The specialized equilibrium is characterized by price equal to cost in factor-bundle production and full employment of both factors. Allowing for endogenous capital mobility, and treating $\hat{P}_f$ as exogenous, these three equations can be used to express the changes in factor prices as:

$$\hat{w} = \frac{1}{\gamma}\left[(\phi + \sigma_f)\hat{P}_f + \phi\theta_{Kf}\hat{S}_K\right] \tag{A3}$$

$$\hat{r} + \hat{S}_K = \frac{1}{\gamma}\left[\sigma_f(\hat{P}_f + \hat{S}_K)\right], \tag{A4}$$

where $\gamma = \phi\theta_{Lf} + \sigma_f > 0$. The concomitant expansion of f production is given by

$$\hat{f} = \epsilon_{Pf}(\hat{P}_f + \hat{S}_K), \tag{A5}$$

where $\epsilon_{Pf} = [\phi\sigma_f\theta_{Kf}]/\gamma$ is a positive, increasing function of ϕ that has a finite limit as ϕ approaches infinity.

Appendix B

Final-Goods Price–Output Effects

The final-goods price–output effect provides the response of M to an increase in P_M, holding factor subsidies constant. From the production function (3),

$$\hat{M} = \alpha\hat{n}. \tag{A6}$$

With pass-through pricing, $\hat{P}_X = \hat{P}_f$ and because x does not respond to a change in price, $\hat{n} = \hat{f}$. Furthermore, differentiating the zero-profit condition for finished manufactures, $P_M M = P_X nx$, yields

$$\hat{P}_M + \hat{M} = \hat{P}_X + \hat{n}. \tag{A7}$$

M.E. Lovely / Journal of International Economics 43 (1997) 463–482 481

In the case of diversified production, $\hat{f} = \eta_{Pf}\hat{P}_f$ from Eq. (A2). Combining these results with (A6) and (A7) provides the price–output response,

$$\hat{M} = \frac{\alpha\eta_{Pf}}{1 - (\alpha - 1)\eta_{Pf}}\hat{P}_M \equiv \frac{\alpha\eta_{Pf}}{D_1}\hat{P}_M. \tag{A8}$$

Thus, a necessary and sufficient condition for the price–output effect to be normal is $D_1 > 0$. In the case of a specialized equilibrium, from Eq. (A5), $\hat{f} = \epsilon_{Pf}\hat{P}_f$. Combining this expression with Eqs. (A6), (A7) provides the price–output response when the price change induces specialization,

$$\hat{M} = \frac{\alpha\epsilon_{Pf}}{1 - (\alpha - 1)\epsilon_{Pf}}\hat{P}_M \equiv \frac{\alpha}{D_2}\epsilon_{Pf}\hat{P}_M. \tag{A9}$$

Thus, a necessary and sufficient condition for the price–output effect to be normal is $D_2 > 0$.

References

Baldwin, R.E., 1995, An economic evaluation of the Uruguay Round Agreements, World Economy 18.

Brecher, R.A., 1983, Second-best policy for international trade and investment, Journal of International Economics 14, 313–320.

Caves, R.E., J.A. Frankel and R.W. Jones, 1990, World trade and payments: An introduction (Scott, Foresman, Glenview, Illinois).

Dixit, A.K. and V. Norman, 1980, Theory of international trade, (Cambridge University Press, Cambridge).

Ethier, W.J., 1982, National and international returns to scale in the modern theory of international trade, American Economic Review 72, 388–405.

Francois, J.F., 1992, Optimal commercial policy with increasing returns to scale, Canadian Journal of Economics 25, 85–95.

Francois, J.F., 1994, Labor force growth, trade, and employment, CEPR Working Paper No. 1069, December.

Grossman, G.M. and E. Helpman, 1991, Innovation and growth in the global economy (MIT Press, Cambridge).

Holtz-Eakin, D. and M.E. Lovely, 1996, Technological linkages, market structure, and optimum production policies, Journal of Public Economics 61, 73–86.

Ide, T. and A. Takayama, 1991, Variable returns to scale, comparative statics paradoxes, and the theory of comparative advantage, in: H. Herberg and N. Van ong, eds., Trade, Welfare, and Economic Policies: Essays in Honor of Murray C. Kemp (University of Michigan Press, Ann Arbor) 67–119.

Jones, R.W., 1967, International capital movements and the theory of tariffs and trade, Quarterly Journal of Economics 81, 1–38.

Kemp, M.C., 1966, The gain from international trade and investment: A neo-Heckscher-Ohlin approach, American Economic Review 56, 788–809.

Markusen, J.R., 1989, Trade in producer services and in other specialized intermediate inputs, American Economic Review 79, 85–95.

Markusen, J.R., 1990, Derationalizing tariffs with specialized intermediate inputs and differentiated final goods, Journal of International Economics 28, 375–383.

Markusen, J.R., 1991, First mover advantages, blockaded entry, and the economics of uneven development, in: E. Helpman and A. Razin, eds., International trade and trade policy (MIT Press, Cambridge) 245–269.

Mayer, W., 1974, Variable returns to scale in general equilibrium theory: A comment, International Economic Review 15, 225–235.

Samurlson, P.A., 1947, Foundations of Economic Analysis (Harvard University Press, Cambridge).

Schott, J.J., 1994, The Uruguay Round: An assessment (Institute for International Economics, Washington, D.C.).

Sullivan, A., 1993, Urban Economics (Irwin, Homewood, Illinois).

Wong, K.-Y, 1990, Factor intensity reversal in a multi-factor, two-good economy, Journal of Economic Theory 51, 434–442.

Wong, K.-Y., 1995, International trade in goods and factor mobility (MIT Press, Cambridge).

Woodland, A.D., 1982, International trade and resource allocation (North Holland, Amsterdam).

59

Technological linkages, market structure, and production policies

Douglas Holtz-Eakin[a,b,*], Mary E. Lovely[c]

[a]Center for Policy Research, Department of Economics, Syracuse University, Syracuse,
NY 13244-1090, USA
[b]NBER, Cambridge, MA 02138, USA
[c]Department of Economics, Syracuse University, Syracuse, NY 13244-1090, USA

Received October 1994; revised version received April 1995

Abstract

Proponents of industrial policy argue that key industries merit subsidies because they generate beneficial externalities. We show that policy must reflect both technological linkages *and* market power in the target industries, the interaction of which may produce an optimal policy including both subsidies *and* taxes on target industries. The optimal policy combination may not be politically or administratively feasible. If so, we show that it may not be desirable to subsidize output in the externality-generating activity on either a fixed or per-unit basis. Thus, technological linkages alone do not lead to the presumption that the externality-generating activity should be subsidized.

Keywords: Industrial policy; Production externalities; Subsidies

JEL classification: F12; H21

1. Introduction

Recent years have witnessed a heated debate over the efficacy of industrial policy, centered on key industries or activities that may generate beneficial interindustry externalities. Proponents of activist policies argue

* Corresponding author. Tel: (315) 443-3115; fax: (315) 443-1081; e-mail: djheakin@maxwell.syr.edu.

74   *D. Holtz-Eakin, M.E. Lovely / Journal of Public Economics 61 (1996) 73–86*

that these interconnections or technological linkages are significant and require government intervention because the private sector is unable to appropriate the gains. Public subsidies would seemingly offset private-sector underinvestment caused by limited appropriability.[1]

We examine formally the optimality of subsidies to industries that generate interindustry spillovers, using a model of vertically-related industries in which final-goods producers realize productivity gains from the specialization of intermediate processes. We set our analysis in the context of a small economy that produces traded final goods and non-traded intermediate inputs.[2] This setting eliminates interjurisdiction spillovers and implies that the government can control the source of the scale economies, which are captured fully by the domestic economy. Trade in intermediate goods, in contrast, would propagate the external economies worldwide, reducing the ability of a single country to influence the externality.[3]

While our framework provides a fertile setting for intervention, we show that policy should not be dictated by technological linkages alone. Of equal importance is the extent of market power in the target industries. Indeed, the interaction of these forces may dictate the need to impose a combination of subsidies *and* taxes, even when there is evidence of substantial external economies. Although we derive our results in the context of a specific model, we believe the lessons apply more broadly. In the presence of market power, there is no presumption that subsidies alone will induce desirable technological spillovers.

Dixit and Stiglitz (1977) (closed economy) and Venables (1982) (small, open economy) demonstrate the need for two policy instruments to reach the optimal scale and diversity of differentiated consumer goods. Dixit and

---

[1] These issues have been most prominent regarding investment in new technologies. The *1994 Economic Report of the President* (pp. 190–191) notes that "... The most important innovations generate spillover benefits for interconnected sectors, creating economic gains well beyond any that eventually accrue to their inventors. ... public actions can offset the effects of underinvestment by the private sector that is caused by limitations on appropriability."

Similar arguments have been raised concerning other spillovers. For example, the Clinton Administration recently endorsed a $1 billion proposal to assist the American advanced flat-panel computer-display screen industry. At least in part, the rationale for such a subsidy rests on the belief that a larger domestic intermediate-good industry will raise productivity of final-good producers. As reported in *The New York Times*, computer screens were chosen for assistance because of their defense uses and because of concerns that the lack of a display-screen industry could weaken the American telecommunications and computer industries (Bradsher, 1994).

[2] Markusen (1991) examines a similar structure in which intermediate goods are non-traded business services. Markusen (1989) shows that when scale economies in final manufactures depend on the number of input varieties produced worldwide, there are gains from trade in these inputs.

[3] Either (1982) emphasizes international returns to scale. Francois (1992, 1994) examines the interaction of scale effects and terms-of-trade effects in policy design.

D. Holtz-Eakin, M.E. Lovely / Journal of Public Economics 61 (1996) 73–86   75

Stiglitz show that in the special case of isoelastic demand for symmetric, differentiated goods, the market produces too little variety but optimal firm scale. More generally, both variety and scale are distorted. Studies of optimal policy with differentiated producer goods have emphasized the analogous case: the production function is written so as to produce a distortion in the number of firms, but not of firm scale (Markusen, 1990, non-traded intermediates, and Francois, 1992, traded intermediates). We extend the examination of differentiated producer goods by treating technological linkages and market power as distinct phenomena, thereby emphasizing the general need for two instruments to influence both variety and scale.

We show that the government generally must offer both an output subsidy and a lump-sum tax or subsidy to control both market power and external economies, a combination that may not be politically or administratively feasible. If lump-sum instruments are precluded, it may not be desirable to subsidize output in the externality-generating activity. Similarly, if the government can offer only a fixed tax or subsidy (e.g. a precommercial development subsidy), the tax may be preferred to the subsidy. Thus, even with limited instruments, there is no presumption that the externality-generating activity should be subsidized.

2. The model

To illustrate the forces at work, we employ a model drawn from Ethier (1982) of a small, open economy producing two final goods. Wheat (W) is supplied by perfect competitors using capital and labor in a constant-returns-to-scale (CRS) technology. 'Manufactures' (M) are produced in stages. First, capital and labor are combined (again with CRS) to produce 'factor bundles'. Factor bundles (f), in turn, are used to produce intermediate 'components'.[4] Lastly, components are transformed into the finished manufactured good.

Fixed endowments of intersectorally-mobile capital and labor combine with the technologies for wheat and factor bundles to define a production possibilities frontier, $W = T(f)$ ($T'(f) < 0$ and $T''(f) \leq 0$). The relative price of factor bundles in terms of wheat (the numeraire) is given by the

---

[4] One need not interpret the terms 'components' and 'assembly' literally. The structure embodies the reliance of final-goods manufacturing on a wide variety of specialized business services and products as inputs. Ethier (1982), for example, emphasizes specialized intermediate inputs to capture the possibility of returns to scale arising from the division of labor. He notes that one could also interpret the intermediate goods as successive manufacturing stages. Markusen (1989, 1991) interprets the intermediate goods as producer services that are knowledge-intensive, requiring a high initial investment in learning.

76   D. Holtz-Eakin, M.E. Lovely / Journal of Public Economics 61 (1996) 73–86

opportunity cost; $P_f = -T'(f)$. The elasticity of P_f with respect to f is denoted ε ($\varepsilon \geq 0$).

Finished manufacturers are costlessly assembled from components according to

$$M = n^\alpha \left[\sum_{i=1}^{n} \frac{x_i^\beta}{n} \right]^{1/\beta}, \tag{1}$$

where x_i is the input of intermediate component i. Two features of (1) are important. The first is imperfect substitutability of differentiated components. The elasticity of substitution between any pair of x_i is $1/(1-\beta)(0 < \beta < 1)$, leading to downward-sloping demand for any single component producer. Higher values of β indicate less differentiation, easier substitutions, more elastic demands, and less market power for any single producer. The second feature to note is that output is increasing in n, the number of distinct components, incorporating the Smithian notion of increased division of labor, as discussed by Ethier (1982) and Romer (1986). The elasticity of output with respect to n is given by $\alpha > 1$, indicating increasing returns to variety.

We assume all components have identical cost functions, leading to identical output (x). With symmetry, the production function collapses to

$$M = n^\alpha x . \tag{1a}$$

This 'reduced form' is not unique to the production function (1). The familiar CES form

$$M = \left[\sum_{i=1}^{n} x_i^\beta \right]^{1/\beta} \tag{1'}$$

also leads to a variant of (1a) in which $\alpha = 1/\beta$; returns to specialization are derived directly from input substitutability. We focus on (1) rather than (1') to permit independent analysis of the distinct phenomena, returns to specialization and producer market power. This distinction is crucial to policy analysis because it implies that there are two distortions in the economy resulting from the production externality and from monopoly power.[5]

The production function (1) captures the notion that access to greater

---

[5] For many questions (e.g. gains from trade in intermediates), this distinction is not crucial in that primary interest lies with the distortion due to an external economy, which is implied by (1') (Markusen, 1989).

D. Holtz-Eakin, M.E. Lovely / Journal of Public Economics 61 (1996) 73–86 77

input variety improves the productivity of manufacturing factors, which can easily be extended beyond factors embodied in the components directly. For example, access to a wider range of producer services may increase managerial productivity. Or, a greater variety of inputs can raise the productivity of resources used in assembly.[6] More generally, while the extent of gains from variety may be related to input substitutability, they need not be determined solely by the parameter β. Our interest lies in the response of products to a range of policy instruments when factors beyond input substitutability influence the level of beneficial spillovers, as implied by (1).

2.1. Pricing and production decisions

Wheat and finished manufactures are tradeable at the world relative price P_M. To produce x units of any component variety requires $ax + b$ ($a, b > 0$) factor bundles. Fixed costs, b, are factor bundles that must be purchased prior to production, and are the source of returns to scale at the firm level. With n varieties of intermediate goods, the aggregate demand for factor bundles is $f = n(ax + b)$.

Government policy may affect either marginal or fixed costs through the provision of a lump-sum subsidy equal to G factor bundles, or an output subsidy of s factor bundles per unit x. Note, however, that $G < 0$ and $s < 0$ are not precluded; the government may levy fixed and output-based taxes on producers of components. In the presence of these policies, the per-firm demand for factor bundles is $(a - s)x + (b - G)$, at a private total cost equal to $P_f\{(a - s)x + (b - G)\}$. Note, however, that the offsetting demand for factor bundles generated by government purchases of $sx + G$, leaving the total bundles required to produce any single variety unchanged at $ax + b$. To avoid complications associated with distortionary taxes, we assume that the government uses a lump-sum instrument to finance the purchase of factor bundles.

We assume that component producers behave as monopolistic com-

---

[6] The production function (1) ignores resources used in assembly. However, a complementary factor, specific to finished manufactures, could easily be incorporated into (1) without altering the structure of our results. For example, one could posit that 'engineers' are required for the assembly of components and that engineers are more productive in the presence of greater options for assembly:

$$M = (nE)^\alpha \left[\sum_{i=1}^{n} \frac{x_i^\beta}{n} \right]^{1/\beta}.$$

Because engineers are assumed to be a specific factor, their presence generates no additional normative issues (Markusen, (1989). This production function also generates a reduced form like (1a), and the competitive equilibrium generally will be characterized by suboptimal scale and variety, as in the case of (1).

78   *D. Holtz-Eakin, M.E. Lovely / Journal of Public Economics 61 (1996) 73–86*

petitors, and that there is free energy into the industry. Component producers equate marginal cost and marginal revenue, setting a price for each component of

$$q = \frac{P_f(a - s)}{\beta} . \tag{2}$$

As β rises, components become less differentiated, the market power of each producer declines, and the markup of price over marginal cost diminishes. Note that s influences the price of components while G does not; the two policy instruments have different influences.

The profit, $qx - P_f((a - s)x + (b - G))$, of each component is driven to zero in equilibrium by free entry and exit. Employing the pricing rule (Eq. (2)) and the zero-profit condition, the scale of production for each component is

$$x = \frac{\beta(b - G)}{(1 - \beta)(a - s)} . \tag{3}$$

Each firm produces more when its variety is more easily substituted by other varieties and hence faces greater competition; i.e. x is increasing in β. The two policy instruments have opposing effects on x; an increase in G reduces x, while an increase in s raises x.

Free entry implies zero profits in the assembly of finished manufactures; $P_M M = qxn$. Since $M = n^\alpha x$, the price of manufactures generates a demand price for components:

$$q = n^{\alpha - 1} P_M . \tag{4}$$

For a given P_M, a higher price for components can be sustained in equilibrium only by an increase in the number of varieties produced.

3. First-best diversity and scale

To begin, we derive the first-best values for x and n. Abstracting from distributional considerations, welfare-improving policies expand the value of domestic production and, thus, the resources available for consumption. The optimal x and n maximize $P_M n^\alpha x + T(f)$ and are characterized by the first-order conditions:

$$P_M n^\alpha = -T'(f)na , \tag{5a}$$

$$\alpha P_M n^{\alpha - 1} x = -T'(f)(ax + b) . \tag{5b}$$

The optimal scale of component production, x, is obtained by equating

D. Holtz-Eakin, M.E. Lovely / Journal of Public Economics 61 (1996) 73–86   79

the additional manufacturing output gained by increasing x with the marginal resource cost (measured in foregone wheat) of expanding each variety by the same increment (see (5a)). Similarly, the optimal diversity is determined by equating the resource cost of a new variety with the value of additional manufacturing output prompted by the new variety (see (5b)). Notice that if $\alpha = 1$, then the latter is simply $P_M x$. In the presence of technological linkages, however, manufacturing output rises by a larger amount when another specialized input is introduced.

Solving yields the optimal output of each variety:

$$x^* = \frac{b}{(\alpha - 1)a},$$ (6)

where an asterisk denotes optimal values. The value of x^* depends on the ratio of fixed to marginal costs, with marginal costs weighted by $\alpha - 1$, the rate at which the economy realizes the external economy. The larger is this rate, the smaller is the optimal output per firm. At the optimum, the per-firm use of factor bundles is $ax^* + b = \alpha b/(\alpha - 1)$, which also declines as α rises. Finally, using (5a), the optimal diversity of components is implicitly defined by

$$n^* = \left(\frac{-T'(f^*)a}{P_M}\right)^{1/(\alpha - 1)}.$$ (7)

4. Laissez-faire equilibrium and the scope for intervention

Using (3), the equilibrium output of each component variety without intervention is

$$x^e = \frac{\beta b}{(1 - \beta)a},$$ (8)

where the superscript 'e' denotes an equilibrium value. The greater the extent of each differentiated-input producer's market power, the lower is the output per firm. Demand for factor bundles by each producer is $ax^e + b = b/(1 - \beta)$. Aggregating demands for factor bundles from all producers of components yields the equilibrium price of factor bundles:

$$P_f^e = -T'(f^e) = -T'(n^e(ax^e + b)) = -T'\left(\frac{n^e b}{1 - \beta}\right).$$ (9)

Producers of components set prices above marginal cost, using a markup of $1/\beta$,

$$q^e = -T'\left(\frac{n^e b}{1 - \beta}\right)\frac{a}{\beta}.$$ (10)

80   D. Holtz-Eakin, M.E. Lovely / Journal of Public Economics 61 (1996) 73–86

Component prices are also constrained by the demand price of producers of finished manufactures. Equating (4) and (10), the equilibrium must satisfy:

$$n^e = \left(-T' \left(\frac{n^e b}{1 - \beta} \right) \frac{a}{P_M \beta} \right)^{1/(\alpha - 1)}. \tag{11}$$

Eq. (11) implicitly defines the number of varieties produced in equilibrium.

As stressed at the outset, market relations are as important as technological linkages in determining the welfare effects of intervention. Market power affects the number of varieties in two ways. First, greater market power (smaller β) implies a higher price of components and, holding P_f fixed, necessitates a larger number of firms to maintain zero profits in finished manufactures assembly. However, P_f is also affected by β (greater market power, smaller per-firm output and lower price for factor bundles) and by changes in n (more firms, higher price for factor bundles). It can be shown that greater market power for each components producer implies a greater number of active firms if $\varepsilon > (1 - \beta)/\beta$. At the formal level, this condition ensures that q^e is a decreasing function of β. More generally, the fact that the features of the equilibrium depend upon ε and β emphasizes the concept that the availability of technological externalities (via n) are dependent upon pricing decisions in both the input (as reflected in ε) and output (as reflected in β) markets.

4.1. Efficiency in equilibrium

Policy intervention must rectify either an inappropriate scale of production of each variety or an inefficient number of varieties, or both. Consider first the scale of production. Comparing (8) and (6) yields:

$$x^e \gtreqless x^* \quad \text{as} \quad \alpha - 1 \gtreqless \frac{1 - \beta}{\beta}. \tag{12}$$

Here, $\alpha - 1$ represents the rate at which returns to diversity are realized in the economy (see Either, 1982). $(1 - \beta)/\beta$ is the proportionate markup over marginal cost, which is used to cover fixed costs. Hence, this term captures the firm's ability to appropriate the surplus generated by returns to diversity. Efficient production of each variety occurs only if firms appropriate the surplus from each variety at exactly the same rate as it is generated in the economy. Moreover, x^e may fall short of, or exceed, x^*. Viewed from a different perspective, to the extent that technological linkages (α) are an important features of the production process, (12) extends the Dixit–Stiglitz dictum to differentiated producer goods: there is no presumption that market power leads to an inefficient restriction in the level of output.

We turn now to the issue of whether the laissez-faire equilibrium provides

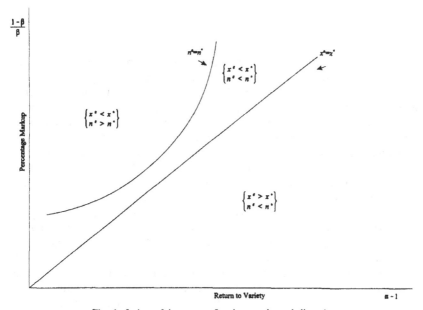

Fig. 1. Laissez-faire versus first-best scale and diversity.

sufficient variety using (11) and (7). These relationships are graphed in Fig. 1, which shows the orderings of x^e and x^* and n^e and n^* for possible values of the external effect $(\alpha - 1)$ and percentage markup $(1 - \beta)/\beta$.[7] As the figure makes transparent, market relations complicate the implications of external effects. As a benchmark, consider the case in which $x^e = x^*$, i.e. the diagonal in Fig. 1.[8] Here, $n^e < n^*$, matching the intuition that the market provides too few varieties of inputs and, hence, too little of the externality. Underprovision of variety stems from the markup over the factor-bundle cost of components. Rearranging (11) yields:

---

[7] The figure reflects $\varepsilon > \alpha - 1$ and $\varepsilon > (1 - \beta)/\beta$. (Note that these conditions coincide for the special case $\alpha = 1/\beta$.) In the language of Ethier (1982), ε is the 'intersectoral effect', while $\alpha - 1$ is the 'scale effect'. $\varepsilon > \alpha - 1$ is necessary to satisfy the second-order condition of the social planning problem. It is also necessary for a normal final-goods price-output effect. (See Markusen, 1989.) As noted in the text, $\varepsilon > (1 - \beta)/\beta$ ensures that n^e rises as the markup rises.

[8] Importantly, fixing the relationship between the external effect and market power by imposing $\alpha = 1/\beta$ ensures that $x^e = x^*$. In this case, as Markusen (1989) shows, the economy produces on the efficient frontier but not, in general, at the optimal point. Because only one distortion is present, only one instrument is needed to correct it.

82   D. Holtz-Eakin, M.E. Lovely / Journal of Public Economics 61 (1996) 73-86

$$P_M = \frac{1}{\beta} \left(\frac{-T'(f^e)a}{(n^e)^{\alpha-1}} \right) . \tag{13}$$

The world price of manufactures constrains production relationships in both the first-best and the laissez-faire equilibrium. As indicated by the right side, however, laissez-faire is distinguished by the markup $(1/\beta)$. Thus, given that the term in parentheses is increasing in n, for expression (13) to hold when $x^e = x^*$, n^e must be less than n^*. With P_M fixed by world markets, the economy adjusts to markup pricing by reducing the production of varieties, the demand for components, and thus the cost of components.

This scenario seemingly underlies interest in subsidies to the manufacturing sector. However, a wider range of outcomes is possible. Fig. 1 indicates that in any instance when $x^e > x^*$, $n^e < n^*$. That is, inefficiently large production of each component is associated with inadequate diversity of inputs. Essentially, for a given level of the external effect $(\alpha - 1)$ the market meets competitive pressure on P_M by producing too few varieties and, hence, lowering demand for factor bundles. Moving toward the first-best would require producing less output per component firm, and meeting competitive pressure by exploiting an increased number of varieties.

As shown in the figure, however, the picture is less clear when $x^e < x^*$. Again, consider a specific value of $\alpha - 1$. As the markup rises (β declines), initially n^e remains below the first-best. Eventually, however, the equilibrium is characterized by two little output per component firm and excessive reliance on returns to diversity in order to meet the world price of finished manufactures. In short, for a given level of technological linkages, market relationships determine the degree to which adequate externalities are produced.

5. Government policy

Eq. (5a) may be interpreted as a first-best rule for the pricing of components, i.e.

$$q^* \equiv P_M(n^*)^{\alpha-1} = -T'(f^*)a . \tag{14}$$

Components should be priced at their social marginal cost. Assume temporarily that there is no distortion of output per firm. A comparison of (7) and (11) indicates that $n^e = n^*$ if components are priced at marginal cost; that is, if $(a - s)/\beta = a$. This suggests an optimal subsidy of $s^* = (1 - \beta)a$. Under these circumstances, the post-subsidy marginal cost is P_f $(a -$

D. Holtz-Eakin, M.E. Lovely / Journal of Public Economics 61 (1996) 73–86 83

$s^*) = P_f \beta a$, which is 'marked-up' by $1/\beta$ to yield marginal cost pricing of components.

It is possible for the market to achieve the optimal output per firm? Substituting s^* into the equilibrium scale (3), equating (3) with the optimal scale (6) and solving for G yields:

$$G^* = b\left(1 - \frac{(1-\beta)}{(\alpha-1)}\right). \tag{15}$$

Thus, s^* and G^* will support the first-best as a competitive equilibrium. The sign of G^* is dictated by the relationship between output per firm with an output subsidy only (denoted x^s) and x^*. At this point,

$$x^s = \frac{b}{(1-\beta)a} \gtreqless x^* = \frac{b}{(\alpha-1)a} \quad \text{as } (\alpha-1) \gtreqless (1-\beta), \tag{16}$$

which relates directly to the conditions under which G^* is employed to raise ($G^* < 0$) or lower ($G^* > 0$) output per firm to the optimal level.

The optimal policies provide another insight. Because fixed costs force pricing above marginal cost to avoid exit, one might extrapolate to a policy that subsidizes fixed costs, permitting marginal cost pricing. The optimal net subsidy *does* equal fixed costs ($s^*x^* + G^* = b$), but s^* and G^* are not both positive. Optimal policy calls for lump-sum *taxes* upon intermediate producers when their market power is too strong ($(1 - \beta) > (\alpha - 1)$). Fixed taxes raise the x necessary to break even while pricing at marginal cost. The availability of two policy instruments is critical to achieving efficient production.

5.1. Alternative policies

We focus on an output subsidy and a lump-sum subsidy/tax offered to producers of intermediate components, but the first-best may be reached using other policy combinations. However, when there is a distortion in x, any successful policy must include at least one of these instruments to alter the ratio of fixed to marginal cost for components producers. In contrast, variety may be influenced in several ways. A subsidy to the production of factor bundles or a subsidy to finished manufactures would have the effect of raising n without altering x.[9] Thus, the first-best may be achieved by using

---

[9] The assumption that the ratio of fixed to marginal costs is invariant to changes in factor prices is crucial in permitting a factor-bundles subsidy to alter variety but not scale. If fixed and variable activities use different factor intensities, an input subsidy may affect scale as well as variety.

an output or lump-sum subsidy/tax to components producers, combined with a subsidy/tax on factor bundles or finished manufactures.[10]

As noted earlier, assuming the familiar technology for finished manufactures, (1′), leads to an equilibrium characterized by optimal firm scale, but too few varieties (Markusen, 1989, 1990). If so, Francois (1992) shows that one instrument can be used to achieve the first-best. This instrument may be an input subsidy (equivalent to a subsidy to factor-bundles) or a finished-manufactures output subsidy. These policies raise the number of components producers without altering the ratio of fixed to marginal cost and, thus, firm scale.[11]

To implement first-best policies one generally must surmount formidable information requirements and political pressures. The government requires detailed knowledge of pricing, costs and external effects in the target industries.[12] Furthermore, it must be able to subsidize firms, even as it simultaneously requires a fixed tax on that sector. It seems unlikely that one could estimate and implement s^* and G^* in a single, comprehensive package.

One might be tempted to 'search' for the optimal policy in a piecemeal fashion. For example, s^* is unambiguously positive; could policymakers incrementally raise subsidies until the beneficial effects were realized? Generally a single instrument does not permit one to reach the efficient production plan. With $G = 0$, the second-best subsidy rate, s', balances the relative benefits of altering scale and diversity and may be negative.[13] Thus, an ad hoc system of subsidies may make matters worse, not better.

Similarly, policymakers may avoid politically unpopular output subsidies and focus instead on policy toward exit and entry, or turn to broad-based provision of inputs like research and development. Our discussion concerning the fixed subsidy G, above, indicates that the use of such policies in

---

[10] Optimal policy will include trade taxes only if the jurisdiction is large enough to affect traded-goods prices (see Markusen, 1990, for the case with local intermediates and Francois, 1992, 1994, for traded intermediates). If the jurisdiction is small, and intermediates are traded, the optimal policy will be laissez-faire.

[11] We thank Joseph Francois for helpful correspondence on alternative policies for the case in which $\alpha = 1/\beta$. Note that an output subsidy offered to components products can induce the socially efficient number of varieties, but will move firm scale away from the optimal level. Thus, a lump-sum instrument will be needed to retain optimal firm scale when component output is subsidized, even if $\alpha = 1/\beta$.

[12] An additional concern is that cases for interventions may involve competition for resources among a number of sources of scale effects. This issue is raised by Dixit and Grossman (1986) in a strategic trade context.

[13] The model does not yield a close-form expression for s'. Details of the analysis of s' are available from the authors.

isolation will not be sufficient to achieve the efficient production policy. The sign of the second-best value of G, G', depends on parameter values.[14] It is not generally possible to recommend in isolation a lump-sum tax or subsidy.

6. Summary

The existence of external effects from production suggests the 'common sense' solution of subsidizing firms to induce sufficient production of beneficial spillovers. Our investigation of optimal policies toward intermediate-good production emphasizes that subsidy policies should not be adopted on the basis of technological considerations alone. Instead, the market structure of the externality-generating sector must be incorporated into policy design. Ideal policies reflect the interaction between external effects and market structure, leading to a mix of lump-sum and output subsidies, and may even involve lump-sum taxes on firms. In the absence of either instrument, the optimal second-best policy may be a fixed or output-based tax. Thus, while laissez-faire may yield either too little or too much of the externality-generating activity, and also either over- or under-exploitation of internal scale economies, as a practical matter it appears optimistic to implement piecemeal policies that move toward an improved allocation of resources. Instead, to intervene productively, policy makers need conclusive information on market structure as well as technological relationships.

There exists an embryonic empirical literature in these areas. Hall (1988), Domowitz et al. (1988), and Shapiro (1987) interpret the evidence as showing substantial pricing above marginal costs in US manufacturing, including those manufactured goods that serve as inputs elsewhere in the economy. To the extent this is accurate, it raises the possibility that there is too little output per firm, but an excessive number of firms in the market (see Fig. 1). However, Caballero and Lyons (1992) argue that manufacturing data reveal important interindustry connections leading to external returns to scale. Evidence of large external economies provides support for the notion that the market underexploits the technological spillovers. These studies, while suggestive, do not provide sufficient empirical guidance for the setting of industrial policy. Providing such support appears to be a valuable area for future research.

[14] Specifically:

$$G' = b\left(\frac{\varepsilon(1 + \beta + \alpha\beta) - (\alpha - 1)(1 - \beta)}{\varepsilon(2 - \alpha) - \alpha(1 - \beta)}\right).$$

86   *D. Holtz-Eakin, M.E. Lovely / Journal of Public Economics 61 (1996) 73–86*

Acknowledgements

We wish to thank Alan Deardorff, Joe Francois, Doug Nelson, Dave Richardson, Nicholas Stern, John Yinger, and two anonymous referees for valuable comments on an earlier draft. Esther Gray, Jennifer Gantt, and Ann Wicks provided valuable aid in preparing the manuscript. This research is part of the National Bureau of Economic Research Program in Public Economics.

References

Bradsher, K., 1994, U.S. to aid industry in computer battle with the Japanese, The New York Times, 27 April, A1.

Caballero, R. and R. Lyons, 1992, External effects in U.S. procyclical productivity, Journal of Monetary Economics 29, 209–225.

Dixit, A.K. and G.M. Grossman, 1986, Targeted export promotion with several oligopolistic industries, Journal of International Economics 21, 233–249.

Dixit, A.K. and J.E. Stiglitz, 1977, Monopolistic competition and optimum product diversity, American Economic Review 67, 297–308.

Domowitz, I., R.G. Hubbard and B. Petersen, 1988, Market structure and cyclical fluctuations in U.S. manufacturing, Review of Economics and Statistics 70, 55–56.

Ethier, W.J., 1982, National and international returns to scale in the modern theory of international trade, American Economic Review 72, 388–405.

Francois, J.F., 1992, Optimal commercial policy with increasing returns to scale, Canadian Journal of Economics 25, 85–95.

Francois, J.F., 1994, Global production and trade: Factor migration and commercial policy with international scale economies, International Economic Review 35, 565–581.

Hall, R., 1988, The relation between price and marginal cost in U.S. industry, Journal of Political Economy 19, 921–947.

Markusen, J.R., 1989, Trade in producer services and in other specialized intermediate inputs, American Economic Review 79, 85–95.

Markusen, J.R., 1990, Micro-foundations of external economies, Canadian Journal of Economics 23, 495–508.

Markusen, J.R., 1991, First mover advantages, blockaded entry, and the economics of uneven development, in: E. Helpman and A. Razin, eds., International Trade and Trade Policy (The MIT Press, Cambridge) 245–269.

Romer, P.M., 1986, Increasing returns and long-run growth, Journal of Political Economy 94, 1002–1037.

Shapiro, M., 1987, Measuring market power in U.S. industry, Mimeo, Yale University.

Venables, A.J., 1982, Optimal tariffs for trade in monopolistically competitive commodities, Journal of International Economics 12, 225–242.

Scale economies, returns to variety, and the productivity of public infrastructure

Douglas Holtz-Eakin[a,b,*], Mary E. Lovely[a]

[a]Center for Policy Research, 426 Eggers Hall, Syracuse University, Syracuse, NY 13244-1090, USA
[b]NBER, Cambridge, MA 02138, USA

Received 2 February 1995; final version received 15 October 1995

Abstract

We examine the productivity of public infrastructure in a general equilibrium context. In our model, infrastructure lowers costs in a manufacturing sector characterized by both firm-level returns to scale and industry-level external returns to variety. Infrastructure alters factor prices, intermediate prices and the allocation of factors across sectors. However, the effect on manufacturing or aggregate output is indeterminate. In particular, our theory suggests that the degree of monopoly power influences public capital's productivity effect. We test the model using state-level, panel data. We confirm the absence of direct effects on output, but find evidence to suggest a positive impact of public capital on manufacturing variety as measured by the number of manufacturing establishments. These results indicate the need for future research on potentially important indirect channels by which public capital affects manufacturing productivity.

Keywords: Public infrastructure; External scale economies

JEL classification: H40; H73; R13

1. Introduction

The impact of publicly provided infrastructure capital on private-sector productivity has attracted considerable attention in recent years. Beginning

---

* Corresponding author. Tel.: 315 443-3115; fax: 315 443-1081; e-mail:djheakin@maxwell.syr.edu.

0166-0462/96/$15.00 © 1996 Elsevier Science B.V. All rights reserved
SSDI 0166-0462(95)02126-4

106   *D. Holtz-Eakin, M.E. Lovely / Reg. Sci. Urban Econ. 26 (1996) 105–123*

with Aschauer (1989), a number of researchers estimated social returns to infrastructure far in excess of those for other investments (e.g. private capital).[1] In response to these claims, a series of increasingly sophisticated econometric studies have focused on the estimated return to public capital, and at this juncture there appears to be little support for a special role for infrastructure in boosting aggregate productivity.[2]

A somewhat surprising feature of this literature is the noticeable absence of formal economic models of the productivity effects of infrastructure.[3] Instead, the empirical literature has centered on estimates of the technical constraints facing firms—in the form of production or cost functions—at the aggregate, regional, or state level.[4] While useful for their 'bottom-line' estimates of productivity effects, these studies shed little light on the mechanism by which infrastructure affects firms, markets, and equilibrium production in each sector of the economy.

Our purpose in this paper is to construct such a model, building into it several features that previous research suggests are important. First, a number of studies have focused on the manufacturing sector, while others have directed attention toward total (private) output. We embed infrastructure within a two-sector model that permits us to account directly for a differential effect between manufactures and non-manufactures. Specifically, we model infrastructure as having direct, cost-saving effects in the manufacturing sector of the economy.[5] As a result, we can answer questions such as: "Is it possible for infrastructure to have cost-saving effects in manufacturing, yet not raise aggregate output?" Second, recognizing that additional infrastructure may reallocate resources among sectors and, as a consequence, alter factor prices, we use a general equilibrium framework. The model incorporates these private-sector responses as well as the direct effect of infrastructure on the stock of productive inputs.

---

[1] See, especially, Munnell (1990a, b).

[2] See Evans and Karras (1994), Garcia-Mila et al. (1995), Holtz-Eakin (1994), Hulten and Schwab (1991), and Tatom (1993).

[3] An exception, albeit quite simple, is Holtz-Eakin and Schwartz (1995), who embed infrastructure within a neoclassical model of state-level economic growth.

[4] Aschauer (1989), Munnell (1990b), Garcia-Mila and McGuire (1992), and Holtz-Eakin (1994) directly estimate the production function. Nadiri and Mamuneas (1994) and Morrison and Schwartz (1992) estimate cost functions for the manufacturing sector. Hulten and Schwab (1991) indirectly examine the effects of infrastructure using growth-accounting techniques for regional manufacturing.

[5] This is consistent with the findings of Morrison and Schwartz (1992) using empirical estimates of flexible cost functions for state-level manufacturing. Despite the cost-saving effect, however, our theoretical results will also be consistent with those of Hulten and Schwab (1991), who argue that a growth-accounting framework indicates little role for infrastructure in determining output.

D. Holtz-Eakin, M.E. Lovely / Reg. Sci. Urban Econ. 26 (1996) 105-123 107

The model has several additional features that highlight the mechanism by which infrastructure affects output. The first is the characterization of scale economies. There are two forms of scale economy in the model: internal scale economies in the production of intermediates, and returns to variety that act as external scale economies in the production of finished manufactures. These scale economies provide an explicit rationale (other than public-goods concerns) for considering public infrastructure provision. A second feature is the treatment of market structure, which plays a crucial role in determining the productivity effect of infrastructure. The empirical research on infrastructure has not acknowledged the role of market structure, but our results indicate that the nature of competition among firms influences both the magnitude and the sign of infrastructure productivity.

The remainder of the paper is organized as follows. In Section 2 we develop our model of the role of infrastructure in the economy. Despite the relatively simple structure of the model, the productivity effects of providing more infrastructure are indeterminant. Hence, in Section 3 we turn to an empirical investigation designed to shed light on the key determinants of the effects of additional infrastructure on manufacturing and non-manufacturing output. Section 4 is a summary with suggestions for further work in this area.

To anticipate the key results, we confirm the absence of significant direct effects on output from infrastructure. However, we find evidence to suggest that public capital may alter productivity through its effect on the number and variety of manufacturing establishments in the local manufacturing base.

2. A model of public infrastructure and equilibrium output

We employ a model of a small, open economy producing two goods – 'wheat' and finished 'manufactures' – drawn from Ethier (1979, 1982). Fixed supplies of capital and labor are intersectorally mobile and are allocated in competitive factor markets in each sector.[6]

Wheat is supplied by perfect competitors using capital and labor in a constant-returns-to-scale technology. Alternatively, capital and labor may

---

[6] Alternatively, the model can be framed using three factors: mobile capital and two immobile factors, land and labor. In this framework, all three factors are used in the production of both wheat and factor bundles, with constant-returns-to-scale technology and no factor-intensity reversals. It is straightforward to show that the price–output response is normal if land and labor are substitutes so that demand for one rises when the price of the other rises. If this condition is met, the opportunity cost of factor bundles in terms of wheat rises as wheat output expands. Consequently, the results derived here for immobile factors carry over to the case of mobile capital.

108   *D. Holtz-Eakin, M.E. Lovely / Reg. Sci. Urban Econ. 26 (1996) 105–123*

be used in another constant-returns-to-scale technology to form 'factor bundles'. Factor bundles are inputs into the production of 'components', or intermediate goods that are necessary for the production of the finished manufactured good.

The limited endowments of capital and labor, and the technology for producing wheat (W) and factor bundles (m) define a transformation function for the economy:

$$W = T(m) , \tag{1}$$

which may be represented by a familiar convex-to-the-origin production possibilities frontier, with $T'(m) < 0$ and $T''(m) \leq 0$. Because wheat and factor bundles are sold under competitive conditions, the relative price of factor bundles in terms of wheat – which serves as our numeraire – is given by the opportunity cost

$$P_m = -T'(m) . \tag{2}$$

Changes in the relative price of factor bundles, P_m, play an important role in what follows. It is useful to summarize the elasticity of P_m with respect to the quantity of bundles used in the non-wheat sector, m, as

$$\xi = \frac{\mathrm{d}P_m}{\mathrm{d}m} \frac{m}{P_m} = \frac{T''(m)m}{T'(m)} \geq 0 . \tag{3}$$

Finished manufactures are costlessly assembled from intermediate manufactured components according to the production function

$$M = n^\alpha \left[\sum_{i=1}^n \frac{x_i^\beta}{n} \right]^{1/\beta} , \tag{4}$$

where x_i is the input of component i into the production of manufactures, M. In the production function (4), α is a measure of scale economies with respect to the range of intermediates, with $\alpha > 1$ indicating increasing returns to variety. Also, components are assumed to be imperfect substitutes; the parameter β ($1 > \beta > 0$) provides a measure of the degree of 'differentiation' between any pair of x_i since the elasticity of substitution between any pair is $1/(1 - \beta)$. Higher values of β indicate greater ease of substitution of components in the assembly process, and hence less differentiation among the components. It is useful to note here that the terms

D. Holtz-Eakin, M.E. Lovely / Reg. Sci. Urban Econ. 26 (1996) 105–123   109

'components' and 'assembly' need not be interpreted literally.[7] Instead, the structure is intended to embody the reliance of final-goods manufacturing on a wide variety of specialized business services and goods as inputs.

In equilibrium, n varieties of components will be produced, and we may use n as an index of the range of economic activity. Thus, we might think of increases in n, ceteris paribus, as indicating a more robust economic environment characterized by a greater variety of active firms. Because a greater variety of intermediate-producing firms enhances the productivity of factors used in finished-manufactures assembly, an important question for policy is the degree to which additional infrastructure increases n.

As in Ethier (1982) and Markusen (1989), we assume that all varieties of components have identical production technologies. Since each variety enters symmetrically into the production of finished manufactures, in equilibrium an identical quantity, x_0, will be supplied of each variety. Thus (4) collapses to

$$M = n^{\alpha} x_0 .$$ (4')

We see from (4') that finished manufactures are linearly homogeneous in x_0 but homogeneous to degree α in n. These economies are external to the finished-manufactures industry since components are assembled into finished manufactures by many competitive firms, each of which takes n as given. This raises the possibility that even if infrastructure policy does not alter x_0, it may raise n and thus enhance productivity.

2.1. Equilibrium and public infrastructure

We assume that wheat and finished manufactures are tradeable; unlimited quantities of either final good may be purchased or sold at the relative price given by P_M. However, we assume that intermediate components are not traded, so capturing the notion that there are services unique to the local economy that contribute to manufacturing.[8] Finished manufactures,

---

[7] Components have been interpreted in several ways. Ethier (1982) emphasizes specialized intermediate inputs. He intends to capture, via the endogenous determination of the number of component varieties, the possibility of returns to scale arising from the division of labor. He notes that, alternatively, one could interpret the intermediate goods as successive manufacturing stages. Markusen (1989) interprets the intermediate goods as producer services that are knowledge-intensive, requiring a high initial investment in learning.

[8] Ethier (1979, 1982) emphasizes traded components. In contrast, Markusen (1991) assumes that intermediates are non-tradeable, identifying them as knowledge-based, specialized business services. Markusen argues that such services are costly to trade internationally or face high tariff barriers. Our emphasis on geographical concentration is similar in spirit to recent analyses of spillover and agglomeration; see, for example, Dekle and Eaton (1994) or Henderson (1994).

110   *D. Holtz-Eakin, M.E. Lovely / Reg. Sci. Urban Econ. 26 (1996) 105–123*

therefore, are assembled from intermediate goods and services produced exclusively in the home jurisdiction.

The imperfect substitutability of components accords some market power to each producer of components. However, we allow free entry into the industry and assume that n is sufficiently large that component producers behave as monopolistic competitors, taking the behavior of other component producers as given.

The number of factor bundles required to produce x units of any variety is $ax + b$ $(a, b > 0)$, indicating returns to scale at the firm level. Infrastructure is tantamount to providing 'factor bundles' (roads, bridges, etc.) to the manufacturing sector, so reducing the private resources needed for production. Of course, government capital may serve to lower either variable costs or fixed costs, or both. If we let s denote the implicit subsidy to variable costs, and let G measure the reduction in fixed costs, then the production of x units of any variety in the presence of infrastructure requires $(a - s)x + b - G$ factor bundles at a private cost of $P_m((a - s)x + b - G)$.

Each component producer sets marginal cost equal to marginal revenue, resulting in a price for each component of [9]

$$P_c = \frac{P_m(a - s)}{\beta}. \tag{5}$$

Note that as β rises, the market power of each component producer declines, and the mark-up of price over marginal cost diminishes as well. The profit, $P_c x_0 - P_m((a - s)x_0 + b - G)$, of each individual component firm is driven to zero in equilibrium by free entry and exit. Thus, using (5) and solving for x_0, the equilibrium output of each firm is

$$x_0 = \frac{\beta(b - G)}{(1 - \beta)(a - s)}. \tag{6}$$

It is useful to note that x_0 is increasing in β; each firm produces more when its variety is more easily substituted for other varieties.

The aggregate demand for factor bundles stems from two sources: component producers and infrastructure provision by the government. With regard to the latter, one possibility is that an expenditure of \$$n$ by the government is needed to provide \$1 of additional infrastructure to each of the n components producers. If so, the government has no special ability to provide infrastructure any 'cheaper' than the private sector. Alternatively,

---

[9] Marginal private cost is $P_m(a - s)$, while marginal revenue is βP_c. The latter may be derived by recognizing that the elasticity of demand for components of cost-minimizing producers of manufactures will be $-1/(1 - \beta)$ and that marginal revenue for component producers is $P_c((1 + \nu)/\nu)$, where ν is the elasticity of demand.

D. Holtz-Eakin, M.E. Lovely / Reg. Sci. Urban Econ. 26 (1996) 105–123   111

infrastructure may be a pure public good; a \$1 expenditure by the government would be sufficient to provide \$1 of additional infrastructure to each of the n intermediate producers. And, of course, the appropriate treatment of infrastructure may lie between these extremes. We capture the range of these possibilities by summarizing total demand for factor bundles as

$$m = n((a - s)x_0 + b - G) + n^{\gamma}(sx_0 + G) . \tag{7}$$

If $\gamma = 0$, G and s are pure public goods, while the case of $\gamma = 1$ corresponds to treating them as pure private goods. Note that (7) summarizes the total resource demand. Regardless of the total purchases by the government, each firm receives a subsidy combination that reduces its variable costs by s and its fixed costs by G.

The domestic supply price of finished manufactures must equal the external price P_M. There are zero profits in the assembly of components into manufactures, implying $P_M M = P_c x_0 n$. Using the relationship $M = n^{\alpha} x_0$, the equilibrium domestic supply price of manufactures is linked to the price of components via

$$P_M = n^{1-\alpha} P_c . \tag{8}$$

An increase in n raises productivity and, therefore, lowers the supply price. An increase in P_c, in contrast, raises P_M.

2.2. The effect of increased public infrastructure

We begin our examination of infrastructure policy by asking whether increasing public infrastructure expands the output of finished manufactures, and then turn to the non-manufacturing sector.[10] To clarify the effects, we abstract from issues of distortionary-tax financing and assume that government spending is funded by lump-sum taxation of households.

2.2.1. Effect on the manufacturing sector

The provision of infrastructure alters the cost structure of each producer of components, altering their preferred levels of output. This may be seen by totally differentiating (6) and using a caret '^' to denote proportionate changes

$$\hat{x}_0 = \frac{-G}{b - G}\hat{G} + \frac{s}{a - s}\hat{s} \equiv -\delta_G \hat{G} + \delta_s \hat{s} . \tag{9}$$

[10] Our focus is on the positive effects of infrastructure. Normative questions are analyzed in Holtz-Eakin and Lovely (1995).

112   D. Holtz-Eakin, M.E. Lovely / Reg. Sci. Urban Econ. 26 (1996) 105-123

Increases in G reduce x_0, with the proportionate change dependent on the ratio of public to privately provided fixed costs. Note that, in contrast, infrastructure provision that has the effect of lowering variable costs will raise output for each component.

Infrastructure provision induces changes in the price of components, the variety of components, and the share of resources devoted to manufacturing. Total differentiation of the remaining equations of the system (5), (7), and (8) yields:

$$\hat{P}_c = \xi \hat{m} - \delta_s \hat{s} \tag{10}$$

and

$$\hat{m} = \phi_n \hat{n} + \phi_x \hat{x} - \phi_s \hat{s} - \phi_G \hat{G} , \tag{11}$$

where

$$\phi_n = \frac{n((a-s)x_0 + b - G) + \gamma n^\gamma (sx_0 + G)}{m} , \tag{12a}$$

$$\phi_x = \frac{n((a-s)x_0 + n^\gamma sx_0)}{m} , \tag{12b}$$

$$\phi_s = \frac{(n - n^\gamma)sx_0}{m} , \tag{12c}$$

$$\phi_G = \frac{(n^\gamma - n)G}{m} , \tag{12d}$$

and

$$\hat{P}_M = 0 = (1 - \alpha)\hat{n} + \hat{P}_c . \tag{13}$$

The price of components is affected directly by the subsidy to variable costs and also by changes in m that influence the relative price of factor bundles (see (10)). If resources are pulled away from wheat production ($\hat{m} > 0$), the price of factor bundles will rise, with the extent of this rise dependent upon the curvature of the production possibility frontier (ξ). We can trace the change in demand for factor bundles ($\hat{m}$) to three sources: changes in the number of components producers, changes in the level of their production, and changes in direct government purchases of factor bundles (see (11)). Eq. (13) embodies the external-price constraint on the supply price of finished manufactures. An increase in the number of components has a negative effect on the supply price (if $\alpha > 1$), which must be offset by the positive effect of an increase in the price of components.

How does infrastructure affect output and productivity in equilibrium? To begin, we focus on changes in G, i.e. infrastructure provision that reduces fixed costs. Solving (9)–(13) yields the proportionate changes in the price

D. Holtz-Eakin, M.E. Lovely / Reg. Sci. Urban Econ. 26 (1996) 105–123   113

of components, factor bundle demand, and the number of component varieties. The resulting changes are

$$\frac{\hat{P}_c}{\hat{G}} = \frac{(\alpha - 1)\xi(\phi_x\delta_G + \phi_G)}{D} > 0 , \tag{14}$$

$$\frac{\hat{m}}{\hat{G}} = \frac{(\alpha - 1)(\phi_x\delta_G + \phi_G)}{D} > 0 , \tag{15}$$

and

$$\frac{\hat{n}}{\hat{G}} = \frac{\xi(\phi_x\delta_G + \phi_G)}{D} > 0 , \tag{16}$$

where $D \equiv \xi\phi_n - (\alpha - 1) > 0$.[11]

Eq. (14) is the key to understanding why an increase in G causes n to rise. The external market for finished manufactures disciplines this small economy. Infrastructure provision pulls primary factors into component production, raising the marginal cost of factor bundles in terms of wheat. Ceteris paribus, component producers pass on the cost increase, but with a mark-up determined by the extent of their market power (β). An increase in component prices must be accompanied by an expansion in varieties if the economy is to remain a competitor in finished manufactures. Because of the mark-up, profits in the components industry are positive at the initial n, inducing entry. Thus, an increase in public infrastructure increases the number of component producers and enhances any external economies of the finished manufactures industry.

Unfortunately, an increase in the number of components producers is not sufficient to guarantee an expansion of the manufacturing sector. Using (4'), the proportionate change in finished manufactures is

$$\hat{M} = \alpha\hat{n} + \hat{x}_0 . \tag{17}$$

As seen in (9), an increase in public infrastructure that reduces the firm's fixed costs lowers the profit-maximizing level of output. Using the solutions for $\hat{n}$ and $\hat{x}_0$,

$$\frac{\hat{M}}{\hat{G}} = \frac{\xi\delta_G(\alpha\phi_x - \phi_n) + \alpha\xi\phi_G + (\alpha - 1)\delta_G}{D} . \tag{18}$$

---

[11] The condition $D > 0$ is necessary for the manufacturing sector to display a positive price–output relationship. We assume $D > 0$ throughout, effectively limiting our analysis to the concave portion of the production frontier for W and M. See Markusen (1989) for a discussion of the features of this frontier.

114   *D. Holtz-Eakin, M.E. Lovely / Reg. Sci. Urban Econ. 26 (1996) 105–123*

A sufficient condition for $\hat{M} > 0$ is that $\alpha\phi_x - \phi_n > 0$ since the other terms in the numerator of (18) are positive. To see the forces at work, consider the effect of initial infrastructure provision by evaluating this expression in the vicinity of $s = 0$ and $G = 0$. In this case, $\hat{M} > 0$ if

$$(\alpha - 1)\left[\frac{ax_0}{b}\right] > 1 . \tag{19}$$

Essentially, the less important are fixed costs, the less the decline in fixed costs affects x_0, and the more likely M is to rise. Alternatively, one may rewrite (19) as

$$(\alpha - 1) > \frac{1 - \beta}{\beta} . \tag{20}$$

The left-hand side of (20) is the rate at which the economy realizes returns to variety (see Ethier, 1982) while the right-hand side is a measure of firms' market power: the percentage mark-up over marginal cost. If the return to variety dominates the ability of firms to capture the returns to restricting output, M will rise. Alternatively, if firms have sufficient market power to enforce greater mark-ups, the contraction of x_0 will dominate and M will fall. Eq. (20) drives home the lesson that the productivity effects of infrastructure depend upon market structure as well as technological factors.

As noted earlier, it may be inappropriate to characterize infrastructure as reducing fixed costs exclusively, suggesting a parallel investigation of the effects of changes in s on the structure and level of output in the manufacturing sector and the economy as a whole. To begin, recall that a subsidy to marginal costs raises the scale of production (x_0) for each producer of components (see (10)). However, unlike G, changes in s also directly affect the pricing decisions of components producers (see (11)). Hence, the predicted impacts differ substantially. Specifically, the effects on the price of components, factor bundles used in manufacturing, and the variety of components are given by

$$\frac{\hat{P}_c}{\hat{s}} = \frac{-(\alpha - 1)[\xi(\phi_x\delta_s - \phi_s) - \delta_s]}{D} \gtrless 0 , \tag{21}$$

$$\frac{\hat{m}}{\hat{s}} = \frac{\phi_n\delta_s - (\phi_x\delta_s - \phi_s)(\alpha - 1)}{D} \gtrless 0 , \tag{22}$$

and

$$\frac{\hat{n}}{\hat{s}} = \frac{-[\xi(\phi_x\delta_s - \phi_s) - \delta_s]}{D} \gtrless 0 . \tag{23}$$

Clearly, to the extent that infrastructure has its effect on marginal costs in the manufacturing sector it will be difficult to predict its impact. Let us consider first the pricing of components. The subsidy directly reduces the

D. Holtz-Eakin, M.E. Lovely / Reg. Sci. Urban Econ. 26 (1996) 105-123 115

marginal cost of factor bundles and, ceteris paribus, lowers P_c. However, if the new equilibrium results in a net increase in m, then the increase in the gross price of factor bundles may outweigh this subsidy.

However, as shown in (22) the direction of impact on total factor usage is unclear, a direct result of the ambiguous effect on variety, (23). Intuitively, an increase in s raises output per producer of components. Other things equal, this increases m, P_m, P_c and, hence, the number of varieties required in equilibrium to meet the external competitive pressures imposed by P_M. However, at the same time, the subsidy directly reduces the price of components (see (5)) and, hence, reduces the number of varieties required to meet trade pressures. The net effect is ambiguous.

Given the ambiguities, it is hardly surprising that manufacturing output may either rise or fall in response to the reduction in variable costs. Formally,

$$\frac{\hat{M}}{\hat{s}} = \frac{\alpha\epsilon\phi_s + \delta_s - \epsilon\delta_s(\alpha\phi_s - \phi_n)}{D} \gtrless 0 . \tag{24}$$

A sufficient condition for $\hat{M} > 0$ is that $\alpha\phi_x - \phi_n < 0$, exactly the opposite of the sufficient condition for G examined above. In this case, if firms have little mark-up power, the subsidy will lead to a relatively small reduction in P_c and have accordingly smaller effects on n. In these circumstances the increases in x_0 will dominate and manufacturing output will rise.

To summarize, our investigation suggests that the effects of infrastructure provision are far from direct and clear-cut. Reductions in fixed costs will have far different effects than reduction in variable costs, and the effects of the latter are quite complex.

2.2.2. Effect on non-manufacturing

With fixed supplies of capital and labor, wheat production rises (falls) as factor bundles are released (acquired) by the manufacturing sector; m and W move in opposite directions. Inspection of (15) and (22) reveals that W will fall as G rises, but increases in s will have an ambiguous effect on non-manufacturing production.

3. Infrastructure and productivity: Empirical analyses

In this section we use the general equilibrium model presented above to guide our empirical analysis of the relationship between infrastructure provision and productivity in the manufacturing and the non-manufacturing sectors. We begin with a discussion of data sources and econometric considerations and then turn to the empirical results.

116   *D. Holtz-Eakin, M.E. Lovely / Reg. Sci. Urban Econ. 26 (1996) 105–123*

3.1. The data

The first step is to choose empirical counterparts to the variables in our highly stylized model. We measure M as output of the manufacturing sector, using the Bureau of Economic Analysis's (BEA) state-by-state series on Gross State Product originating in the private sector. Similarly, W is measured as the output of the non-manufacturing sector from the same source. While it may be tempting to consider each major group within the manufacturing sector separately, data limitations (especially private capital) preclude such an approach. Moreover, we have no theoretical guidance for untangling the differential responses of each subgroup to expanded infrastructure provision. However, such disaggregation may be a fruitful area for future research.

A distinguishing feature of our approach is the important role played by variety in the intermediates sector. In the theory, the number of firms, n, corresponds exactly to variety since no two firms produce exactly the same variety of input. Obviously, our data do not identify 'intermediate varieties'; indeed, they do not contain direct estimates of activity at each stage of production. The manufacturing sector is, however, extensively interlinked, with the products of each sector (e.g. steel) serving as inputs to the production of other sectors (e.g. autos). And, at least to some extent, each production facility has its own set of activities. Hence, we use data on the number of manufacturing establishments as a proxy for the range of varieties contributing to manufacturing productivity. These data are obtained from the quintennial Census of Manufactures for each of the 48 contiguous states for the years 1972, 1977, 1982 and 1987.

Several issues arise in our use of these data. First, as with our output measures, it would be desirable to distinguish between producers of final goods and producers of intermediates, but such a distinction is simply not possible. Second, we would like to guard against the possibility that an increase in the number of establishments does not represent a rise in the variety of activities. For example, consider two states, one with 100 establishments concentrated in a single activity and the other with 80 establishments distributed evenly across the range of manufacturing sectors. It seems inappropriate to identify the former state as having greater variety than the latter.

With this in mind, we develop a measure of the dispersion of manufacturing establishments across activities. For each state, we compute the coefficient of variation (CV) of the number of manufacturing establishments across two-digit Standard Industrial Classification (SIC) codes. Note that if there are the same number of establishments in each SIC code, and hence a great variety of manufacturing activity, the CV will be equal to zero. In

D. Holtz-Eakin, M.E. Lovely / Reg. Sci. Urban Econ. 26 (1996) 105–123 117

contrast, if establishments are concentrated in a few, or even a single, area, the CV will be quite large.[12]

We turn now to our measures of public and private inputs. Public capital stocks are estimates of the stock of state and local government capital in each state as constructed by Holtz- Eakin (1993). (The exclusion of federal government capital is unimportant in practice since it is largely devoted to military capital.) These data include the total real capital in each state for each year, and also individual estimates for capital devoted to specific government functions such as schools, streets and highways, etc. In large part, we focus on total public capital in our analysis. However, because this measure includes capital such as public school buildings, which may not be included in common definitions of infrastructure, we test the sensitivity of our results to using a narrower measure of public capital which we call 'core infrastructure'. Core infrastructure is measured as the sum of capital in streets and highways, sanitation and sewerage systems, and utilities.

For private inputs, estimates of private-sector capital in each state and sector are taken from Munnell (1990b). Labor inputs are measured using BEA data on full-time and part-time wage and salary employees in each state and sector.

3.2. Econometric considerations

In what follows we will be interested in equations that have the generic form

$$y_{it} = x_{it}\beta + \gamma_t + \mu_{it},$$ (25)

where i indexes states, t indexes years, y is the logarithm of, for example, manufacturing output, x is a vector of (logarithms of) explanatory variables including public sector capital, γ_t is a year-specific intercept, and μ_{it} is a regression disturbance term.

In analyzing the effects of infrastructure, Holtz-Eakin (1994) demonstrates the importance of controlling for unobserved heterogeneity among the states. In short, because more productive states have a greater ability to undertake public works, ceteris paribus, cross-sectional heterogeneity in productivity will generate variation in public capital. In the presence of this reverse causality, ordinary least squares will yield inconsistent estimates of

---

[12] One issue that arises is the treatment of zeros. One might wish to concentrate on variety *given* that there is some activity at all (i.e. exclude zeros). Also, for confidentiality reasons some establishments are not identified in the Census of Manufactures. In practice, the exclusion of zeros has little impact on the character of the results. However, with the latter issue in mind, we concentrate on the CV computed excluding zeros.

118   *D. Holtz-Eakin, M.E. Lovely / Reg. Sci. Urban Econ. 26 (1996) 105–123*

the parameters. To confront this difficulty, we augment our basic estimating equations with f_i, a state-specific intercept. Importantly, the state-specific effects are time-invariant, capturing the effects of location, climate, mineral endowments, and so forth. Thus, the equations become

$$y_{it} = x_{it}\beta + \gamma_t + f_i + \mu_{it} \ . \tag{26}$$

To control for the state effects, we employ standard fixed-effect techniques that estimate the parameters using the variation 'within' each state over time. Specifically, we transform the data into deviations from state-specific means, yielding

$$\tilde{y}_{it} = \tilde{x}_{it}\beta + \gamma_t + \mu_{it} \ , \tag{27}$$

where $\bar{y}_i$ is the mean value of y_{it} for state i, $\bar{x}_i$ is defined analogously, $\tilde{y}_{it} \equiv y_{it} - \bar{y}_i$, and $\tilde{x}_{it} \equiv x_{it} - \bar{x}_i$. As indicated by the absence of the f_i from Eq. (27), the use of deviations eliminates the state-specific effects.[13]

3.3. Results

It is now widely recognized that there is a positive correlation between infrastructure and output. In the context of our data, this finding is confirmed; a regression of the logarithm of manufacturing output on the logarithm of public capital yields a coefficient (standard error) of 0.637 (0.127), while a similar regression for non-manufacturing private output yields a coefficient of 0.360 (0.0877).[14,15]

Our theoretical model assumes that public capital does not directly affect non-manufacturing. Its only influence is through its effect on private sector inputs ('factor bundles') to the sector. Thus, as a first check, we examine the effect of public capital, K_g, on W, controlling for private sector labor, L_W, and capital, K_W, in non-manufacturing. Looking at the data yields:

$$\tilde{W} = 0.326\tilde{K}_W + 0.744\tilde{L}_W - 0.00776\tilde{K}_g \ . \tag{28}$$
$$(0.0623) \quad (0.0661) \quad (0.0343)$$

These results support the notion that public capital's direct productivity effect, if one exists, arises in the manufacturing sector.

Our model suggests that infrastructure affects manufacturing through a variety of channels. The first of these is by altering the preferred scale of

---

[13] See Hsiao (1986) for a discussion of fixed-effect estimations.

[14] Each regression reported herein controls for state effects, and contains an intercept and dummy variables for the years 1977, 1982 and 1987. Heteroskedasticity-consistent (Huber) standard errors are reported in parentheses.

[15] Using our narrower measure of core infrastructure capital does not alter the character of the relationship. The respective estimates are 0.489 (0.113) and 0.362 (0.0750).

D. Holtz-Eakin, M.E. Lovely / Reg. Sci. Urban Econ. 26 (1996) 105–123 119

production for each firm in the manufacturing sector. Recall, from what we found above, that to the extent that infrastructure subsidizes fixed costs, x_0 will fall, while to the extent that it reduces variable costs we anticipate greater output. We do not have a direct measurement of intermediate output per firm, but we can examine the impact of infrastructure on output per establishment in the manufacturing sector, M/n. Examination of Eq. (4′) indicates that this does not directly yield an estimate of x_0. Instead,

$$M/n \equiv x_0' = n^{\alpha-1}x_0 , \tag{29}$$

suggesting that if we first control for a variation in n, the effect of infrastructure on x_0' and x_0 will coincide. Implementing this strategy, we regress output per manufacturing establishment on the logarithms of the number of establishments and public capital (K_g). The result is

$$\tilde{x}' = 0.0332\tilde{n} + 0.0608\tilde{K}_g , \tag{30}$$
$$\quad (0.113) \quad (0.116)$$

indicating a small, imprecisely estimated impact of additional infrastructure on output per firm.[16] In the context of the theoretical model, the result suggests that the reduction in fixed costs embodied in infrastructure nearly offsets the concomitant reduction in variable costs.[17]

As noted earlier, we wish to check the robustness of our results using our CV measure of the dispersion of establishments across SIC codes. To do so, we interact n with our CV measure, σ. Recall that a larger value of σ is associated with lower variety; hence, we expect this interaction term to have a negative sign. Our augmented regression is[18]

$$\tilde{x}' = 0.163\tilde{n} - 0.0379\widetilde{\sigma n} + 0.0147\tilde{K}_g . \tag{31}$$
$$\quad (0.121) \quad (0.00934) \quad (0.107)$$

[16] Our theoretical model suggests also that n is determined simultaneously with x. Recall that endogeneity in the cross-section will likely manifest itself as fixed effects, and our equations control for this feature of the data. Variations in n and x over time remain, however, suggesting that it might be desirable to apply an instrumental variables technique to (30). (Similar considerations apply in other circumstances below.) Unfortunately, it is difficult to construct a variable affecting the number of establishments that is unrelated to output per establishment, especially given the paucity of data at our disposal. Hence, we do not pursue this route.

[17] Also, the point estimate of α implied by Eq. (30) is 1.033, but this coefficient is imprecisely estimated. Using core infrastructure yields similar results. One might be concerned that the specification in (30) treats public capital as a pure public good. Notice, however, that entering public capital in per-firm units would not affect its coefficient. Instead, only the coefficient on the growth of firms (and our estimate of α) would be affected (rising toward 1.1).

[18] We could include the level of σ as well as its interaction with n. This reduces the precision of the individual estimates, but does not alter their qualitative character.

120   *D. Holtz-Eakin, M.E. Lovely / Reg. Sci. Urban Econ. 26 (1996) 105–123*

The interaction variable is statistically significant and indicates a positive relationship between the richness of the local environment and output per establishment. With regard to public capital, however, expanding our control for variety has little impact on the small, positive, imprecisely estimated effect on output per establishment.[19]

The second major channel by which infrastructure may operate is through the equilibrium number of firms. A simple regression of the logarithm of the number of manufacturing establishments on (log) public capital yields a coefficient of 0.557 (0.0882); the data reveal a positive and significant correlation between public capital and the number of establishments.[20] One objection to this procedure is that it fails to control for the resources available to the manufacturing sector. Augmenting the regression with private capital (K_P) and labor (L_P) in the state yields:

$$\tilde{n} = -0.202\tilde{K}_P + 0.828\tilde{L}_P + 0.169\tilde{K}_g . \tag{32}$$
$$(0.0683) \quad (0.0815) \quad (0.0500)$$

Our theory does not provide an interpretation of each coefficient in this reduced form, but the regression continues to indicate that public capital does more than transfer private resources to the manufacturing sector. Infrastructure appears to contribute significantly to the growth of the number of manufacturing establishments.[21]

Thus far, the picture that emerges is one in which public capital has little effect on the level of production per establishment, but an upward effect on the number of firms in manufacturing. As a check on the model, however, note that infrastructure provision should influence total manufacturing output only through its effect on output per firm and the number of varieties. The first of these effects appears to be roughly zero. Thus, if we control for the private inputs (factor bundles) used to produce x_0 and the number of firms, public capital should have little residual explanatory power. We use manufacturing capital per firm and labor per firm to proxy for the factor content of x_0 and implement this strategy, yielding the regression

$$\tilde{M} = 0.300\tilde{k}_M + 0.892\tilde{l}_M + 0.995\tilde{n} - 0.132\tilde{K}_g , \tag{33}$$
$$(0.0426) \quad (0.0877) \quad (0.0678) \quad (0.0675)$$

---

[19] We may derive an estimate of α from (31) by differentiating with respect to n and evaluating the result at the mean value of σ (1.173). The result implies an α of 1.12.

[20] Again using core infrastructure, public capital does not alter the basic conclusion. The estimates are 0.399 (0.0821).

[21] Again, focusing on infrastructure capital alone gives qualitatively similar results.

where lower case letters denote per-firm values, e.g. $k_M \equiv K_M / n$. In Eq. (33) the per-firm levels of capital and labor (our controls for 'factor bundles' per firm) have a strong (and not surprising) influence on the level of manufacturing output. Similarly, the number of manufacturing establishments translates into greater output.[22] Notice, however, that after controlling for these features, additional public capital does not lead to greater manufacturing output; indeed, the point estimate is negative.[23]

Consistent with our earlier discussion, we augment Eq. (33) with our CV measure to improve the control for returns to variety. As above, the interaction with the CV measure enters significantly:

$$\tilde{M} = 0.287\tilde{k}_M + 0.881\tilde{l}_m + 1.04\tilde{n} - 0.134\widetilde{\sigma n} - 0.144\tilde{K}_g . \qquad (34)$$
$$(0.0423) \quad (0.0865) \quad (0.0675)(0.00633) \quad (0.0639)$$

In (34), the controls for firm-level resources $(\tilde{k}_M$ and $\tilde{l}_M)$ continue to display an important role.[24] However, the alternative specification does not alter our calculations regarding public capital.

Eqs. (33) and (34) are modified versions of the standard 'production function' approach to analyzing the productivity effects of public infrastructure, and the absence of direct effects from K_g are consistent with the findings of that literature. However, viewing the data through the lens of our equilibrium model suggests that the existing analyses do not capture an important feature of the data. While additional public infrastructure may have little direct effect on manufacturing output, the results presented above suggest an important effect on the number of manufacturing firms. More generally, the character of these results suggests that the focus should shift from the effect of infrastructure on the *level* of manufacturing activity to its effects on the *composition* of activity. To the extent that increases in the range of manufacturing yield returns to variety, public infrastructure may raise the productivity of manufacturing-sector inputs.

4. Summary

In this paper we have sought to analyze the productivity effects of public infrastructure in the context of a general equilibrium model. Our model was

---

[22] The implied value of α here is 0.995, somewhat smaller than that estimated by Eq. (30) or (31).

[23] As above, entering the public capital in per-firm units does not alter this conclusion. See footnote 17. Also, while the magnitudes differ, the point estimates derived using core infrastructure capital are quite similar in character.

[24] As before, including the dispersion of establishments as a control raises the implied estimate of α, here raising it from 0.995 to 1.02. We obtain similar results if we use the core infrastructure or if we enter the level of σ directly into (34).

constructed in accordance with several features of the empirical literature on infrastructure productivity: potentially different effects on the manufacturing and non-manufacturing sectors, potential cost reductions in manufacturing, and returns to scale in manufacturing. By its nature our equilibrium model accounts for factor price changes induced by the provision of infrastructure.

The analytics of our model suggest that infrastructure has few unambiguous effects. Instead, the results hinge upon the degree to which publicly provided capital reduces the fixed costs of production or provides a subsidy to variable costs. Furthermore, the magnitudes of the key effects are sensitive to the market structure in which producers operate.

Framing our empirical investigation of public capital in the context of the model indicates little in the way of direct output effects from infrastructure, supporting previous production function studies. However, our results suggest a more subtle role for public capital, working through increases in the number of manufacturing establishments. Taken at face value, the results show no productivity effects outside the manufacturing sector, and no influence on output per establishment. However, infrastructure increases the number of individual establishments, thus raising manufacturing output. Moreover, to the extent that the increase in establishments carries external returns, manufacturing productivity rises as well. Hence, our results are consistent with cost-saving and productivity effects in manufacturing.

Our study represents a first step in the use of equilibrium models to analyze infrastructure, and our results await further corroboration. However, they also point to several promising areas for future research: the role of infrastructure in the dynamics of firm creation and destruction, the measurement of external effects and returns to variety, and the differential effects of infrastructure in more disaggregate analyses.

Acknowledgements

We thank seminar participants at the American Economic Association meetings and Syracuse University, John Quigley, Dave Richardson, David Wildasin, and an anonymous referee for helpful comments on an earlier draft. Karin D'Agostino, Jennifer Gantt, Esther Gray, Ann Wicks, and Jodi Woodson were invaluable in their assistance in preparing the manuscript.

References

Aschauer, D., 1989, Is public expenditure productive?. Journal of Monetary Economics 23, 177–200.

D. Holtz-Eakin, M.E. Lovely / Reg. Sci. Urban Econ. 26 (1996) 105–123 123

Dekle, R. and J. Eaton, 1994, Agglomeration and the price of land: Evidence from the prefectures, National Bureau of Economic Research, Working Paper No. 4781.

Ethier, W.J., 1979, Internationally decreasing costs and world trade, Journal of International Economics 9, 1–24.

Ethier, W.J., 1982, National and international returns to scale in the modern theory of international trade, American Economic Review 72, 388–405.

Evans, P. and G. Karras, 1994, Are government activities productive? Evidence from a panel of U.S. states, The Review of Economics and Statistics 76, 1–11.

Garcia-Mila, T. and T. McGuire, 1992, The contribution of publicly provided inputs to states' economies, Regional Science and Urban Economics 22, no. 2.

Garcia-Mila, T., T. McGuire and R. Porter, 1995, The effect of public capital in state-level production functions reconsidered, The Review of Economics and Statistics, in press.

Henderson, V., 1994, Externalities and industrial development, National Bureau of Economic Research Working Paper No. 4730.

Holtz-Eakin, D., 1993, State-specific estimates of state and local government capital, Regional Science and Urban Economics 23, 185–210.

Holtz-Eakin, D., 1994, Public sector capital and the productivity puzzle, The Review of Economics and Statistics 76, 12–21.

Holtz-Eakin, D. and A.E. Schwartz, 1995, Infrastructure in a structural model of economic growth, Regional Science and Urban Economics 25, 131–151.

Holtz-Eakin, D. and M. Lovely, 1995, Technological linkages, market structure, and optimum production policies, Journal of Public Economics, in press.

Hulten, C. and R. Schwab, 1991, Public capital formation and the growth of regional manufacturing industries, National Tax Journal 44, 121–134.

Hsiao, C., 1986, Analysis of panel data (Cambridge University Press, Cambridge).

Markusen, J.R., 1989, Trade in producer services and in other specialized intermediate inputs, American Economic Review 79, 85–95.

Markusen, J.R., 1991, First mover advantages, blockaded entry, and the economics of uneven development, in: E. Helpman and A. Razin, eds., International trade and trade policy (The MIT Press, Cambridge, MA).

Morrison, C. and A.E. Schwartz, 1992, State infrastructure and productive performance, National Bureau of Economic Research Working Paper No. 3981.

Munnell, A., 1990a, Why has productivity growth declined? Productivity and public investment, New England Economic Review, January/February, 3–22.

Munnell, A., 1990b, How does public infrastructure affect regional economic performance?, in: A. Munnell, ed., Is there a shortfall in public capital investment? (Federal Reserve Bank of Boston, Boston, MA).

Nadiri, I.M. and T. Mamuneas, 1994, The effects of public infrastructure and R&D capital on the cost structure and performance of U.S. manufacturing industries, The Review of Economics and Statistics 76, 22–37.

Tatom, J., 1993, The spurious effect of public capital formation on private sector productivity, Policy Studies Journal 2, 391–395.

Information, agglomeration, and the headquarters of U.S. exporters

Mary E. Lovely[a,1], Stuart S. Rosenthal[b,*], Shalini Sharma[c]

[a] *Department of Economics, Syracuse University, Syracuse, NY 13244-1020, USA*
[b] *Department of Economics, Syracuse University, Syracuse, NY 13244-1020, USA*
[c] *Department of Economics, University of Toronto, Toronto, ON, Canada M5S 3G7*

Received 21 June 2002; accepted 23 September 2003
Available online 16 March 2004

Abstract

Although longstanding arguments suggest that the need to acquire information contributes to spatial concentration of employment, few studies have provided evidence on this point. This paper addresses this issue by examining the spatial concentration of headquarter activity of exporters. Exporting requires specialized knowledge of foreign markets and should, therefore, contribute to spatial concentration. We test this idea by applying differencing methods to 4-digit industry-level data for the fourth quarter of 2000. Results suggest that when foreign market information is difficult to obtain, exporter headquarter activity is more agglomerated. Results also indicate that the sensitivity of agglomeration to foreign trading environments depends on the underlying characteristics that define countries as "difficult."
© 2004 Elsevier B.V. All rights reserved.

JEL classification: R10; R12; F00; F23
Keywords: Agglomeration; Exporting; Information

1. Introduction

The need for industry to acquire information underlies a number of theoretical explanations of agglomeration that have become standard in the economics literature.[2]

---

* Corresponding author. Tel.: +1-315-443-3809; fax: +1-315-443-1081.
E-mail addresses: melovely@maxwell.syr.edu (M.E. Lovely), ssrosent@maxwell.syr.edu (S.S. Rosenthal).
[1] Tel.: +1-315-443-9048.
[2] See Quigley (1998) for a survey of the theoretical literature on the micro-foundations of agglomeration economies.

0166-0462/$ - see front matter © 2004 Elsevier B.V. All rights reserved.
doi:10.1016/j.regsciurbeco.2003.09.002

168   *M.E. Lovely et al. / Regional Science and Urban Economics 35 (2005) 167–191*

As early as 1920, Marshall (1920) suggested that establishments concentrate spatially in part because of external economies of scale arising from knowledge spillovers and labor market pooling.[3] Knowledge spillovers arise when firms learn from their neighbors and clearly depend on the need to acquire information. Labor market pooling arises when firms are able to hire skilled labor more easily in areas populated with companies that rely on similarly skilled workers. To the extent that workers provide information—as with accountants, lawyers, and the like—the value of labor market pooling also depends on the need to acquire information. Finally, Alonso (1972) and others have noted that many industries concentrate spatially because of a common desire to locate close to the source of a key input, such as timber or mineral deposits. To the extent that information is a key input, areas with information-oriented facilities—such as libraries, government offices, and universities—offer "natural advantages" (e.g., Ellison and Glaeser, 1997) that also flow from the need to acquire information.

Yet, despite longstanding beliefs that the need to acquire information fosters agglomeration, only a handful of studies have provided empirical evidence on this point. Of these, perhaps the most compelling is that of Jaffe et al. (1993), who demonstrate that patent citations attenuate with distance from the company with the original patent.[4] Another important study of innovative activity, by Audretsch and Feldman (1996), uses a spatial Gini coefficient to measure geographic concentration. Their results indicate that innovative activity is substantially more concentrated than overall production and that industries that emphasize research and development tend to be more spatially concentrated.[5]

The goal of this paper is to add to this literature by examining the spatial concentration of headquarter activity of exporters. Exporting requires specialized knowledge of foreign markets and contacts abroad. Such information is costly to obtain, especially when exporting to countries that do not have open and easily accessed markets. Moreover, evidence suggests that export-specific information needs to be updated on a continuing basis.[6] Therefore, for all of the reasons noted above, the need to acquire information should contribute to spatial concentration of headquarter activity among exporters.

---

[3] Marshall (1920) also emphasized the importance of shared intermediate inputs. These ideas have been expanded and embellished upon by Krugman (1991) and others, but the essential ideas articulated by Marshall (1920) have remained.

[4] To be precise, Jaffe et al. (1993) show that patent citations are 5–10 times as likely to come from the same SMSA as control patents.

[5] Studies in the trade literature also implicitly examine the linkage between information and spatial concentration of activity. For example, Aitken et al. (1997) examine Mexican manufacturing firms and find evidence that spillovers associated with exporting are economically important and derive from the presence of multinational enterprises. In contrast, using U.S. plant-level data, Bernard and Jensen (2001) test the hypothesis that proximity to other exporting plants raises the probability of exporting, but find no evidence of such behavior.

[6] Using data from Colombia, Roberts and Tybout (1997) find that a plant that exported in the prior year is up to 60 percentage points more likely to export in the current period. But, by the time a plant has been out of the export market for 2 years, its probability of exporting differs little from that of a plant that has never exported. Roberts and Tybout suggest that this pattern is consistent with the need to update export-specific information on a recurring basis, although they also note that these patterns could arise because of increasing costs associated with updating old export products. Bernard and Jensen (2001) find a similar pattern of transitions using a sample of U.S. manufacturing plants, estimating that prior-year exporting raises the probability of exporting in the current period by 36%, but that exporting two years prior raises the current-period exporting probability by only 10.5%.

M.E. Lovely et al. / Regional Science and Urban Economics 35 (2005) 167–191 169

We test this idea by applying differencing methods to 4-digit industry-level data using the *iMarket* Inc. "MarketPlace" database for the fourth quarter of 2000. Our primary strategy is to compare the spatial concentration of headquarter activity among exporting manufacturing establishments to the concentration of those firms that do not export, treating each industry as a separate observation. The degree of spatial concentration within an industry-class is measured using Ellison and Glaeser's (1997) Gamma index of spatial agglomeration.

We begin by regressing the *level* of exporter headquarter spatial concentration and also that of domestic-only headquarter agglomeration on export shares to "difficult" countries—countries for which the cost of obtaining export-specific information is likely to be high. Regressors are also included for a variety of industry characteristics that capture broader underlying determinants of industry spatial concentration. To control for unobserved attributes of a given export sector and industry, we repeat the regressions for each export sector using a *single-differenced* measure of agglomeration. This measure is obtained by subtracting branch-level agglomeration by export status from the corresponding headquarter concentration measure. Finally, our most robust specification uses a *twice-differenced* measure of agglomeration obtained by further subtracting domestic-only agglomeration from that of the export sector. This controls for additional unobserved industry attributes and also provides a convenient way to test for the relative effect of trade with difficult countries on the export sector as compared to the domestic-only sector.

An important feature of our work is the manner in which we classify countries as having a "difficult" trading environment for U.S. exporters. Because definitions of "difficult" trading environments are not standard, we estimate our models separately for five different measures of difficult trading environments. The classification we experiment with first is based on the degree to which a country is integrated into the world economy (*Integration*). In this case, a country is classified as difficult if it has below average trade per dollar of GDP after controlling for the size of the country (a measure used by the World Bank in its "integration index") and proximity to economic activity outside of the country (weighted by the inverse distance between the country and its potential trading partners). Alternative measures depend on the level of political freedom in the country, GATT membership, whether the country is subject to U.S. trade sanctions, and country credit rating.

Our most important finding is that geographic concentration of exporter headquarter activity in the U.S. relative to the domestic sector does appear to increase with the share of an industry's exports destined for countries with difficult trading environments. However, the evidence to support this conclusion is sensitive to the manner in which a foreign country is deemed difficult. Political freedom, GATT membership, and the presence of trade sanctions have little discernible effect on the agglomeration of U.S. exporter headquarters. On the other hand, industries exporting to countries that are poorly integrated into the world economy tend to have more highly agglomerated exporter headquarter activity at the state level, while industries trading with countries with poor credit ratings tend to have more highly agglomerated exporter headquarter activity at the county and zipcode levels. Taken as a whole, these results support the idea that the need to acquire information contributes to agglomeration. In addition, these results suggest that not all

170   *M.E. Lovely et al. / Regional Science and Urban Economics 35 (2005) 167–191*

information is alike, which presumably contributes to the different patterns of agglomeration generated by the alternative measures of foreign country trading environments.

The next section presents the Ellison and Glaeser (1997) measure of spatial concentration used in this study. Thereafter, we describe our data and discuss the main estimating equation, differencing procedures, and related specification issues. Section 6 contains results, while Section 7 concludes.

2. Conceptual measures of agglomeration

There are a number of statistics that one might employ to characterize the degree of agglomeration among manufacturing industries. A natural candidate is the spatial Gini coefficient, defined as $G_j \equiv \Sigma_i(s_{ij} - m_i)^2$, where s_{ij} is location i's share of employment for manufacturing industry j and m_i is location i's share of total manufacturing employment. This statistic is employed by Krugman (1991) and Audretsch and Feldman (1996), among others. It takes on a value of zero when an industry is allocated across space in exactly the same way as total employment. It takes on a value close to one (depending on the size of the industry itself) when the industry is completely concentrated in one location.

As Ellison and Glaeser (1997) note, however, $G > 0$ does not necessarily imply that the industry in question exhibits agglomeration. Suppose that an industry is made up of a small number of large plants, and that there is no agglomerative force—either an externality or a natural advantage—leading to concentration. In this case, G will take on a large value simply because of the industrial organization of the industry. The spatial Gini coefficient, therefore, does not distinguish between concentration arising from industrial structure and concentration arising from systematic agglomerative externalities or natural advantage. In our work, the total number of exporter headquarter facilities is small in many industries, and the issues emphasized by Ellison and Glaeser clearly arise.

To address this problem, Ellison and Glaeser propose the following index of concentration:

$$\gamma = \frac{G - \left(1 - \sum_i m_i^2\right)H}{\left(1 - \sum_i m_i^2\right)(1 - H)},$$ (1)

where $H = \Sigma_j z_j^2$ is a Herfindahl index of the J plants in the industry, with z_j representing the employment share of the jth plant.[7] The expected value of the Ellison–Glaeser Gamma

---

[7] Ellison and Glaeser (1997) obtain γ by demonstrating that the expected value for G is $\gamma(1 - \Sigma m_i^2)(1 - H) + (1 - \Sigma m_i^2)H$. In addition, note that for a perfectly competitive industry with a large number of small plants, H and Σm_i^2 both approach zero and γ approaches G. In this case, G measures spatial concentration without any contamination associated with industrial organization.

M.E. Lovely et al. / Regional Science and Urban Economics 35 (2005) 167–191   171

index is zero when the spatial allocation of employment is random. Thus, the index has the appealing feature of permitting comparisons between the actual pattern of spatial concentration and the concentration that would be expected to arise from a random allocation of employment. We use the index defined in Eq. (1) to measure agglomeration in the work to follow.

3. Agglomeration of exporting and non-exporting employment

We compute the Ellison–Glaeser index using information from Dun and Bradstreet (D&B), included in the *iMarket*'s MarketPlace database for the fourth quarter of 2000.[8] The complete version of the data set contains establishment-level information on over 12 million establishments (over 700,000 manufacturing establishments) in the United States.[9] We use a more manageable and affordable version of the data set in which the data are aggregated up to the zipcode level.[10]

The database contains information on number of establishments, employees, sales, and type of site, among other characteristics, by SIC code for each zipcode, county, and state in the United States.[11] In all cases, we classify the industry to which an establishment belongs based on the establishment's primary SIC code. Exporting status is contained in the Harris Infosource database, which is matched by *iMarket* to the D&B database and included in the MarketPlace file.[12] Establishments are classified as exporters if exporting occurs from any site within the firm.

As a rough check on the degree to which the *iMarket* data is representative of exporting establishments in the United States, we compare the D&B/Harris information to data compiled by the U.S. Department of Commerce in 2001. The Foreign Trade Division of the U.S. Census Bureau prepares a profile of U.S. exporting companies by linking individual company identifiers reported on documents filed for export clearances to

---

[8] *iMarket* is a commercial data vendor. *iMarket* obtains the core data from Dun and Bradstreet, another commercial data vendor, and then matches the D&B data with a wide variety of data from other data vendors. Additional details on the MarketPlace database are provided in Rosenthal and Strange (2001).

[9] Firms requesting not to be in the database are omitted from the data file. Partly for that reason, the D&B database, while extensive, does not contain the entire universe of establishments in the United States.

[10] Additional details on the Dun and Bradstreet (D&B) MarketPlace file are provided at the Dun and Bradstreet web site, www.dnb.com. As described by Dun and Bradstreet, there are several important benefits to firms from listing themselves in the D&B database and obtaining a DUNS identification number. In particular, DUNS identification numbers are rapidly becoming a standard identification device in the economy, and many companies, including the Federal Government, require that clients obtain a DUNS number as a precondition for engaging in trade.

[11] In contrast, the Census of Manufacturing (CM) and County Business Patterns (CBP), the data sets used by Ellison and Glaeser (1997), are designed as representative surveys. However, the public use versions of the CM and CBP both suffer from restrictions on the type of firms and employment data reported, including top-coding problems. Access to confidential files at a Census research station avoids these limitations, but access is costly both financially and in that individuals must work on site at one of a small number of such research stations in the country. In contrast, there is no top-coding in the *iMarket* database.

[12] Harris InfoSource compiles information on locations and other characteristics of the establishments from exclusive relationships with local, state and national agencies, including the National Association of Manufacturers. Companies are then profiled in detail by in-house researchers before inclusion.

172   *M.E. Lovely et al. / Regional Science and Urban Economics 35 (2005) 167–191*

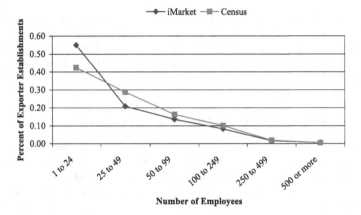

Fig. 1. *iMarket* and census data: size distribution of single site manufacturing exporters. (Sources: census data—U.S. Department of Commerce, 2001; Table 1 *iMarket* data—see text.)

Census' centralized company information database.[13] However, the Census profile does not disaggregate multi-site firms into their component establishments, while the *iMarket* multi-site data are only available in a form that cannot be aggregated back to the firm level. For that reason, we limit our comparison of the two data sources to single-site companies for which no issues of aggregation arise. As Fig. 1 shows, the employment size distribution of single-site manufacturing exporters is quite similar in the Census profile and the *iMarket* database.

Although the comparison in Fig. 1 is based on single-site firms, for all of the analysis to follow, we now focus entirely on multi-site companies. We do this for two reasons. First, multi-site companies account for 77% of employment among exporters in our data. Second, a central goal of this paper is to identify the extent to which the need to acquire export specific information—as opposed to materials—affects the spatial concentration of industrial activity. Export specific information, however, pertains primarily to administration and marketing and is processed at headquarter and sales facilities within a company. It is desirable, therefore, to highlight the impact of exporting on the spatial concentration of headquarter activity. The headquarters of multi-site companies are directly observable in the D&B data which facilitates analysis of these issues.[14] In contrast, all single site firms necessarily locate both production and headquarter activity at the same site making it more

---

[13] Approximately 82% of total export value for 1998 and 84% for 1999 were linked to specific companies. For more information, see U.S. Department of Commerce (2001).

[14] In our data, a headquarters is defined as a center of a firm's operations, administration, or marketing activity, and it may or may not also be the site of manufacturing operations. In this regard, a headquarters in the iMarket data is more general than the central decision making authority in the firm. But this is desirable for our work because sales offices and regional administrative centers also need to obtain foreign country specific information in order to contribute to a firms' exporting activities.

M.E. Lovely et al. / Regional Science and Urban Economics 35 (2005) 167–191   173

difficult to isolate the influence of export specific information on the spatial pattern of economic activity.[15]

For these reasons, in the empirical work to follow, we calculate γ separately for different sub-categories of multi-site firms: exporter headquarter employment, exporter branch employment, domestic-only headquarters employment, and domestic-only branch employment. In each case, separate measures of H and G are used for each industry sub-group. As such, each sub-group is treated as a separate "industry" and γ measures the level of excess agglomeration (or dispersion) of employment in that sub-group relative to what would otherwise be expected given the size distribution of establishments in the sub-group.

4. Empirical strategy

As noted earlier, in our data headquarters engage in information oriented administrative, managerial, and marketing activities. In addition, some headquarters have production facilities on site. Accordingly, agglomeration of exporter headquarter employment is sensitive to natural advantages and agglomeration economies that affect both the cost of marketing products to domestic and foreign destinations as well as to those that affect production costs.

In order to isolate the impact of information specific to the marketing of products to foreign countries, it is necessary to strip away the influence of other determinants of headquarter agglomeration. We begin by regressing the level of exporter headquarter agglomeration (γ_j^{HQe}) on proxies for reliance on export-specific information (E) and other determinants of agglomeration (X),

$$\gamma_j^{HQe} = \beta_E^{HQe} E_j + \beta_X^{HQe} X_j + \varepsilon_j^{HQe} \tag{2}$$

where j denotes industry ($j = 1, \ldots, J$), β_E^{HQe} and β_X^{HQe} are vectors of estimated coefficients, and ε_j^{HQe} is a vector of error terms, assumed to be independent and identically distributed. Provided X_j is sufficiently well specified, estimates of Eq. (2) yield consistent measures of the influence of E_j on the agglomeration of exporter headquarter employment. As indicated in the Introduction, we expect this effect to be positive. In addition, to the extent that domestic-only companies value proximity to exporters, we may also obtain a positive effect of E_j when domestic-only headquarter agglomeration is substituted as the dependent variable, though presumably of a lesser magnitude.

A difficulty with this approach, of course, is that X may not control for enough factors to ensure an unbiased and consistent estimate of β_E^{HQe}. To address that concern, we decompose the error term in Eq. (2) into five parts and employ differencing methods to

---

[15] As a robustness check, we also examined the spatial concentration of employment among single-site companies. As anticipated, the blending of headquarter and manufacturing activity obscures the role of export specific information on the location of decision making activity among manufacturers. See Sharma (2001) for results.

further remove unobserved effects. This approach is based on the following decomposition of the error term from Eq. (2):

$$\varepsilon_j^{HQ_e} = \theta_j^{NA_{Shipping,d}} + \theta_j^{NA_{Shipping,e}} + \theta_j^{NA \& AS_{Production}} + \theta_j^{Info_{Sales \& Management}} + u_j^{HQ_e}, \qquad (3)$$

where $\theta_j^{NA_{Shipping,d}}$ and $\theta_j^{NA_{Shipping,e}}$ reflect the influence of unobserved natural advantages pertinent to shipping of product to domestic and foreign customers, respectively, $\theta_j^{NA \& AS_{Production}}$ captures the influence of unobserved natural advantages and agglomerative spillovers that affect production costs among all members of the industry, and $\theta_j^{Info_{Sales \& Management}}$ captures the influence of localized information pertinent to the marketing and sales of products for all members of the industry. The remaining error component, $u_j^{HQ_e}$, is idiosyncratic to the export headquarter sector.

Differencing exporter headquarter and exporter branch agglomeration yields

$$\gamma_j^{HQ_e} - \gamma_j^{Branch_e} = \left(\beta_E^{HQ_e} - \beta_E^{Branch_e} \right) E_j + \left(\beta_X^{HQ_e} - \beta_X^{Branch_e} \right) X_j$$
$$+ \left\{ \theta_j^{Info_{Sales \& Management}} + \left(u_j^{HQ_e} - u_j^{Branch_e} \right) \right\} \qquad (4)$$

where, as a first approximation, unobserved industry attributes related to natural advantages in shipping and production are stripped away. Eq. (4) is more robust than Eq. (2). But it should also be noted that Eq. (4) addresses a slightly different question. Specifically, Eq. (4) estimates the influence of E_j on the agglomeration of exporter headquarter employment *relative* to the agglomeration of exporter branch employment, $\beta_E^{HQ_e} - \beta_E^{Branch_e}$. On the other hand, consider that E reflects information related to marketing to foreign countries, while the spatial concentration of branch plant activity is generally thought to be sensitive primarily to production technology and shipping costs. For these reasons, E is expected to have little systematic effect on branch-plant agglomeration ($\beta_E^{Branch_e}$ is likely to be close to zero), and we expect $\beta_E^{HQ_e} - \beta_E^{Branch_e}$ to be positive.[16] Moreover, as before, a similar interpretation holds for the domestic-only sector when domestic agglomeration is substituted for the dependent variable.

In a similar fashion, differencing exporter headquarter agglomeration and domestic-only headquarter agglomeration yields:

$$\gamma_j^{HQ_e} - \gamma_j^{HQ_d} = \left(\beta_E^{HQ_e} - \beta_E^{HQ_d} \right) E_j + \left(\beta_X^{HQ_e} - \beta_X^{HQ_d} \right) X_j$$
$$+ \left\{ \theta_j^{NA_{Shipping,e}} + \left(u_j^{HQ_e} - u_j^{HQ_d} \right) \right\}. \qquad (5)$$

To the extent that $\theta_j^{NA_{Shipping,d}}$, $\theta_j^{NA\&AS_{Production}}$, and $\theta_j^{Info_{Sales \& Management}}$ are common to all headquarter establishments, these unobserved effects are differenced away in Eq. (5). As such, it is clear that differencing export and domestic headquarter agglomeration accomplishes two distinct tasks. First, Eq. (5) is more robust than Eq. (2) because unobserved factors common to all headquarters are removed. In addition, we obtain a

---

[16] As reported below, the specifications in Eqs. (2) and (3) generally yield similar estimates of the coefficient on E, consistent with the idea that E has little direct effect on branch plant agglomeration.

M.E. Lovely et al. / Regional Science and Urban Economics 35 (2005) 167–191   175

direct estimate of $\beta_E^{HQ_e} - \beta_E^{HQ_d}$. This enables us to test whether exporting to difficult countries has a greater effect on the export sector relative to the domestic-only sector.

Finally, differencing off branch plant agglomeration from Eq. (5) further removes the influence of $\theta_j^{NA_{Shipping,d}}$. Accordingly, we also estimate:

$$
\begin{aligned}
(\gamma_j^{HQ_e} &- \gamma_j^{Branch_e}) - (\gamma_j^{HQ_d} - \gamma_j^{Branch_d}) \\
&= \left[\left(\beta_E^{HQ_e} - \beta_E^{Branch_e} \right) - \left(\beta_E^{HQ_d} - \beta_E^{Branch_d} \right) \right] E_j \\
&+ \left[\left(\beta_X^{HQ_e} - \beta_X^{Branch_e} \right) - \left(\beta_X^{HQ_d} - \beta_X^{Branch_d} \right) \right] X_j \\
&+ \left[\left(u_j^{HQ_e} - u_j^{Branch_e} \right) - \left(u_j^{HQ_d} - u_j^{Branch_d} \right) \right].
\end{aligned}
\tag{6}
$$

This specification is the least sensitive to unobserved industry effects and, in that respect, is the most robust model that we estimate. Given our earlier arguments about the likely strength of E_j on agglomeration in the four segments, we expect its estimated coefficient in Eq. (6) to be positive.

A final issue related to the model above concerns the interpretation of the estimated coefficients, β_E^i. Our proxies for an industry's reliance on export-specific information, E_j, are calculated using the distribution of the industry's exports across countries. The distribution of industry exports is influenced by differences in endowments, technology, and trade practices between the U.S. and all countries with which it trades. Although agglomeration may raise the level of productivity in the U.S. industry as a whole, it is unlikely to influence foreign productivity and, hence, the pattern of U.S. exports across countries. For that reason, we treat the distribution of an industry's exports as exogenous and interpret the coefficients as providing evidence of the causal effect of trade patterns on the agglomeration of individual industries.[17]

5. Variables

5.1. Measuring the trading environment of foreign countries

In order to estimate the model above, we need a measure of the foreign trading environment faced by each industry, as represented by E_j. We start from the premise that the challenges of exporting depend on the degree to which a given industry's exports are shipped to countries with difficult trading environments. Country characteristics that make exporting more difficult include those that are policy induced, such as opaque product

---

[17] This need not be the case for other industry attributes. To be precise, from a more general perspective, industry characteristics can affect the propensity of an industry to agglomerate, but agglomeration can also affect characteristics of the industry. This is particularly relevant for those X measures that proxy for an industry's reliance on shared intermediate inputs and product innovation. In these cases, it is possible that the coefficient estimates more accurately reflect equilibrium relationships rather than causal effects of industry attributes on agglomeration.

176   *M.E. Lovely et al. / Regional Science and Urban Economics 35 (2005) 167–191*

standards, tariffs or import licenses, and those that are structural, such as geographic re-moteness, poor infrastructure, or a weak legal system. Because no simple measure charac-terizes the full set of barriers that exporters face, we create a summary measure of a country's revealed openness by comparing its actual trade volume to the trade volume we would ex-pect given its size and location. Countries that trade more than "expected" are then charac-terized as integrated into the world economy, while those that trade less reveal trade frictions.

To calculate a country's expected trade volume (expressed as trade relative to GDP), we run the following regression:

$$\log\left(\frac{\text{Exports}_j + \text{Imports}_j}{\text{GDP}_j}\right) = \theta_0 + \theta_1\log(\text{Population}_j) + \theta_2\log\left(\sum_i GDP_i/D_{ij}\right) + e_j \quad (7)$$

where Exports_j, Imports_j, and GDP_j are export, import, and GDP values for a given country j, and Population_j is country j's population (all based on 1994 data from the World Bank's "World Development Indicators CD-ROM"). The measure $\Sigma_i GDP_i/D_{ij}$ reflects the proximity of country j to the economic activity of potential trading partners, where D_{ij} is the distance between country j's capital and the capitals of all countries $i = 1, ..., I$ to which country j exports.

Ordinary least squares estimates of Eq. (7) for 121 countries are presented in Table 1. Observe that the elasticity with respect to population (θ_1) is negative and highly significant as expected: small countries cannot provide for all of their needs and must engage in trade. Similarly, the elasticity with respect to proximity to trading partners (θ_2) is positive and highly significant, also as anticipated: countries in close proximity to economic activity of potential partners face lower transactions costs and are more likely to engage in trade. The R^2 value is 41.2%, suggesting that country size and proximity to trading partners explain a large fraction of variation in trade across countries.

Negative residuals in Eq. (7) indicate that a country has a smaller than expected level of international trade (per dollar of GDP) given the country's population and proximity to markets. Accordingly, in the work to follow, we characterize countries for which the residuals from Eq. (7) are negative as "difficult" and assign a value of 1 to these countries. Countries with positive residuals are assigned a value of 0. These 1/0 values are then weighted by the share of industry j's exports destined to each country, producing a measure that varies by industry. We refer to this measure as *Integration* in the discussion to follow. For these calculations, export shares are based on 1992 industry export values from the NBER Import–Export Database.[18]

5.2. Controls for other determinants of agglomeration

We also include controls to capture the influence of factors unrelated to trade that contribute to agglomeration for both exporters and non-exporters alike, the **X** matrix in Eqs. (2)–(6). For these purposes, we use several variables recently developed by

---

[18] In total, 442 countries have positive exports in the NBER import–export database. We use 1992 export share values because firm location decisions are likely to reflect past business conditions. See Feenstra (1997) and the NBER website http://www.nber.org) for a detailed data description.

M.E. Lovely et al. / Regional Science and Urban Economics 35 (2005) 167–191 177

Table 1
Trade share results dependent variable: log of trade share[a]

	Log of population	Log of "market size"[b]	Constant
	− 0.269	0.349	− 6.24
	(− 7.27)	(6.34)	(− 2.90)
Number of countries	121		
Root MSE	0.670		
R^2	0.412		

[a] Trade share for country j is calculated by dividing exports plus imports by GDP.
[b] Log of market size is calculated by forming $M_j = \log(\Sigma_{i=1} GDP_i/Distance_{ij})$ where $i = \{1,...,I\}$ are the set of countries in 1992 from which country j received imports, GDP_i is country i's GDP, $Distance_{ij}$ is the distance in miles between the capitals of country j and i, and $1,...,I$ includes 121 countries present in the World Bank database. These countries include all of the major developed nations and developing countries throughout the world.

Rosenthal and Strange (2001) that are available for all of the industries for which the trade measure is also present. Variable definitions, summary statistics, and data sources are provided in Appendix A. Because the primary role of these variables is to control for factors that might otherwise obscure the influence of export-specific effects, our discussion of the components of the X matrix both here and elsewhere in the paper is brief. Bear in mind also that our primary strategy for controlling for factors unrelated to trade that influence agglomeration is by differencing and twice-differencing the agglomeration measures in the manner outlined earlier.

The first set of X variables control for natural advantage and transportation costs. This set uses information from the BEA Input–Output tables and includes energy cost per dollar shipment, natural resource cost per dollar shipment, and water costs per dollar shipment. To the extent that industries concentrate because of a desire to reduce input costs, we expect these variables to be positively related to industry agglomeration. To control for the importance of transportation costs in location decisions, we also include inventories per dollar shipment. Industries that produce highly perishable products face high shipping costs per unit distance and, therefore, seek locations close to their markets. With multiple markets, such industries will tend to display less agglomeration, cet. par.

Two variables are used to proxy for input sharing: manufactured inputs per dollar shipment, and non-manufactured inputs per dollar shipment. Theory suggests that reliance on shared inputs should increase the industry's geographic concentration, so we expect both of these factors to positively affect agglomeration. To control for the importance of knowledge spillovers related to product research and development (as opposed to marketing of exports), we include a measure of innovations per dollar of shipments, expecting industries that are highly innovative to have higher levels of agglomeration.[19]

---

[19] In earlier version of the paper we experimented with controls for the educational characteristics of the industries and also the ratio of production to non-production workers in the industry. These measures were intended to proxy for labor market pooling. However, the education variables are available only at the 3-digit level and were not available for a number of industries for which the trade measures were otherwise present. The ratio of production to non-production workers, in contrast, although present for all industries, was never significant in any of the models after differencing the data. For these reasons these variables were dropped from the analysis.

178 *M.E. Lovely et al. / Regional Science and Urban Economics 35 (2005) 167–191*

6. Results

6.1. Summary measures

Table 2 presents the summary measures of state-level agglomeration for different segments of the 4-digit industries.[20] Observe that employment at domestic-only firms tends to be more spatially concentrated than exporter employment: the average gamma value for exporters is 0.037 while the average value for non-exporters is 0.047. The same pattern is evident when agglomeration is measured separately for headquarter and branch employment. Averaging across industries, however, is sensitive to outliers. For that reason, Table 3 reports the percentage of industries for which state-level employment is more agglomerated among exporters relative to domestic-only plants. Measures are analyzed grouping together headquarter and branch employment (the "Headquarter and Branch" column), and again focusing on just headquarter employment. Among all manufacturing industries (the top row of Table 3), employment is more agglomerated among exporters relative to domestic-only plants in 38.6% of industries for branch and headquarter employment combined, and 33.9% of industries for just headquarter employment. Table 3 also reports analogous measures for each of the twenty 2-digit SIC manufacturing industries. In nearly every case, the majority of 4-digit industries belonging to the broader 2-digit industry display more agglomeration among domestic-only plants relative to exporters. On the surface, these summary measures are not consistent with the idea that the need to acquire export-specific information fosters agglomeration.

6.2. Agglomeration with branch and headquarter employment combined

To explore these patterns further, Table 4 presents regressions results of the state-level agglomeration measures without distinguishing between headquarter and branch employment.[21] These equations are estimated with robust standard errors and are clustered on 2-digit SIC codes. Consider first the influence of variables that control for determinants of agglomeration apart from export-specific factors. Examining the table, it is clear that these variables appear to have more influence in the domestic-only sector as compared to the exporter sector. Variables that have the most significant effect on agglomeration are the natural resource measures that proxy the importance of natural advantages and related shipping costs (natural resource and water expenditures), and also

---

[20] Both here and in the tables to follow we focus on only a subset of the 459 4-digit industries. This is because for a number of industries multi-site headquarter establishments are not present at the 4-digit level in our data, or nearly so. To be precise, of the 459 4-digit industries, 5 have zero multi-site exporter headquarters sites, 8 have only one such site, and another 42 have nearly all employment concentrated at one site as indicated by a Herfindahl (H) measure in excess of 0.5. Among these industries the Herfindahl measure approaches (or is equal to) unity and the Gamma index is not well defined in Eq. (1). For that reason, these industries are dropped from the analysis. Note also, that these industries account for only 3% of total employment found at exporter headquarter sites in our data.

[21] The number of industries analyzed in Table 4 and the tables to follow is reduced relative to the industry counts in Tables 2 and 3 because the trade share variable is missing for a number of industries.

Table 2
Summary measures of state-level agglomeration in different manufacturing segments[a,b]

Variable name	Manufacturing segment	Number of observations	Mean	Std. dev.	Min	Max
γ_{state}	All establishments	404	0.0451	0.0660	−0.0187	0.4993
γ_{state}^{Export}	Export establishments	404	0.0369	0.0854	−0.0611	0.9995
$\gamma_{state}^{Domestic}$	Non-exporting establishments	404	0.0471	0.0723	−0.0521	0.4572
$\gamma_{state}^{Export,HQ}$	Headquarter employment at export establishments	404	0.0260	0.1317	−0.1673	0.9866
$\gamma_{state}^{Domestic-Only,HQ}$	Headquarter employment at domestic-only establishments	403	0.0553	0.1196	−0.2223	0.9185
$\gamma_{state}^{Export,Branch}$	Branch employment at export establishments	397	0.0129	0.1901	−3.1114	0.7500
$\gamma_{state}^{Domestic-Only,Branch}$	Branch employment at domestic-only establishments	404	0.0488	0.0906	−0.3050	0.6983

[a] All values are computed using 2000:4 *iMarket* MarketPlace Data.
[b] All values calculated using data disaggregated to the 4-digit SIC level.

inventories per dollar of shipments which proxies perishability of products, and therefore, shipping costs as well.[22] These results are broadly consistent with those of Rosenthal and Strange (2001).[23]

Table 4 indicates *Integration* is insignificant for exporters and domestic-only plants alike, which suggests that the need to collect export-specific information does not promote agglomeration. However, as discussed earlier, our theory pertains primarily to headquarter agglomeration, which is not isolated in Table 4. In the next section, we explore the relationship between trading environments and headquarter and branch agglomeration separately. We also develop and test several alternative measures of which foreign countries are difficult locations for exporters.

6.3. Alternative classifications of the trading environment

Four alternative measures of whether a country has a difficult trading environment are now considered, each of which targets a different set of policies or circumstances that might make it difficult to do business with a given country. A complete listing of how each country's trading environment is classified based on the different measures of *Difficult* is provided in Appendix B. For each definition of *Difficult* a separate measure of the share of an industry's exports destined for difficult countries is calculated as described above. Data sources and summary statistics of the export shares for the different measures are provided

---

[22] Industries that produce perishable products must ship their products to market quickly and tend to be less agglomerated for that reason.
[23] Note that Rosenthal and Strange (2001) do not take exporting into account or the division of activities into headquarter and branch establishments.

180   *M.E. Lovely et al. / Regional Science and Urban Economics 35 (2005) 167–191*

Table 3
Comparison of 4-digit SIC state-level agglomeration of exporting and non-exporting establishments[a]

SIC	Industry description	Number of 4-digit industries	Headquarter and branch employment — Percent of Industries for which $\gamma_{state}^{Export} > \gamma_{state}^{Domestic}$	Headquarter employment only — Percent of Industries for which $\gamma_{state}^{Export,HQ} > \gamma_{state}^{Domestic\text{-}Only.HQ}$
20–39	All Manufacturing Industries	404	0.386	0.339
20	Food and kindred products	39	0.436	0.436
21	Tobacco products	3	0.667	0.333
22	Textile mill products	19	0.684	0.368
23	Apparel and other textile products	27	0.222	0.259
24	Lumber and wood products	14	0.357	0.357
25	Furniture and fixtures	11	0.545	0.273
26	Paper and allied products	17	0.294	0.118
27	Printing and publishing	13	0.385	0.154
28	Chemicals and allied products	28	0.321	0.464
29	Petroleum and coal products	4	0.250	0.250
30	Rubber and miscellaneous plastics	15	0.400	0.333
31	Leather and leather products	8	0.125	0.500
32	Stone, clay and glass products	19	0.421	0.158
33	Primary metal industries	23	0.435	0.391
34	Fabricated metal products	35	0.371	0.314
35	Industrial machinery and equipment	51	0.412	0.353
36	Electronic and other electrical equipment	32	0.281	0.281
37	Transportation equipment	12	0.167	0.417
38	Instruments and related products	17	0.353	0.471
39	Miscellaneous manufacturing industries	17	0.647	0.412

[a] All values are computed using 2000:4 *iMarket* MarketPlace Data.

in Tables 5a–c. In creating each variable, we attempted to find country information for 1994, the date of the World Bank data used to calculate population and trade measures for the *Integration* measure. When this was not possible, we used the available data closest in time to 1994.

Freedom weights export shares based on whether a given country has a poor record on political rights and civil liberties. Political rights and civil liberties are often linked to economic freedoms and, thus, countries that deny these rights and liberties are likely to be difficult export destinations. This measure is based on the 1993–1994 Freedom House Annual Survey of Freedom.[24]

Not GATT weights export shares by whether or not a destination country is a signatory to the GATT on January 1, 1994. This measure tests the importance of official trade agreements that are clearly intended to facilitate trade among nations.

---

[24] The freedom index is obtained from Freedom House, Annual Survey of Freedom, Country Scores, for 1993–94. The raw index takes on values of 1, 2, or 3, with higher values indicating lesser freedoms. Using these data, we set Difficult equal to 1 if the raw index equaled 3 and 0 otherwise.

Table 4
State-level agglomeration of all firms, exporters, and non-exporters (numbers in parentheses are *t*-ratios based on robust standard errors with clustering on 2-digit SIC codes)

	All firms	Exporters	Non-exporters
Share of exports to countries that are	0.045	0.073	0.002
not globally integrated (*Integration*)	(1.00)	(0.87)	(0.04)
Innovations per $ shipment	− 1.811	− 2.51	− 1.024
	(− 1.76)	(− 1.99)	(− 0.89)
Manufactured inputs per $	0.054	0.052	0.059
shipment	(0.59)	(0.52)	(0.69)
Non-manufactured inputs per $	− 0.107	− 0.034	− 0.087
shipment	(− 1.78)	(− 0.47)	(− 1.34)
Natural resource expenses per $	0.118	0.062	0.183
shipment	(2.16)	(1.25)	(3.52)
Energy expenses per $ shipment	− 0.052	− 0.095	− 0.070
	(− 0.27)	(− 0.38)	(− 0.44)
Water expenses per $ shipment	2.38	0.970	3.44
	(1.54)	(0.52)	(2.53)
Inventories per dollar shipment	0.194	0.134	0.240
(non-perishability)	(2.23)	(1.55)	(2.55)
Constant	− 0.002	− 0.004	− 0.011
	(− 0.07)	(− 0.15)	(− 0.44)
Number of industries	345	345	345
Root mean square error	0.061	0.073	0.068
R^2	0.085	0.037	0.094

Sanction weights export shares by whether or not a country is subject to a broad U.S. trade sanction through 1993. Such sanctions, of course, reflect policies intended explicitly to make it difficult to do business with a given country.

Finally, *Risk* weights export shares by the perceived financial risk associated with doing business with the destination country. Risk, in this case, is based on credit ratings constructed by a private company, *Institutional Investor* for 1998. These country credit ratings account for both access to private capital markets and the terms of that access, and serve as a measure of the institutional maturity of the country.[25] As can be seen in Table 5a, the various measures of foreign trading environments capture different aspects of the international economy. Using the *Integration* measure, on average 8.5% of industry exports are destined for "difficult" countries. Using the *Risk* measure, only 1.3% of industry exports, on average, are destined for "difficult" countries. Table 5b indicates that the alternative 1–0 characterizations of whether countries are "difficult" are not highly correlated. The correlation between characterizations of countries using *Integration* and *Risk* is only 0.25. When the binary characterizations are

---

[25] The credit rating measure is a continuous variable ranging from 0 to 100, where a value of 100 implies a perfect credit rating while a number close to zero implies a poor credit rating. We transform the raw form of this variable by subtracting it off from 100 such that countries with the worst credit rating are coded 100 and those with the best rating are coded 0. We specify countries as having a difficult trading environment if our adjusted index is above the 75th percentile by setting Difficult to 1 and otherwise set Difficult to 0. The trade share variable was then calculated as before.

182   M.E. Lovely et al. / Regional Science and Urban Economics 35 (2005) 167–191

Table 5a

Variable definitions, data sources, and summary measures of export share variables

Variable name	Definition	Time period and data source	Number of observations	Mean	Std. dev.	25th percentile	75th percentile
Integration	Share of industry exports to countries with smaller than average world trade given the size of the country	1994; World Bank "World Development Indicators" CD-ROM	345	0.085	0.068	0.043	0.107
Freedom	Share of industry exports to countries that have a poor record on political rights and civil liberties	1993–1994; Freedom House (2001) Annual Survey of Freedom	345	0.049	0.060	0.014	0.061
Not GATT	Share of industry exports to countries that are not signatories to the GATT agreement	January 1, 1994; World Trade Organization (2001) and U.S. Central Intelligence Agency (1992)	345	0.062	0.058	0.026	0.079
Risk	Share of industry exports to countries that are characterized as high risk by the Institutional Investor	1998; Institutional Investor, (2001), Country Credit Ratings	345	0.013	0.028	0.002	0.013
Sanction	Share of industry exports to countries subject to world trade sanctions	1994; Hufbauer et al. (1990) and updates by authors	345	0.007	0.012	0.002	0.010

Table 5b

Correlation of alternative measures of *difficult* trading environments *across Countries* (based on 141 countries for *Integration*; 149 for *Sanction*, *Freedom*, *Not GATT*, 118 for *Risk*)

	Integration	Freedom	Not GATT	Risk	Sanction
Integration	1				
Freedom	0.110	1			
Not GATT	0.006	0.293	1		
Risk	0.248	0.407	0.082	1	
Sanction	0.087	0.343	0.353	0.160	1

M.E. Lovely et al. / Regional Science and Urban Economics 35 (2005) 167–191   183

Table 5c
Correlation of alternative measures of *weighted export shares* to difficult trading environments *across industries* (based on 345 industries)

	Integration	Freedom	Not GATT	Risk	Sanction
Integration	1				
Freedom	0.357	1			
Not GATT	0.369	0.826	1		
Risk	0.487	0.397	0.302	1	
Sanction	0.317	0.379	0.307	0.245	1

weighted by industry trade shares (Table 5c), the correlation between any pair of measures tends to rise. The correlation between the weighted trade shares based on *Integration* and *Risk* rises to 0.49, which still indicates separate information is captured by each measure.

6.4. Headquarter agglomeration

Tables 6a and b present estimates of the difference-in-difference models outlined in Section 4. Each model is estimated separately using each of the five different measures of the trading environment. Each specification is also estimated with agglomeration measured at three different levels of geography, state, county, and zipcode. All of the models were estimated with robust standard errors in addition to clustering based on 2-digit SIC industry codes. To conserve space, only the trading environment coefficient is presented from each regression. It should be emphasized, therefore, that each coefficient in Tables 6a and b is drawn from a separate regression.

Consider Table 6a first. This table presents results based on the specifications in Eqs. (2) and (4), headquarter agglomeration and headquarter less branch agglomeration, respectively. Estimates are provided separately for exporters and non-exporters for each specification. Observe that for both specifications (headquarter and headquarter less branch), the coefficients on *Integration* are positive and significant for the exporter models regardless of whether agglomeration is measured at the state, county, or zipcode level. In contrast, among non-exporters, *Integration* is insignificant in all cases. This is in contrast to the findings in Table 4 and is consistent with the idea that exporting information burdens feed back to affect the spatial concentration of exporter headquarter activity in the U.S.

Results based on the credit risk variable (*Risk*) are also positive and marginally significant in some instances. This is especially apparent at the county level where the estimated coefficients on *Risk* for both the headquarter and the headquarter-less-branch models are roughly 0.47 with t-ratios roughly equal to 1.8. The *Risk* variable may have some effect at the zipcode level as well, but the evidence here is weaker. In contrast, estimates of the coefficient on *Risk* for the non-exporters both at the county level and for the other levels of geography are much smaller and clearly insignificant.

Results from specifications based on *Freedom, NotGATT,* and *Sanction* as indicators of the trading environment are less compelling. Although the coefficients on these variables are positive in all of the specifications, in no case are the estimates clearly significant for the export sector. In light of the results based on the *Integration* and *Risk* measures, this

Table 6a

Alternative classifications of difficult countries: agglomeration of multi-site headquarter establishments (numbers in parentheses are t-ratios based on robust standard errors with clustering on 2-digit SIC codes)[a]

	State-level agglomeration				County-level agglomeration				Zipcode-level agglomeration			
	Exporters		Non-exporters		Exporters		Non-exporters		Exporters		Non-exporters	
	HQ	HQ–Branch	HQ	HQ–Branch	HQ	HQ–Branch	HQ	HQ–Branch	HQ	HQ–Branch	HQ	HQ–Branch
Share of exports to countries that are not globally integrated (*Integration*)	0.231 (1.82)	0.269 (2.55)	−0.038 (−0.56)	0.029 (0.33)	0.190 (2.05)	0.216 (2.24)	0.049 (1.04)	0.037 (0.50)	0.146 (2.02)	0.156 (1.98)	0.034 (1.48)	0.027 (0.59)
Share of exports to countries that are not free (*Freedom*)	0.272 (1.30)	0.269 (1.20)	0.260 (2.28)	0.175 (1.41)	0.224 (1.22)	0.276 (1.49)	0.154 (2.02)	0.123 (1.41)	0.211 (1.18)	0.232 (1.24)	0.037 (1.38)	0.038 (1.14)
Share of exports to countries that are not members of GATT (*Not GATT*)	0.247 (1.13)	0.328 (1.44)	0.265 (2.18)	0.273 (2.76)	0.216 (1.29)	0.257 (1.52)	0.162 (2.05)	0.117 (1.60)	0.177 (1.29)	0.200 (1.41)	0.071 (1.47)	0.052 (1.67)
Share of exports to countries that have bad investor ratings (*Risk*)	0.483 (1.01)	0.498 (1.40)	0.108 (0.52)	0.014 (0.04)	0.472 (1.83)	0.477 (1.79)	0.130 (0.79)	0.138 (0.70)	0.385 (1.58)	0.369 (1.40)	−0.006 (−0.09)	0.023 (0.23)
Share of exports to countries that are subject to world trade sanctions (*Sanction*)	2.09 (1.37)	1.97 (1.21)	1.34 (1.90)	1.49 (1.70)	1.73 (1.34)	2.01 (1.56)	1.07 (1.76)	0.959 (1.72)	1.58 (1.24)	1.68 (1.29)	0.466 (1.33)	0.613 (1.68)

[a] Each estimate in the table is taken from a separate regression. All other variables in this table and Tables 6b and 6c including the squared share of exports to difficult countries are included in the model but estimates for those variables and summary measures for the regressions are suppressed to conserve space.

M.E. Lovely et al. / Regional Science and Urban Economics 35 (2005) 167–191   185

Table 6b
Alternative classifications of difficult countries: difference in agglomeration of multi-site headquarter establishments[a] exporter–non-exporter (numbers in parentheses are *t*-ratios)

Alternative measures	State level agglomeration		County level agglomeration		Zipcode level agglomeration	
	HQ	HQ–Branch	HQ	HQ–Branch	HQ	HQ–Branch
Share of exports to countries that are not globally integrated (*Integration*)	0.263 (1.93)	0.245 (2.10)	0.142 (1.41)	0.179 (1.69)	0.111 (1.48)	0.128 (1.78)
Share of exports to countries that are not free (*Freedom*)	0.016 (0.09)	0.096 (0.56)	0.069 (0.46)	0.150 (0.92)	0.174 (1.05)	0.194 (1.13)
Share of exports to countries that are not members of GATT (*Not GATT*)	− 0.021 (− 0.10)	0.042 (0.21)	0.054 (0.34)	0.140 (0.79)	0.106 (0.79)	0.148 (1.09)
Share of exports to countries that have bad investor ratings (*Risk*)	0.378 (1.09)	0.455 (2.53)	0.342 (2.04)	0.332 (2.01)	0.391 (2.16)	0.338 (1.79)
Share of exports to countries that are subject to world trade sanctions (*Sanction*)	0.756 (0.52)	0.468 (0.49)	0.667 (0.53)	1.03 (1.14)	1.11 (0.84)	1.05 (0.78)

[a] Each estimate in the table is taken from a separate regression. All other variables in Table 4 are included in the model but estimates for those variables and summary measures for the regressions are suppressed to conserve space.

pattern underscores that not all measures of a foreign country's trading environment provide the same information.

Table 6b repeats the analysis in the prior table but with a more rigorous specification that differences domestic-only agglomeration from exporter agglomeration, Eqs. (5) and (6). This specification strips away common unobserved industry-wide factors that influence agglomeration in both the export and non-export sectors. This differencing more clearly identifies the influence of trading environments on exporter headquarter agglomeration relative to the non-exporter segment of the economy. Estimates are provided for agglomeration measured at the state, county, and zipcode levels, and all models are estimated with robust standard errors and clustering at the 2-digit SIC level.

Immediately apparent, the estimated coefficients on *Integration* are once again positive and significant at the state level. A similar pattern holds for county and zipcode, but the results are weaker. *Risk* is similarly positive and clearly significant in each of the models except for the first column for which the *t*-ratio is 1.09. In contrast, the coefficients on *Freedom, NotGATT,* and *Sanction* are always insignificant.

Two important findings emerge from these results. First, there is evidence to suggest that foreign country trading environments do feed back to affect headquarter agglomeration of exporters in the United States. But it matters how we characterize the foreign country trading environment. Measures based on political freedom, GATT membership, and trade sanctions appear to have little effect. This may indicate that these factors do not increase the difficulty of gaining information about how to do

186   *M.E. Lovely et al. / Regional Science and Urban Economics 35 (2005) 167–191*

Table 6c
Combined impact of alternative classifications of difficult countries: difference in agglomeration of multi-site headquarter establishments[a] exporter–non-exporter (numbers in parentheses are t-ratios)

Alternative measures	State level agglomeration		County level agglomeration		Zipcode level agglomeration	
	HQ	HQ–Branch	HQ	HQ–Branch	HQ	HQ–Branch
Share of exports to countries	0.244	0.201	0.092	0.147	0.044	0.080
that are not globally	(1.80)	(1.68)	(1.04)	(1.43)	(0.87)	(1.34)
integrated (*Integration*)						
Share of exports to countries	0.093	0.218	0.230	0.158	0.340	0.244
that have bad investor	(0.35)	(1.15)	(2.41)	(1.60)	(2.11)	(1.42)
ratings (*Risk*)						

[a] Each column of estimates in the table is taken from a regression that includes *both* of the alternative measures of hard-to-do-business with foreign countries. All other variables in Table 4 are included in the model but estimates for those variables and summary measures for the regressions are suppressed to conserve space.

business with foreign countries. On the other hand, trade share measures based on whether the foreign country is integrated into the world economy and measures based on the foreign country's credit rating—a proxy for the financial risk of doing business with the foreign country—do positively affect U.S. exporter headquarter agglomeration. These factors, it seems, do increase the informational burdens associated with exporting.[26]

Recall that Tables 5b and c report the correlation between the different trade share measures, both with respect to the 1–0 coding of whether individual countries are *Difficult* (Table 5b) and when weighted by export flows to produce the trade share measures in the regressions (Table 5c). The correlation in the coding of whether foreign countries are *Difficult* based on the *Integration* and *Risk* measures is 0.248 (Table 5b), while the correlation coefficient between the trade share measures based on *Integration* and *Risk* is 0.49 (Table 5c). It is clear, therefore, that although these two variables are correlated, they nevertheless bring different information to the model. Accordingly, Table 6c repeats the specifications from Table 6b but in this case includes both the *Integration* and *Risk* measures in each of the models in order to identify their independent effects.[27]

Results from Table 6c suggest that both the integration of foreign trading partners into the world economy and the financial risk of doing business with foreign countries significantly influence headquarter agglomeration among U.S. exporters. However, the effects differ. *Integration* has its largest and most significant effects with respect to state-level agglomeration of exporter headquarter activity, with effects declining in magnitude

---

[26] As a further robustness check, we estimated all of the models in the paper omitting the X vector. This omission had little effect on the export share coefficients. Those results are not presented to conserve space.

[27] The models in Table 6c were also estimated including all five alternative measures of the trading environment. However, in each case, *Freedom*, *NotGATT*, and *Sanction* were completely insignificant and results from those regressions are not reported for that reason.

and significance as the geographic scope narrows. *Risk*, on the other hand, displays the opposite pattern. *Risk* has a small and insignificant coefficient with agglomeration measured at the state level but a much larger and significant effect at the county and zipcode levels.

7. Conclusion

The need to acquire information underlies several longstanding theoretical arguments for why manufacturing industries in our economy are so spatially concentrated. Such arguments include knowledge spillovers whereby companies learn from their neighbors, pooling of skilled labor to the extent that such labor provides information (e.g., lawyers, accountants, and consultants), and even natural advantages to the extent that government facilities, libraries, and universities are natural sources of information around which companies may want to locate. Yet despite widespread belief that reliance on information promotes agglomeration, empirical evidence on this point has been limited.

This paper fills part of that gap by comparing the spatial concentration of headquarter activity of exporters to that of non-exporters. Exporting requires specialized knowledge of foreign markets that is difficult and expensive to obtain. This should, therefore, increase spatial concentration of headquarter activity among exporters relative to the domestic-only sector. We test this idea using 4-digit industry-level data for the fourth quarter of 2000 from *iMarket's* MarketPlace database.

We find that foreign country political freedom, GATT membership, and the presence of trade sanctions have little discernible effect on the agglomeration of U.S. exporter headquarters. On the other hand, industries that export to countries that are poorly integrated into the world economy have more highly agglomerated exporter headquarter activity at the state level. Industries that export to countries with poor credit ratings—a proxy for the financial risk of doing business with such countries—have more highly agglomerated exporter headquarter activity at the county and zipcode levels. Taken as a whole, these results support the idea that the need to acquire information contributes to agglomeration.[28]

Acknowledgements

We thank Sukkoo Kim, Jeffrey Bergstrand, Vernon Henderson, and anonymous referees for helpful comments on an earlier version of this paper. Any remaining errors, of course, are the responsibility of the authors.

---

[28] As a final perspective, several previous studies have emphasized that a country's own trade policy can affect the spatial concentration of domestic economic activity (e.g., Krugman (1991), Krugman and Livas Elizondo (1996), and Hanson (1996)). Our results suggest that foreign as well as domestic policies have the potential to influence the spatial organization of domestic economic activity.

Appendix A. Variable definitions, data sources, and summary measures of X matrix

Variable name	Definition	Time period and data source	Number of observations	Mean	Std. dev.	Min	Max
Innovations per $ shipment	Number of new products in 1982 trade magazines divided by dollar value of shipments (in $1,000,000)	1982 U.S. SBA Innovation Data Base and 1992 Annual Survey of Manufacturers from NBER	459	0.0049	0.0030	0.000	0.0259
Manufactured inputs per $ shipment	Cost of materials other than manufactured inputs, energy, natural resources, and water per dollar of shipments	1992 BEA Input–Output Tables and 1992 Annual Survey of Manufacturers from NBER	459	0.3502	0.1166	0.0063	0.6572
Non-manufactured inputs per $ shipment	Cost of material other than manufactured inputs, energy, natural resources, and water per dollar of shipments	1992 BEA Input–Output Tables and 1992 Annual Survey of Manufacturers from NBER	459	0.0819	0.0675	−0.1119	0.6557
Natural resource expenses per $ shipment	Cost of natural resource inputs per dollar of shipments	1992 BEA Input–Output Tables	459	0.0357	0.1026	0.000	0.7923
Energy expenses per $ shipment	Cost of energy inputs per dollar of shipments	1992 BEA Input–Output Tables	459	0.0208	0.0232	0.0022	0.2405
Water expenses per $ shipment	Cost of water inputs per dollar of shipments	1992 BEA Input–Output Tables	459	0.0018	0.0029	0.000	0.0238
Inventories per $ shipment (non-perishability)	Dollar value of end-of-year inventories per dollar of shipments	1992 Annual Survey of Manufacturers from NBER	459	0.1446	0.0634	0.0209	0.5053

M.E. Lovely et al. / Regional Science and Urban Economics 35 (2005) 167–191   189

Appendix B. Classification of foreign country trading environments by alternative measures (1=difficult and 0=not difficult)

Country	Inte-gration	Free-dom	Not Gatt	Risk	Sanc-tion	Country	Inte-gration	Free-dom	Not Gatt	Risk	Sanc-tion
AFGHAN		1	1	1	0	DJIBOUTI	0	1	1		0
ALBANIA	1	0	1	1	0	DOM_REP	0	0	0	0	0
ALGERIA	0	1	1	0	0	ECUADOR	1	0	1	0	0
ANGOLA	0	1	1	1	0	EGYPT	1	1	0	0	0
ARAB_EM	0	1	1	0	0	EQ_GNEA	0	1	1		0
ARGENT	1	0	0	0	0	ETHIOPIA	1	0	1	1	1
ASIA_NES	0	1	1		0	FIJI	0	0	0		0
AUSTRAL	0	0	0	0	0	FINLAND	0	0	0	0	0
AUSTRIA	1	0	0	0	0	FRANCE	0	0	0	0	0
BAHAMAS	1	0	1		0	FR_IND_O	0	0	1		0
BAHRAIN	0	1	0	0	0	GABON	0	0	0	0	0
BARBADO	0	0	0	0	0	GAMBIA	1	1	0		0
BELIZE	1	0	0		0	GERMAN	0	0	0	0	0
BEL_LUX	0	0	0	0	0	GHANA	1	0	0	0	0
BENIN	0	0	0	1	0	GREECE	1	0	0	0	0
BERMUDA	0	0	1		0	GREENLD		0	0		0
BNGLDSH	1	0	0	0	0	GUATMALA	1	0	0	0	0
BOLIVIA	1	0	0	0	0	GUINEA	1	1	1	1	0
BRAZIL	1	0	0	0	0	GUYANA	0	0	0		0
BULGARIA	1	0	1	0	0	G_BISAU	1	0	1		0
BURKINA	1	0	0	1	0	HAITI	1	1	0	1	0
BURMA	0	1	0	0	1	HONDURA	1	0	1	1	0
BURUNDI	1	1	0		0	HONGKONG	0	0	0	0	0
CAMBOD	1	1	1		0	HUNGARY	0	0	1	0	0
CAMEROON	1	1	0	1	0	ICELAND	1	0	0	0	0
CANADA	0	0	0	0	0	INDIA	1	0	0	0	0
CHAD	1	1	0		0	INDONES	0	0	0	0	0
CHILE	0	0	0	0	0	IRAN	1	1	1	0	1
CHINA	0	1	1	0	0	IRAQ	0	1	1	1	1
COLOMBIA	1	0	0	0	0	IRELAND	0	0	0	0	0
CONGO	0	0	0	1	0	ISRAEL	0	0	0	0	0
COS_RICA	1	0	0	0	0	ITALY	0	0	0	0	0
CUBA		1	0	1	1	IVY_CST	0	1	0	0	0
CYPRUS	1	0	0	0	0	JAMAICA	0	0	0	0	0
CZECHO	0	0	0	0	0	JAPAN	0	0	0	0	0
C_AFRICA	1	0	0		0	JORDON	0	0	1	0	0
DENMARK	1	0	0	0	0	KENYA	1	1	0	0	0
KIRIBATI	0	0	0		0	QATAR	0	1	1	0	0
KOREA_N		1	1	1	1	ROMANIA	0	0	0	0	0
KOREA_S	0	0	0	0	0	RWANDA	0	1	0	0	0
KUWAIT	0	0	0	0	0	SALVADR	1	0	0	0	0
LAO	1	1	1		0	SAMOA	0	0	1		0
LEBANON	0	0	1		0	SD_ARAB	0	1	1	0	0
LIBERIA	0	1	1	1	0	SENEGAL	0	0	0	0	0
MACAU		0	0		0	SEYCHEL	1	0	1	0	0
MADAGAS	1	0	0		0	SIER_LN	1	1	0	1	0
MALAWI	1	1	0	1		SINGAPR	0	0	0	0	0

(continued on next page)

Appendix B (continued)

Country	Inte-gration	Free-dom	Not Gatt	Risk	Sanc-tion	Country	Inte-gration	Free-dom	Not Gatt	Risk	Sanc-tion
MALAYSIA	0	0	0	0	0	SOMALIA	0	1	1		1
MALI	1	0	0	1	0	SPAIN	0	0	0	0	0
MALTA	0	0	0	0	0	SRL_LKA	1	0	0	0	0
MAURITN	0	1	0		0	ST_K_NEV	0	0	0	1	0
MEXICO	0	0	0	0	0	SUDAN	1	1	1	1	1
MONGOLA	0	0	1		0	SURINAM	0	0	0		0
MOROCCO	0	0	0	0	0	SWEDEN	0	0	0	0	0
MOZAMBQ	1	1	0	1	0	SWITZLD	0	0	0	0	0
MRITIUS	0	0	0	0	0	SYRIA	1	1	1	0	1
NEPAL	1	0	1	0	0	S_AFRICA	0	0	0	0	1
NETHLDS	0	0	0	0	0	TANZANIA	0	1	0	1	0
NEW_CALE		0	1		0	THAILAND	0	0	0	0	0
NEW_GUIN	0	0	1	0	0	TOGO	1	1	0	1	0
NEW_ZEAL	0	0	0	0	0	TRINIDAD	0	0	0	0	0
NICARAGA	1	0	0	1	0	TUNISIA	0	1	0	0	0
NIGER	1	0	0		0	TURKEY	1	0	0	0	0
NIGERIA	0	1	0	1	0	UGANDA	1	1	0	1	0
NORWAY	0	0	0	0	0	UKINGDOM	0	0	0	0	0
N_ANTIL		0	0		0	URUGUAY	1	0	0	0	0
OMAN	0	1	1	0	0	USSR	0	0	1	0	0
PAKISTAN	1	0	0	0	0	US_NES		0	0		0
PANAMA	0	0	1	0	0	VENEZ	0	0	0	0	0
PARAGUA	0	0	1	0	0	VIETNAM	1	1	1	0	1
PERU	1	0	0	0	0	YEMEN_N	0	0	1		0
PHIL	0	0	0	0	0	YUGOSLAV	0	0	1	0	0
POLAND	0	0	0	0	0	ZAIRE	1	1	0	1	0
PORTUGAL	1	0	0	0	0	ZAMBIA	0	0	0	1	0
						ZIMBABWE	1	0	0	0	0

References

Aitken, B., Hanson, G.H., Harrison, A.E., 1997. Spillovers, foreign investment, and export behavior. Journal of International Economics 43, 103–132.

Alonso, W., 1972. Location theory. In: Edel, M., Rothenberg, J. (Eds.), Readings in Urban Economics. Macmillan, New York.

Audretsch, D.B., Feldman, M., 1996. R&D spillovers and the geography of innovation and production. American Economic Review 86, 630–640.

Bernard, A.B., Jensen, J.B., 2001. Why some firms export. NBER Working Paper 8349, Cambridge, MA.

Ellison, G., Glaeser, E.L., 1997. The geographic concentration of US manufacturing industries: a dartboard approach. Journal of Political Economy 105, 889–927.

Feenstra, R.C., 1997. U.S. exports, 1972–1994, with state exports and other U.S. data. NBER Working Paper 5990, Cambridge, MA.

Freedom House, 2001. Annual Survey of Freedom: 1972–73 to 1999–00. http://www.freedomhouse.org/ratings.

Hanson, G.H., 1996. Localization economies, vertical organization, and trade. American Economic Review 86, 1266–1278.

Hufbauer, G.C., Schott, J.J., Elliott, K.A., 1990. Economic Sanctions Reconsidered: History and Current Policy, second edition. Institute for International Economics, Washington, DC.

Institutional Investor, 2001. Country Credit Ratings 1998. http://www.iiplatinum.com/rr/countrycredit/ccr/1998.

M.E. Lovely et al. / Regional Science and Urban Economics 35 (2005) 167–191   191

Jaffe, A.B., Trajtenberg, M., Henderson, R., 1993. Geographic localization of knowledge spillovers as evidenced by patent citations. Quarterly Journal of Economics 108, 577–598.

Krugman, P., 1991. Geography and Trade. The MIT Press, Cambridge MA.

Krugman, P., Livas Elizondo, R., 1996. Trade policy and third world metropolis. Journal of Development Economics 49, 137–150.

Marshall, A., 1920. Principles of Economics. MacMillan, London.

Roberts, M.J., Tybout, J.R., 1997. The decision to export in Colombia: an empirical model of entry with sunk costs. American Economic Review 87, 545–564.

Rosenthal, S.S., Strange, W.C., 2001. The determinants of agglomeration. Journal of Urban Economics 50, 191–229.

Sharma, S., 2001. Three essays on the economics of agglomeration. Unpublished PhD dissertation, Syracuse University.

Quigley, J., 1998. Urban diversity and economic growth. Journal of Economic Perspectives 12, 127–138.

United States Central Intelligence Agency, 1992. The GATT System: Spectrum of Country Relationships.

United States Department of Commerce, United States Census Bureau, Foreign Trade Division, 2001, "A Profile of U.S. Exporting Companies, 1998–1999, http://www.census.gov/foreign-trade/.

World Trade Organization, 2001. The 128 countries that had signed GATT by 1994. http://www.wto.org/thewto_e.

Decomposing China–Japan–U.S. trade: Vertical specialization, ownership, and organizational form[☆]

Judith M. Dean [a], Mary E. Lovely [b,*], Jesse Mora [a]

[a] *Office of Economics, U.S. International Trade Commission,*[1] *USA*
[b] *Department of Economics, Syracuse University, Syracuse, NY 13244-1090, USA*

ARTICLE INFO

Article history:
Received 24 June 2009
Received in revised form 20 August 2009
Accepted 26 August 2009

JEL classification:
F14
F15

Keywords:
Trade
Asia
Regional integration
Fragmentation
FDI

ABSTRACT

We use the US International Trade Commission's uniquely detailed 1995–2007 Chinese Customs data to better understand the pattern of trade between China and its two largest trading partners, Japan and the United States. Our review finds that only a small share of these flows can be characterized as arm's length, one-way trade in final goods. Instead, we find extensive two-way trade, deep vertical specialization, concentration of trade in computer and communication devices, and a prominent role for foreign-invested enterprises. While these characteristics define both bilateral relationships, important differences between the two pairs do emerge, suggesting that trade costs influence the method by which multinationals choose to integrate their production with China. Consequently, we argue that dialogue on East Asian trade liberalization should include the possibility of significant production gains for the US from its inclusion in any regional agreements.

© 2009 Elsevier Inc. All rights reserved.

1. Introduction

China's ongoing transitions, from bureaucratic socialism to market economy and from a rural to an urban society, have transformed the country into a global economic power.[2] This transition has affected virtually every aspect of the world economy—which goods are made, what they cost, and the wages earned by those engaged in their production. The impact of China's economic emergence on its trading partners, however, goes well beyond the textbook treatment of liberalization of trade in final goods. Widely recognized is China's unique mode of entry, characterized by unprecedented foreign direct investment inflows and heavy reliance on processing inputs as the fuel for explosive trade growth.[3]

These unique features of China's global engagement suggest that rather than simply changing *where* goods are made, China's opening permitted shifts in *how* goods are made. Trade theorists have emphasized two aspects of these shifts in the organization of production—the fragmentation of the production process and the internalization decisions of multinational

☆ We thank Dylan Carson and Fred Distefano for assistance with compilation of data. We also benefited from comments by Michael Plummer, Ryuhei Wakasugi, and other participants in the China–Japan–US: Deeper Integration Pre-Conference in January 2009 and Conference in May 2009.
* Corresponding author. Tel.: +1 315 443 9048.
E-mail address: melovely@maxwell.syr.edu (M.E. Lovely).
1 The views expressed here are those of the authors. They do not necessarily represent the views of the USITC or the views of any of the individual Commissioners.
2 Naughton (2007) emphasizes the dual nature of China's transition and its implications.
3 Dean et al. (2008) emphasize China's unique trade profile. They report that the current dollar value of China's exports plus imports rose from $280.9 billion in 1995 to $1760.4 billion in 2006, a growth of about 537%.

1049-0078/$ – see front matter © 2009 Elsevier Inc. All rights reserved.
doi:10.1016/j.asieco.2009.08.003

J.M. Dean et al./Journal of Asian Economics 20 (2009) 596–610   597

firms. Fragmentation of production, sometimes referred to as "slicing of the value chain," is viewed as a consequence of trade liberalization in developing countries (e.g. Jones & Kierzkowski, 2001) as well as a determinant of the welfare effects of that liberalization on all partners (e.g. Deardorff, 2001, 2005). Similarly, the internalization decisions of multinationals, specifically the choice to produce inputs abroad through a foreign subsidiary versus purchasing inputs from an unaffiliated foreign subcontractor, not only arise from the liberalization of trade and investment policies, but also themselves shape the overall pattern of economic activity and its rewards.[4]

In this paper, we use uniquely detailed 1995–2007 China Customs data to better understand the pattern of trade between China and two of its largest and most advanced trading partners, the United States and Japan, emphasizing the distinct nature of these flows. The analysis reveals the extent to which bilateral trade is due to fragmented production and foreign-invested enterprises (FIEs), as well as the organizational form of China's processing trade relationships with Japan and the US. Using recent theoretical models as lenses through which we explore the bilateral trade flows, we uncover commonalities and differences in the production sharing strategies of American and Japanese firms, as evidenced in bilateral trade patterns.

Section 2 presents an overview of US–China and Japan–China bilateral trade. We quantify aspects of these trade flows that do not fit into neoclassical explanations, specifically the importance of processing trade and the significant role of FIEs. In Section 3, we focus on trade in production "fragments," highlighting transport costs as a factor driving differences in the share of processing trade across the two bilateral relations. We also discuss new evidence on the vertical specialization of China's exports to the US and Japan. We turn then to exploring the role of foreign enterprises in China's bilateral trade flows in Section 4. We ask if the trade data provide insight into how American and Japanese firms serve the local market and whether transport costs and product differentiation illuminate the differences. Finally, in Section 5, we exploit a unique feature of the China Customs data to explore the organizational form of multinational firms engaged in processing trade, specifically comparing flows to the US with those to Japan. We conclude by summarizing our comparisons of the bilateral relationships and drawing implications for further research on the distributional gains from offshoring and for further dialogue on an East Asian regional trade and investment agreement.

2. Unique features of China–Japan–US trade

Commercials relations with China are important both to the United States and to Japan. By 2007, China was the third most important export destination and the top source of imports for the United States. Similarly, China was the second most important export destination and the top source of imports for Japan. China's official trade data[5] records exports and imports at the HS 8-digit level, by country of final consumption and country of origin, respectively.[6] These data are disaggregated by transport mode, customs regime, firm-type, incentive zone, and intra-provincial location of producer/consumer.[7] Table 1 shows China's bilateral import and export values and growth rates over the 1996–2007 period. In current dollars, the value of China's exports to all destinations grew at an average annual growth rate of 20.9%. Exports to the United States grew somewhat faster, at an average annual growth rate of 21.7%, while exports to Japan grew more slowly, at an average annual rate of 11.5%. In comparison to the growth of exports to the European Union (24.5%) and ASEAN (22.3%), the growth of Chinese exports to Japan is relatively low.[8]

China's imports from all sources also grew at a rapid rate over the period, averaging growth in current dollars of 18.3%. Imports from both the United States and Japan grew more slowly, averaging 14.1% and 14.9%, respectively, only slightly below the growth of imports from the EU15. Over the same period, Chinese imports from ASEAN grew much more rapidly, at an annual average of 23.3%.

The relatively rapid growth of net exports to the United States is reflected in the US trade deficit with China, which grew at an average annual rate of 28.1% from 1996 to 2007. Over the same period, Japan saw rapid growth in its trade surplus with China, which changed from a small deficit in 1996 to a $31.9 billion surplus in 2007. As with Japan, China's trade with ASEAN grew rapidly, with ASEAN's small trade deficit in 1996 shifting to a surplus of $14.2 billion by 2007.

Japan and the United States are extremely important to China's trade growth over the past decade. As shown in Fig. 1a, by 2007 the United States was the most important individual-country market for Chinese exports, moving up from the third largest destination in 1996. Hong Kong received the second largest share of exports by value, although some of these goods were re-exported.[9] Japan received the third largest share, importing more than twice as much as the next larger importer of Chinese goods, South Korea. There is some evidence of an East Asian supplier network even in these aggregate trade statistics. Japan, South Korea, and Taiwan are China's largest import sources, followed by the United States (Fig. 1b). While

---

[4] Recent contributions to the literature are reviewed by Helpman (2006) and Antràs and Rossi-Hansberg (2009).
[5] These data were purchased from China Customs Statistics Information Center in Hong Kong. Detailed information can be found at http://www.hktdc.com/info/mi/ccs/en/.
[6] Data are also recorded by country of immediate destination and most recent point of departure. The two sets of location records allow the identification of entrepôt trade.
[7] Locations are usually counties (districts) within provinces (province-level cities).
[8] References to the EU refer specifically to the EU15 comprised of Austria, Belgium, Denmark, Finland, France, Germany, Greece, Ireland, Italy, Luxembourg, Netherlands, Portugal, Spain, Sweden, and the United Kingdom.
[9] Our Chinese dataset allows us to observe re-exports through Hong Kong and to identify and attribute them to their final destinations. However, the size of the share of exports with Hong Kong as their final destination suggests that some exports destined for other markets may still be included in these figures.

598 *J.M. Dean et al./Journal of Asian Economics 20 (2009) 596–610*

Table 1
China–Japan–US exports, imports, and trade balance, billions of current US dollars.

Country[a]	China's exports by destination			China's imports by origin			China's trade balance	
	1996	2007	AAGR	1996	2007	AAGR	1996	2007
US	26.7	232.7	21.7	16.2	69.5	14.1	10.5	163.3
Japan	30.9	102.1	11.5	29.2	134.1	14.9	1.7	−31.9
ASEAN[b]	10.3	94.2	22.3	10.9	108.4	23.3	−0.6	−14.2
EU15	19.8	221.3	24.5	19.9	106.1	16.4	0.0	115.3
ROW	63.4	567.7	22.0	60.4	452.4	20.1	3.0	115.3
World	151.2	1217.9	20.9	136.5	870.1	18.3	14.7	347.8

Source: Authors' calculations using official Chinese Customs data.
AAGR = average annual growth rate.
[a] For exports (imports), country refers to the final destination (original source) country where goods are consumed (produced). For example, exports passing though Hong Kong but destined for the US are entered as exports to the US (not Honk Kong).
[b] ASEAN includes Brunei, Indonesia, Cambodia, Laos PDR, Malaysia, Myanmar, Philippines, Singapore, Thailand and Vietnam.

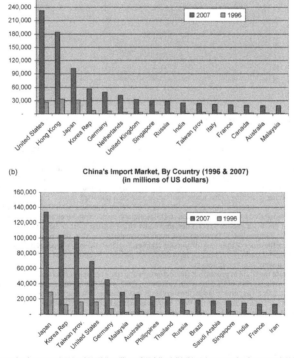

Fig. 1. (a) China's export market, by country (1996 and 2007) (in millions of US dollars). (b) China's import market, by country (1996 and 2007) (in millions of US dollars).

J.M. Dean et al./Journal of Asian Economics 20 (2009) 596–610   599

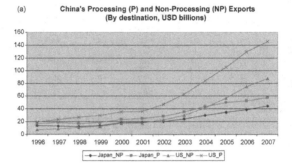

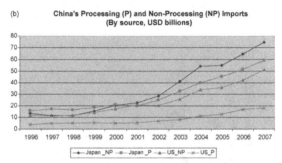

Fig. 2. (a) China's processing (P) and non-processing (NP) exports (by destination, USD billions). (b) China's processing (P) and non-processing (NP) imports (by source, USD billions).

these four countries were also the top four sources in 1996, the growth of imports from the three East Asian countries as a whole has been notably stronger than import growth from the US.

Processing trade, the import of intermediates for assembly and transformation in China and their subsequent re-exporting, lies behind much of the growth in China's imports and exports.[10] In China's customs statistics, processing imports and exports consist of two types: those declared as entering or exiting China under the "processing and assembly" regime; those declared as entering or exiting China under the "processing with imported inputs" regime.[11] Under processing and assembly, ownership of the imported inputs is retained by the foreign exporting firm. Under processing with imported inputs, ownership is transferred to the local producer in China. Imports declared under either processing regime can only be used for production of goods for export. Exports declared under either regime must embody processing imports, but may also embody domestic intermediates. Exporters and importers undertaking this kind of production and trade declare shipments under one or the other of these two processing regimes. Together, these two types of processing trade comprise a large share of total bilateral trade with China for both developed partners. In 2007, 62.5% of China's exports to the US and 56.6% of those to Japan were processing exports.

Fig. 2a and b illustrate the trend in processing and non-processing trade between China and the US, and China and Japan. Fig. 2a shows the dramatic take-off of US-Sino trade volumes in 2001, particularly with respect to processing trade. While there is a similar rise in China's exports to Japan, the increase is much smaller. There are several factors that account for this "take-off" in 2001. With China's accession to the WTO, there was a sharp increase in FDI inflows from both the US and Japan. Between 2001 and 2002 alone, the flow of US and Japanese FDI projects grew by 29% and 35%, respectively.[12] As will be

[10] See Hammer (2006).

[11] These are coded as customs regime 14 and 15, respectively, in China Customs Statistics.

[12] See 2006 Annual FDI data from the US and Japan, provided by the Chinese Ministry of Commerce: http://www.fdi.gov.cn/pub/FDI_EN/Statistics/AnnualStatisticsData/default.jsp.

shown below, much of the increase in China's processing exports shown in Fig. 2a is due to rapid growth in exports from FIEs. China's WTO accession also meant the partial phase-out of textile and apparel restraints under the Agreement on Textiles and Clothing. This may account for part of the differential in growth of non-processing exports to the US relative to Japan, since Japan had no quantity restraints on these products.

Turning to Fig. 2b, we see that the rise in Chinese processing exports to the US was not matched by a rise in processing imports from the US. Japan, rather than the US, experienced a dramatic increase in its processing exports to China from 2001 onward. The rapid growth in non-processing imports from both countries is likely due in part to significant reductions in consumer goods prices with WTO accession (Ianchovichina & Martin, 2004). As will be discussed below, a large part of the growth in processing imports is again due to FIEs. But the differential growth of processing imports from Japan relative to the US suggests again that Japan may be a key source of inputs for China in the global supply chain.

Fig. 3 shows China's top ten exports to and imports from the United States and Japan, respectively. On first glance, the top ten appear to be consistent with factor endowment similarities of the US and Japan: six of the top exports and six of the top imports are shared by the two bilateral flows. Particularly striking, however, is the importance of two-way trade between China and the US, and China and Japan, particularly in two product categories. In 2007, HS 85 (electrical machinery, sound, and television equipment) and HS 84 (nuclear reactor, boilers, machinery, and parts thereof) comprised 46.4% and 35.7% of China's exports to the US and Japan, respectively. These two categories also accounted for 33.5% and 50.2% of China's imports from the US and Japan, respectively. Deeper exploration into these categories reveals that trade in HS 84 is predominately trade in computers and computer parts, while HS 85 trade consists primarily of mobile phones and television parts. Thus, the bilateral commercial relations are dominated by two-way trade in a narrow set of products.

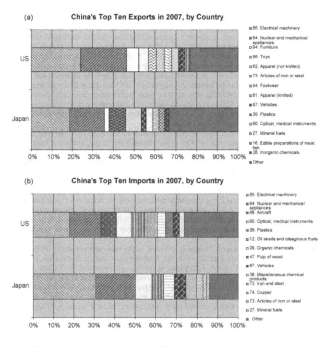

Source: Author's calculations using official Chinese Customs data.

Fig. 3. (a) China's top ten exports in 2007, by country. (b) China's top ten imports in 2007, by country.*Source:* Author's calculations using official Chinese Customs data.

J.M. Dean et al./Journal of Asian Economics 20 (2009) 596–610   601

Table 2
Export similarity indices, various country pairs.

	Similarity of exports to China[a]	
	1996	2007
Japan/US	0.36	0.42
EU/US	0.44	0.48
EU/Japan	0.41	0.44
Tigers/Japan	0.56	0.52
Tigers/US	0.32	0.34
ASEAN[b]/Japan	0.20	0.30
ASEAN[b]/US	0.18	0.25

[a] Finger and Kreinin (1979) export similarity index, calculated using the HS 8-digit Chinese mirror import data.
[b] ASEAN excluding Singapore, and including East Timor.

Using the Finger–Kreinin (1979) export similarity index (ESI), we explore the overlap between US and Japanese exports to China.[13] The first row of Table 2, reveals that in 1996, a little over one-third of US exports to China were matched by similar Japanese exports to China. By 2007, this overlap had risen to 42%. Not surprisingly, US–EU ESI is even higher (44%) in 1996, and rises to 48% by 2007. These findings are suggestive of a factor-proportions view of trade patterns. However, Table 2 also shows that Japanese exports to China are actually much more similar to those of the Asian Tigers than to those of the US or the EU, with an ESI of over 50% in both years. Further evidence of an East Asian supply network is the last row of Table 2, which shows a dramatic increase in the similarity between Japan and ASEAN exports to China during this period.

To explore the extent to which US–China and Japan–China two-way trade is in differentiated products, we use the Grubel–Lloyd (1975) index of intra-industry trade (IIT).[14] Table 3 shows IIT for the SITC 2-digit industries in which China has the largest global trade (exports plus imports). Comparing the first two top panels, we see that Japan's trade with China is more heavily composed of IIT (27.6%) than is American trade with China (14.2%). Individual sectors also show large differences. In electrical machinery and equipment (SITC 76) 52% of trade between China and Japan is IIT, compared to only 7.5% between China and the US. In office processing machines (SITC 75) the figures are 42.5% and 10.7%, respectively. In fact, in eight out of these ten industries, IIT is a higher share of Japan–China trade than US–China trade. Xing (2007) finds similar patterns of high IIT for China's bilateral trade with Japan compared to the US, at both the aggregate and industry levels for the 1980–2004 period. Table 3 also shows that the pattern and magnitudes of China–Japan IIT across sectors are very similar to those for China–ASEAN IIT (bottom left panel). For both bilateral pairs, half of the trade in telecommunications, over 40% of trade in office equipment, and one-third of trade in electrical machinery and professional instruments is IIT. In contrast, the pattern and magnitudes of China–US and China–EU15 IIT across these industries are highly correlated, and show little similarity to China's bilateral IIT with either Japan or ASEAN.

Trade mediated by FIEs operating in China, many in special economic zones, is significant for both Japan and the US. Fig. 4 shows bilateral exports and imports by firm type. In 1996, exports to both the US and Japan were split fairly evenly between exports by state-owned enterprises (SOEs) and FIEs (Fig. 4a and b). By 2007, however, FIEs controlled over 65% of exports from China to both countries, with SOEs providing a falling share. Since 2001, as private enterprises have been allowed to proliferate, the share of exports through these firms has grown, exceeding 10% of total exports to both the US and Japan by 2007. Many organizational forms are classified as private enterprises, including limited liability corporations, share-holding corporations, partnerships, and unincorporated businesses.

American and Japanese exports to China show somewhat different profiles. While more than half of exports from each country were destined for foreign-invested enterprises inside China by 2007, this form of trade was more dominant in the Japan–China relationship (Fig. 4c and d). In 2007, 72% of China's imports from Japan went to FIEs, compared with 58% of China's imports from the US. As in the case of China's exports, SOEs play a declining role in import flows while private enterprises have increased in importance.

Using neoclassical trade theory as a lens, observing relative factor endowments sheds little light on substantive differences between China's manufacturing trade with the United States and its trade with Japan. Both developed countries are abundantly endowed with capital, both physical and human, compared with China. In 2007, real GDP per capita in the United States and Japan was $38,338 and $40,656, respectively.[15] As of 2005, almost 60% of the American labor force had some form of tertiary education, as did 40% of the Japanese labor force. In contrast, China's 2007 GDP per capita was $1791, and only about 7% of its labor force had tertiary education in 2005. While the United States, with 0.6 ha of arable land per person, is relatively well endowed with land compared with Japan (0.03 ha/person) and to China

---

[13] ESI is calculated as $ESI_t^{a,b} = \sum_p \min(s_{t,p}^{a,c}, s_{t,p}^{b,c})$, where a = country 1, b = country 2, c = destination country, p = export product, and s = share of exports of product p in total exports to destination country c. Its values range from 0 to 1.
[14] The IIT index is calculated at the SITC 5-digit level as $IIT_j = \{1 - (|X_j - M_j|/(X_j + M_j))\} \times 100$ (where j refers to the jth SITC industry), and aggregated up to the SITC 2-digit industry level using trade weights. It's values range from 0 to 100.
[15] All data in this paragraph, with the exception of Chinese education data are from the World Bank's 2007 World Development Indicators and values are expressed in constant 2000 US dollars. The Chinese tertiary education data are from China's *Yearbook of Labour Statistics* for 2006.

602 J.M. Dean et al./Journal of Asian Economics 20 (2009) 596–610

Table 3
China's exports and imports by country (USD, mn) and intra-industry trade (IIT) index (%) in 2007.

SITC	Description[a]	Japan				US			
		Exports	Imports	Balance	IIT Index[b]	Exports	Imports	Balance	IIT Index[b]
77	Electrical machinery	11,666	37,027	(25,362)	32.2%	19,054	10,836	8,218	28.1%
76	Telecommunications and sound recording	7,762	5,581	2,182	52.2%	36,847	1,435	35,412	7.5%
75	Office and processing machines	10,085	3,911	6,173	42.5%	38,165	2,152	36,013	10.7%
84	Articles of apparel and clothing	16,499	128	16,371	1.4%	18,737	20	18,717	0.2%
87	Professional instruments	2,122	7,884	(5,762)	35.3%	3,664	3,591	73	45.0%
74	General industrial machinery	3,896	5,896	(2,000)	48.2%	8,718	3,517	5,201	41.9%
89	Miscellaneous manufactured articles, n.e.s.	4,401	1,915	2,486	25.9%	21,610	1,175	20,435	5.3%
67	Iron and steel	2,122	7,702	(5,580)	13.5%	4,454	754	3,700	16.5%
28	Metalliferous ores and metal scrap	115	1,974	(1,859)	1.7%	6	3,156	(3,150)	0.2%
65	Textile yarn and related products	3,152	3,154	(2)	21.6%	6,075	547	5,528	9.9%
Subtotal		61,819	75,171	(13,352)		157,329	27,182	130,147	
Total trade		101,379	133,777	(32,398)	27.6%	232,570	69,267	163,302	14.2%

SITC	Description[a]	ASEAN				EU15			
		Exports	Imports	Balance	IIT Index[b]	Exports	Imports	Balance	IIT Index[b]
77	Electrical machinery	12,473	42,520	(30,047)	32.9%	21,044	14,246	6,798	35.9%
76	Telecommunications and sound recording	9,796	3,699	6,098	48.3%	29,646	2,786	26,860	17.1%
75	Office and processing machines	8,678	14,019	(5,342)	47.9%	39,165	1,485	37,679	7.3%
84	Articles of apparel and clothing	5,032	98	4,935	3.1%	19,954	333	19,622	3.3%
87	Professional instruments	2,405	867	1,538	29.8%	3,241	4,566	(1,325)	29.5%
74	General industrial machinery	4,080	1,858	2,222	38.9%	9,064	12,526	(3,462)	45.7%
89	Miscellaneous manufactured articles, n.e.s.	2,381	1,890	491	33.9%	13,095	1,195	11,901	11.9%
67	Iron and steel	7,964	231	7,732	4.7%	9,039	3,706	5,333	26.7%
28	Metalliferous ores and metal scrap	5	4,537	(4,532)	0.2%	451	3,679	(3,227)	0.4%
65	Textile yarn and related products	5,839	703	5,136	18.3%	6,348	1,075	5,273	19.3%
Subtotal		58,653	70,421	(11,768)		151,049	45,597	105,451	
Total trade		94,066	108,223	(14,158)	30.1%	221,263	105,955	115,308	22.1%

Source: Authors' calculations using official Chinese Customs data, and HS 2007 to SITC Rev. 4 concordance from WITS. Excludes HS 98 and HS 99.

[a] Top ten industries based on size of Chinese global trade flows (imports + exports), excluding petroleum, in descending order.
[b] The intra-industry trade index is Grubel and Lloyd index (1975), calculated at the SITC 5-digit level and aggregated to SITC 2-digit.

(0.11 ha/person), this difference cannot explain variations in the manufacturing trade compositions of the two countries with China.

Reliance on theoretical guides other than neoclassical explanations is necessitated by the characteristics of bilateral trade flows we have highlighted in this section. While neoclassical models focus on trade in final goods, much of the actual flows are in intermediate goods. Equally important, neoclassical models do not explain the decision of firms to engage in foreign investment, exporting to and importing from the source country. To address these features of US–China and Japanese–China trade, we next consider models that seek to explain fragmentation of the production process into distinct vertically arranged tasks. We probe these explanations for clues to differences in the observed flows between the two trade pairs.

3. Production fragmentation and vertical specialization

Jones and Kierzkowski (2001) provide a useful definition of production fragmentation as the decomposition of production into separable component blocks connected by service links. In their discussion of the causes of fragmentation, they emphasize the importance of reductions in the costs of service links between fragments. Advances in telecommunications have reduced the costs of cross-border coordination, thereby encouraging the decomposition and offshoring of production blocks. Deardorff (2001) examines the link between the factor intensity of fragment production and factor prices in possible production locations (fragmentation across cones of diversification). Like Jones and Kierzkowski, Deardorff emphasizes the cost of fragmentation, noting that if coordination costs are large, offshoring of production fragments may not occur. Given the geographic proximity of Japan to China, we might anticipate that service links and production coordination are less costly for Japanese firms than for American firms. For both countries, however, China's trade liberalization, its encouragement of processing trade, and its incentives for foreign direct investment may all be viewed as policies that integrate China into both countries' supply chains.

The two-way trade discussed in part 1 may be horizontal trade in similar goods, "vertical" trade in similar goods of different qualities, or vertical trade in intermediate goods, exported and imported as part of a sequential supply chain. Measures such as the IIT index are designed to capture the first two types of two-way trade, but are not likely to capture trade in fragments, as these are, by definition, not similar. Fragments are distinguished from each other by their degree of

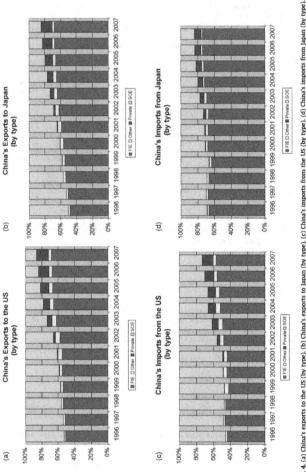

Fig. 4. (a) China's exports to the US (by type). (b) China's exports to Japan (by type). (c) China's imports from the US (by type). (d) China's imports from Japan (by type).

604 *J.M. Dean et al./Journal of Asian Economics 20 (2009) 596–610*

processing at different stages of production.[16] Given the limitations of using only trade data to draw inferences regarding production fragmentation and integration, we turn to evidence presented by Dean, Fung, and Wang (2008) (DFW hereafter) that draws on multiple information sources to measure trade in intermediates and the foreign content of China's exports.

DFW provide a detailed analysis of how China's trade is shaped by production fragmentation. They develop a method to identify imported intermediates using the Chinese Customs Regime Data and the UN Broad Economic Classification, as well as the 1997 and 2002 Chinese benchmark IO tables. About 77% of China's imports in 2002 were processing or normal intermediate imports.[17] More than half of these imported intermediates were from Japan and the Four Tigers, while only about 18% came from the US and the EU. Japan alone accounted for 19% of China's imported intermediates and 23% of China's imported processing intermediates. The figures for the US were only 7.6% and 6.3%, respectively. While Japan's share was roughly stable between 1997 and 2002, the US share fell, with respect to both processing and normal intermediate imports during that time.

Several factors may explain China's greater reliance on Japan, as well as other Asian countries, than on the US as the source of intermediate inputs. An obvious factor is transportation costs and geographic location. Just as Mexico provides a nearby location for processing and assembly for American firms, China provides a nearby location for labor-intensive fragments of Japanese, Taiwanese, and Korean designed and marketed products. In a formal model, Yi (2003) shows that small differences in trade costs matter when production must be done sequentially. He considers a technology with three sequential stages, two of which may be produced offshore but the last must be produced close to firm headquarters. Because some trade costs have to be paid on gross value or weight rather than just that added at an individual stage, small differences in these costs can have large effects on fragmentation and trade volumes. Yi focuses on tariffs specifically, but tariffs are unlikely to drive China's processing trade because intermediates imported under the processing regime are tariff exempt. However, transportation costs play a similar role, as weight accumulates during a sequential production process. Thus, differences in transportation costs could explain the differences we observe in China's trade with Japan and with the US.

DFW determine the vertical specialization in Chinese exports for 1997 and 2002, using two methods. The first method combines the newly identified imported intermediates with the official Chinese benchmark input–output table. The second method goes one step further, and uses the Koopman, Wei, and Wang (2008) technique to split the official input–output table—allowing processing exports to be imported-input-intensive in production relative to normal exports and domestic sales. In 2002, China's aggregate exports were characterized by significant vertical specialization, with foreign content estimated to be between 25% and 46%. DFW find a lower bound estimate of the foreign content of China's exports to the US and Japan of 28% and 25%, respectively; upper bound estimates are 55% and 46%, respectively. These results suggest that China's exports to the US have a somewhat higher foreign content, on average, than those to Japan.

From China's point of view, the US and Japan are also sources for very different imports.[18] In 2002, the US accounted for more than half of Chinese aggregate imports of special industrial equipment, more than one-third of its imported fertilizers, more than one-quarter of its agricultural imports, and about 60% of its imported computers. Japan accounted for 45% of China's imported radio, TV, and communications equipment; about 30% of China's imports of special industrial equipment, electric machinery and equipment, parts and accessories for motor vehicles, and metal products; and more than one-quarter of China's metal working machinery imports.

Comparing the 2002 bilateral trade data more closely we find that about 74% of China's imports from Japan were intermediate goods, while only 60% of China's imports from the US were intermediates. Nearly half of the intermediates imported from Japan came in under the processing regime, which indicates that they were re-exported after processing, while only about one-quarter of those from the US did. In contrast, nearly 68% of China's exports to the US were under the processing regime, while only 58% to Japan were processing exports. China's processing imports from both the US and Japan are dominated by electronic elements and devices in value terms. However, other key processing imports from the US include leather, fur and down products, and chemicals, while those from Japan include cotton textiles and other electric machinery. China's largest normal intermediate imports from the US (agriculture, paper products, and chemical fertilizers) also contrast with the largest from Japan (basic chemicals and steel pressing).

In sum, we find evidence suggestive of global supply chains with Japan as a principal source for China's imported intermediates, and the US as a key destination for China's exports of products embodying imported intermediates. While the largest flows for both pairs occur in the electronics and machinery industries, there are substantive differences that emerge from the detailed data.

4. Foreign-invested enterprises

Evidence presented in the previous section attests to the importance of fragmented production to China's overall relationship with the US and Japan. An equally important aspect is its reliance on foreign-invested enterprises as the source of import demand and export supply. Fueled by reforms that legalized various types of non-state-owned enterprises but retained limitations on domestic credit, FIEs became the main vehicle for China's integration into the global economy.

---

[16] In the IIT literature, "vertical" IIT refers to differences in product quality, not to differences in stages of production (Greenaway et al., 1995). The SITC classifies products such that only a small number of 5-digit lines include products at different stages of production.

[17] Dean et al. (2008) focus on trade in 2002 because that year matches the most recent benchmark input–output tables, which they use extensively in their analysis of the vertical specialization of China's trade.

[18] The data for this paragraph and the next are from Dean et al. (2008). We thank them for giving us access to these data.

128　　*International Economic Integration and Domestic Performance*

J.M. Dean et al./Journal of Asian Economics 20 (2009) 596–610　　　　　　605

Currently, FIEs consist of fully-funded foreign enterprises (FFEs), Sino-foreign contractual joint ventures (CJVs) and Sino-foreign equity joint ventures (EJVs). American and Japanese firms have invested heavily in foreign affiliates in China, both to gain access to Chinese labor for processing and as a platform to serve the growing Chinese consumer market. From 1998 to 2007, American foreign direct investment in China averaged $3.9 billion per year. Over the same period, Japanese foreign direct investment in China averaged somewhat more, $4.3 billion per year. Though far outweighed by FDI from Hong Kong, these investments are large, persistent, and indicative of the rapid integration of production between China, Japan, and the US.

　　Why firms choose to operate foreign affiliates rather than service a market through exports from the home country is the subject of a large theoretical literature. Markusen (1984) explains "horizontal FDI" as the outcome of a trade-off between proximity to a local market and the concentration of production in one location. Serving a foreign market through a local affiliate replicates the home production process abroad but saves on transport costs. However, if there are economies of scale in production, exporting may be more profitable than serving the local market through FDI because production remains concentrated in a single location. This horizontal approach is extended and tested by Brainard (1997), Markusen and Venables (1998, 2000), and Helpman, Melitz, and Yeaple (2004), among others.

　　When we consider how transport costs might drive differences across industries in horizontal FDI, we note that Krugman (1980) identifies a "home-market effect" for industries producing differentiated final products. While transport costs lead firms to locate production as close as possible to final consumers, fixed costs associated with differentiating products in response to consumer tastes encourage the concentration of production in a single location. In that case, there is a tendency for a differentiated-products industry to concentrate in the country with the larger market for home varieties, making the home country the net exporter of differentiated goods.

　　Hanson and Xiang (2004) test the home-market effect with international trade data organized into two groups of industries: those with high transport costs and more differentiated products and those with low transport costs and less

Table 4
Characteristics of Chinese imports, by origin and type, 2007, industries identified by Hanson and Xiang (2004).

SITC	Industry	Japan (as share of total trade)		US (as share of total trade)	
		Ordinary trade	Processing trade	Ordinary trade	Processing trade
Industries with low transport costs and low production differentiation					
514	Nitrogen compounds	62.9	31.8	69.6	13.6
541	Pharmaceuticals	85.0	6.7	77.5	6.1
726	Printing machinery	66.1	1.8	58.9	0.7
751	Office machines	69.1	3.6	74.7	0.2
752	Computers	36.7	41.2	81.7	3.2
759	Computer parts	6.6	74.6	15.3	60.4
761	Televisions	70.1	10.4	75.9	8.2
762	Radios	77.5	9.1	2.7	1.2
764	Audio speakers	18.0	60.0	43.4	42.2
881	Cameras	14.9	34.8	66.4	7.1
882	Camera supplies	37.8	50.4	60.2	33.8
884	Optical lenses	25.0	71.1	47.3	37.9
885	Watches and clocks	8.6	84.3	24.8	69.4
	Weighted average	25.9	55.3	63.9	19.1
Industries with high transport costs and high product differentiation					
621	Rubber and plastics	43.5	50.7	63.6	27.6
625	Tires	89.3	4.8	69.4	3.9
634	Wood panels	54.6	44.9	32.7	64.6
635	Wood manufacturing	38.2	48.3	68.4	23.1
641	Paper and paperboard	44.1	47.6	69.8	26.4
642	Paper products	29.3	60.5	34.8	57.1
661	Cement	92.8	6.8	96.3	2.4
662	Clay	69.9	24.1	81.1	1.5
663	Mineral manufacturing	43.5	48.9	43.5	30.2
665	Glassware	12.8	84.4	45.7	33.4
666	Pottery	45.5	49.0	36.6	17.5
671	Pig iron	19.6	80.4	99.6	0.4
672	Iron ingots	64.2	33.6	91.9	1.0
673	Iron bars	43.0	52.6	31.9	59.1
674	Iron sheets	38.4	57.5	61.4	33.8
676	Steel rails	60.1	35.0	0.2	98.2
677	Iron wire	50.8	43.0	46.9	47.7
678	Iron tubes	69.9	16.4	82.5	9.6
679	Iron castings	40.3	55.6	13.9	79.0
812	Sanitary and plumbing	39.9	40.7	74.8	9.9
821	Furniture	91.8	4.7	51.9	25.6
	Weighted average	45.0	49.8	65.1	25.9

Source: Authors' calculations using official Chinese Customs data.

Table 5
China's exports, by destination and type, 1996 and 2007.

Country	Year	Processing[a] exports/total exports (%)	FIE[b] exports/total exports (%)	FIE processing exports/total processing exports (%)
World	1996	55.8	40.7	62.9
	2007	50.7	57.1	84.4
US	1996	72.0	50.6	64.0
	2007	62.5	68.3	86.2
Japan	1996	55.8	48.2	69.6
	2007	56.6	67.7	86.9
ASEAN	1996	41.3	30.4	59.1
	2007	42.7	49.6	81.7
EU15	1996	49.9	35.4	60.4
	2007	51.9	58.3	84.4
ROW	1996	53.2	36.2	60.1
	2007	45.7	51.4	83.3

Source: Authors' calculations using official China Customs data.

[a] Processing includes the processing and assembly and processing with imported materials customs regimes.
[b] FIE includes Sino-foreign contractual joint ventures, Sino-foreign equity joint ventures, and fully-funded (wholly-owned) foreign enterprises.

differentiated products. In Table 4, we provide characteristics of Chinese imports from Japan and the US, for industries divided into the two groups identified by Hanson and Xiang. Because transport costs to China are much larger for American firms, we might expect to see the influence of firm-level fixed costs more clearly in Japan–China trade and thus, the influence of the home-market effect in these flows. The left panel provides the share of Chinese imports from Japan that are ordinary imports and the share that are processing imports, for the 3-digit SITC industries classified as having low transport cost/low differentiation (top panel) and high transport cost/high differentiation (bottom panel).[19] Interestingly, we see that China's imports from Japan of the highly differentiated products are much more likely to be ordinary trade, and less likely to be processing trade, than the low-differentiation products. This evidence suggests that, for Japan-Sino trade, the home-market effect may indeed explain some of the differences in the ordinary trade shares across industries.

In contrast, the same comparison using US values in Table 4 shows very little difference between the two industry groups. China's imports from the US in both these categories are more likely to be ordinary trade, and less likely to be processing intermediates than are China's imports from Japan. Moreover, for imports from the US, the share of trade that is ordinary trade is nearly identical across the two industry groups. That no difference appears between high-differentiation and low-differentiation industries suggests that transport costs between the US and China dominate sourcing decisions.

Because the horizontal FDI literature focuses on the mode of entry into a foreign market, some empirical studies rely on detailed information on foreign affiliates' sales to the host country domestic market. As noted by Greaney and Li (this issue), there are significant differences in the extent to which American and Japanese firms use their Chinese subsidiaries to serve the local market. Their analysis reveals that in 2003 70% of sales by US majority-owned non-bank manufacturing affiliates in China were to the local market. Less than 8% of their sales were exports to the US. In contrast, in 2003 only 46% of sales by Japanese majority-owned non-bank manufacturing affiliates in China were to the local market, while 34% of sales were exports to Japan. These data are consistent with Markusen's (1984) framework, in that transportation costs are larger for American firms than for Japanese firms and, thus, may be an explanation for the greater intensity with which American firms use local affiliates to serve the Chinese market.

An alternative approach for understanding firms' decisions to invest abroad is a focus on "vertical FDI." This approach builds on the work of Helpman (1984), who shows that if there are increasing returns to scale in "headquarter services" and cross-country differences in factor prices, a firm may split the production of headquarter services and manufacturing across countries. Helpman's model predicts that the extent of multinational activity will be increasing in relative factor endowment differences across countries. Empirical evidence on the vertical explanation for multinational activity is provided by Yeaple (2003a) and Hanson, Mataloni, and Slaughter (2005).[20]

The foreign affiliate sales patterns in Greaney and Li (this issue) highlight the importance of vertical FDI, especially for Japanese firms, which export more than half of their Chinese production. In comparing this evidence to information provided by detailed trade data, it is essential to note that FIE exports to the US (or Japan) will include both exports by US (Japanese) affiliates, and also exports by non-US (non-Japanese) affiliates. The Chinese trade data do not distinguish FIE exports by the parent company's source country. Thus, an FIE exporting to the US (Japan) may have a parent in any country, including the US (Japan). Nevertheless, evidence from the trade data does reinforce the view that vertical motives are an important reason for

---

[19] Using a concordance between SITC (Rev. 2) and HS codes, these shares were then averaged using trade volumes as weights.
[20] Some analyses, such as Yeaple (2003b), combine both the vertical and horizontal motive for foreign investment and emphasize complementarities between the two forms of activity.

FDI into China. Table 5 shows the share of China's exports to various destinations that is classified as processing trade, the share carried out by FIEs, and the share of processing trade that is performed by FIEs. Processing trade carried out by FIEs is clearly evidence of vertical FDI activity. From Table 5, we find that Chinese exports to the US are somewhat more likely to be processing exports than are exports to Japan (62.5% versus 56.6%). Coupled with the evidence presented above from Greaney and Li (this issue), this figure indicates that a large share of Chinese exports to the US flows from non-US foreign affiliates, again providing evidence of an Asian supply chain. Secondly, again looking at Table 5, we see that for both the US and Japan, a remarkably high share of total exports is carried out by FIEs: 68.3% for exports to the US and 67.7% for exports to Japan in 2007. Thirdly, and perhaps less surprisingly, the majority of processing trade is performed through FIEs, as 86.2% of processing exports come from FIEs to the US and 86.9% to Japan in 2007. Less obvious, however, is the extent to which total FIE trade is processing trade. Detailed examination of the data shows that, for many industries, FIEs do very little trade other than processing importing and exporting.

5. Contractual frictions and organizational form

While the importance of processing trade is evidence that firms have broken the production process into several fragments, some component production is done within the firm while some involves arm's length transactions. Recent theories of organization and trade, drawing upon models of contractual frictions, seek to understand which activities take place within the firm's boundaries. Thus, they address a narrower aspect of the data: whether production of intermediates takes place inside the firm (in-sourcing) or outside the firm (outsourcing). They presume that production is fragmented, rather than trying to explain how fragmented it is.

Simply observing the extent to which trade is mediated by foreign-invested enterprises does not capture the extent to which an American or Japanese firm controls production decisions. However, some insight into firm boundaries can be obtained through use of the separate data on processing and assembly (P&A), which is conducted mostly by SOEs and FIEs; and processing with imported materials (PWIM), which is largely conducted by FIEs. As noted earlier, the key distinction between these two customs regimes is control over inputs: with P&A, the producer in China receives materials and processes them according to orders taken from the foreign firm, while with PWIM, the producer in China firm has full control of decisions related to input sourcing, production, trading, and financing. The Chinese firm involved in these relationships may be an SOE, an FIE, or a private domestic enterprise.

Use of this Chinese Customs distinction to study firm boundaries was exploited by Feenstra and Hanson (2005), who develop their approach from recent advances in the study of imperfect contracts. Since production of final goods may require highly customized and specialized intermediate inputs to be produced by input suppliers, its quality may not be verifiable by a third party. In such a case, the final good producer and the input supplier may find it impossible to write a complete contract specifying the price–quality relationship. Moreover, even if such a contract could be written, it may not be enforced by the judicial system. Thus, the division of the economic surplus from production and use of the input may be subject to ex post bargaining between the final good producer and the input supplier/producer. This potentially results in what, in the literature, is called a "hold up" problem: distortions in the incentives for investment and effort in input production because the producer is able to get only a fraction of the returns to her investment or effort. If so, the input supplier will provide less investment or effort than is optimal for maximization of the joint production surplus. Such a situation may also characterize resources provided by the final good producer.

Helpman (2006) argues that "intermediate inputs under the direct control of the final good producer suffer less from agency problems than intermediate inputs that require the engagement of suppliers." Also, the effective bargaining power of the final good supplier is higher under integration than under outsourcing as under the former the final good supplier has some control over inputs and can recover some of its value if bargaining fails. This is good from the point of view of getting the resources provided by the final good producer as close to the optimum level (that which maximizes the joint surplus from production) as possible, but it adversely affects the level of activity of the input producer. Thus incentives are closer to optimal under integration when goods require intensive use of headquarter services (provided by the final good producer) in their production, while outsourcing is better when goods require intensive use of specialized inputs (provided by the intermediate good producer). If (1) headquarter services are capital intensive and input production is labor intensive, and if (2) the two have to be combined in the same country to produce a specific tradable intermediate input used in the production of a given non-tradable final good (and there are many different intermediate and final goods), then we should see, *ceteris paribus*, a positive correlation between the share of intra-firm imports of a country and the capital abundance of the exporting country (Antràs, 2003; Helpman, 2006).

Note that intra-firm imports are correlated with vertical FDI while inter-firm imports are correlated with offshore outsourcing. With vertical FDI, inputs are being produced in the same multinational firm as the final output. This is not so with offshore outsourcing. Thus, according to this theory, in less capital-abundant countries such as China and India, we should see relatively more offshore outsourcing than offshoring through FDI. Of course, legal institutions are weaker in these countries than in the more capital-abundant countries, and that will be an offsetting force as it influences contract enforcement.

How well these theories fare with actual experience in China is the subject of Feenstra and Hanson's (2005) exploration of ownership and control in Chinese processing trade. They build a simple model of international outsourcing and apply it to China. They consider a multinational firm that has decided to set up an *export-processing* plant in a low-wage country. In this

608 *J.M. Dean et al./Journal of Asian Economics 20 (2009) 596–610*

Table 6
Processing exports by input control and factory ownership (% of total processing exports).

Country	Control over inputs	Ownership of factory			
		1996		2007	
		Foreign[a]	Chinese[b]	Foreign[a]	Chinese[b]
US	Foreign (processing and assembly[c])	3.3	26.5	10.4	8.3
	Chinese (process with imported materials[d])	60.7	9.5	75.9	5.4
Japan	Foreign (processing and assembly[c])	13.3	17.8	15.9	8.0
	Chinese (process with imported materials[d])	56.3	12.6	71.1	5.0

Source: Authors' calculations using official Chinese Customs data.

[a] Foreign ownership is made up of Sino-foreign contractual joint ventures, Sino-foreign equity joint ventures, and fully-funded (wholly-owned) foreign enterprises.
[b] Chinese ownership is made up of state-owned enterprises, collective enterprises, private enterprises, individual-owned industrial or commercial firms, customs broking enterprises, and other.
[c] The foreign firm retains ownership over the imported intermediates.
[d] The Chinese importing firm has ownership over the imported intermediates.

arrangement, the firm sends intermediate inputs to a processing factory, which converts the inputs into finished goods and then exports the final output. The decisions facing the multinational include who should own the processing factory and who should control input-purchase decisions the factory makes. They posit that parties use control rights over productive assets to ameliorate hold up problems created by incomplete contracts. Their model predicts that the joint surplus generated by the partnership depends on model parameters, including the specificity of investments and contracting costs, which they estimate.

Feenstra and Hanson (2005) do not observe the value of surplus from outsourcing activities directly. Rather, they use the share of processing trade accounted for by each contractual type to represent the probability that a particular contractual arrangement is chosen.[21] Comparing these shares in China's total processing exports over the period 1997–2002, they find that multinational firms tend to split factory ownership and input control with local managers. The most common form, as evidenced by trade shares, is to have foreign factory ownership but Chinese control over input purchases.

Following Feenstra and Hanson (2005), we calculate the shares of processing trade by contractual type for 1996 and 2007. In Table 6, multinationals engaged in export processing tend to split factory ownership and input control with local managers. A little over one-quarter of processing exports to the US come from Chinese owned factories operating under P&A arrangements (foreign control of inputs), while nearly two-thirds come from foreign owned factories operating under PWIM arrangements (local control of inputs). A similarly small share of processing exports to Japan (17.8%) come from Chinese owned factories operating under P&A arrangements, while the largest share (56.3%) comes from foreign owned factories operating under PWIM arrangements. These results indicate similar patterns across the two bilateral relationships and are close to the results found by Feenstra and Hanson for all trade in the 1997–2002 period: 27% of processing exports produced in Chinese factories under P&A arrangements and 49.6% produced in Chinese factories under PWIM arrangements.

Looking at data from 2007 in Table 6, however, we do see some changes in contractual arrangements over the decade. The dominant form of processing trade continues to be foreign-owned factories with Chinese managers controlling input decisions. This type accounts for more than three-quarters of processing exports to the US and nearly as much to Japan. However, the second largest form—processing and assembly by Chinese firms—dwindles in share. Instead, there is a growing share of processing exports by foreign-owned firms with foreign control over inputs. This pattern appears with respect to both destination countries, but more dramatically with respect to the US.[22]

Further differences between the US and Japan emerge when we dig a bit deeper in the data and distinguish between foreign firms by type. As noted above, not all FIEs operate under the same organizational forms. In fully-funded enterprises, foreign control over production decision is complete. With an equity joint venture or contractual joint venture, control is shared between the foreign investor and the Chinese partner. In Table 7, we see that processing exports by foreign-owned firms destined for Japan are more likely to come from firms with foreign control over inputs than those destined for the US, regardless of firm type. But there is also variation across firm types. When the exporter is an FFE, so that the foreigner has complete ownership of the firm, the share of processing exports to the US under processing and assembly is 15% (8.9/59.7), in contrast to about 20% for exports to Japan. When foreign ownership is shared, as under an EJV, about 7% of processing exports to the US are from firms with foreign control over inputs, in contrast to 27% of exports to Japan. Finally, when joint ownership is stipulated only contractually (CJV), the shares of processing exports to the US and to Japan under processing and assembly

[21] They assume that ownership and control are chosen to maximize joint surplus plus an i.i.d. extreme value random error that varies across contractual types.
[22] Part of this dominance of foreign ownership and foreign control over inputs may be explained by the post-1996 ease in Chinese FDI restrictions, leading to a surge in the establishment of wholly-owned foreign subsidiaries (FFEs).

J.M. Dean et al./Journal of Asian Economics 20 (2009) 596–610   609

Table 7
Processing exports by input control and foreign ownership type (% of total processing exports).

Country	Control over inputs	Foreign ownership type 2007		
		FFE[a]	CJV[b]	EJV[c]
US	Foreign (processing and assembly)	8.9	0.3	1.0
	Chinese (process with imported materials[e])	59.7	1.3	15.1
Japan	Foreign (processing and assembly[d])	10.4	0.8	4.7
	Chinese (process with imported materials[e])	52.1	1.4	17.4

Source: Authors' calculations using official Chinese Customs data.

[a] FFE is a fullly-funded (wholely-owned) foreign enterprise.
[b] CJV is a contractual joint venture.
[c] EJV is an equity joint venture.
[d] The foreign firm retains ownership over the imported intermediates.
[e] The Chinese importing firm has ownership over the imported intermediates.

are 23% and 57%, respectively. This decomposition suggests that foreign firms undertaking processing exports to Japan are progressively more likely to retain control over inputs, as their control over the ownership of the firm declines.

6. Implications for regional integration

A detailed look at trade between China and two of its largest trading partners, the United States and Japan, finds that only a small share of these flows can be characterized as arm's length, one-way trade in final goods. Instead, we find extensive two-way trade, deep vertical specialization, concentration of trade in computer and communication devices, and a prominent role for foreign-invested enterprises. While these characteristics define both bilateral relationships, some important differences between the two pairs do emerge. China's imports from Japan are most likely destined for an FIE within China, and more likely to be processing than non-processing trade; its processing imports are roughly balanced with Chinese processing exports to Japan. In comparison, China's imports from the US are somewhat less likely to be destined for an FIE within China, and most likely to be non-processing trade; its processing imports are outsized by Chinese processing exports to the US. Even as both Japan and the US experienced rapid growth in non-processing exports to China after 2001, Japan's processing exports to China increased apace while US processing exports grew far more slowly. The picture that emerges is one where China is in the midst of a global production chain, with Japan as a principal source of imported intermediates, and the US as a principal destination for exports embodying imported intermediates. This impression is reinforced by Wakasugi, Ito, and Tomiura (2008), who find a sharp decline in Japan's share of the world manufacturing value added between 1996 and 2004, a sharp increase for China and no change for the US.

While this evidence is often interpreted as support for the view that Japan is more deeply "integrated" with China, we stress that trade flows provide only a limited window into production fragmentation as they do not trace products through the production cycle. While it may certainly be the case that some Japanese firms are more likely to export components and parts to China for processing than are similar US firms, the evidence is also consistent with a relatively greater reliance by US-based firms on production of components within China, and thus relatively smaller flows of processing exports from the US to China. In other words, larger trade costs may lead US-based multinationals to choose direct investment over exporting relatively more often than do Japanese-based firms.

Trade costs may also be an explanation for evidence of a "home-market effect" at work in the Japan–China relationship that we do not find in the US–China relationship. China's imports from Japan of highly differentiated products are much more likely to be ordinary trade than are less differentiated products, a difference not evident in US–China flows. Transport costs between the US and China may be large enough to outweigh the benefits of concentrating production within the US and serving China via exporting. For Japan, transportation costs are lower and thus serving the Chinese market through domestic production may more often be the profit maximizing strategy.

Although the US and Japan face different trade costs and, thus, appear to pursue somewhat different strategies for integrating with China, each will gain from shifting some fragments of production to a country where they can be produced at lower cost. Grossman and Rossi-Hansberg (2008) emphasize the productivity effect of offshoring and the possibility that these productivity gains raise wages for unskilled as well as skilled workers in the high-wage country. An important question is how the extent of this shift in response to differential transport costs affects the distribution of gains in the high-wage country. Does it matter for source country unskilled wages if more or less of the value chain is offshored?

Our findings also suggest a new perspective on the costs to the US of an East Asian free trade area that does not include the United States. There is an emerging consensus view of East Asia as a highly interdependent producer of final goods for North American consumption. Athukorala and Yamashita (2008) characterize the US–China trade imbalance as a structural phenomenon resulting from the emergence of China as a final assembly center for East Asian production networks, largely for North American consumption. Consequently, Athukorala (2005) argues that East Asian growth is increasingly reliant on extra-regional trade, mainly as a destination for its exports, strengthening the case for global, rather than regional, trade and investment policy making. Our findings add a somewhat different shading to these arguments, while retaining the case for global, over regional, liberalization. We have documented the many commonalities between China's bilateral trade with the US and that with Japan. While reliance on exports to Chinese processors may differ, production fragmentation and input processing are important for American producers as well as for Japanese producers. Thus, dialogue on regional trade liberalization should expand beyond a view of the US mainly as a final goods consumer; it should include discussion of gains for the US through greater production efficiency from production fragmentation and gains to East Asia through processing trade creation with the US.

References

Antràs, P. (2003). Firms, contracts, and trade structure. *Quarterly Journal of Economics, 118*(4), 1375–1418.
Antràs, P., & Rossi-Hansberg, E. (2009). Organizations and trade. *Annual Review of Economics, 1*, 43–64.
Athukorala, P.-C. (2005). Production fragmentation and trade patterns in East Asia. *Asian Economic Papers, 4*(3), 1–27.
Athukorala, P.-C., & Yamashita, N. (2008). *Global production sharing and US-China trade relations*. Departmental Working Paper 2008-22. Canberra: Australian National University, Economics, RSPAS.
Brainard, S. L. (1997). An empirical assessment of the proximity-concentration trade-off between multinational sales and trade. *American Economic Review, 84*, 520–544.
Dean, J., Fung, K. C., & Wang, Z. (2008). *How vertically specialized is Chinese trade?* Office of economics working paper 2008-09D Washington: US International Trade Commission.
Deardorff, A. (2001). Fragmentation across cones. In S. Arndt & H. Kierzkowski (Eds.), *Fragmentation*. Oxford: Oxford University Press.
Deardorff, A. (2005). *Gains from trade and fragmentation*. Mimeo: University of Michigan, Ann Arbor.
Feenstra, R. C., & Hanson, G. H. (2005). Ownership and control in outsourcing to China: Estimating the property rights theory of the firm. *Quarterly Journal of Economics, 120*(2), 729–762.
Finger, J., & Kreinin, M. M. (1979). A measure of 'export similarity' and its possible uses. *Economic Journal, 89*, 905–912.
Greaney, T. M., & Li, Y. (this issue). Assessing foreign direct investment relationships between China, Japan, and the United States. *Journal of Asian Economics.*
Greenaway, D., Hine, R., & Milner, C. (1995). Vertical and horizontal intra-industry trade: A cross industry analysis for the UK. *Economic Journal, 105*, 1505–1518.
Grossman, G. M., & Rossi-Hansberg, E. (2008). Trading tasks: A simple theory of offshoring. *American Economic Review, 98*(5), 1978–1997.
Grubel, H. G., & Lloyd, P. J. (1975). *Intra-industry trade: The theory and measurement of international trade in differentiated products*. New York: John Wiley.
Hammer, A. (2006). *The dynamic structure of US-China trade, 1995–2004*. Office of Economics working paper 2006-07A. Washington: US International Trade Commission.
Hanson, G. H., Mataloni, R. J., & Slaughter, M. J. (2005). Vertical production networks in multinational firms. *Review of Economics and Statistics, 87*(4), 664–678.
Hanson, G. H., & Xiang, C. (2004). The home-market effect and bilateral trade patterns. *American Economic Review, 94*(4), 1108–1129.
Helpman, E. (1984). A simple theory of international trade with multinational corporations. *Journal of Political Economy, 92*, 451–471.
Helpman, E. (2006). Trade, FDI, and the organization of firms. *Journal of Economic Literature, 44*, 589–630.
Helpman, E., Melitz, M. J., & Yeaple, S. R. (2004). Export versus FDI with heterogeneous firms. *American Economic Review, 94*, 300–316.
Ianchovichina, E., & Martin, W. (2004). Economic impacts of China's accession to the WTO. In D. Bhattasali, S. Li, & W. Martin (Eds.), *China and the WTO*. Washington: World Bank and Oxford University Press.
Jones, R. W., & Kierzkowski, H. (2001). A framework for fragmentation. In S. Arndt & H. Kierzkowski (Eds.), *Fragmentation*. Oxford: Oxford University Press.
Koopman S Robert, Wei, S.-J., & Wang, Z. (2008). *How much of Chinese exports are really made in China?* NBER working paper 14109 Cambridge, Massachusetts: National Bureau of Economic Research.
Krugman, P. (1980). Scale economies, product differentiation, and the pattern of trade. *American Economic Review, 70*(5), 950–959.
Markusen, J. R. (1984). Multinationals, multi-plant economies, and the gains from trade. *Journal of International Economics, 16*, 205–226.
Markusen, J. R., & Venables, A. J. (1998). Multinational firms and the new trade theory. *Journal of International Economics, 46*, 183–203.
Markusen, J. R., & Venables, A. J. (2000). The theory of endowment, intra-industry and multi-national trade. *Journal of International Economics, 52*, 209–234.
Naughton, B. (2007). *The Chinese economy: Transitions and growth*. Cambridge, Massachusetts: MIT Press.
Wakasugi, R., Ito, B., & Tomiura, E. (2008). Offshoring and trade in East Asia: A statistical analysis. *Asian Economic Papers, 7*, 101–124.
Xing, Y. (2007). Foreign direct investment and China's bilateral intra-industry trade with Japan and the US. *Journal of Asian Economics, 18*, 685–700.
Yeaple, S. R. (2003a). The role of skill endowments in the structure of US outward FDI. *The Review of Economics and Statistics, 85*, 726–734.
Yeaple, S. R. (2003b). The complex integration strategies of multinationals and cross country dependencies in the structure of FDI. *Journal of International Economics, 60*, 293–314.
Yi, K.-M. (2003). Can vertical specialization explain the growth of world trade? *Journal of Political Economy, 111*(1), 52–102.

The home-market effect and bilateral trade patterns: A reexamination of the evidence

Cong S. Pham [a,*], Mary E. Lovely [b], Devashish Mitra [c]

[a] School of Accounting, Economics and Finance, Deakin University, 221 Burwood Highway, Burwood, 3125 Victoria, Australia
[b] Department of Economics, Syracuse University, Eggers Hall, Syracuse, NY 13244, United States
[c] Department of Economics, Syracuse University, 133, Eggers Hall, Syracuse, NY 13244, United States

ARTICLE INFO

Article history:
Received 20 June 2013
Received in revised form 22 October 2013
Accepted 22 October 2013
Available online 9 November 2013

JEL classification:
F12
F14

Keywords:
Gravity equation
Home-market effect
Zero trade flows

ABSTRACT

This paper finds that the evidence for the home market effect (HME) found by Hanson and Xiang (AER, 2004) is sensitive to the way the dependent and the independent variables are constructed. Second, we also find that the HME evidence goes away when we estimate their difference-in-difference gravity model on a truncated sample of positive trade flows. With Eaton–Tamura–Tobit, Heckman, and Helpman–Melitz–Rubinstein estimation of the gravity equation using Hanson and Xiang's data, we are unable to find any evidence for the HME. Finally, the HME evidence is also absent for a sample of Canadian provinces' exports to U.S. states. All of our results, taken together, do not reject the existence of the HME in general but rather suggest that the HME results found by Hanson and Xiang may not be robust.

© 2013 Elsevier Inc. All rights reserved.

1. Introduction

Hanson and Xiang (2004) develop a multi-sector, monopolistic competition model and use it to reveal a systematic relationship between the strength of the home-market effect and industry characteristics.[1,2] The multisectoral nature of their model, by suggesting "treatment" and "control" sectors, allows them to devise a difference-in-difference gravity approach to empirically test the home-market effect. The home-market prediction is that industries with high transport costs and low substitution elasticities (more highly differentiated products) will tend to be more concentrated in large countries than industries with low transport costs and high substitution elasticities. Hanson and Xiang treat the former industries as "treatment" industries and the latter as "control" industries. Using this innovative approach, they are able to address major econometric concerns about earlier tests of the home-market effect, including possible correlation between industry demand and supply shocks and a failure to control for "remoteness" of exporting and importing countries, both of which can lead to biased coefficient estimates. Because Hanson and Xiang's approach provides a novel and potentially quite useful methodological breakthrough, we examine the robustness of their findings to changes in data handling, changes in sample, and changes in estimation procedure. Overall, the

---

* Corresponding author. Tel.: +61 3 924 46611.
  E-mail addresses: cpham@deakin.edu.au (C.S. Pham), melovely@maxwell.syr.edu (M.E. Lovely), dmitra@maxwell.syr.edu (D. Mitra).
[1] HME: the home-market effect; OLS: ordinary least squares; ET-Tobit: Eaton–Tamura Tobit.
[2] Note that the HME hypothesis is an important prediction of new trade theory and new economic geography. Empirical studies on the HME include for example Head and Ries (1998), Behrens et al. (2009) and Kamal, Lovely, and Ouyang (2012). It is important here not to view the HME hypothesis in international trade as analogous or similar to the equity home bias puzzle in international finance. The latter refers to the fact that individuals and institutions in most countries hold modest amounts of foreign equity in their portfolios. See, for instance, French and Poterba (1991), Jinlan (2009) and Fugazza, Giofre, and Nicodano (2011).

1059-0560/$ – see front matter © 2013 Elsevier Inc. All rights reserved.
http://dx.doi.org/10.1016/j.iref.2013.10.005

C.S. Pham et al. / International Review of Economics and Finance 30 (2014) 120–137   121

weight of evidence from reasonable amendments to the Hanson–Xiang methodology and from a large number of robustness check runs against the presence of a significant home-market effect in trade flows.

Our observation is that in a difference-in-difference gravity specification in which there is a constant and/or a squared term for the independent variable of interest and both the dependent and independent variables are in ratios (differences in log values) for exporting country pairs, the method used to eliminate redundant observations affects both the sign and magnitude of the coefficient estimated for the independent variable of interest. Since each exporting country pair should only enter the sample once for a given destination country (and for a given treatment and control pair), some method for choosing one out of the two permutations associated with each pair of exporting countries must be used. Unfortunately, there exists no theoretical guidance about what the configuration of exporter pairs in the dependent variable or/and the independent variable must be. Our empirical analysis confirms that the configuration of exporter pairs powerfully affects the HME regression results. Specifically, when we apply Hanson and Xiang's difference-in-difference gravity specification using different configurations of exporter pairs we obtain completely conflicting results about the HME. In most specifications there is no evidence of the HME. When the HME is found in a few specifications it is reduced by more than 50%.

Second and importantly, we find that the data used by Hanson and Xiang are characterized by the pervasive presence of zero trade flows and that the strategy Hanson and Xiang use to incorporate information on zero trade flows into their analysis influences their empirical findings. Specifically, when the dependent variable is in double ratios (ratio of ratios), its value is powerfully affected by the value imputed to zero trade flows (even if the value to which each zero is set is small). Unfortunately, there is neither theoretical nor empirical justification for choosing a particular value to impute to zero trade flows, even though Hanson and Xiang follow many researchers in setting these values to unity. As expected, the influence of these imputed values on the inferences one may draw from estimation rises as the number of zero values in the trade data rises.

When we drop observations that contain zero trade values from the Hanson and Xiang sample we find no evidence of a home-market effect in the difference-in-difference gravity regression. Truncated OLS, Tobit-Style, Heckman and Helpman–Melitz–Rubinstein estimators of the gravity equation, which are methods better suited to samples with many zero values and are applied with intercept, without intercept and with intercept that varies depending on the way the explanatory variable of interest is configured, also do not yield support for the home-market effect.

We also look for the evidence of the HME using a sample of Canadian provinces' exports to U.S. states. This exercise is motivated by the fact that there exists established evidence of clustering of economic activity in Canadian largest provinces. Yet we also don't find any evidence of the HME under different econometric specifications.

Looking at different theoretical models that generate the HME hypothesis, we also provide some explanations for the absence of the HME. We show that in Hanson and Xiang's model the HME is determined not only by factors such as trade costs and the elasticity of substitution between varieties but also factors such as the tastes of exporting countries and the intensity of scale economies of industries. Failing to take into account those factors may explain why we have found no evidence of the HME or even the evidence of a reversed HME.

Finally, it is important to point out that, taken together, our results suggest that the HME evidence found by Hanson and Xiang may not be robust. However, our results must not be taken as evidence rejecting the HME hypothesis of the new trade theory or new economic geography models in general. Rather, the results of the econometric exercises in this paper must be seen as contributing to the discussion about the applicability of suitable econometric methods in future empirical studies of the HME effect.

2. Sensitivity of the difference-in-difference gravity specification to configuration of country pairs

The econometric specification Hanson and Xiang rely on to test the home-market effect is the following cross-section, difference-in-difference regression:

$$V_{jhk} = \ln\left(\frac{S_{mjk}/S_{mhk}}{S_{ojk}/S_{ohk}}\right) = \alpha + \beta f\left(Gdp_j/Gdp_h\right) + \varphi\left(X_j - X_h\right) + \theta \ln\left(d_{jk}/d_{hk}\right) + \varepsilon_{mojhk} \tag{1}$$

where Gdp_l $(l = j, h)$ is exporter l's market size (as measured by its gross domestic product) and d_{lk} $(l = j, h)$ is the distance between the exporting country l and the destination country k. $(X_j - X_h)$ is a vector of control variables that determine relative production costs for industries m, high-transport-cost and low-substitution elasticity industries, and industries o, low-transport-cost and high-substitution-elasticity industries, in exporter j relative to that in exporter h. This vector also includes level differences in standard gravity dummy variables such as common border and common language. The dependent variable V is composed of four export values with S_{dlk} $(d = m, o$ and $l = j, h)$ denoting exports of country l to destination country k in industry d.

The function $f(Gdp_j/Gdp_h)$ captures the relative number of product varieties in the exporting country pair. Hanson and Xiang show that this ratio of product varieties can be approximated by a linear function of polynomials of two alternative relative market size measures: $\text{Ln}(Gdp_j/Gdp_h)$ or $(Gdp_j/Gdp_h) - 1$. As Hanson and Xiang show theoretically, an estimated coefficient for β that is positive and statistically significant is evidence of HME, or whether larger countries export more of high transport cost, low substitution elasticity goods.

122   *C.S. Pham et al. / International Review of Economics and Finance 30 (2014) 120–137*

In their estimation results, Hanson and Xiang include regressions that include the market size measure and its square, following their derivation of an approximation for the relative number of product varieties. For their first market size measure, $Ln(Gdp_j/Gdp_h)$, the resulting estimating equation is:

$$V_{jhk} = \ln\left(\frac{S_{mjk}/S_{mhk}}{S_{ojk}/S_{ohk}}\right) = \alpha + \beta f\left(Gdp_j/Gdp_h\right) + \delta\left[\ln\left(Gdp_j/Gdp_h\right)\right]^2 + \varphi\left(X_j - X_h\right) + \theta \ln\left(d_{jk}/d_{hk}\right) + \varepsilon_{mojhk}. \tag{2}$$

Table 5 of Hanson and Xiang provides estimation results for this equation, using both market size measures and for regressions that drop the squared term.

It is straightforward to show that in the presence of the constant term α and the squared term $[Ln(Gdp_j/Gdp_h)]^2$, the coefficient estimates are sensitive to how the countries are arranged by pairs, i.e., which country is represented in the numerator and which in the denominator of these ratio variables. Suppose pairs of exporting countries are configured for estimation such that Gdp_j is *not always* greater than Gdp_h, as would be the case if the econometrician dropped one of the two occurrences (permutations) of each pair randomly. Let each pair (j, h) be denoted by $p \in P$ where P is the set of all exporting country pairs, with each pair appearing only once in the set (because one of the two occurrences of each pair has been dropped randomly). Let the coefficient estimates be obtained from the following OLS minimization problem:

$$\underset{\omega}{Min} \sum_{p\in P}\sum_{k}\sum_{m}\sum_{o}\varepsilon_{mojhk}{}^2 = \sum_{p\in P}\sum_{k}\sum_{m}\sum_{o}\{V_{mojhk} - \alpha - \beta\ln\left(Gdp_j/Gdp_h\right) - \delta\left[\ln\left(Gdp_j/Gdp_h\right)\right]^2 - \prod_{mojhk}\}^2 \tag{3}$$

where ω is the vector of all coefficients to be estimated and $\prod = \varphi(X_j - X_h) + \theta \, Ln(d_{jk}/d_{hk})$.

Of the above set P where the second occurrence of each pair has been dropped randomly, let NG be its subset that consists of all country pairs where the GDP of the country in the numerator is greater than the GDP of the country in the denominator. Now, consider an alternative method where we start out creating and arranging all our available data prior to estimation as follows: Rather than dropping the second occurrence of each pair randomly, keep all those possible observations of pairs of exporting countries where the GDP of the country in the numerator is greater than the GDP of the country in the denominator. As in the random procedure, this alternative method results in each pair being represented only once in the sample for any given good and destination. The minimization problem using this new alternative sample can now be written in terms of the old set of observations, P as follows:

$$\underset{\omega}{Min} \sum_{p\in NG}\sum_{k}\sum_{m}\sum_{o}\{V_{mojhk} - \alpha - \beta\ln\left(Gdp_j/Gdp_h\right) - \delta\left[\ln\left(Gdp_j/Gdp_h\right)\right]^2 - \prod_{mojhk}\}^2$$
$$+ \sum_{p\in NG}\sum_{k}\sum_{m}\sum_{o}\{-V_{mojhk} - \alpha + \beta\ln\left(Gdp_j/Gdp_h\right) - \delta\left[\ln\left(Gdp_j/Gdp_h\right)\right]^2 + \prod_{mojhk}\}^2. \tag{4}$$

Estimation of Eqs. (3) and (4) clearly can yield different coefficient estimates of β, even though they both apply OLS to the same dataset. Identical coefficient estimates will only be obtained when the constant term *and* the squared term are excluded from the regression.[3]

Figs. 1 and 2 illustrate graphically why the difference in the two maximization problems (3) and (4) may result in very different OLS estimates. Specifically, both figures represent the OLS regression of X on Y. Both the dependent variable and the independent variable are constructed as the ratio of country j's variable to country h's same variable in log value as is the case in the difference-in-difference gravity equation. The only difference between the two figures is the way the country pairs are configured. In Fig. 1 the pairs are configured in such a way that the country with larger value is always in the numerator of *the dependent variable*, which is reflected by the fact that all the observations are located in the area in which $Y = Ln(y_j/y_h) > 0 \leftrightarrow y_j > y_h$. On contrary, the pairs are matched randomly in Fig. 2 and consequently the observations are located both above and below the horizontal axis. It is noteworthy to see that the two figures contain exactly the same information about the relationship between Y and X and that observations A, B and C in nonrandom configuration become A*, B* and C* in random configuration of country pairs.[4]

Figs. 1 and 2 show that the OLS estimates (both the intercept and the slope) change or not depending on whether the estimator is run with or without a constant. Without a constant there is no change in the OLS estimates independently of the way the dependent variable is configured because whether country pairs are configured randomly or not observations move in a symmetric way with respect to the origin (for examples A, B and C become A*, B* and C*) as well as with respect to the OLS fitted line without a constant. When the OLS estimator is applied with a constant however the symmetric movement is only with respect to the origin but not to the OLS fitted line with a constant. In the example above not only the intercept changes in magnitude but also the slope of the OLS regression moves from being positive (Fig. 1) to being negative (Fig. 2).

---

[3] It is also straightforward to see from minimization problem (4) that reconfiguring pairs such that the GDP of the country in the numerator is always greater than the GDP of the country in the denominator and reconfiguring pairs such that the GDP of the country in the denominator is greater than the GDP of the country in the numerator yield the same coefficient estimates of β.

[4] This example is used to illustrate how the configuration of country pairs matters for the OLS estimator with a constant. Observations A, B, and C are chosen so that the configuration of country pairs influence not only the intercept but also the magnitude and the sign of the slope of the OLS estimator.

C.S. Pham et al. / International Review of Economics and Finance 30 (2014) 120–137   123

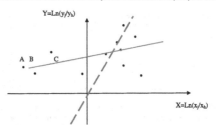

Fig. 1. OLS estimation with and without the intercept using a non random configuration of the dependent variable Ln(yⱼ/yₕ).

It is important to note that the argument laid down in the paragraph above also applies to the configuration of *the independent variable X*. In other words, the way the independent variable X, which is also the ratio of a variable of two different countries in log value, is created also influences both the intercept and the slope of the OLS estimator with a constant.

The set of regression results of Hanson and Xiang's paper is only one of many possible sets of results. The configuration of country pairs used by Hanson and Xiang is characterized by the fact that Gdp_j is sometimes but not always greater than Gdp_h *and* the numerator in the dependent variable (i.e. S_{mjk}/S_{mhk}) is sometimes but not always greater than the denominator in the dependent variable (i.e. S_{ojk}/S_{ohk}).[5] In order to confirm that the regression results vary from one configuration to another we actually reconfigure these pairs in different ways and examine how the OLS estimates of the difference-in-difference gravity change as a result.[6] Specifically, we investigate how the difference-in-difference estimates are sensitive to the configuration of country pairs with respect to the independent variable or the dependent variable. Table 1 reports the results of the difference-in-difference gravity regression using Hanson and Xiang's sample. The standard errors are bootstrapped. These specifications correspond to Table 5 in Hanson and Xiang. Yet, the configuration of country pairs differs from Hanson and Xiang's configuration. In cases A and B we only keep observations for which GDP_j (i.e. the numerator of the independent variable of interest) is always greater than GDP_h (i.e. the denominator of the independent variable of interest). In cases C, D and E we configure country pairs in such a way that the dependent variable is greater than zero for 25%, 50% and 75% of the total number of observations, respectively. These 25%, 50% and 75% of the total of number of observations are chosen randomly.

Unlike the results obtained when pairs are dropped randomly in Hanson and Xiang, Table 1 shows that a different data arrangement leads to findings that are sensitive to specification. As seen in case A, there is no evidence of the HME when we use Ln(Gdp_j/Gdp_h) as the market size measure and its squared term is also included. In contrast, results in case B, estimated using the reordered sample and Hanson and Xiang's preferred specification, do support the HME, as do the two specifications using (Gdp_j/Gdp_h) − 1 as the market size measure. In these cases, though, the magnitude of the estimated effect is smaller: 21% smaller in the estimates shown in column (3). So far the reconfiguration of country pairs is carried out with respect to the independent variable of interest. When we configure country pairs with respect to the dependent variables in three different ways (cases C, D and E) using Hanson and Xiang's preferred econometric specification the HME evidence disappears but in one case. Yet in case C the magnitude of the HME evidence is reduced by half. In cases D and E there is no evidence of the HME.

As a way of reducing the effect that the configuration of country pairs has on the difference-in-difference gravity estimates we also apply a more flexible specification in which the intercept is allowed to vary depending on whether the numerator of the independent variable of interest (GDP_j) is greater or smaller than the denominator (GDP_h). Specifically, we apply the following specification of the difference-in-difference gravity equation:

$$V_{jhk} = \ln\left(\frac{S_{mjk}/S_{mhk}}{S_{ojk}/S_{ohk}}\right) = \alpha_0 + \alpha_1 * Config + \beta \ln\left(Gdp_j/Gdp_h\right) + \varphi\left(X_j - X_h\right) + \theta \ln\left(d_{jk}/d_{hk}\right) + \varepsilon_{mojhk} \qquad (5)$$

where *Config* is a dummy variable equal to 1 if $Gdp_j > Gdp_h$ and to zero otherwise.[7] Again Table 2 shows that the gravity estimates of the HME are sensitive to the configuration of country pairs in the dependent and/or the independent variable. It is only in case B that there is evidence of the HME. In other cases the evidence is against the existence of the HME.

So far all the results confirm our argument that different configurations of country pairs yield completely different gravity estimates of the HME. Thus, it is important next to investigate the likelihood of finding the HME when we apply the

---

[5] We have carefully checked the Stata programs and the data we received from Hanson and Xiang. We note that the independent variable Ln(Gdp_j/Gdp_h) in their data takes both negative and positive values.

[6] We also run the difference-in-difference gravity regression with the independent variable Ln(Gdp_j/Gdp_h) created so that the higher GDP is always in the denominator. As expected, the coefficient estimate of β is the same as when the independent variable always has the higher GDP in the numerator.

[7] See Appendix A for an illustration of why gravity Eq. (6), which includes dummy variable $\alpha_1 * Config$, still yields different estimates depending on how country pairs are configured. Note that when we include squared term $[\text{Ln}(Gdp_j/Gdp_h)]^2$ in gravity specification (6) it is interacted with the dummy variable *Config*.

124 C.S. Pham et al. / International Review of Economics and Finance 30 (2014) 120–137

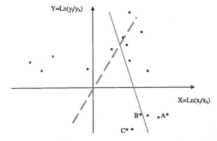

Fig. 2. OLS estimation with and without the intercept using random configuration of the dependent variable $Ln(y_j/y_h)$.

difference-in-difference gravity estimator to different samples of data. These samples differ by the way in which country pairs are reconfigured. Specifically, starting with the data used by Hanson and Xiang we first generate a random variable x_1. For those observations falling into the top half of x_1 we reverse the order of country pairs. The data are saved each time a random variable x_1 is generated and the reconfiguration carried out. We generate a random variable x_1 and reconfigure the data 100 times to obtain our base sample. We estimate the HME 1000 times with this base sample. Each time before the HME is estimate a random variable x_1 is generated and the data reconfigured in the same way as described above.

We present in Table 3 the results of the difference-in-difference gravity equation after 1000 runs are carried out using the two new samples of data. We can see that there is evidence of the likelihood of the HME. The mean of the HME estimates with the HME variable being $Log(Gdp_j/Gdp_h)$ and $(Gdp_j/Gdp_h) - 1$ is 0.348 and 0.074, respectively. These values are 20% lower than the HME estimate obtained by Hanson and Xiang.

It is noteworthy that with 1000 runs we don't find the HME estimates that include the HME estimates we obtained earlier in Tables 1 and 2. It is not difficult to see why it is the case. First note that the data have a total of 19 countries that belong to three different preferential trading arrangements: 15 members of European Economic Community (now E.U.), Australia and New Zealand (British Commonwealth) and U.S. and Canada (U.S. Canada Free Trade Area). Consequently, there is a total of 2^{107} different ways in which country pairs can be constructed.[8] Thus, the results from 1000 runs clearly are far from representing the whole distribution of the HME estimates resulting from 2^{107} different configurations of country pairs.[9]

In sum, the analysis of this section shows that there exists a mixed evidence of the HME. The evidence varies depending on the way country pairs are configured. In probabilistic sense, the HME, when it is found, is 20% lower than what Hanson and Xiang found.

3. Sensitivity of the difference-in-difference specification to treatment of zero values

An important feature of the sample used by Hanson and Xiang is the substantial presence of zero trade flows, as documented in Table 4. For example, if only a single-differenced gravity equation is used, the dependent variable contains at least one zero value in 45.9% of the total number of 173,910 observations. If a difference-in-difference specification is used, a zero occurs in at least one of the four components of the dependent variable in 62.3% of the observations.[10]

Given the pervasive presence of zero trade flows, it is of critical importance to know if evidence of the HME is robust to the truncation. We first estimate the difference-in-difference regressions using only non-zero trade values. The pooled sample is reduced by more than 60% from 1,396,395 to 527,053 observations. Table 5A and B reports the results when we configure the country pairs randomly and when we configure them such that the GDP of the larger country is in the numerator, respectively. As we can see, in all cases but one there is no evidence of the HME. The estimated coefficient on the ratio of exporter-pair GDP is of smaller magnitude (in absolute value) than when the sample includes zero trade values. It is never both positive and statistically significant. When the estimated coefficient is significant, as in column 2 of Table 5B, it is negative rather than positive. Importantly, the coefficient on the difference in distance is negative but not statistically significant in all cases, which result

---

[8] Given n countries the total number of possible permutations of country pairs is $2^{[n \cdot (n-1)/2]}$. For example, if there are two countries A and B the total number of configurations is $2^{[2 \cdot (2-1)/2]} = 2$ (i.e. AB or BA). If there are three countries A, B and C the total number of configurations is $2^{[3 \cdot (3-1)/2]} = 8$ (i.e. AB, AC, BC; AB, AC, CB; AB CA BC; BA AC BC; BA, AC, CB; BA CA BC; BA CA BC; BA CA CB). Note that the total number of possible configurations of country pairs is 2^{107} but not $2^{[19 \cdot (19-1)/2]} = 2^{171}$. This is because we can pair only countries of the same preferential trading agreement.

[9] Note that in order to obtain estimates that represent the distribution of the HME estimates from 2^{107} different configurations we need to carry out 2^{107} and more runs, which is clearly not feasible especially when the sample consists of more than 1.5 million observations.

[10] Since the data used by Hanson and Xiang are disaggregated at the 3-digit SITC classification, it is not surprising to have such a high percentage of zero trade flows.

C.S. Pham et al. / International Review of Economics and Finance 30 (2014) 120–137   125

Table 1
Difference-in-difference gravity regressions, pooled sample. Different configurations of country pairs.

Regressors	A		B		C		D		E	
	1	2	1	2	1	2	1	2	1	2
$Ln(Gdp_j/Gdp_h)$	−0.057		0.333***		0.184***		0.131		0.027	
	(−0.84)		(3.23)		(4.68)		(1.12)		(0.31)	
$[Ln(Gdp_j/Gdp_h)]^2$	0.124***									
	(2.81)									
$(Gdp_j/Gdp_h) - 1$		−0.051		0.046		−0.023		−0.023		−0.051
		(−0.54)		(1.49)		(−0.61)		(−0.71)		(−1.31)
$[(Gdp_j/Gdp_h) - 1]^2$		0.006								
		(0.68)								
Distance	−0.280***	−0.271***	−0.290***	−0.286 **	−0.160***	−0.324***	−0.327***	−0.326***	−0.321***	−0.314***
	(−6.13)	(−4.60)	(−5.21)	(−6.62)	(−5.14)	(−6.26)	(−6.07)	(−6.46)	(−6.30)	(−7.95)
Common language	−0.431***	−0.362***	−0.446***	−0.412 **	−0.317***	−0.445***	−0.504***	−0.447***	−0.504***	−0.443***
	(−3.31)	(−2.47)	(−3.78)	(−3.42)	(−4.33)	(−2.96)	(−3.13)	(−3.18)	(−3.76)	(−3.59)
Common border	0.911***	0.836***	0.918***	0.875***	0.269***	0.873***	0.955 **	0.876 **	0.856***	0.767***
	(9.30)	(9.47)	(10.80)	(9.34)	(4.83)	(8.98)	(9.48)	(9.06)	(9.72)	(9.34)
Capital/worker	1.761***	1.852***	1.920***	1.998***	0.838***	2.652***	2.522 **	2.650 **	2.546***	2.577***
	(4.00)	(4.48)	(5.64)	(5.59)	(4.37)	(5.89)	(5.70)	(6.07)	(5.33)	(6.67)
Wage	−1.887***	−1.740***	−1.897***	−1.798***	−0.872***	−1.691***	−1.838***	−1.690***	−1.647***	−1.512***
	(−7.49)	(−7.03)	(−8.37)	(−8.11)	(−5.97)	(−6.49)	(−6.35)	(−5.91)	(−4.18)	(−5.20)
Area/population	0.212***	0.142**	0.181***	0.133	0.051	−0.131	−0.013	−0.131	−0.100	−0.194*
	(2.28)	(2.08)	(2.32)	(1.76)	(1.58)	(−1.31)	(−0.13)	(−1.53)	(−1.06)	(−2.00)
Average education	−3.375***	−3.804***	−3.336***	−3.663***	−1.003***	−4.199***	−3.729***	−4.198***	−3.490***	−3.811***
	(−7.99)	(−9.09)	(−8.95)	(−7.01)	(−4.18)	(−6.95)	(−6.81)	(−7.72)	(−6.21)	(−6.02)
Constant	0.199	0.381***	0.031	0.254*	2.907***	0.825***	0.720***	0.824***	1.455***	1.547***
	(1.45)	(2.53)	(0.23)	(1.78)	(65.9)	(10.52)	(7.55)	(9.63)	(22.3)	(23.55)
R-squared	0.107	0.109	0.106	0.104	0.05	0.046	0.07	0.07	0.07	0.07
No of obs.	1,396,395	1,396,395	1,396,395	1,396,395	1,396,395	1,396,395	1,396,395	1,396,395	1,396,395	1,396,395

Notes: (1) This table replicates the estimation in Table 5 of Hanson and Xiang (2004), using their sample and estimation method. However, rather than eliminating redundant country-pair observations randomly, we configure country pairs in five different ways. In cases A and B those observations for which $Gdp_j < Gdp_h$ are eliminated. In case C those observations for which the denominator in the dependent variable is greater than the numerator are eliminated. In case D only 25% of those observations that are randomly chosen and for which the denominator is greater than the numerator in the dependent variable are eliminated. Finally in case E 50% of those observations that are chosen randomly and for which the denominator in the dependent variable is greater than the numerator are eliminated.
(2) The dependent variable is, for a pair of countries, log relative exports in a treatment industry minus log relative exports in a control industry. Each regression includes dummy variables for the industry match. Other variables are expressed as differences or log differences for a country pair.
(3) T-statistics are given in parentheses and are calculated from *bootstrapped* standard errors that have been adjusted for correlation of errors across observations that share the same pair of exporting countries. *, ** and *** denotes 10%, 5% and 1% level of significance, respectively.

suggests that while distance substantially reduces trade there is no strong evidence that its impact is greater for treatment than for control industries.

So far in all gravity specifications used the configuration of country pairs influence the gravity estimates. Consequently, we cannot make any conclusion about the existence of the HME. We now apply the difference-in-difference gravity regression without the constant to the non-zero sample. It is important to note that it is *only* when the gravity equation excludes the constant *and* the squared term in the HME variable (i.e. $[Log(Gdp_j/Gdp_h)]^2$) that the gravity estimates are unique and are not sensitive to how country pairs are configured. Specifically, also rely on the following difference-in-difference gravity specification:

$$V_{jhk} = \ln\left(\frac{S_{mjk}/S_{mhk}}{S_{ojk}/S_{ohk}}\right) = \beta f\left(Gdp_j/Gdp_h\right) + \varphi\left(X_j - X_h\right) + \theta \ln\left(d_{jk}/d_{hk}\right) + \varepsilon_{mojhk}. \quad (6)$$

The results, which are reported in Table 5C, clearly show that there is no evidence of HME in all specifications. While not presented the results we obtain when we include in the squared term in the HME variable (i.e. $Ln(Gdp_j/Gdp_h)^2$ or $[(Gdp_j/Gdp_h) - 1]^2$) show no evidence of the HME.

We now perform two additional robustness checks using Hanson and Xiang's sample of nonzero trade only and the single-difference gravity specification without a constant. The single-difference gravity specification is the following:

$$\ln\left(S_{djk}/S_{dhk}\right) = \beta f\left(Gdp_j/Gdp_h\right) + \varphi\left(X_j - X_h\right) + \theta \ln\left(d_{jk}/d_{hk}\right) + \varepsilon_{mojhk} \quad (7)$$

where d denotes either a treatment (m) or a control (o) industry. First, we estimate the single-difference gravity Eq. (7) for each of the 21 treatment and 13 control industries. The results, which are reported in Table 6 and correspond to Table 4 in Hanson and Xiang, show that the average coefficient on exporter GDP for treatment industries and for the control industries is 1.06 and 1.04, respectively. The difference in these estimates between the treatment and control industries is insignificant. Thus, there is no

126 C.S. Pham et al. / International Review of Economics and Finance 30 (2014) 120–137

Table 2
Difference-in-difference gravity equation, pooled sample. Different configurations of country pairs.

Regressors	A		B		C		D		E	
	1	2	1	2	1	2	1	2	1	2
$\text{Ln}(Gdp_j/Gdp_h)$	0.189		0.429***		0.042		−0.093		−0.069	
	(0.42)		(3.20)		(0.32)		(−0.73)		(−0.70)	
$[\text{Ln}(Gdp_j/Gdp_h)]^2$	0.111									
	(0.75)									
$[\text{Ln}(Gdp_j/Gdp_h)]^2 * Config$	−0.169									
	(−0.59)									
$(Gdp_j/Gdp_h) - 1$		0.015		0.085***		−0.045		−0.072*		−0.052*
		(0.26)		(3.42)		(−1.10)		(−1.88)		(−1.84)
$[(Gdp_j/Gdp_h) - 1]^2$		−0.909*								
		(−1.91)								
$[(Gdp_j/Gdp_h) - 1]^2 * Config$		0.913*								
		(1.92)								
Distance	−0.271***	−0.261***	−0.274***	−0.265***	−0.326***	−0.324***	−0.315***	−0.310***	−0.262***	−.0257***
	(−4.97)	(−4.82)	(−5.07)	(−4.94)	(−6.26)	(−6.33)	(−6.35)	(−6.42)	(−6.44)	(−6.50)
Common language	−0.416***	−0.375***	−0.421***	−0.376***	−0.508***	−0.486***	−0.504***	−0.481***	−0.446***	−0.424***
	(−3.33)	(−2.93)	(−3.31)	(−3.04)	(−3.74)	(−3.73)	(−3.73)	(−3.95)	(−3.74)	(−3.74)
Common border	0.889***	0.863***	0.893***	0.839***	0.949***	0.907***	0.854***	0.808***	0.631***	0.593***
	(10.3)	(9.91)	(10.13)	(9.39)	(10.19)	(9.38)	(9.35)	(8.64)	(8.52)	(7.83)
Capital/worker	1.669***	1.620***	1.700***	1.733***	2.476***	2.498***	2.481***	2.412***	1.934***	1.862***
	(4.35)	(4.34)	(4.70)	(4.45)	(5.88)	(5.93)	(5.85)	(5.92)	(5.63)	(5.64)
Wage	−1.891***	−1.815***	−1.901***	−1.785***	−1.822***	−1.756***	−1.631***	−1.582***	−1.330***	−1.292***
	(−8.23)	(−7.79)	(−8.39)	(−7.91)	(−6.50)	(−6.23)	(−5.42)	(−5.47)	(−5.35)	(−5.48)
Area/population	0.256***	0.235**	0.242**	0.213**	−0.0002	−0.049	−0.075	−0.103	−0.05	−0.065
	(2.51)	(2.24)	(2.29)	(2.39)	(−0.00)	(−0.58)	(−0.92)	(−1.30)	(−0.78)	(−1.05)
Average education	−3.138***	−3.330***	−3.131***	−3.408***	−3.779***	−4.047***	−3.540***	−3.693***	−2.655***	−2.761***
	(−6.69)	(−8.07)	(−7.39)	(−8.66)	(−7.49)	(−7.53)	(−6.75)	(−6.73)	(−6.20)	(−6.28)
Constant	−0.178	−0.264	−0.211	−0.059	0.549***	0.524***	1.203***	1.217***	1.902***	1.882***
	(−0.66)	(−1.37)	(−1.28)	(−0.43)	(2.77)	(3.05)	(6.04)	(7.44)	(11.71)	(14.27)
Constant * Config	−0.149	0.391*	0.037	−0.453*	0.367	0.627*	0.523	1.217***	0.519	0.627***
	(−0.39)	(1.67)	(0.15)	(−1.88)	(1.01)	(2.01)	(1.32)	(7.44)	(1.57)	(2.37)
R-squared	0.07	0.07	0.07	0.06	0.06	0.07	0.06	0.07	0.05	0.05
No of obs.	1,396,395	1,396,395	1,396,395	1,396,395	1,396,395	1,396,395	1,396,395	1,396,395	1,396,395	1,396,395

Notes: (1) This table replicates the estimation in Table 5 of Hanson and Xiang (2004), using their sample and estimation method. However, rather than eliminating redundant country-pair observations randomly, we configure country pairs in five different ways. In cases A and B those observations for which $Gdp_j < Gdp_h$ are eliminated. In case C those observations for which the denominator in the dependent variable is greater than the numerator are eliminated. In case D only 25% of those observations that are randomly chosen and for which the denominator is greater than the numerator in the dependent variable are eliminated. Finally in case E 50% of those observations that are chosen randomly and for which the denominator in the dependent variable is greater than the numerator are eliminated.

(2) The dependent variable is, for a pair of countries, log relative exports in a treatment industry minus log relative exports in a control industry. Each regression includes dummy variables for the industry match. Other variables are expressed as differences or log differences for a country pair.

(3) T-statistics or z-statistics are given in parentheses and are calculated from standard errors that have been adjusted for correlation of errors across observations that share the same pair of exporting countries. *, ** and *** denotes 10%, 5% and 1% level of significance, respectively.

evidence of the HME as Hanson and Xiang found when using sample of both non zero and zero trade flows. Second, we estimate single-difference gravity Eq. (8) for each of 273 (21 ∗ 13) treatment and control industry pairs:

$$\ln\left(S_{mjk}/S_{ohk}\right) = \beta f\left(Gdp_j/Gdp_h\right) + \varphi\left(X_j - X_h\right) + \theta \ln\left(d_{jk}/d_{hk}\right) + \varepsilon_{mojhk}. \tag{8}$$

For comparative purpose Table 7 presents in columns 2 and 3 the regression results in Hanson and Xiang (i.e. Table 7 in their study) and the estimates of gravity Eq. (8) in columns 4 and 5. Importantly, the coefficient on relative exporter GDP is found to be

Table 3
HME estimates under different random configurations of exporter pairs.

Hanson and Xiang's full sample				
Form of the independent variable	Mean	Std. dev.	Minimum	Maximum
$\log(Gdp_j/Gdp_h)$	0.348	0.000039	0.3479	0.3481
$(Gdp_j/Gdp_h) - 1$	0.0741	0.00035	0.0729	0.0755

Notes: (1) Data in base configuration 1 are obtained using the following steps.
Step 1: Starting with the exact sample used by Hanson and Xiang we generate a random variable x_1. Step 2: For those observations for which values of x_1 falling into its top 50% percentile we reverse the order of countries in the pair while keeping the other observations unchanged. Step 3: We repeat step 2 100 times.
(2) Table 3 reports the mean and the standard deviation of the HME estimates after 1000 runs. In each run a random x_1 variable is generated.

C.S. Pham et al. / International Review of Economics and Finance 30 (2014) 120–137   127

Table 4
Presence of zero trade values in Hanson and Xiang's sample.

	The dependent variable	Percentage	No. of observations
	Standard gravity		
Zero trade	Exp_{jk}	35.90%	11,086
Positive trade		64.10%	19,820
Total		100.00%	30,906
	Single-difference gravity		
Zero trade for one component of the dependent variable	Exp_{jk}/Exp_{lk}	30.70%	53,425
Zero trade for both components of the dependent variable		15.20%	26,447
Positive trade for both components of the dependent variable		54.10%	94,038
Total		100.00%	173,910
	Difference-in-difference gravity		
Zero trade for one component of the dependent variable	$(Exp_{mjk}/Exp_{ojk})/(Exp_{mlk}/Exp_{olk})$	23.00%	320,908
Zero trade for two components of the dependent variable		23.10%	321,806
Zero trade for three components of the dependent variable		11.10%	154,325
Zero trade for all four components of the dependent variable		5.20%	72,303
Positive trade for four components of the dependent variable		37.70%	527,053
Total			1,396,395

Notes: (1) In the data used by Hanson and Xiang, there are 107 exporter pairs and 56 importers (i.e. 58 importers minus 2) observed for 34 industries (i.e. 13 control and 21 treatment industries). Thus the total number of *possible* observations is 203,728 (i.e. 107 • 56 • 34) in the single-difference gravity equation and 1,635,816 (i.e. 107 • 56 • 21 • 13) in the difference-in-difference gravity equation. Table 4 only reports the percentage of zero trade flows in the sample of 21 treatment and 13 control industries for which data on the independent variables are available.
(2) In the formulas of the dependent variable *j*, *l* and *k* denote the exporting countries and importing destination while *m* and *o* denote the industries of treatment and control groups, respectively.

positive in only 147 (53.8%) of the cases, which is roughly equal to the probability of obtaining a head when flipping a coin. When it is positive it is statistically significant at 10% for only 20.9% of the cases. On contrary to Hanson and Xiang there is no evidence that the HME is strongest for the matches of more restrictive and control industries and weakest for matches involving less

Table 5
Difference-in-difference gravity regression – sample of non-zero trade values.

Regressors	A		B		C	
	1	2	1	2	1	2
$Ln(Gdp_j/Gdp_h)$	0.107		0.163*		0.054	
	(1.25)		(1.67)		(0.77)	
$(Gdp_j/Gdp_h) - 1$		0.034		0.014		0.008
		(1.08)		(0.51)		(0.34)
Distance	−0.059	−0.058	−0.066	−0.066	−0.063	−0.062
	(−0.96)	(−0.95)	(−1.09)	(−1.08)	(−1.03)	(−1.02)
Common language	−0.271***	−0.258***	−0.269***	−0.251***	−0.271***	−0.259***
	(−2.52)	(−2.44)	(−2.52)	(−2.34)	(−2.52)	(−2.42)
Common border	0.721***	0.708***	0.709***	0.678***	0.727***	0.711***
	(8.12)	(7.88)	(8.02)	(7.32)	(8.08)	(7.54)
Capital/worker	1.153***	1.131***	1.354***	1.321***	1.303***	1.309***
	(3.87)	(3.68)	(5.03)	(4.82)	(4.42)	(4.37)
Wage in low-skill industries	−1.234***	−1.198***	−1.215***	−1.149***	−1.211***	−1.179***
	(−6.05)	(−6.20)	(−6.51)	(−6.27)	(−6.07)	(−6.23)
Area/population	0.367***	0.359***	0.312***	0.289***	0.323***	0.305***
	(6.05)	(6.04)	(6.33)	(5.89)	(6.77)	(6.45)
Average education	−2.630***	−2.651***	−2.711***	−2.871***	−2.787***	−2.861***
	(−6.41)	(−6.65)	(−7.88)	(−8.41)	(−7.69)	(−8.31)
Constant	−0.131	−0.174	−0.209*	−0.078	No	No
	(−1.31)	(−1.45)	(−1.82)	(−0.79)		
R-squared	0.10	0.10	0.10	0.10	0.078	0.079
No of obs.	527,053	527,053	527,053	527,053	527,053	527,053

Notes: (1) This table shows estimation results from Hanson and Xiang's preferred specification, when we drop observations for which one element of the dependent variable is zero. See notes to Table 1 for estimation details. A denotes cases when the sample is chosen by eliminating redundant pairs randomly. B denotes cases when the sample is chosen by retaining country pairs such that the GDP of the country in the numerator is greater than the GDP of the country in the denominator.
(2) Case C shows estimation results from Hanson and Xiang's difference-in-difference gravity specification when we drop observations for which one element of the dependent variable is zero *and* the regression does not include a constant. Please note that without a constant the estimates remain the same independently of the way country pairs are configured.
(3) The results are essentially the same when we include a squared term (i.e. $[Ln(Gdp_j/Gdp_h)]^2$ or $[(Gdp_j/Gdp_h) - 1]^2$) in the single-difference gravity regression. These results are available from the authors upon request.
(4) T-statistics or z-statistics are given in parentheses and are calculated from standard errors that have been adjusted for correlation of errors across observations that share the same pair of exporting countries. *, ** and *** denotes 10%, 5% and 1% level of significance, respectively.

128   C.S. Pham et al. / International Review of Economics and Finance 30 (2014) 120–137

Table 6
Single-difference gravity estimates – sample of non-zero trade.

Low-transport industries		High-transport industries			
SITC	Relative GDP	SITC	Relative GDP	SITC	Relative GDP
541	0.729	671	1.251	677	1.181
	(9.35)		(8.37)		(8.61)
752	1.15	621	1.138	672	0.934
	(11.24)		(12.81)		(6.31)
761	0.989	674	1.624	635	0.839
	(9.61)		(15.7)		(15.38)
884	0.711	679	1.046	673	1.239
	(4.27)		(14.37)		(17.09)
764	1.139	665	1.042	821	1.15
	(13.67)		(14.04)		(20.6)
762	0.841	663	0.946	634	0.787
	(7.89)		(9.89)		(8.79)
759	0.902	666	1.265	661	0.516
	(7.40)		(26.49)		(4.66)
514	0.894	678	1.528	662	1.021
	(10.10)		(19.5)		(11.21)
881	1.072	642	1.006		
	(16.06)		(15.25)		
751	0.866	812	1.039		
	(6.57)		(19.93)		
882	1.453	625	0.956		
	(11.10)		(14.6)		
885	1.451	676	0.578		
	(22.77)		(4.48)		
726	1.382	641	1.258		
	(19.43)		(9.09)		

Notes: These are the OLS estimates of the HME by industry using truncated sample of nonzero trade flows when the OLS estimator does not include a constant. The average coefficient on exporter GDP is 1.04 and 1.06 for the control and treatment industries, respectively.

restrictive treatment and control industries. Overall, there is no evidence of the HME when we use Hanson and Xiang's nonzero sample and apply the single-difference gravity equation without a constant.

We now look into how the HME estimates of the sample of nonzero bilateral trade flows vary when country pairs are randomly reconfigured 1000 times. We apply the same method of random reconfiguration as in Section 1. The results of the HME estimates are presented in Table 8 and show that when the HME variable is $Log(Gdp_j/Gdp_h)$ and $(Gdp_j/Gdp_h) - 1$ the mean of the HME estimates from 1000 runs is 0.054 and 0.029, respectively. Thus, while the HME evidence is found its magnitude is small and 80% lower than the HME evidence we previously obtained using Hanson and Xiang's full sample (i.e. Table 3). In sum, observations of zero trade flows clearly are behind the results of the HME when country pairs are randomly reconfigured 1000 times and the mean of the HME of these 1000 runs is computed.

We now investigate the extent to which the HME evidence, when it is found, differs by groups of exporter pairs. Theoretically, the HME is increasing in the size of the exporting country. Consequently, we expect to find a strong evidence of the HME for the pairs of countries that differ substantially in their GDP. Yet, countries that differ substantially in their GDP may also differ substantially in unobservable factors that correlate with relative GDPs of exporter pairs, which may bias the results. Four our purpose we define three groups of country pairs: low GDP–low GDP group, low GDP–high GDP group and high GDP–high GDP group. The following countries are classified as countries of high GDP: Australia, France, Germany, UK, Italy, the Netherlands,

Table 7
Summary of industry-by-industry regression results.

		Hanson and Xiang's results		Results of gravity specification without a constant	
		Share of regression with		Share of regression with	
	Number of cases	$\beta > 0$	p-Value < 0.1	$\beta > 0$	p-Value < 0.1
All industry matches	273	0.875	0.582	0.538	0.209
More restrictive treatment – More restrictive control	54	1.000	0.741	0.648	0.296
Less restrictive treatment – More restrictive control	72	0.986	0.75	0.681	0.292
More restrictive treatment – Less restrictive control	63	0.762	0.46	0.413	0.159
Less restrictive treatment – Less restrictive control	84	0.726	0.429	0.440	0.119

Notes: (1) As in Hanson and Xiang the list of more restrictive treatment 3-digit industries is 666, 678, 625, 676, 677, 672, 673, 661 and 662. The list of more restrictive control 3-digit control industries is 541, 752, 761, 764, 762 and 759.

C.S. Pham et al. / International Review of Economics and Finance 30 (2014) 120–137   129

Table 8
HME estimates under 1000 different random configurations of exporter pairs.

Hanson and Xiang's sample of nonzero trade flows

Form of the independent variable	Mean	Std. dev.	Minimum	Maximum
$\log(Gdp_j/Gdp_h)$	0.0544	0.00074	0.0542	0.0546
$(Gdp_j/Gdp_h) - 1$	0.0296	0.00082	0.0275	0.0317

Notes: (1) Data in base configuration 1 are obtained using the following steps.
Step 1: Starting with the exact sample used by Hanson and Xiang we generate a random variable x_1. Step 2: For those observations for which values of x_1 falling into its top 50% percentile we reverse the order of countries in the pair while keeping the other observations unchanged. Step 3: we repeat step 2 100 times. Table 3 reports the mean and the standard deviation of the HME estimates after 1000 runs. In each run a random x_1 variable is generated.

Spain, US and Canada. The other countries are considered to be low GDP economies. A pair consisting of a low GDP exporter and a high GDP exporter, two low GDP exporters and two high GDP exporters belongs to the low GDP–high GDP group, low GDP–low GDP group and high GDP–high GDP group, respectively.

The HME estimates from 1000 runs for each group of exporters are presented in Table 9. When we use Hanson and Xiang's full sample the means of HME coefficient estimates for the low GDP–low GDP group, low GDP–high GDP and high GDP–high GDP are found to be 0.842, 0.268 and 0.082, respectively. When only the nonzero sample is used the means of HME estimates for the three groups are 0.279, 0.032 and −0.107, respectively. The results clearly suggest that the inclusion of zero trade flows accounts for the significant HME evidence when the full sample of data is used. The results also run counter to our prediction that the HME evidence must be largest for the low GDP–high GDP group.

In order to preserve information on zero trade flows, Hanson and Xiang assume countries with zero bilateral imports of a good actually import minute quantities (see footnote 16 in Hanson and Xiang). As a common practice in studies using the gravity equation (Eichengreen and Irwin (1995, 1997), Felbermayr and Kohler (2006, 2007) and Lederman and Ozden (2007)), Hanson and Xiang impute a value of 1 for these observations. The evident dilemma of this strategy is that there is no guidance on what value the researcher should impute to a zero trade flow. Since the only purpose of setting zero trade flows to a positive value is to allow the dependent variable to be defined once it is expressed as a natural log, it is clear that any positive number can do the job. As innocent as adding a one may seem, this choice makes a substantial difference when applied to the difference-in-difference approach. Seemingly small differences in imputed values result in largely different values for the dependent variable when one or more components of the dependent variable are zero. For example, $Ln\left(\frac{S_{jk}}{S_{hk}+1}\right)$ is much smaller than $Ln\left(\frac{S_{jk}}{S_{hk}+0.000001}\right)$ when $S_{jk} \neq 0$ and $S_{hk} = 0$.

Using Hanson and Xiang's data and specification, we find that evidence of the HME is indeed sensitive to the value imputed to zero flows. The coefficient estimate for $Ln(Gdp_j/Gdp_h)$ is found to be decreasing in the imputed values. Specifically, it increases from 0.420 to 1.451 as the imputed value decreases from 1 to $1^{(-7)}$. Moreover as the imputed value gets closer to zero, the estimated coefficient for $Ln(Gdp_j/Gdp_h)$ shows no sign of converging to a certain value.[11]

It is possible that the sensitivity of the estimates in the single-difference and difference-in-difference gravity equation is specific to the data used. To investigate this possibility, we employ Monte-Carlo simulations to see if the sensitivity in the Hanson and Xiang estimation applies to different data samples. Specifically, we simulate data for exports of 50 countries to 51 destinations with zero trade flows being generated based on the Heckman sample selection model as follows[12]:

$$y_{1jk}^* = \exp\left(x_{1j} + x_{2jk}\right) * \eta_{jk} = \exp\left(x_{1j} + x_{2jk}\right) + \varepsilon_{1jk} \tag{9}$$

$$y_{2jk}^* = \exp\left(x_{1j} + x_{2jk} + x_{3jk}\right) + \varepsilon_{2jk} \tag{10}$$

where $\varepsilon_{1jk} \equiv (\eta_{jk} - 1) * \exp(x_{1j} + x_{2jk})$, $\eta_{jk} \sim$ lognormal$(1, \exp(x_{1j} + x_{2jk}))$, $x_{1j} \sim N(0,1)$, $\varepsilon_{2jk} \sim N(0, 9)$, and Cov$(\varepsilon_{1jk}, \varepsilon_{2jk}) = 0.5$. x_{1j} is the continuous variable for a country's exporter specific while x_{2jk} and x_{3jk} are dummy variables which are exporter–importer specific – i.e. $x_{2jk} = x_{2kj}$ and $x_{3jk} = x_{3kj}$.[13] It is noteworthy that x_{3jk} is the exclusion restriction variable. The sample selection equation, Eq. (10), determines whether observations in the gravity equation, Eq. (9), are equal to zero or not:

$$y_{1jk} = y_{1jk}^* \quad \text{if} \quad y_{2jk}^* > 0 \quad \text{or} \tag{11}$$

---

[11] Regression results of the single-difference and difference-in-difference gravity equation with different imputed values for zero trade flows are not presented here but are available upon request from the authors.
[12] Helpman et al. (2008) provide a theoretical explanation for the existence of substantial and asymmetric zero trade flows observed in the aggregate trade data. In their model, zero trade flows occur when even the most productive firm of a country does not find it profitable to export to a destination because of exporter-importer specific trade costs.
[13] Recent studies (i.e. Santos and Tenreyro, 2006; Martin and Pham Cong, 2008) show that in the presence of heteroscedasticity the gravity equation yields substantial bias. Since our simulations are carried out in order to investigate how the regression results of the single-difference gravity equation are sensitive to the value imputed for zero flows, we set the variance of η_j such that there is no heteroscedasticity problem when the gravity equation (Eq. (5)) is estimated with the dependent variable in log form. Estimating the gravity equation with the dependent variable in log form is the most popular method in the literature. The sample selection equation (Eq. (6)) results in approximately 25% zero values in the dependent variable.

Table 9
HME estimates under 1000 random configurations of exporter pairs and by groups of exporters.

Group configuration	Sample	Percentage of zero obs.	No of obs.	Form of the independent variable	Mean	Std. dev.	Minimum	Maximum
Low GDP–Low GDP	H&X's full sample	78%	402,420	$\log(Y_j/Y_h)$	0.842	0.00045	0.8408	0.8441
Low GDP–Low GDP	H&X's full sample	78%	402,420	$(Y_j/Y_h) - 1$	0.249	0.0037	0.2364	0.2613
Low GDP–High GDP	H&X's full sample	66%	735,735	$\log(Y_j/Y_h)$	0.268	0.00007	0.2676	0.2681
Low GDP–High GDP	H&X's full sample	66%	735,735	$(Y_j/Y_h) - 1$	0.079	0.00066	0.0771	0.0812
High GDP–High GDP	H&X's full sample	35%	240,240	$\log(Y_j/Y_h)$	0.082	0.00023	0.0815	0.0829
High GDP–High GDP	H&X's full sample	35%	240,240	$(Y_j/Y_h) - 1$	0.029	0.002	0.0223	0.0345
Low GDP–Low GDP	H&X's nonzero sample	0%	102,813	$\log(Y_j/Y_h)$	0.279	0.0013	0.2748	0.2839
Low GDP–Low GDP	H&X's nonzero sample	0%	102,813	$(Y_j/Y_h) - 1$	0.122	0.0059	0.1035	0.1417
Low GDP–High GDP	H&X's nonzero sample	0%	268,394	$\log(Y_j/Y_h)$	0.0342	0.00015	0.0336	0.0347
Low GDP–High GDP	H&X's nonzero sample	0%	268,394	$(Y_j/Y_h) - 1$	0.0296	0.00079	0.0267	0.0318
High GDP–High GDP	H&X's nonzero sample	0%	155,846	$\log(Y_j/Y_h)$	−0.107	0.00027	−0.1079	−0.1061
High GDP–High GDP	H&X's nonzero sample	0%	155,846	$(Y_j/Y_h) - 1$	−0.0503	0.0017	−0.0561	−0.0449

Notes: (1) The following countries are considered to belong to the high-GDP group: Australia, France, Germany, UK, Italy, the Netherlands, Spain, US and Canada. The other countries are considered to belong to the low GDP group.

$$y_{1jk} = 0 \text{ if } y^*_{2jk} \leq 0 \tag{12}$$

Along the lines of Hanson and Xiang, we assume that 50 exporters belonging to the same FTA form 2500 exporting-country pairs for each of the 51 destinations. We simulate the data 10,000 times and estimate the following single-difference gravity equation:

$$\ln\left(\frac{y_{1jk}+a}{y_{1hk}+a}\right) = \beta_0 + \beta_1\left(x_{1j}-x_{1h}\right) + \beta_2\left(x_{2jk}-x_{2hk}\right) + \left(\varepsilon_{1jk}-\varepsilon_{1hk}\right) \tag{13}$$

where $j \neq h$. Different chosen values of a are 1, $1^{(-1)}$, $1^{(-3)}$, $1^{(-5)}$ and $1^{(-7)}$.[14] Simulation results, which are presented in Table 10, show that the single-differenced gravity regression yields estimates that are very sensitive to the value of a. The bias of the coefficient estimates of the gravity equation goes from −50% to +17% as the value chosen for a decreases. The bias is decreasing in the chosen value of a, which is consistent with the result we obtain using Hanson and Xiang's data. Importantly, there is no evidence of convergence in the estimates.

Another notable problem with single-differenced gravity estimation is that when the magnitude of the bias happens to be small (i.e. when a is set to 0.00001) the standard deviation of the Monte Carlo estimates is very large. A standard deviation of 0.1739, for example, means that the coefficient estimates of x_{1j} of the single-gravity equation vary from 47% below to 66% above the true value. These simulation results suggest that methods other than differencing may be better choices when working with a gravity specification. Other results reported in Table 9 show that the ET-Tobit estimator and the Heckman sample-selection estimator yield estimates with reasonably small bias and small standard deviation.

4. Investigating the home market effect: new methods

In this section we are to estimate the HME using methods that outperform in our simulations above the difference-in-difference estimator used by Hanson and Xiang. Our observation is that when the form of the dependent variable is double ratio – i.e. $\text{Ln}[((S_{mjk} + 1) / (S_{mhk} + 1)) / ((S_{ojk} + 1) / (S_{ohk} + 1))]$ – the percentage of observations for which at least one component of the dependent variable is a zero value is largest and represents 62.3% of the sample compared to 45.9% in case of the single-difference gravity specification. In order to have to deal with less zero observations we apply the truncated OLS, ET-Tobit, Heckman and Helpman–Melitz–Rubinstein estimators using a single-difference gravity specification.

First, we rely on the truncated OLS estimation of the gravity equation using the following specification:

$$\text{Ln}\left(\frac{S_{jkl}}{S_{hkl}}\right) = \alpha + \beta \ln\left(Gdp_j/Gdp_h\right) + \eta[\ln\left(Gdp_j/Gdp_l\right)] * Treatment_i + \varphi\left(X_j-X_h\right) + \theta \ln\left(d_{jk}/d_{hk}\right) + \varepsilon_{jhkl} \tag{14}$$

where $Treatment_i$ is equal to 1 if the industry i belongs to the treatment group and zero if it belongs to the control group, as defined by Hanson and Xiang.

Second, we rely on the threshold Tobit model, which is a standard strategy for dealing with zero trade values in the literature. This model was first introduced by Eaton and Tamura (1994) in gravity model estimation and later was adopted by numerous

---

[14] It is important to note that y_{1l} – the simulated dependent variable – has a mean and variance approximately equal to 2.5 and 6.1, respectively while the dependent variable in the actual data used by Hanson and Xiang has a mean and a variance equal approximately to 10,000 and 50,000, respectively.

Table 10
Monte Carlo simulations of single-difference gravity equation.

	Bias in the estimates of the single-difference gravity equation				
	$a = 1$	$a = 0.1$	$a = 0.001$	$a = 0.00001$	$a = 0.0000001$
x_1 (continuous variable)	−0.5778	−0.3285	−0.1186	0.0219	0.1687
	(0.0228)	(0.0457)	(0.1052)	(0.1739)	(0.2366)
x_2 (dummy variable)	−0.5414	−0.2918	−0.0898	0.0576	0.2114
	(0.0302)	(0.0678)	(0.1634)	(0.2632)	(0.3616)
	Truncated OLS		ET-Tobit	Heckman	
x_1 (continuous variable)	0.0928		0.0688	0.1350	
	(0.0286)		(0.0283)	(0.0379)	
x_2 (dummy variable)	0.0956		0.0488	0.1392	
	(0.0415)		(0.0438)	(0.0497)	

Notes: The standard deviation of the estimates is given in parentheses. The Truncated OLS estimator is OLS regression of the single-difference gravity equation using only non-zero trade flows. When the ET-Tobit estimator and the Heckman estimator are used to estimate the single-difference gravity equation, observations for which both the numerator and the denominator of the dependent variable are zero are dropped from the regression.

studies using the gravity equation such as Head and Ries (1998), Trindade and Rauch (2002) and Dalgin, Trindade and Mitra (2007). Specifically, we estimate the following:

$$\ln\left(\frac{S_{jkl}}{S_{hkl}} + v\right) = Max[\alpha + \beta \ln\left(Gdp_j/Gdp_h\right) + \eta[\ln\left(Gdp_j/Gdp_l\right)] * Treatment_l + \varphi\left(X_j - X_h\right) + \theta \ln\left(d_{jk}/d_{hk}\right) + \varepsilon_{jhkl}, \ln(v)].$$

(15)

In Eq. (11) we estimate jointly the threshold v, η and other coefficients in the single-difference gravity equation by maximum likelihood. The ET-Tobit specification (11) has an added advantage over the difference-in-difference gravity used by Hanson and Xiang. Since v is estimated jointly we do not face the difficult task of justifying the value of a imputed to zero observations.[15]

Our third strategy is a Heckman-style estimation of the gravity equation, as used in Helpman, Melitz, and Rubinstein (2008) and in Lederman and Ozden (2007). Specifically we estimate the following gravity equation:

$$\ln\left(\frac{S_{jkl}}{S_{hkl}}\right) = \alpha + \beta \ln\left(Gdp_j/Gdp_h\right) + \eta\left[\ln\left(Gdp_j/Gdp_l\right)\right] * Treatment_l + \varphi\left(X'_j - X'_h\right) + \theta \ln\left(d_{jk}/d_{hk}\right) + \varepsilon_{jhkl}.$$

(16)

Whether the dependent variable of gravity Eq. (16) is equal to zero depends on the sample selection Probit equation:

$$\Pr\left(\frac{S_{jkl}}{S_{hkl}} > 0 | \Theta\right) = \Phi\{\left(\alpha + \beta \ln\left(Gdp_j/Gdp_h\right) + \eta[\ln\left(Gdp_j/Gdp_l\right)] * Treatment_l + \varphi\left(X_j - X_h\right) + \theta \ln\left(d_{jk}/d_{hk}\right)\right\}$$

(17)

where Θ stands for the set of observed variables and Φ is the c.d.f. of the unit-normal distribution.[16]

Finally, we also estimate the single-difference gravity a la Helpman et al. (2008). Specifically, the econometric specification is:

$$\ln\left(S_{jkl}/S_{hkl}\right) = \alpha + \beta f\left(Gdp_j/Gdp_h\right) + \eta[\ln\left(Gdp_j/Gdp_h\right)] * Treatment_l + \varphi\left(X'_j - X'_h\right) + \theta \ln\left(d_{jk}/d_{hk}\right)$$
$$+ \rho\left(\frac{InverseMill_{jk}}{InverseMill_{hk}}\right) + \mu(Z) + \delta\left(Z^3\right) + \varepsilon_{jhkl}$$

(18)

where *InverseMill* and Z, which are obtained from standard gravity equations, control for sample selection bias and firm heterogeneity, respectively.[17]

It is noteworthy to emphasize that we apply regressions (15), (16), (17) and (18) in three different ways: with a constant (i.e. α), without a constant, and with a constant that varies depending on whether the numerator of the independent variable of

---

[15] For Eqs. (15), (16) and (17) when both $S_{jkl} = S_{hkl} = 0$ the dependent variable is not defined and consequently the corresponding observations are excluded from the sample. When either S_{hkl} or S_{jkl} is equal to zero the dependent variable is created with the numerator being less than the denominator. We also follow this approach for our Heckman-style regressions.

[16] Vector $(X_j - X_h)$ of the probit equation is different from vector $(X'_j - X'_h)$ of gravity Eq. (16) by the exclusion restriction, which is chosen to be the level difference in the dummy for *common language*. This method is applied by Helpman et al. (2008).

[17] Specifically, following Helpman, Melitz and Rubinstein we first estimate the Probit equation predicting whether or not country j (h) and country k have trade with each other. From the Probit equation estimates we obtain $\hat{p}_{jk}(\hat{p}_{hk})$ the predicted probability of exports from $j(h)$ to k. For exporter j and importer k, the inverse Mills ratio is equal to $\hat{v}^*_{jk} \equiv \phi\left(\hat{z}^*_{jk}\right)/\Phi\left(\hat{z}^*_{jk}\right)$ where ϕ and Φ denote the density and the c.d.f. of the of the unit-normal distribution, respectively and $\hat{z}^*_{jk} = \Phi^{-1}\left(\hat{p}_{jk}\right)$. The variable controlling for firm heterogeneity is defined as $z_{jk} \equiv \hat{v}^*_{jk} + \hat{z}^*_{jk}$. These formulas similarly apply to exporter h and importer k. Finally we define Z in single-difference gravity (14) as follows: $z = z_{jk}/z_{hk}$.

Table 11
Difference-in-difference gravity equation, various methods, Hanson and Xiang sample.

Regressors	Truncated OLS			ET-Tobit		
	1	2	3	1	2	3
Ln(Gdp$_j$/Gdp$_h$)	1.046***	0.984***	1.045***	1.324***	1.338***	1.245***
	(14.44)	(10.85)	(15.08)	(5.38)	(6.46)	(15.06)
[Ln(Gdp$_j$/Gdp$_h$)] ∗ Treatment$_t$	−0.010	−0.032	−0.030	−0.037	0.034	0.044
	(−0.13)	(−0.43)	(−0.39)	(−0.39)	(0.30)	(0.43)
Distance	−1.270***	−1.268***	−1.271***	−1.384***	−1.250***	−1.264***
	(−24.47)	(−24.57)	(−24.48)	(−14.17)	(−12.59)	(−15.63)
Common language	0.897***	0.983***	0.898***	1.434***	0.959***	0.896***
	(15.54)	(15.45)	(15.51)	(3.73)	(7.74)	(10.22)
Common border	0.399***	0.398***	0.404***	0.0911	0.386**	0.388***
	(5.51)	(5.57)	(5.62)	(0.41)	(4.86)	(4.72)
Capital/worker	0.727***	0.719***	0.762***	1.382***	0.418	0.563***
	(4.41)	(4.32)	(4.77)	(2.55)	(1.48)	(2.54)
Wage in low-skill industries	0.197	0.201	0.197	0.569	0.121	0.194
	(1.26)	(1.29)	(1.26)	(1.50)	(0.56)	(0.86)
Area/population	−0.170***	−0.165***	−0.177***	−0.058	−1.249***	−1.264***
	(−4.44)	(−4.16)	(−4.66)	(−0.57)	(−12.59)	(−15.63)
Average education	0.956***	0.883***	0.907***	0.386	1.715***	1.361***
	(3.42)	(3.15)	(3.10)	(0.85)	(3.46)	(3.70)
Constant	−0.022	0.110	No	0.101	−0.369	No
	(−0.37)	(0.92)		(1.12)	(−1.06)	
Constant ∗ Config	No	−0.234	No	No	0.101	No
		(−1.27)			(0.32)	
R^2	0.47	0.46	0.46	–	–	–
No of obs.	94,038	94,038	94,038	147,463	147,463	147,463

Notes: (1) It is important to point out that in Table 9 when the regression includes a constant it also includes, as in Hanson and Xiang, industry-pair dummies. When the regression does not include a constant we also exclude industry-pair dummies.
(2) T-statistics or z-statistics given in parentheses, calculated with adjustment for clustering on exporter pairs. *, ** and *** denotes 10%, 5% and 1% level of significance, respectively.

interest (GDP$_j$) is greater or smaller than the denominator (GDP$_h$). In these regressions we expect the estimated coefficient for η to be positive if there is evidence of the HME. Results of the truncated OLS and the Eaton–Tamura Tobit are presented in Table 11 while the results of the Heckman and Helpman, Melitz and Rubinstein regressions are presented in Table 12. In all cases, the coefficient estimates for η are negative, and in one case, negative and statistically significant. Thus, alternative estimators for the gravity equation, which yield relatively small bias and standard deviation in Monte Carlo simulations, provide no evidence of the HME.[18]

5. Investigating the home-market effect using Canada–US data

In this section we investigate the home-market effect using data on exports of manufactures from the Canadian provinces to the U.S. states.[19] Given our above findings, it is important to investigate whether the home-market effect operates at smaller units, such as the Canadian provinces. In our specific context, it is useful to note some additional advantages of using this dataset. First, the clustering of economic activity in Canada is substantial and well documented in the literature. This phenomenon is believed to be caused, among other factors, by the home-market effect. Thus, we look for the evidence of the HME not as an ad-hoc statistical practice but because there is strong evidence of economic clustering in Canadian provinces. Second, observation units within a country like Canadian provinces are ideal data in the difference-in-difference gravity specification, which requires we only match exporters similar in terms of production costs and other determinants of relative exports. As in Section 4, we estimate the HME using truncated OLS, ET-Tobit, Heckman and HMR estimators.

The results, which are presented in Tables 13 and 14, show no evidence of the HME in all specifications. In no cases the HME coefficient is found to be of positive sign. In most cases the HME coefficient is negative and statistically significant at 1% level. Thus, larger Canadian provinces are not found to export more in industries characterized by high level of product differentiation and high transport cost. Since different datasets might reveal different trade patterns, we need to be careful about interpreting the

---

[18] While not presented the regression results of specifications (15), (16), (17) and (18) in which we interact the *Treatment* dummy with all other explanatory variables yield essentially the same results about the HME.
[19] The export data of Canadian provinces are available from Canada's Business and Consumer Site created and maintained by Industry Canada: http://strategis.ic. gc.ca/sc_mrkti/tdst/engdoc/tr_homep.html. Specifically, they are data on exports of Canadian provinces to U.S. states from 1994 to 2003 in 50 HS four-digit classifications associated with 10 SITC 2 classifications (661, 662, 626, 664, 666, 652, 672, 674, 678, and 676) of the treatment group and in 20 HS four-digit classifications associated with 9 SITC 2 classifications (541, 542, 516, 751, 759, 761, 764, 726, and 881). It is useful to note that the United States absorbs more than 80% of total Canadian exports. Data on other characteristics of Canadian provinces are available from Canadian Socio-Economic Information Management System (CANSIM) database. Specifically, we use data on average hourly earnings in manufacturing for employees paid by hour, educational attainment of Canadian provinces, and fixed residential capital stock from CANSIM's Table 281-0029, Table 282-0004, and Table 030-0002 respectively.

C.S. Pham et al. / International Review of Economics and Finance 30 (2014) 120–137   133

Table 12
Difference-in-difference gravity equation, various methods, Hanson and Xiang sample.

Regressors	Heckman			Helpman–Melitz–Rubinstein		
	1	2	3	1	2	3
$Ln(Gdp_j/Gdp_h)$	0.980***	0.929***	1.064***	0.557***	0.486***	1.070***
	(12.97)	(9.86)	(14.56)	(6.21)	(4.67)	(15.07)
$[Ln(Gdp_j/Gdp_h)]$ * $Treatment_t$	−0.168**	−0.171**	−0.024	−0.023	−0.026	−0.023
	(−2.01)	(−2.05)	(−0.31)	(−0.30)	(−0.34)	(−0.30)
Distance	−1.221***	−1.220***	−1.363***	−1.002***	−1.001***	−1.336***
	(−22.81)	(−20.17)	(−27.27)	(−17.86)	(−18.09)	(−25.94)
Common language						
Common border	0.454***	0.452***	0.622***	0.278***	0.278***	0.594***
	(6.04)	(6.06)	(9.09)	(3.72)	(3.67)	(8.83)
Capital/worker	0.446***	0.436	0.620***	0.590***	0.567***	0.493***
	(2.59)	(0.70)	(3.68)	(3.25)	(3.09)	(2.80)
Wage in low-skill industries	0.103	0.110	0.123	−0.136	−0.125	0.097
	(0.65)	(0.69)	(0.75)	(−0.90)	(−0.83)	(0.59)
Area/population	−0.202***	−0.200***	−0.153***	−1.059	−0.057	−0.117***
	(−4.75)	(−4.54)	(−4.02)	(−1.64)	(−1.49)	(−2.83)
Average education	0.361	0.321	0.983***	0.316	0.261	1.053***
	(1.14)	(1.01)	(3.31)	(1.15)	(0.97)	(3.52)
Constant	−0.571***	−0.472***	No	2.007***	2.132***	No
	(−4.15)	(−2.53)		(7.73)	(7.98)	
Constant * Config	No	−0.184	No	No	−0.253	No
		(−0.95)			(−1.60)	
Inverse Mill's ratio				−3.8e−06***	−3.7e−06***	−3.47e−07
				(−3.05)	(−3.05)	(−0.33)
Z				−1.856***	−1.836***	−0.73
				(−7.95)	(−8.15)	(−1.31)
Z^3				0.05***	0.049***	−0.002
				(5.47)	(5.38)	(−0.18)
R^2	–	–	–	–	–	–
No of obs.	147,463	147,463	147,463	147,463	147,463	147,463

Notes: (1) T-statistics or z-statistics given in parentheses, calculated with adjustment for clustering on exporter pairs. *, ** and ** denotes 10%, 5% and 1% level of significance, respectively.

Table 13
Difference-in-difference gravity equation, various methods, sample of Canadian provinces' exports to the U.S. states.

Regressors	Truncated OLS			ET-Tobit		
	1	2	3	1	2	3
$Ln(Gdp_j/Gdp_h)$	1.675***	1.596***	1.671***	1.129***	1.252***	1.810***
	(23.27)	(19.91)	(23.22)	(14.26)	(14.93)	(27.81)
$[Ln(Gdp_j/Gdp_h)]$ * $Treatment_t$	−0.887***	−0.884***	−0.890***	−0.129***	−0.052	−0.616***
	(−22.29)	(−22.13)	(−22.47)	(−4.06)	(−1.48)	(−25.08)
Distance	−0.469***	−0.464***	−0.473***	−1.124***	−1.132***	−0.842***
	(−10.87)	(−10.75)	(−10.97)	(−21.70)	(−21.44)	(−23.34)
Common language	0.839***	0.820***	0.834***	−2.346***	−2.233***	−1.012***
	(6.05)	(5.93)	(6.02)	(−14.55)	(−14.09)	(−8.85)
Common border	0.698***	0.704***	0.693***	0.263***	0.280**	0.370***
	(7.32)	(7.38)	(7.29)	(2.38)	(2.48)	(4.95)
Capital/worker	−1.464***	−1.232***	−1.910***	−8.538***	−8.245***	−0.754***
	(−4.73)	(−3.63)	(−7.78)	(−27.84)	(−25.86)	(−3.95)
Wage in low-skill industries	−6.590***	−6.764***	−7.029***	−1.616	−1.368	1.103
	(−6.67)	(−6.56)	(−7.16)	(−1.49)	(−1.23)	(1.40)
Area/population	−0.590***	−0.549***	−0.705***	−1.788***	−1.699***	−0.005
	(−8.27)	(−7.26)	(−13.27)	(−27.85)	(−25.06)	(−0.12)
Average education	4.618***	4.551***	4.878***	10.644***	10.594***	3.830***
	(7.57)	(7.41)	(8.14)	(17.60)	(17.18)	(9.02)
Constant	0.130**	0.024	No	−4.152***	−3.689***	No
	(2.44)	(0.35)		(−50.11)	(−34.31)	
Constant * Config	No	0.286**	No	No	−0.781***	No
		(2.15)			(−6.75)	
R^2	0.45	0.45	0.45			
No of Obs.	7221	7221	7221	44,196	44,196	44,196

Notes: (1) T-statistics or z-statistics given in parentheses, calculated with adjustment for clustering on exporter pairs. *, ** and ** denotes 10%, 5% and 1% level of significance, respectively.

134   *C.S. Pham et al. / International Review of Economics and Finance 30 (2014) 120–137*

Table 14
Difference-in-difference gravity equation, various methods, sample of Canadian provinces' exports to the U.S. states.

Regressors	Heckman			Helpman–Melitz–Rubinstein		
	1	2	3	1	2	3
$Ln(Gdp_j/Gdp_h)$	1.936***	1.805***	2.071***	1280***	1.181***	1.541***
	(23.41)	(18.72)	(27.00)	(13.17)	(10.91)	(17.16)
$[Ln(Gdp_j/Gdp_h)] \cdot Treatment_i$	−0.831***	−0.832***	−0.819***	−0.689***	−0.689***	−0.731***
	(−20.28)	(−20.31)	(−20.23)	(−15.62)	(−15.62)	(−16.78)
Distance	−0.495***	−0.491***	−0.552***	−0.129**	−0.133***	−0.338***
	(−10.67)	(−10.59)	(−11.87)	(−2.25)	(−2.33)	(−6.90)
Common language						
Common border	0.732***	0.745***	0.751***	0.116	0.130	0.446***
	(7.45)	(7.57)	(7.62)	(1.03)	(1.17)	(4.40)
Capital/worker	1.834***	1.832***	1.661***	0.613***	0.646***	1.395***
	(8.09)	(8.09)	(7.64)	(2.45)	(2.58)	(5.98)
Wage in low-skill industries	−2.664***	−2.907***	2.757***	0.103	−0.134	−1.519***
	(−4.50)	(−4.86)	(9.52)	(1.03)	(−0.21)	(−2.54)
Area/population	0.245***	0.220***	0.210***	0.196***	0.175***	0.219***
	(4.23)	(3.74)	(11.97)	(3.38)	(2.99)	(3.75)
Average education	−1.987***	−1.333	−3.616***	−2.731***	−2.204***	−1.097
	(−2.36)	(−1.52)	(−14.38)	(−3.35)	(−2.64)	(−1.40)
Constant	0.273***	0.132*	No	−1.325***	−1.389***	No
	(4.60)	(1.65)		(−7.33)	(−7.51)	
Constant • Config	No	0.340**	No	No	0.277*	No
Inverse Mill's ratio		(2.65)			(2.08)	
z				−0.024***	−0.025***	−0.009
				(−3.26)	(−.342)	(−1.40)
				1.535***	1.494***	0.523***
z^3				(10.31)	(10.06)	(11.27)
				−0.076***	−0.075***	−0.094***
				(−5.11)	(−5.00)	(−6.36)
R^2	–	–	–	–	–	–
No of obs.	43,521	43,521	43,521	43,521	43,521	43,521

Notes: (1) T-statistics or z-statistics given in parentheses, calculated with adjustment for clustering on exporter pairs. *, ** and ** denotes 10%, 5% and 1% level of significance, respectively.

results above. Specifically, the results above suggest at most that the evidence supporting the HME, found by Hanson and Xiang at the country level, may not hold at sub-national (province or state) levels.

6. The reverse home market effect: potential explanations

Despite the rare evidence of the HME in a few specifications our elaborate econometric analysis above, when taking into account the effects of the configuration of exporter pairs *and* the prevalent presence of zero trade flows, has overwhelmingly attested to the absence of the HME or to the reverse HME. It is important at this stage to provide some alternative explanations to why it might be the case. One important result that Hanson and Xiang and *explicitly* recognize from their model is that the HME is a function not only of the trade cost τ_i and the elasticity of substitution σ_i and but also preference and technology parameters.[20]

It is also important to point out that a number of theoretical models, which built on Krugman (1980) and are less general than Hanson and Xiang's model, have showed that the HME is not pervasive and may be reversed when a model takes into account the difference in trade costs among industries, the difference in tastes across countries that are endogenously determined or difference in scale economies across industries. For example, Davis (1998) showed that if the difference in trade costs between the homogeneous good and the differentiated variety industries are the same the HME may not occur at all. Yu (2005) shows that tastes matter for the existence of the HME. Behrens, Lamorgese, Ottaviano, and Tabuchi (2009) show that in presence of sector specific intensity of increasing returns to scale the HME prediction only holds under some conditions.[21]

The strategy used by Hanson and Xiang in which the HME is identified by selecting the industries of the treatment and control group *only* based on their trade costs and their elasticity of substitution does not control for the fact that the preferences/tastes of exporters selected *and* the intensity of increasing returns to scale of treatment and control industries selected are not the same. Pairing only countries belonging to the same FTA can control for differences in exporter industry tariffs that determine the export

[20] Specifically, they wrote: "From theory, we do not know whether $\bar{n}_{mj}/\bar{n}_{mh}$ will be increasing or decreasing in Y_j/Y_h, the relative market size of the two countries. This relationship depends in part on the distribution of *preference* and *technology* parameters across countries." (Italics added).
[21] How technology across industries determines the HME was also briefly analyzed by Krugman (1980) as a potential extension of his model. Specifically Krugman pointed out that if there are two classes of goods *alpha* and *beta* with many potential products within each class and if the production of *alpha* goods is characterized by increasing returns to scale while the production of *beta* goods is characterized by constant returns to scale, then the HME *only* applies to the *alpha* goods. Specifically, whichever country has the larger market for the *alpha* goods will be a net exporter of these goods. Clearly, this result also implies that the intensity of increasing returns to scale determines whether or not the HME occurs.

flows but not for the differences in tastes that may correlate with the GDPs of exporting countries and for the difference in the intensity of increasing returns to scale that is present at the industry level. Intuitively, tastes may cause the HME empirical evidence to be reversed if small countries spent a smaller share of their GDP spent on products of high trade costs and low elasticity of substitution (i.e. products of the treatment group) than large countries. The intensity of increasing returns to scale may cause the HME evidence to be reversed if some products of high trade costs and low elasticity of substitution are characterized by low intensity of increasing returns to scale than products of low trade costs and high elasticity. The incentive that firms in industries characterized by high trade costs have in reallocating in large markets in order to realize saving in these trade costs may be reduced or even reversed by the fact that some of the industries with high trade costs are characterized by low intensity of increasing returns to scale and consequently firms do not need to be large to cover the fixed costs of production. Important studies like Morrison and Siegel (1997, 1999) have showed that the intensity of increasing returns to scale in U.S. manufacturing production varies substantially from one industry to another. Consequently, the necessity to control for different level of scale economies in the econometric specification is required to be able to correctly identify the HME.[22] We leave it for our future work.

7. Conclusion

In this paper, we reexamine closely the empirical evidence in support of the home-market effect in Hanson and Xiang (2004). We first show that their difference-in-difference gravity specification produces estimates that are sensitive to the way the independent variable is created when a constant term or a squared term of the independent variable of interest is included in the regression. Our empirical analysis using Hanson and Xiang's sample shows that the difference-in-difference gravity specification in which the dependent variable or/and the independent variable is constructed using different configurations of exporter pairs yields completely conflicting results on the HME.

Second and more importantly, we show that the trade data used by Hanson and Xiang are characterized by the pervasive presence of zero trade flows and that difference-in-difference estimation yields no evidence of the HME in the truncated sample of positive trade flows. There is no evidence of the HME when we use this non-zero truncated sample and estimate the single-difference gravity equation without a constant for each of 21 treatment and 13 control industries as well as for each of 273 treatment–control industry pairs. While there is evidence of the HME in the full sample, we question the strategy of adding one to each zero trade flow observation that Hanson and Xiang rely on to preserve information. Monte Carlo simulations show that the single-difference and difference-in-difference gravity equation yield estimates that are very sensitive to the exact value added to convert zeros into positive trade flows. These simulations also suggest that alternative estimators such as the truncated OLS, ET-Tobit and Heckman sample-selection estimators have smaller bias and standard deviation for coefficients estimated in a gravity framework. When we apply these techniques (truncated OLS, ET-Tobit and Heckman) to the gravity equation using Hanson and Xiang's data, we do not find support for the HME.

Given the well-documented evidence of clustering of economic activity in Canadian largest provinces we also look for the HME using a sample of Canadian provinces' exports to the U.S. states. Regardless of the econometric specifications used we find no evidence of the HME in the patterns of exports of Canadian provinces. In sum, the weight of the evidence, in our view, thus tilts away from a role for home-market size as a determinant of sectoral trade flows.

We also provide potential explanations to why methods that improve on Hanson and Xiang's difference-in-difference gravity specification by addressing the problems of configuration of country pairs and the prevalent presence of zero trade flows in the data do not yield empirical evidence in support of the HME. It is our argument that these methods remain far from perfect because they fail to control for unobservable factors such as differences in preferences of exporters and differences in the degree of scale economies at the industry level. These are the potential reasons for which we found no evidence of the HME or evidence of a reverse HME.

Finally, we also would like to make two important qualifications. First, one should not interpret our results about the absence of the HME evidence or of the reverse HME as a rejection of the HME hypothesis of the new trade theory and new economic geography models in general. Rather, the results suggest that the results of the HME evidence found in Hanson and Xiang might not be robust. Second, the econometric exercises used in this paper can be considered as the stepping stones to better econometric methods for the identification of the HME in future studies.

Acknowledgments

We thank Gordon Hanson and Chong Xiang for graciously making their data and programs available to us and for helpful correspondence on these issues.

---

[22] Specifically, after controlling for agglomeration externalities in the estimation of a dynamic cost function Morrison and Siegel (1997) found the evidence of both increasing returns to scale and decreasing returns to scale. The industry exhibiting the highest level of increasing returns to scale is Chemical and Allied Products (SIC 28) while Lumber and Wood Products industry (SIC 24) even exhibits decreasing returns to scale.

Appendix A

We are to show that the gravity specification that includes a constant and a dummy variable *Config* denoting whether the independent variable

Ln(Gdp_j/Gdp_h) is greater than zero or not (i.e. *Config* = 1 if Ln(Gdp_j/Gdp_h) > 0 and *Config* = 0 if Ln(Gdp_j/Gdp_h) ≤ 0) still yields different gravity estimates depending on how the independent variable is constructed. Specifically, we apply the following gravity equation

$$\ln\left(Y_j/Y_h\right) = \alpha + \mu Config + \beta \ln\left(Gdp_j/Gdp_h\right) + \varepsilon_{jh}$$

to three different datasets as presented in Table A.1 below. It is noteworthy that cases A, B, and C have the same set of information about the relationship between Ln(Y_j/Y_h) and Ln(Gdp_j/Gdp_h). The difference is only the way the independent (and dependent) variables are created. To make our analysis simple we assume that each sample has only five observations. The way the data are constructed is exactly the same across the three samples with respect to observations 1, 4 and 5.

	Case A			Case B			Case C		
Obs	Ln(Y_j/Y_h)	Ln(Gdp_j/Gdp_h)	Config	Ln(Y_j/Y_h)	Ln(Gdp_j/Gdp_h)	Config	Ln(Y_j/Y_h)	Ln(Gdp_j/Gdp_h)	Config
1	2	1	1	2	1	1	2	1	1
2	−3	−1	0	3	1	1	−3	−1	0
3	0.5	−0.5	0	0.5	−0.5	0	−0.5	0.5	1
4	−1	2	1	−1	2	1	−1	2	1
5	−0.5	3	1	−0.5	3	1	−0.5	3	1

The OLS minimization problem applying to the three cases is as follows:

$$Case\ A : Min(\alpha,\mu,\beta) = [2-(\alpha+\mu(1)+\beta(1))]^2 + [-3-(\alpha+\mu(0)+\beta(-1))]^2 + [0.5-(\alpha+\mu(0)+\beta(-0.5))]^2$$
$$+ [-1-(\alpha+\mu(1)+\beta(2))]^2 + [-0.5-(\alpha+\mu(1)+\beta(3))]^2 \tag{A1}$$

$$Case\ B : Min(\alpha,\mu,\beta) = [2-(\alpha+\mu(1)+\beta(1))]^2 + [3-(\alpha+\mu(1)+\beta(1))]^2 + [0.5-(\alpha+\mu(0)+\beta(-0.5))]^2$$
$$+ [-1-(\alpha+\mu(1)+\beta(2))]^2 + [-0.5-(\alpha+\mu(1)+\beta(3))]^2 \tag{A2}$$

$$Case\ C : Min(\alpha,\mu,\beta) = [2-(\alpha+\mu(1)+\beta(1))]^2 + [-3-(\alpha+\mu(0)+\beta(-1))]^2 + [-0.5-(\alpha+\mu(1)+\beta(0.5))]^2$$
$$+ [-1-(\alpha+\mu(1)+\beta(2))]^2 + [-0.5-(\alpha+\mu(1)+\beta(3))]^2. \tag{A3}$$

It is easy to see that the minimization problem is not the same in all three cases. Comparing Eqs. (A1) and (A2) shows that it is observation 2 that explains the difference in the OLS minimization problem in Case A and Case B. Similarly, observations 2 and 3 result in the difference of the OLS minimization problem in cases B and C. Finally, the OLS minimization problem in cases A and C differs by configuration of the independent and dependent variables in observation 3. Since the minimization problem is not the same in all the three cases the estimates of α, μ and β will be different.

The regression results in three cases that we obtain from Stata and are presented below show that we indeed obtain different estimates of α, μ, and especially β.

Case A: −1.82 + 3.52 *Config* − 0.76 Ln(Gdp_j/Gdp_h)
Case B: −0.34 + 4.16 *Config* − 1.68 Ln(Gdp_j/Gdp_h)
Case C: −3.47 + 4.25 *Config* − 0.47 Ln(Gdp_j/Gdp_h).

Thus, the example above shows that allowing the intercept to vary depending on whether the numerator of the independent variable of interest (GDP_j) is greater or smaller than the denominator (GDP_h) still yields different estimates of the gravity equation.

Table A.1

	Case A			Case B			Case C		
Obs	Ln(Y_j/Y_h)	Ln(Gdp_j/Gdp_h)	Config	Ln(Y_j/Y_h)	Ln(Gdp_j/Gdp_h)	Config	Ln(Y_j/Y_h)	Ln(Gdp_j/Gdp_h)	Config
1	2	1	1	2	1	1	2	1	1
2	−3	−1	0	3	1	1	−3	−1	0
3	0.5	−0.5	0	0.5	−0.5	0	−0.5	0.5	1
4	−1	2	1	−1	2	1	−1	2	1
5	−0.5	3	1	−0.5	3	1	−0.5	3	1

C.S. Pham et al. / International Review of Economics and Finance 30 (2014) 120–137   137

References

Behrens, Kristian, Lamorgese, Andrea R., Ottaviano, Gianmarco I. P., & Tabuchi, Takatoshi (2009). Beyond the home market effect: Market size and specialization in a multi-country world. *Journal of International Economics, 79*, 259–265.
Dalgin, Muhammed, Trindade, Victor, & Mitra, Devashish (2007). Inequality, nonhomothetic preferences and trade: A gravity approach. *Southern Economic Journal, 74*(3), 747–774.
Eaton, Jonathan, & Tamura, Akiko (1994). Bilateralism and Regionalism in Japanese and U.S. Trade and Direct Foreign Investment Patterns. *Journal of Japanese and International Economies, 8*(4), 478–510.
Eichengreen, Barry, & Irwin, Douglas A. (1995). Trade blocs, currency blocs and the reorientation of world trade in the 1930s. *Journal of International Economics, 38*, 1–24.
Eichengreen, Barry, & Irwin, Douglas A. (1997). The role of history in bilateral trade flows. In Jeffrey A. Frankel (Ed.), *The regionalization of the world economy.* Chicago: University of Chicago Press.
Felbermayr, Gabriel J., & Kohler, Wilhelm (2006). Exploring the intensive and extensive margin of world trade. *Review of World Economics, 142*(4), 642–674.
Felbermayr, Gabriel J., & Kohler, Wilhelm (2007). Does WTO membership make a difference at the extensive margin of world trade? *CESifo working paper no. 1898.*
French, Kenneth, & Poterba, James (1991). Investor diversification and international equity market. *American Economic Review, 81*(2), 222–226.
Fugazza, Carolina, Giofre, Maela, & Nicodano, Giovanna (2011). International diversification and industry-related labour income risk. *International Review of Economics and Finance, 20*, 764–783.
Hanson, Gordon H., & Xiang, Chong (2004). The home market effect and bilateral trade patterns. *American Economic Review, 94*(4), 1108–1129.
Head, Keith, & Ries, John (1998). Immigration and trade creation: Econometric evidence from Canada. *Canadian Journal of Economics, 31*(1), 47–62.
Helpman, Elhanan, Melitz, Marc, & Rubinstein, Yona (2008). Estimating trade flows: Trading partners and trading volumes. *Quarterly Journal of Economics, CXXIII*(2), 441–487.
Jinlan, Ni (2009). The effects of portfolio size on international equity home bias puzzle. *International Review of Economics and Finance, 18*(3), 469–478.
Kamal, Fariha, Lovely, Mary E., & Ouyang, Puman (2012). Does deeper integration enhance spatial advantages? Market access and wage growth in China. *International Review of Economics and Finance, 23*, 59–74.
Krugman, Paul (1980). Scale economies, product differentiation and the pattern of trade. *American Economic Review, 70*(5), 950–959.
Lederman, Daniel, & Ozden, Carglar (2007). Geopolitical interests and preferential access to U.S. markets. *Economics and Politics, 19*(2), 235–258.
Martin, Will and Pham Cong S. (2008). Estimating the gravity equation when zero trade flows are important. Mimeo.
Morrison, Catherine J., & Siegel, Donald (1997). External capital factors and increasing returns in U.S. manufacturing. *Review of Economics and Statistics, 79*(4), 647–654.
Morrison, Catherine J., & Siegel, Donald (1999). Scale economies and industry agglomeration externalities: A dynamic cost function approach. *American Economic Review, 89*(1), 272–290.
Santos, Silvas J., & Tenreyro, Silvana (2006). The log of gravity. *The Review of Economics and Statistics, 641-58.*
Trindade, Victor, & Rauch, James (2002). Ethnic Chinese networks in international trade. *Review of Economics and Statistics, 84*(1), 116–130.
Yu, Z. (2005). Trade, market size, and industrial structure: Revisiting the home-market effect. *Canadian Journal of Economics, 38*, 255–272.

Cong S. Pham is Lecturer in Economics at the School of Accounting, Economics and Finance, Deakin University. Before joining Deakin University from 2005 to 2008 he was working as a Consultant in the Development Research Group, the World Bank in Washington D.C. His research areas are international trade, applied econometrics and economic development. Dr. Cong S. Pham has published in well-known journals like JIE and REStat. He holds a Ph.D. in Economics from Syracuse University.

Devashish Mitra is Professor of Economics and Cramer Professor of Global Affairs at Syracuse University. He is a Fellow of the CESifo network and IZA, and Research Professor, Ifo Institute. He is Coeditor of Economics and Politics, and Associate Editor of the EER, JDE, JIE, IREF and IJBE. He is also on the editorial boards of the RIE, ISRN Economics and Economies. His research areas are international trade, political economy and development economics. He has published in well-known journals like the AER, REStat, EJ, JIE, JDE etc. He holds a Ph.D. in Economics from Columbia University.

Mary E. Lovely is Professor of Economics and Eggers Faculty Scholar at Syracuse University. She is a Fellow of the CESifo network and is co-editor of the *China Economic Review.* Her research areas are international trade, development economics and public economics. Mary Lovely has published in well-known journals such as the JIE, JDE, JPubEc, REStat etc. She earned her Ph.D. in Economics at the University of Michigan, Ann Arbor.

PART III

ENVIRONMENTAL POLICY IN THE OPEN ECONOMY

Are foreign investors attracted to weak environmental regulations? Evaluating the evidence from China[☆]

Judith M. Dean [a,*,1], Mary E. Lovely [b], Hua Wang [c]

[a] U.S. International Trade Commission, United States
[b] Department of Economics, Syracuse University, United States
[c] Development Research Group, The World Bank, United States

ARTICLE INFO

Article history:
Received 13 April 2007
Received in revised form 19 November 2008
Accepted 30 November 2008

JEL classifications:
F18
F23
Q56

Keywords:
Foreign investment
Pollution
Environmental regulation
China

ABSTRACT

At the center of the pollution haven debate is the claim that foreign investors from industrial countries are attracted to weak environment regulations in developing countries. Some recent location choice studies have found evidence of this attraction, but only for inward FDI in industrial countries. The few studies of inward FDI in developing countries have been hampered by weak measures of environmental stringency and by insufficient data to estimate variation in firm response by pollution intensity. This paper tests for pollution haven behavior by estimating the determinants of location choice for equity joint ventures (EJVs) in China. Beginning with a theoretical framework of firm production and abatement decisions, we derive and estimate a location choice model using data on a sample of EJV projects, Chinese effective levies on water pollution, and Chinese industrial pollution intensity. Results show EJVs in highly-polluting industries funded through Hong Kong, Macao, and Taiwan are attracted by weak environmental standards. In contrast, EJVs funded from non-ethnically Chinese sources are not significantly attracted by weak standards, regardless of the pollution intensity of the industry. These findings are consistent with pollution haven behavior, but not by investors from high income countries and only in industries that are highly polluting. Further investigation into differences in technology between industrial and developing country investors might shed new light on this issue.

Published by Elsevier B.V.

1. Introduction

"While studies based on U.S. data provide us with some of the most convincing evidence for a regulatory impact on economic activity – i.e. a pollution haven effect – convincing evidence for or against the pollution haven hypothesis must employ international data" M. Scott Taylor (2004).

☆ Partial funding for this research was provided by the World Bank. We would like to thank Xuepeng Liu for compiling the EJV data and Cory Davidson for research assistance. We have benefited from helpful suggestions regarding data and estimation from K.C. Fung, Meredith Crowley, Andrew Bernard, Keith Head, Jan Ondrich, John List, Stuart Rosenthal, and Scott Taylor. We are also grateful for comments from seminar participants at the 2004 NBER ITI Summer Institute, 2004 American Economic Association meetings, 2003 Econometric Society Summer meetings, Fall 2003 Midwest International Economics meetings, 2003 Northeast Universities Development Conference, Williams College, Dartmouth College, University of Minnesota, Cornell University, University of Maryland, 2004 UC Santa Barbara UNCTEE Workshop, and the World Bank Trade Seminar.
* Corresponding author. Tel.: +1 202 205 3051.
E-mail addresses: Judith.Dean@usitc.gov (J.M. Dean), melovely@maxwell.syr.edu (M.E. Lovely), hwang1@worldbank.org (H. Wang).
1 The views in this paper are those of the authors. They do not necessarily represent the views of the U.S. International Trade Commission or any of its individual Commissioners.

0304-3878/$ – see front matter. Published by Elsevier B.V.
doi:10.1016/j.jdeveco.2008.11.007

One of the most contentious issues debated today is whether inter-country differences in environmental regulations are turning poor countries into "pollution havens." The main argument is that stringent environmental standards in industrial countries lead to the relocation of dirty goods production away from high income countries toward developing countries, where standards are relatively weak.[2] A convincing test of the pollution-haven hypothesis (PHH) would surely examine foreign direct investment (FDI) outflows from industrial countries to all host countries. In lieu of such a formidable endeavor, researchers have searched for evidence of what Taylor (2004) calls a "pollution haven effect," the deterrence of exports or capital inflows by tighter environmental regulation. Existence of a pollution haven effect is necessary, but not sufficient, for the PHH to hold. While higher environmental costs must affect trade and investment flows for pollution havens to appear, these cost effects may be outweighed by other factors determining international flows.

Early empirical studies do find FDI in pollution-intensive industries, but find little evidence that it had been influenced by relative environmental standards or had flowed relatively faster into

2 A corollary is that developing countries may purposely undervalue environmental damage to attract more FDI. While these views assume that relatively weaker environmentalstandards in developing countries are inappropriate, such standards may reflectoptimal policy responses to differences in marginal costs and benefits (Dean, 2001).

2   J.M. Dean et al. / Journal of Development Economics 90 (2009) 1–13

developing countries.[3] More recently, Eskeland and Harrison (2003) examine the pattern of industrial country FDI across industries within Mexico, Venezuela, Morocco, and Cote d'Ivoire, but find little evidence to support PHH. Javorcik and Wei (2004) analyze the investment choices of multinational firms locating across Eastern Europe and the former Soviet Union. Although they find some evidence that FDI is deterred by tight standards, their results are not robust to alternative proxies for environmental stringency. In contrast, studies focusing on the location of investment in the United States find evidence consistent with the PHH. Keller and Levinson (2002), List and Co (2000), and List et al. (2004) all find that regulatory costs deter investment in relatively stringent U.S. states. These U.S. studies argue that lack of evidence for PHH in earlier studies may be due to a failure to account for endogeneity and measurement error.

This paper tests for evidence of pollution haven behavior by foreign investors in China, incorporating the methodological insights of these recent studies. Building upon Copeland and Taylor (2003) firm production and abatement model, we derive a model of FDI location choice in the presence of inter-provincial differences in environmental stringency, amended to include agglomeration and factor abundance. We assemble a new dataset of 2886 manufacturing equity joint venture (EJV) projects in China,[4] across 28 3-digit ISIC industries during 1993–1996, and estimate this model using conditional and nested logit. These data permit us to examine differences in investors' responses based on source and pollution intensity.[5] We use data on actual collected water pollution levies to construct a measure of provincial environmental stringency, drawing on annual Chinese environmental and economic censuses. This detailed information on the levy system allows us to address endogeneity concerns directly.

Turning the spotlight on investment flows into a low-standard, developing country is essential. The U.S. is a high standard, industrial country and it receives the vast majority of its capital inflows from other industrial countries. Thus, the behavior observed in the U.S. may not characterize FDI flows into developing countries, the focus of concern in the pollution haven debate (Blonigen and Wang, 2005). China provides an advantageous site for such an investigation. Significant Chinese trade and investment liberalization in 1992 spurred vast FDI inflows from many source countries (Broadman and Sun, 1997; Shuguang et al., 1998) and made China the single largest recipient of FDI flows to the developing world in 1995 (UNCTAD, 1996). China's national price-based, well-developed water pollution control system makes it unique among developing countries with severe pollution problems.[6] The enormity and scope of FDI into China reduce the likelihood that environmental costs are the driving force behind them. However, environmental stringency varies dramatically across Chinese provinces. Thus, if reductions in compliance costs matter to investors, PH behavior will be evident in their location choice across China.

Our analysis addresses three important issues raised in the recent literature. First, the impact of regulatory costs varies across industries by pollution intensity (Copeland and Taylor, 1994; Taylor, 2004). Attempts to find such differential effects have been hampered by lack of detail on investment flows or by small sample sizes. Our large sample of projects and our disaggregated Chinese industrial emissions intensity data allow us to test for differences in firm response by pollution intensity.[7] Second, poor proxies for environmental strin-

gency can lead to measurement error and endogeneity bias (Keller and Levinson, 2002). Lack of data on environmental policy in developing or transition economies has led researchers to use either indirect measures of stringency (e.g., signing an international environmental treaty) or outcome measures (e.g. pollution abatement costs). Using Chinese collected pollution levies and official water pollution-tax formula, we are able to measure provincial environmental stringency and control for endogeneity arising from industrial concentration.[8] Third, omission of corruption and other location-specific attributes can lead to a spurious relationship between FDI and environmental stringency (Javorcik and Wei, 2004; Fredriksson et al., 2003; Keller and Levinson, 2002). Careful modeling of firm production and abatement decisions, inclusion of location fixed effects, and corrections for the effects of state ownership allow us to reduce the possibility of omitted variable bias.[9]

Results suggest important links between the investor's source country, the pollution intensity of the industry, and PH behavior. For the sample of projects from non-ethnically Chinese (non-ECE) source countries, we find no significant evidence of pollution haven behavior, regardless of the pollution intensity of the industry. However, projects in highly polluting industries from ethnically Chinese (ECE) sources are significantly deterred by pollution taxes. These findings provide evidence of PH behavior by foreign investors in China, but not by investors from high income countries and only in industries that are highly polluting. The results also point to a new direction for inquiry in the PHH debate: investigating whether differences in technology between industrial and developing country investors might be a critical factor in explaining PH behavior.

2. FDI and environmental stringency in China

The distribution of foreign investment within China is highly uneven, as it is in most host countries.[10] Henley et al. (1999) report that 80% of cumulative FDI inflows is located in one of China's ten eastern provinces. This distribution clearly reflects the influence of special incentive programs[11] and the policy of gradual opening pursued before new guidelines were issued in 1992.[12] However, as Huang (2003) notes, in comparison to other countries at similar stages of development, FDI inflows to China are remarkable for their wide distribution among industries and provinces.[13]

The pattern of clustering of investors from different source countries is distinctive.[14] According to Henley et al. (1999), between 1985 and 1996, 66.4% of FDI into China came from ECE sources: Hong Kong, Macao, and Taiwan. While dispersed throughout China, FDI from these sources, especially from Hong Kong, concentrated in the southern coastal provinces.[15] Much of this investment involved labor-intensive processing of

---

[3] See surveys of the literature by Dean (1992, 2001) and Copeland and Taylor (2004).
[4] In their investigation of FDI inflows to China, Amiti and Javorcik (2008) use more recent data that provide information on the number of foreign firms by province and by industry. These data are not publicly available.
[5] The current study is a revised version of Dean et al. (2005).
[6] In 2006, China's freshwater lakes and 40% its 7 major rivers were heavily polluted (SEPA, 2007).
[7] Adapting the framework in Dean et al. (2002a,b, 2004, 2005), Di (2007) provides some firm level evidence of a PH effect for investors in dirty industries. Unlike Dean et al., Di covers only 4 industries, uses US abatement costs to proxy pollution intensity, and does not test for differential responses by source country.

[8] Di uses only a single year of levy data, and, ignoring the official pollution tax formula, incorporates it incorrectly.
[9] Di acknowledges omitted variable problems, but does not introduce appropriate corrections.
[10] For evidence of FDI clustering, see Ondrich and Wasylenko (1993) and Head and Mayer (2004).
[11] China began accepting FDI in 1979, and established 4 SEZs in 2 provinces in 1980. Although 14 coastal cities received FDI incentives in 1984, by 1986 most of these were available anywhere in China to foreign enterprises that produced for export or brought advanced technology (Head and Ries, 1996).
[12] See Tseng and Zebregs (2002). In 1992 China removed a number of sectoral and regional FDI restrictions and decentralized approval (Lardy, 1994). New 1995 rules "encouraged" investment using new technology or equipment for pollution control, and "prohibited" highly polluting processes (Henley et al., 1999).
[13] In the 1995 Industrial Census, no industry received more than 10% of total FDI. While interior regions received only 13% of cumulative FDI from 1992 to 1998, that exceeded all FDI inflows to India during the same period.
[14] In Chinese official publications ECE (non-ECE) FDI is designated as "Chinese" ("Foreign") FDI.
[15] ECE investors may also have family or business interests which influence their location choice.

J.M. Dean et al. / Journal of Development Economics 90 (2009) 1–13   3

imported inputs for re-export. The remaining 33.6% of FDI came from non-ECE sources: mainly OECD countries, with the largest shares from the US (8%) from Japan (8%). Much of this investment was by transnational corporations to produce goods for the Chinese market.

We compiled data for a sample of EJV investments undertaken during 1993–1996 using project descriptions available from the Chinese Ministry of Foreign Trade and Economic Cooperation (various years).[16] The full sample includes 3854 projects, or 3.4% of the total EJV projects entered into during this period, valued at $2.4 billion, or roughly 1% of the value of all EJV inflows into China in the period. While complete data showing FDI by province, type and year are not available, we were able to obtain the provincial distribution of total EJV projects for 1993–95.[17] The simple correlation between the provincial distributions of sample EJV projects and total EJV projects (summed over 1993–95) is 0.90, suggesting that our sample is fairly representative of the overall distribution of EJVs across provinces.

Table 1 and Fig. 1 show the distribution of the 2886 manufacturing EJVs in the sample across provinces, by source and by 2-digit ISIC industrial sector, respectively. Provinces are grouped into five regions: coastal, northeast, central, southwest, and northwest.[18] While the patterns of investment differ, Table 1 shows that both ECE and non-ECE partners engage in EJVs in all provinces. Investment in the southern coastal region is predominantly ECE, while investment in the northern coastal region is split more equally between sources. Fig. 1 suggests that industrial concentration is generally low, with most provinces receiving investment in a wide range of sectors. The most pronounced specialization occurs in the northwest region, where natural-resource based activities dominate.

Fig. 2 shows the distribution of sample EJVs across ISIC 3-digit industries by source and pollution intensity. Since about two-thirds of total FDI in this time period is of ECE origin, it is not surprising that ECE FDI accounts for about 60–70% of the FDI in most sectors. However, the pattern of investment across industries is very similar for ECE and non-ECE FDI, with only a few sectors where one source is dominant.[19] The average water pollution intensity of Chinese industries is measured as chemical oxygen demand (COD) emissions (kg) per 1000 yuan real output.[20] COD emissions are highly correlated with other water pollutants and account for the majority of Chinese pollution tax revenues (Wang and Wheeler, 2005). Most ECE and non-ECE projects are concentrated in the least polluting industries. While a higher share of non-ECE EJVs are in industries with very low and very high pollution intensity, the simple correlation between the distributions is 0.90.[21]

The water pollution levy system is the most fully developed mechanism in the Chinese pollution control regime.[22] The discharge levy faced

Table 1
Equity joint venture sample, by province, 1993–1996.

Province	Number of projects	Projects from ECE sources (%)	Average Utilized FDI * ($10,000)	Average Utilized FDI* (%)
Coastal				
Beijing	248	50.4	55,358.7	8.1
Fujian	95	91.6	30,247.2	4.4
Guangdong	325	77.8	91,830.7	13.4
Hainan	19	68.4	6495.6	1.0
Hebei	99	52.5	22,430.3	3.3
Jiangsu	565	55.6	16,2205.0	23.7
Shandong	400	57.3	73,166.0	10.7
Shanghai	114	47.4	44,075.3	6.4
Tianjin	68	25.0	25,944.6	3.8
Zhejiang	176	61.9	34,860.3	5.1
Northeast				
Heilongjiang	62	61.3	8339.0	1.2
Jilin	76	55.3	9593.8	1.4
Liaoning	166	38.0	37,875.8	5.5
Inland				
Anhui	34	55.9	5200.6	0.8
Henan	85	76.5	8357.3	1.2
Hubei	41	41.5	7461.8	1.1
Hunan	110	72.7	26,248.5	3.8
Jiangxi	76	85.5	8284.1	1.2
Shanxi	8	25.0	1822.4	0.3
Southwest				
Guangxi	36	72.2	9858.3	1.4
Guizhou	6	50.0	437.0	0.1
Sichuan	21	57.1	5301.9	0.8
Yunnan	8	62.5	1064.1	0.2
Northwest				
Gansu	0		0	0.0
Inner Mongolia	11	72.7	1812.0	0.3
Ningxia	3	66.7	365.7	0.1
Qinghai	2	50.0	150.5	0.0
Shaanxi	27	37.0	5734.8	0.8
Tibet	0		0	0.0
Xinjiang	5	40.0	526.3	0.1
Total	2886	100	685,047.0	100

*Period averages. Values are in $10,000 (1990). Source: Ministry of Foreign Trade and Economic Cooperation (various years), and author calculations. See text discussion and Appendix A for more details.

---

[16] EJVs are LLCs incorporated in China, in which foreign investors hold equity. See Fung (1997).
[17] The number of total EJV projects (approved contracts), by province and year, were taken from the provincial reports in the Local Economic Relations and Trade chapter of the Almanac.
[18] These national groups are similar to Demurger et al. (2002), with their coastal and metro groups combined.
[19] The tobacco industry is monopolized by the Chinese government and heavily regulated.
[20] COD measures the oxygen consumed by chemical breakdown of organic and inorganic matter in water. A comparison of 1995 COD intensities for China (Dean and Lovely, 2008) and 1987 biological oxygen demand (BOD) for the US (Hettige et al., 1995) shows a high correlation. In both countries paper is the most water-polluting, followed by food/beverages a distant second, followed by chemicals, non-ferrous metals and leather. The remaining industries have relatively low water-pollution intensities.
[21] Chinese data for ISIC 33 (wood products and furniture) are missing. About 3.9% (2.4%) of the ECE (non-ECE) EJVs are in this sector. Since estimates for the US are relatively low (Hettige et al. (1995), we classify these EJVs in the low-polluting group.
[22] Chinese air pollution regulation was not as well developed in the mid-1990s and disaggregated air levies were not available for analysis. However, U.S. and Chinese industries show similar rankings for air pollution intensity.

by a polluter depends on the pollutant, volume of emissions, and concentration. Because concentration standards are set jointly at the national and provincial level, they vary across provinces and, hence, may influence location choice. If the pollutant concentration of a firm's wastewater exceeds the local concentration standard, a levy is applied.[23] The tax rate for each pollutant is set at the national level and does not vary by industry. For each plant, a potential levy is calculated for each pollutant, and the actual levy imposed is the greatest of these potential levies.

Dasgupta et al. (1997) conclude from plant-level data that these fines are typically consistent with the form dictated by regulatory statutes. Thus, we combine the regulatory formula and data on total collected levies and wastewater to create a measure of *de facto* provincial stringency—the average collected levy per ton of wastewater.[24] Conditional on the emissions intensity of provincial output, this measure is a function only of the stringency of provincial *de facto* regulation. Provinces that commonly reduce the levy below its *de jure* level will receive fewer tax revenues, and, all else equal, will have lower measured stringency. Table 2 shows period average data on collected levies, wastewater effluent intensity, and the share of wastewater meeting the provincial standard for each province.

---

[23] In 1993, a fee on all wastewater was imposed by the national government.
[24] We thank David Wheeler and the World Bank staff for access to these data.

4   J.M. Dean et al. / Journal of Development Economics 90 (2009) 1–13

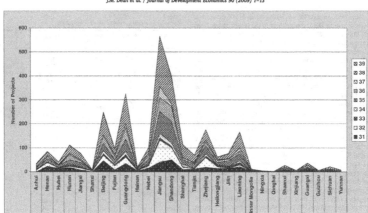

Fig. 1. Distribution of EJV sample by province and industry, 1993–1996.

Evidence from previous studies suggests that FDI in China has concentrated in higher income provinces (e.g. Cheng and Kwan, 2000) and that these provinces have *more* stringent environmental regulation (Dean, 2002; Wang and Wheeler, 2003). The maps in Fig. 3 show the average water pollution levy and the share of sample EJVs across provinces. In 1993 and 1996, the sample EJVs clustered on the coast, with a few inland and almost none in the west. In 1993, there was wide variation in the levies, with the highest rates along the coast. By 1996 much of the map had darkened, indicating an increase in the levies across most parts of the country. These maps suggest a positive unconditional

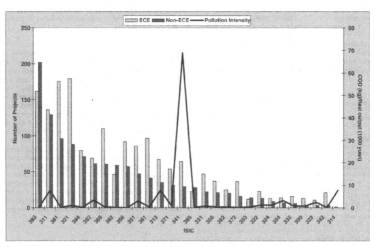

Fig. 2. Distribution of EJV sample by industry, source and pollution intensity 1993–1996.

J.M. Dean et al. / Journal of Development Economics 90 (2009) 1–13 5

Table 2
Provincial characteristics: period averages (1993–1996).

Province	Cons. p.c. (yuan)	Water levy (yuan/ton wastewater)	Effluent intensity (COD/000 tons wastewater)	Share of wastewater meeting standard	Domestic entrepr. FDI (000s)	Cum. real FDI ($ billion)	Skilled labor (%)	Unskilled labor (%)	Highways (km/km² area)	Inland waterway (km/km² area)	Telephones per 000 people	SEZ or OCC	Indus. output from SOE (%)
Coastal													
Beijing	2972	0.09	0.20	0.66	9.4	1986.7	33	14	0.72	0.000	129.02	1	51
Fujian	2522	0.08	0.33	0.42	14.3	4347.0	8	28	0.37	0.031	37.76	1	23
Guangdong	3104	0.11	0.25	0.55	29.2	13862.7	12	22	0.42	0.059	68.98	1	25
Hainan	1928	0.09	0.59	0.45	1.5	1297.1	12	25	0.40	0.009	32.21	1	53
Hebei	1458	0.05	0.29	0.69	22.7	543.2	9	22	0.27	0.000	20.62	1	38
Jiangsu	2197	0.06	0.20	0.68	40.5	4069.9	13	21	0.25	0.233	39.49	1	23
Shandong	1662	0.10	0.94	0.48	26.5	2814.5	10	24	0.33	0.012	20.36	1	30
Shanghai	5869	0.06	0.12	0.77	11.9	3422.1	30	14	0.57	0.317	125.54	1	46
Tianjin	3018	0.12	0.36	0.70	9.1	1002.4	23	16	0.34	0.007	79.39	1	41
Zhejiang	2478	0.10	0.26	0.70	36.5	1198.8	9	22	0.34	0.106	47.78	1	19
Northeast													
Heilongjiang	2394	0.06	0.32	0.53	18.9	419.5	15	18	0.10	0.000	31.87	0	73
Jilin	2027	0.06	0.58	0.53	13.2	321.4	18	17	0.15	0.006	37.09	0	65
Liaoning	2573	0.08	0.24	0.67	29.0	2004.3	14	16	0.29	0.004	41.71	0	49
Inland													
Anhui	1426	0.08	0.36	0.49	24.1	338.4	7	30	0.24	0.040	14.05	0	41
Henan	1183	0.06	0.52	0.48	23.6	431.8	9	24	0.29	0.007	11.53	0	40
Hubei	1745	0.04	0.22	0.60	23.4	674.8	11	25	0.26	0.042	19.97	0	49
Hunan	1587	0.05	0.21	0.57	25.6	460.8	9	21	0.27	0.047	16.39	0	48
Jiangxi	1338	0.04	0.23	0.49	18.4	283.5	8	26	0.20	0.029	12.96	0	50
Shanxi	1430	0.06	0.23	0.49	11.5	103.7	12	20	0.21	0.001	18.61	0	49
Southwest													
Guangxi	1452	0.07	0.62	0.45	12.9	910.0	8	22	0.17	0.019	11.94	1	50
Guizhou	1070	0.03	0.21	0.41	7.7	88.1	6	35	0.18	0.010	6.71	0	71
Sichuan	1408	0.04	0.23	0.46	41.3	735.8	7	25	0.18	0.014	10.75	0	44
Yunnan	1379	0.09	0.51	0.31	7.9	109.0	5	35	0.18	0.004	9.14	0	73
Northwest													
Gansu	1118	0.05	0.13	0.47	7.2	44.3	10	40	0.08	0.013	15.41	0	72
Inner Mongolia	1511	0.05	0.97	0.40	9.9	77.5	13	23	0.04	0.001	22.76	0	68
Ningxia	1430	0.04	0.43	0.44	1.8	10.7	11	35	0.16	0.008	23.13	0	74
Qinghai	1539	0.02	0.08	0.51	1.6	4.8	11	44	0.02	0.000	18.11	0	83
Shaanxi	1274	0.07	0.19	0.65	13.3	480.2	12	26	0.19	0.005	16.36	0	61
Tibet	1127	na	na	na	0.3	2.0	3	70	0.02	0.000	9.94	0	80
Xinjiang	1852	0.12	0.74	0.37	6.9	66.4	14	25	0.02	0.000	22.16	0	71

Source: Environmental data from a World Bank dataset, compiled from *Chinese Environmental Yearbook*, various years. Other provincial data from *China Statistical Yearbook*, various years, and calculations by authors. See Appendix A for more details. Cumulative real FDI (1980 dollars) from Coughlin and Segev (2000).

relationship between the average provincial levies and the share of EJV projects locating in a province. They also suggest that any empirical analysis must account for regional clustering.

3. Modeling foreign investor behavior

Given the global surge in FDI into China following its 1992 trade and foreign investment liberalization, we take the decision to invest in China as exogenous. We consider a multinational firm that wants to invest one unit of capital somewhere in China. The firm's objective is to choose the host province that yields the highest profit. Profit depends, among other factors, on the cost of emissions. A provincial pollution policy is defined as the schedule of fines the firm faces for wastewater emissions and emissions intensity. Since Chinese provincial fine schedules exempt below-threshold emissions intensity, the cost of emissions to the firm depends on the firm's emissions intensity choice. We treat foreign firms as price takers with respect to provincial pollution policy at the time of their location decision. The firm can obtain information on the fine schedule, as well as the average rate that has been levied by inspectors in each province. This information is incorporated directly into our approach.

3.1. Production, emissions, and profits

We consider a firm that jointly produces two outputs, good X and polluted wastewater emissions Z, using variable inputs of unskilled

labor, L, skilled labor, H, and a vector of intermediate (locally-provided) services, s. The capital input is embodied in the original investment and is fixed in the short run. We assume that the firm can abate the concentration of pollutants in its wastewater, so emission intensity is a choice for the firm. Accordingly, the firm can allocate an endogenous fraction, θ, of its inputs to abatement activity. This implies that abatement and production use factors in the same proportion. If $\theta = 0$, there is no abatement and, by choice of units, each unit of output generates one unit of pollution. The joint production technology for firm i operating in industry j is:

$$X_{ij} = \left(1 - \theta_{ij}\right)G^{j}\!\left(L_{ij}, H_{ij}, I_{ij}(s)\right), Z_{ij} = \varphi^{ij}\!\left(\theta_{ij}\right)G^{j}\!\left(L_{ij}, H_{ij}, I_{ij}(s)\right). \quad (1)$$

The function $I(s)$ aggregates local service varieties into an intermediate input for the foreign firm. We assume that G is increasing and concave, and $0 \le \theta \le 1$, $\phi(0) = 1, \phi(1) = 0$.

To derive an estimating equation, we follow Copeland and Taylor (2003) and assume that the relation between abatement activity and emissions takes a constant elasticity form, $\phi^{ij}(\theta) = (1 - \theta)^{1/\alpha_{ij}}$, where $0 \le \alpha_{ij} \le 1$. This function captures the efficiency with which the firm's abatement inputs reduce emissions; the larger α_{ij} is, the less efficient is the firm in abating pollution. Abatement efficiency may vary across industries because industrial production processes differ, with some processes resulting in large volumes of emissions (e.g. paper and

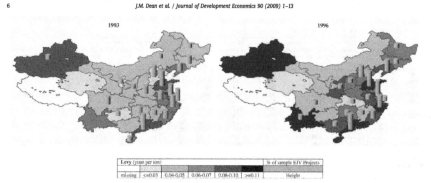

Fig. 3. Source: EJV distribution constructed from the sample EJV data. Average provincial pollution levy constructed from World Bank dataset, compiled from *Chinese Environmental Yearbook*, various years. See Appendix A for more details.

paper products). Additionally, abatement efficiency will vary among firms within an industry if investors from different source countries use different production technologies.[25] Using this form for abatement technology, we can eliminate θ and invert the joint production technology to obtain a net production function in which emissions are treated as an input:

$$X_{ij} = Z_{ij}^{\alpha_{ij}} \left[G^j \left(L_{ij}, H_{ij}, I_{ij}(s) \right) \right]^{(1-\alpha_{ij})}. \tag{2}$$

Let factor prices be given by the vector $\mathbf{w} = (\tau, u, h, \bar{p}_s)$, where τ is the marginal tax rate for emissions, u the wage for unskilled labor, h the wage for skilled labor, and $\bar{p}_s$ a price index for locally-provided services. All factor prices vary across provinces, including the marginal emissions tax rate. We assume that the firm adjusts its emissions by altering the effluent concentration of its wastewater. Using the structure of the Chinese levy system, the fine for non-compliant firms in province k is[26]

$$F_{ijk} = R \left(\frac{E_{ij} - E_k}{E_k} \right) W_{ij}, \tag{3}$$

where F_{ijk} is the total fine levied on firm i in industry j if it locates in province k. Here, R is the national tax rate on the discharge factor (given in brackets), E_{ij} is the effluent concentration in firm i's wastewater, E_k is the allowable concentration standard set by province k, and W_{ij} is firm i's wastewater. For firms exceeding the standard, the marginal levy on emissions from Eq. (3), denoted by τ_k, is $\tau_k = R/E_k$, which varies by province. Under this levy system, the total fine paid by a non-compliant firm operating in province k can be expressed as $F_{ij} = (\tau_k E_{ij} - R)W_{ij} = \tau_k Z_{ij} - RX_{ij}$. Therefore, the cost function for a firm operating in province k with the production function (2) is $C^{ij}(\mathbf{w}_k, R, X_{ij})$.

Let the producer price for a unit of X_j be denoted by p_j. For any non-compliant firm, the maximum profit that can be earned in province x is the solution to:

$$\pi_{ijk} \left(p_j, \mathbf{w}_k, R \right) = \max p_j X_{ij} - C^{ij} \left(\mathbf{w}_k, R, X_{ij} \right). \tag{4}$$

A firm will choose the investment location that offers the highest feasible profit given local factor prices.

3.2. Pollution taxes and profits

Using Eq. (4), we can explore how cross-province differences in the emissions concentration standard influence the maximum profit that an investor can earn in that province, *ceteris paribus*. A stricter provincial concentration standard implies a higher marginal levy rate, which enters the profit function through τ_k. Variable cost is non-decreasing in factor prices and profits are non-increasing in cost.[27] Therefore, profits are non-increasing in τ_k. Using the Envelope Theorem, the impact of a higher pollution tax on profit reflects the firm's optimal level of emissions: $\partial \pi_{ijk}(p_j, \mathbf{w}_k, R)/\partial \tau_k = -Z_{ijk}$. Because the decline in profit from a higher pollution tax is the emissions level itself, it follows that firms that are large polluters will be more sensitive to variation in pollution taxes when choosing a location for investment.

From Eq. (2) and noting that the firm chooses emissions such that the value of the marginal product of emissions equals the pollution tax, the firm's chosen pollution intensity (PI), defined as emissions per unit value of output, can be expressed as $PI_{ijk} = Z_{ijk}/p_j X_{ijk} = \alpha_{ij}/\tau_k$. Thus, a firm's pollution intensity is increasing in its abatement parameter α_{ij} and the response to pollution taxes should vary in accordance with the firm's pollution intensity. These observations lead to the following hypothesis, which we test using provincial variation in pollution levies.

Hypothesis. A stricter environmental standard, all else equal, decreases profits. This profit effect is larger (i) for firms in industries that are more pollution intensive in production; and (ii) within industries, for firms whose capital investment embodies less efficient abatement technology.

To test (i) we allow the responsiveness of firms to pollution taxes to differ by the pollution intensity of their industry. We test (ii) by allowing the responsiveness of firms to pollution taxes to differ by source group, controlling for the pollution intensity of the investor's industry.

---

[25] Evidence suggests that most innovation in pollution control equipment has occurred in OECD countries (Lanjouw and Mody, 1996) and that firms tend to purchase pollution control equipment from domestic suppliers (Popp, 2006).
[26] For further details on the Chinese levy system, see Wang and Wheeler (2005).

[27] See Varian (1992).

J.M. Dean et al. / Journal of Development Economics 90 (2009) 1–13   7

4. Econometric method

4.1. Econometric model and estimation

While the exact functional form of the profit function in Eq. (4) is unknown, we assume that potential profit is a multiplicative function of its arguments and, thus, linear in logs.[28] Decomposing Eq. (4) and distinguishing the levy τ_k, other variables that are observable at the provincial level, $\mathbf{V_K}$, and variables observable at the regional level, $\mathbf{V_R}$, profits for firm i can be expressed as[29]:

$$\ln \pi_{ik} = a_0 + a_1 \ln \tau_k + \mathbf{b'V_K} + \mathbf{c'V_R}. \qquad (5)$$

Clearly provincial characteristics, such as investment incentives and transport costs, influence the location decision. Following Head and Ries (1996) and Cheng and Kwan (2000), we add incentives as a proportionate shift factor to the profit function. We also introduce variables that capture transportation and telecommunications costs. Finally, we relax the assumption that firms receive the same price in every province. The literature indicates that some firms, particularly those with partners based in the US and Japan, produce for the local market, so we introduce measures of local income and market size.

Assuming that potential profits are subject to shocks to local conditions (ξ_{ik}) that are specific to firm-province pairs, and that ξ_{ik} follows a Type I Extreme Value distribution, the probability, P_{ik}, that investor i chooses province k where k is a member of choice set K is given by

$$P_{ik} = \frac{\exp(\ln \pi_{ik})}{\sum_{k \in K} \exp(\ln \pi_{ik})}, \qquad (6)$$

where we represent $\ln \pi_{ij}$ by Eq. (5). Eq. (6) is estimated using data on 2886 manufacturing EJVs undertaken during 1993–1996 across 28 provinces and 27 3-digit ISIC industries. Baseline results are obtained using conditional logit. To test hypothesis (i), we allow the pollution levy parameter to vary by industrial pollution intensity. To test hypothesis (ii), we estimate Eq. (6) for ECE and non-ECE subsamples, separately.[30] Because Malaysia, Indonesia, and the Philippines have large ethnically Chinese populations, the few projects from these countries are included in the ECE subsample.[31]

Given investors' geographic links to coastal provinces, clustering of prior investment and natural resources, and the gradual nature of the opening process from the coast inward, the assumption of independence of irrelevant alternatives may not hold for China.[32] To allow for correlation among provinces in the same geographic region, we estimate a nested logit model. This allows for dependence among the unobservable aspects of profitability among provinces in a given region. The location choice becomes a two-level decision—choosing a region in China, and then a specific province within that region. We estimate the nested logit model using full information maximum likelihood estimation.

4.2. Data description

Summary data for provincial characteristics are shown in Table 2, with definitions and sources provided in the Appendix A. Although wages by skill level are not available, a distribution of the labor force by education categories is available for each province from the 1990

Population Census and a 1% sample of the population performed in 1995.[33] Since inter-provincial labor mobility is low, we assume that relative labor supplies determine relative wages in each province. Defining unskilled labor as those who are illiterate or have less than primary level education and skilled labor as those with senior secondary education or beyond, we calculate the percentage of unskilled and skilled labor relative to the percentage of semi-skilled labor (those with primary and junior secondary level education).

The profit function also depends on the price of locally produced intermediate services. Head and Ries (1996) argue that agglomeration in China is the result of localization economies from concentrations of intermediate service providers. Adopting their framework, we assume the market for local services is monopolistically competitive and that foreign firms use a composite of these services. The equilibrium number of intermediate suppliers then depends on the final-good price, the number of foreign firms to which they may sell, and the number of domestic firms that must undertake the costly upgrading necessary to serve foreign firms. This framework can be used to derive a price index for locally-provided service intermediates, which is a function of previous foreign investment and the number of potential local intermediate service suppliers. Previous foreign investment is measured as the real value of provincial cumulative FDI from 1983 to the year before the project is undertaken. Availability of potential intermediate service suppliers is measured by the number of domestic enterprises.

As in other studies, we include several measures of infrastructure. Transport infrastructure is proxied by the length of roads and inland waterways (both adjusted for provincial size), while telecommunications are proxied by the number of urban telephone subscribers relative to population. FDI incentives are included using a dummy that takes a value of one if there is a special economic zone (SEZ) or open coastal city (OCC) in the province. This variable does not vary during the 1993–1996 period.

Using the data on COD-intensity of Chinese industrial output, we create three dummy variable indicators of water pollution intensity (PI). About 60% of the EJV projects in the sample are in industries designated as low polluters, with a PI of less than 1 kg per thousand yuan output (1990 yuan). Another 24% of the sample are in industries with $1 < \text{PI} < 3.5$, and are classified as medium polluters. The final 16% are in industries with $\text{PI} > 7$, and are denoted high polluters. This classification scheme is motivated by low within-group variation, but high between-group variation in PI.

4.3. Addressing environmental stringency and endogeneity

Environmental stringency may itself be endogenous, thus blurring the relationship between stringency and FDI location choice. One source of endogeneity might be two-way causality. Foreign investors might negotiate pollution levies with local authorities prior to choosing where to invest. This would imply that the levy itself is a function of the location choice of the firm. As the OECD (2005) states, there is evidence that local Environmental Protection Boards (EPBs) often negotiate the levels of fees with firms. In addition, EPBs are often impeded from fully enforcing environmental regulations, when local leaders believe the non-compliant enterprises are important for the local economy.

However, the OECD study notes that negotiations between the EPBs and firms take place *after* the EPBs issue notices to collect discharge fees. Thus, such negotiations occur *after* location, production, and emissions decisions have been made by the firm and following an inspection by local authorities (Wang and Wheeler, 2005). In addition, recent evidence shows that state-owned enterprises (SOEs) have more bargaining power than other firms and that this has led to significantly lower environmental levies for SOEs relative to foreign-invested and Chinese private firms (Wang et al., 2003; Wang and Jin, 2006; Wang and Wheeler, 2005). This evidence suggests that two-way causality is

---

[28] The cost function is commonly assumed to be generalized Cobb-Douglas (e.g. Head and Mayer, 2004).

[29] The subscript j is suppressed for clarity.

[30] There is no source for 12% of projects in 1996, 17% in 1995, 10% in 1994, and 3% in 1993. Since most FDI inflows at this time were ECE, these projects were designated ECE. Our results are not sensitive to this assumption.

[31] Omission of these projects from the analysis did not affect our results.

[32] This clustering may also differ systematically for ECE and non-ECE investors—an outcome consistent with the foreign-investor information disadvantage stressed by List et al. (2004) in their interpretation of results for the US.

[33] We interpolate between these years to develop a time series.

unlikely to be a problem when it comes to a foreign investor's location choice. While enforcement does vary across provinces, evidence from Wang and Wheeler (2005) shows that better enforcement does significantly increase average collected *plant-level* water pollution levies. Thus, our collected levy variable should correctly signal *de facto* stringency, due to tighter regulations, better enforcement or both.

But the influence of SOEs points to the importance of controlling for corruption and a second possible source of endogeneity—omitted variable bias. Fredriksson et al. (2003) and Javorcik and Wei (2004) argue that corruption may imply lower environmental charges, but may also imply a less attractive location in which to invest. Thus, if corruption is omitted, low levies may not attract FDI even if the PHH is true. A similar bias may arise if income is omitted. Higher incomes may imply more stringent environmental regulations, but may also imply a larger local market and better infrastructure. If these variables are omitted, high levies might not deter FDI, even if PHH were true.

The use of a lag should prevent any contemporaneous correlation between the levy and the error term. However, in light of the evidence on bargaining power of SOEs, we proxy corruption using controls for state ownership. Since large reductions in state ownership may signal a commitment to liberalization and less potential for corruption, we include growth in the share of provincial output from SOEs as a location choice determinant. In addition, since the appeal of higher incomes and investment incentives may be reduced if commerce is heavily concentrated in SOEs, we interact both incentives and consumption per capita with the degree to which the economy is *non-state-owned*. As a final defense against omitted variable bias, we introduce regional and provincial fixed effects to capture other province-specific features that might impact FDI location choice. With a short time-series, these fixed effects reduce our ability to estimate the influence of provincial characteristics that change slowly over time, but they greatly reduce the scope for correlation between the error term and the levy.

A third source of endogeneity is measurement error in the proxy for environmental stringency. To see this, suppose that of the *N* firms located in a province, firms 1 to *n* emit wastewater up to standard and, thus, do not pay a fine. Using Eq. (3) and the definition of *τ*, the average provincial collected levy is:

$$\frac{TL_{kt}}{W_{kt}} = \tau_k \cdot \left[\sum_{j=n+1}^{N} w_{it}(E_{it} - E_{kt}) \right] \quad (7)$$

where TL_{kt} are total collected levies and $w_{it} = W_{it}/W_{kt}$. As Eq. (7) indicates, the average collected levy in province *k* is the product of (i) the marginal pollution tax, which reflects provincial policy only, and (ii) the weighted average deviation of firm effluent intensity from the provincial standard, which reflects industrial composition in the province as well as the tax. A more stringent provincial standard (a decrease in E_{kt}) will always imply a higher average collected levy, *cet. par.* However, a higher share of pollution-intensive industries could raise E_{it}, and therefore the average collected levy, even if E_{kt} is constant.

Table 2 provides some evidence that this is important. The average collected levy in both Zhejiang and Xinjiang is 0.12 yuan per ton of wastewater—one of the highest in China. Zhejiang has a relatively low average effluent intensity (0.36 tons COD per thousand tons wastewater) and 70% of its wastewater met its concentration standard. In contrast, Xinjiang has one of the highest average effluent intensities (0.74) and only 37% of its wastewater met its concentration standard. For this reason, in addition to the regional and provincial fixed effects, we control for the average provincial effluent intensity in Eq. (6) as a proxy for the bracketed term in Eq. (7).

5. Results

We estimate Eq. (6) using conditional logit and nested logit methods. In both approaches, we estimate the model for the full sample and for

each of the source-specific subsamples, ECE and non-ECE. As suggested by our theory, we allow the effect of regulation to vary by the pollution intensity of the industry in which the investment occurs.

5.1. No evidence of a pollution haven effect on average

Table 3 reports the conditional logit results for the full sample. Model (1) incorporates regional fixed effects to control for unobserved correlates of environmental stringency. Average collected levy and average effluent intensity are lagged one year to represent predetermined information, available to an investor at the time of the location decision. The estimated coefficient for the average levy in model (1) is very small and insignificant. Therefore, ignoring the variation in pollution intensity across industries, we find no support for a pollution-haven effect in our full sample. We do find strong regional effects, however, indicating that EJVs are much less likely to locate in the southwest and northwest regions, relative to the central (omitted) region.

We expect all investors to be attracted to provinces with large stocks of FDI (agglomeration) and potential suppliers (local firms), as well as special incentives and good infrastructure. These priors are supported by the full sample.[34] Estimates in model (1) also indicate a strong attraction to provinces with relatively abundant skilled workers, and provinces where state-ownership is shrinking rapidly. We also expect that firms seeking to sell into the local market will be attracted to areas that have rich and growing local markets, as measured by provincial consumption per capita and real provincial GDP growth. EJVs appear to be attracted to fast-growing markets, but high incomes have no significant impact in model (1).

Model (2) of Table 3 allows for province-specific effects that deviate from those captured by the regional dummies, providing an additional defense against omitted variable bias.[35] Notably, the estimated average levy coefficient now is negative, but it remains insignificant. Thus, inclusion of provincial fixed effects does not change the lack of support for a PH effect in the full sample. For most of the other explanatory variables, the results in model (2) mirror those in model (1). However, there are a few exceptions. The estimated coefficient for average effluent intensity is now negative and significant, and for consumption per capita is now positive and significant. Thus, investors are indeed attracted to cleaner provinces with higher incomes. Model (2) also suggests a much stronger attraction to rapid growth, incentives, and abundant semi-skilled labor. While model (2) does render local firms and agglomeration insignificant, there is little variation in these variables over this short time period.

5.2. The pollution intensity of the industry matters

Hypothesis (i) suggests that the attraction of low levies will be stronger for highly polluting industries. In model (3) of Table 3, the PI dummy indicators are interacted with the average levy and average effluent intensity to test whether these groups respond differently to pollution standards. We find that the pollution levy is not a significant deterrent for firms in industries with low pollution intensity. The estimated coefficient for firms in medium pollution intensity industries is negative, but also not significant. However, investors in highly polluting industries are significantly less likely to choose a province with a high levy. This finding is consistent with haven-

---

[34] The estimated coefficient for telephone coverage is negative and significant, but may simply be a poor proxy for telecommunications infrastructure. Other authors have found similar results using various measures of telephones.

[35] For each region with *n* provinces, (*n* − 1) provincial fixed effects are introduced (though not shown in Table 2).

J.M. Dean et al. / Journal of Development Economics 90 (2009) 1–13   9

Table 3
EJV provincial location choice: conditional logit, full sample[1,2].

	(1) Coefficient	z	(2) Coefficient	z	(3) Coefficient	z	(4) Coefficient	z
Provincial variables (in logs)								
Levy[3]	0.01	0.10	−0.06	−0.45				
Av. effluent intensity[3]	0.09	1.27	−0.43**	−3.44				
Levy[3]*low polluter					0.13	1.04	0.03	0.24
Levy[3]*medium polluter					−0.11	−0.75	−0.18	−1.07
Levy[3]*high polluter					−0.38*	−2.48	−0.42**	−2.59
Av. EI[3]*low polluter					−0.02	−0.21	−0.46**	−4.01
Av. EI[3]*medium polluter					0.15	1.68	−0.31*	−2.36
Av. EI[3]*high polluter					0.27**	2.87	−0.11	−0.90
Local firms	0.46**	6.77	0.25	1.31	0.45**	6.73	0.28	1.48
Agglomeration	0.35**	8.91	−0.02	−0.17	0.35**	8.94	−0.02	−0.22
Ratio skilled labor	1.26**	8.45	−2.44**	−5.36	1.27**	8.54	−2.38**	−5.24
Ratio unskilled labor	−1.17**	−3.51	−1.81**	−4.94	−1.15**	−3.46	−1.78**	−4.88
Weighted SEZ or OCC[4,5]	1.19**	4.54	2.44**	2.74	1.21**	4.65	2.50**	2.80
Weighted consumption P.C.[5]	0.11	0.48	1.78**	4.56	0.12	0.53	1.79**	4.59
Real provincial growth[4,6]	1.27**	2.82	2.26**	3.56	1.19**	2.69	2.21**	3.51
Change in state ownership	−2.10**	−2.81	−1.85**	−2.12	−2.12**	−2.84	−1.97*	−2.27
Telephones	−1.38**	−10.84			−1.39**	−10.96		
Roads	0.31**	3.41			0.32**	3.44		
Inland navigable waterways	0.12**	7.11			0.12**	7.09		
Regional fixed effects								
Coast	0.38*	2.10	3.02**	3.83	0.39*	2.14	3.00**	3.79
Northeast	0.36*	2.36	−0.80	−1.55	0.39**	2.53	−0.80	−1.56
Southwest	−1.28**	−7.98	−1.66**	−3.28	−1.29**	−8.11	−1.70**	−3.36
Northwest	−0.33	−1.61	−0.04	−0.07	−0.34	−1.66	−0.05	−0.09
Provincial fixed effects[7]	No		Yes		No		Yes	
Obs	80,808		80,808		80,808		80,808	
Log likelihood	−7862.65		−7795.52		−7856.85		−7789.34	
LR test	2286.71**		3642.45**		2319.69**		3654.81**	

[1]**, *, and † indicate significance at the 1%, 5%, and 10% levels, respectively. [2]Gansu and Tibet excluded since no foreign investment located there during the time period. [3]Variable is lagged one year. [4]Variable not in logs. [5]Weighted by (1 − share of industrial output from SOEs). [6]Three-year moving average. For each region with n provinces, (n − 1) provincial fixed effects are introduced.

Table 4
EJV provincial location choice: conditional logit, ECE and non-ECE samples[1,2].

	ECE sample (3) Coefficient	z	(4) Coefficient	z	Non-ECE sample (3) Coefficient	z	(4) Coefficient	z
Provincial variables (in logs)								
Levy[3]*low polluter	0.15	0.90	0.10	0.57	0.04	0.19	0.02	0.07
Levy[3]*medium polluter	−0.15	−0.77	−0.17	−0.83	−0.13	−0.55	−0.12	−0.41
Levy[3]*high polluter	−0.54**	−2.84	−0.54**	−2.69	−0.18	−0.72	−0.19	−0.53
Av. EI[3]*low polluter	0.04	0.43	−0.47**	−3.14	−0.04	−0.34	−0.31	−1.71†
Av. EI[3]*medium polluter	0.17	1.38	−0.38*	−2.19	0.18	1.32	−0.10	−0.48
Av. EI[3]*high polluter	0.24†	1.91	−0.20	−1.21	0.32*	2.35	0.09	0.46
Local firms	0.35**	4.53	0.37	1.48	0.67**	4.57	0.31	0.99
Agglomeration	0.47**	10.16	−0.09	−0.67	0.08	1.12	−0.06	−0.32
Ratio skilled labor	0.46**	2.61	−3.60**	−5.91	2.77**	9.90	−0.27	−0.36
Ratio unskilled labor	−1.33**	−3.46	−2.40**	−5.33	−1.06†	−1.72	−0.73	−1.09
Weighted SEZ or OCC[4,5]	0.57†	1.67	2.06†	1.77	2.07**	4.97	1.95	1.35
Weighted consumption p.c.[5]	0.08	0.27	1.59**	3.19	0.84*	2.22	3.35**	4.88
Real Provincial Growth[4,6]	0.93†	1.66	2.52**	3.07	1.62*	2.24	1.09	1.06
Change in state ownership	−2.41*	−2.36	−2.90**	−2.51	−2.74*	−2.22	−1.72	−1.22
Telephones	−1.17**	−7.51			−2.22**	−9.62		
Roads	0.30**	2.43			0.52**	3.56		
Inland navigable waterways	0.18**	7.59			0.06*	2.37		
Regional fixed effects								
Coast	0.47*	1.96	4.80**	4.64	0.57†	1.93	0.50	0.39
Northeast	0.15	0.72	−0.86	−1.30	1.09**	4.31	−0.44	−0.50
Southwest	−1.41**	−7.49	−1.54**	−2.42	−1.00**	−3.46	−1.26	−1.44
Northwest	−0.43†	−1.59	0.19	0.23	0.05	0.17	−0.86	−1.08
Provincial fixed effects[7]	No		Yes		No		Yes	
Obs	47,964		47,964		32,844		32,844	
Log likelihood	−4658.07		−4592.50		−3101.31		−3066.65	
LR test	1343.27**		2231.13**		1023.23**		1684.05**	

[1]**, *, and † indicate significance at the 1%, 5%, and 10% levels, respectively. [2]Gansu and Tibet excluded since no foreign investment located there during the time period. [3]Variable is lagged one year. [4]Variable not in logs. [5]Weighted by (1 − share of industrial output from SOEs). [6]Three-year moving average. [7]For each region with n provinces, (n − 1) provincial fixed effects are introduced.

10   *J.M. Dean et al. / Journal of Development Economics 90 (2009) 1–13*

seeking behavior, but also supports the view that such behavior is conditioned by pollution intensity.[36]

These results are robust to the inclusion of provincial fixed effects. In model (4), we find significant PH behavior among investors in highly polluting industries but not among investors in industries with low or medium pollution intensity. As before, inclusion of provincial fixed effects controls for provincial characteristics correlated with effluent intensity and consumption per capita. All three types of polluters are attracted to cleaner provinces and provinces with higher incomes.

5.3. The source country of the investor matters

Hypothesis (ii) suggests that the attraction of weak environmental regulations depends on the technological sophistication of the firm within a given industry. There is some evidence from firm surveys that non-ECE investors transfer more advanced technology in their Chinese investments than do investors from ECE countries.[37] Our hypothesis is that the levy will have a stronger deterrent impact on ECE firm location decisions than on non-ECE firms, all else equal. To investigate this, we estimate models (3) and (4) for the 1713 (1173) projects funded by ECE (non-ECE) investors, separately.[38]

Model (3) in Table 4 shows the results for the split sample. Higher standards do not affect the location decision for ECE investors in low or medium polluting industries, but are a negative and significant deterrent for investors in highly polluting industries. Higher standards have no significant impact on location choice for non-ECE investors, regardless of pollution intensity. Importantly, these results are robust to the inclusion of provincial fixed effects, as shown in model (4). As with the full sample, the inclusion of fixed effects indicates that both investors groups are attracted to cleaner, higher income provinces. We conclude that ECE investors are deterred by more stringent pollution standards, but only when investing in pollution intensive activities. In contrast, non-ECE investors do not engage in significant pollution-haven seeking behavior within China.[39]

5.4. The investment decision is nested

It is possible that the decision to locate EJVs in China is a nested one. Strong regional effects in the conditional logits suggest a nested decision, and Hausman tests rejected the null hypothesis of the independence of irrelevant alternatives. Thus, we estimate a nested logit specification. The investor is assumed to first choose the region in which to invest and then the province within that region.[40] We include

---

[36] Wald tests indicated no significant difference between the responses of low- and medium-intensity polluters, but a significant difference between the response of high-intensity polluters and those of other two groups.
[37] Survey data on EJVs in China (Brandt and Zhu, undated) indicated that during 1987–1993, 35% (5%) of EJVs with Hong Kong investors were required to transfer advanced technology (a patent) from a foreign parent, in contrast to 76% (29%) of EJVs with developed country investors. Similarly 6% of EJVs from Hong Kong were required to manufacture certain components or final products in China, in contrast to 42% of EJVs with developed country investors. We thank Susan Zhu for making this information available.
[38] Because the South Asian projects may reflect round-tripping concerns, the models were rerun omitting these projects. The results were unaffected. We thank K.C. Fung for bringing this to our attention.
[39] Dean and Lovely (2008) show that water and air pollution intensities are not highly correlated across industries. Thus, EJV firms still might be deterred by air pollution regulations, if air pollution was more stringently regulated or more costly to abate. We have no evidence regarding the latter, but we know Chinese air regulations were less well developed, and collected levies from water pollution exceeded those from air pollution (Wang and Wheeler, 2005). This suggests that, *de facto*, water pollution was more stringently regulated than air pollution.
[40] Modeling the choice to locate in China at all would require a three-tiered nest and national measures of stringency (which are not available). Since existing research stresses the importance of non-environmental motivations for investing in China in the 1990s, we believe omitting the prior decision does not bias our results.

Table 5
EJV provincial location choice: nested logit, by source[12].

	Full sample		ECE		Non-ECE	
	(1)		(2)		(3)	
	Coeff	z	Coeff	z	Coeff	z
Provincial variables (in logs)						
Levy[3]*low polluter	0.08	0.67	0.02	0.11	−0.01	−0.05
Levy[3]*medium polluter	−0.15	−0.97	−0.11	−0.56	−0.15	−0.58
Levy[3]*high polluter	−0.37*	−2.14	−0.53**	−2.51	−0.15	−0.55
Av. EI[3]*low polluter	0.15**	2.52	0.21**	2.81	0.21*	2.41
Av. EI[3]*medium polluter	0.23**	3.49	0.29**	3.20	0.27**	2.59
Av. EI[3]*high polluter	0.33**	4.96	0.42**	5.08	0.35**	3.03
Local firms	0.56**	7.11	0.46**	5.12	0.66**	4.01
Agglomeration	0.34**	9.89	0.44**	10.72	0.09	1.34
Ratio skilled labor	1.38**	11.80	0.65**	4.35	2.77**	11.37
Ratio unskilled labor	−0.71**	−2.73	−0.74*	−2.31	−1.29*	−2.26
Weighted SEZ or OCC[45]	1.43**	4.82	0.62	1.46	2.06**	4.65
Weighted consumption p.c.[5]	0.05	0.13	0.18	0.41	1.37*	2.32
Real provincial growth[6]	1.63**	3.34	1.16†	1.79	2.41**	3.07
Change in state ownership[4]	−2.23**	−2.56	−1.97†	−1.88	−1.42	−0.89
Telephones	−1.21**	−7.03	−1.06**	−5.13	−2.26**	−7.83
Roads	0.32**	3.39	0.36**	2.95	0.55**	3.93
Inland navigable waterways	0.11**	6.72	0.17**	7.55	0.07**	2.70
Regional variables						
Average consumption p.c.	0.48	1.40	0.30	0.75	−0.51	−0.52
Average population	0.02	1.12	0.01	0.57	−0.04	−1.32
Average annual real growth[6]	3.73**	4.01	5.65**	4.77	1.17	0.82
IV parameters						
Coast	1.38**	8.95	1.63**	6.85	1.51**	3.60
Northeast	0.72**	3.17	1.04**	4.03	1.11**	3.51
Inland	0.80**	2.84	1.24**	3.79	1.26**	2.63
Southwest	1.66**	6.85	2.00**	5.99	1.54**	4.05
Northwest	0.69**	2.06	0.87*	2.19	1.49**	3.02
Obs	80,808		47,964		32,844	
Log likelihood	−7848.62		−4648.31		−3102.07	
LR test	3536.24**		2119.50**		1613.21**	
LR test: IV parameters=1	64.94**		143.91**		26.20**	

[1] **, *, and † indicate significance at the 1%, 5%, and 10% levels, respectively.
[2] Gansu and Tibet excluded since no foreign investment located there during the time period.
[3] Variable is lagged one year.
[4] Not in logs.
[5] Weighted by (1 − share of industrial output from SOEs).
[6] Three-year moving average. Not in logs.

regional averages of consumption per capita, population, and real income growth as determinants of regional choice.

Table 5 presents the nested logit results for the full sample and both subsamples, incorporating pollution intensity. If the investor's decision is not nested, then the estimated inclusive value (IV) parameters should be equal to one. The last row of Table 5 shows that this null hypothesis is rejected for the full sample and each of the source sub-samples. As further verification of the nested logit specification, the IV parameters for both sub-samples are within the range consistent with the maintained assumption of stochastic profit maximization.[41] Results for the full sample (model 1) show that investors are attracted to regions with high annual real income growth. While this holds true for ECE investors, non-ECE investors' decisions are not significantly influenced by any of these regional attributes.

The results in Table 5 confirm that the levy plays no significant role in determining the choice of province for investors in low pollution intensity industries. The estimated levy effect is negative for investors in industries of medium pollution intensity, but these coefficients are never statistically significant. However, there is a negative and significant response to the levy by investors in highly polluting industries for the full sample. When the sample is split by source, it is clear that this result is

---

[41] See Ondrich and Wasylenko (1993) and Kling and Herriges (1995).

J.M. Dean et al. / Journal of Development Economics 90 (2009) 1–13   11

Table 6
Elasticity of unconditional probabilities with respect to change in selected own province characteristics.

Province characteristics	Elasticities					
	Guangdong		Henan		Inner Mongolia	
	ECE	Non-ECE	ECE	Non-ECE	ECE	Non-ECE
Pollution levy (high polluter)	−0.48	−0.14	−0.54	−0.16	−0.52	−0.16
# Local firms	0.41	0.63	0.47	0.69	0.45	0.70
Agglomeration	0.40	0.09	0.45	0.09	0.43	0.10
Skilled labor	0.58	2.66	0.66	2.88	0.64	2.94
Unskilled labor	−0.67	−1.24	−0.76	−1.34	−0.73	−1.37
Incentives[1,2]	0.42	1.48				
Consumption per capita[1]	0.16	1.32	0.18	1.43	0.18	1.46
Real provincial growth	1.04	2.31	1.28	2.50	1.14	2.55
SOE growth	−1.74	−1.36	−2.01	−1.47	−1.94	−1.50
Inland navigable waterways/area	0.15	0.07	0.17	0.07	0.17	0.07
Roads/area	0.32	0.53	0.37	0.57	0.36	0.58

[1] Incentives and consumption per capita weighted by the share of output from non-SOEs.
[2] Of these three provinces, only Guangdong had any SEZs or had Open Coastal Cities between 1993 and 1996.

driven by the ECE sample.[42] Non-ECE investors are negatively but not significantly influenced by the levy, regardless of the pollution intensity of the industry. Thus, the nested logit analysis supports the conclusion that only ECE investment in highly polluting industries is significantly deterred by stringent pollution regulation.

To compare the effects of environmental stringency relative to other determinants of FDI location choice, we compute the elasticities of the unconditional probability of locating in three provinces (Table 6). These elasticities are based on the nested logit coefficients in Table 5 and the unconditional probabilities evaluated at the means of the provincial variables. Guangdong is a relatively high income province with high average pollution levies, a high level of agglomeration, a high percentage of wastewater meeting the provincial standard, and a relatively low average effluent concentration. Henan and Inner Mongolia are moderate and low income provinces, respectively, with progressively lower levies and less agglomeration, higher average effluent concentrations, and lower percentages of wastewater meeting the provincial standard.

The first row of Table 6 shows that while both ECE and non-ECE investors in highly-polluting industries have an inelastic response to changes in the own province average levy, the ECE elasticities are about three times larger than those of non-ECE investors. A one percent increase in Guangdong's average levy decreases the likelihood of locating there by 0.48% for ECE investors, but only 0.14% for non-ECE investors. The impact of a one percent change in Henan's or Mongolia's levy on the likelihood that ECE investors will locate there is somewhat higher than for Guangdong, indicating a greater sensitivity to marginal changes in levies in low stringency areas.

In all three provinces, ECE investors show a large, elastic response to an increase in the local growth rate and to the rate of decline in state ownership. A one percent reduction in state ownership increases the probability that an ECE investor locates in Guangdong by 1.7%, while a one percent increase in the provincial growth rate increases the probability by 1%. These elasticities are even larger for Inner Mongolia and Henan, where state ownership is high and diminishing slowly, and where income growth is slow. ECE FDI is more attracted by an increase (decrease) in the relative supply of skilled (unskilled) labor in all three provinces than by reductions in the average pollution levy. These results suggest that educating the work force and increasing privatization are potentially more useful tools for attracting ECE FDI than reducing environmental stringency.

Non-ECE FDI also shows an elastic response to changes in state ownership, and a relatively large inelastic response to changes in the number of local suppliers. In contrast to ECE investment, non-ECE FDI

is highly responsive to changes in the abundance of skilled labor and to increased real provincial income growth. A one percent increase in the ratio of skilled labor raises the likelihood of choosing Guangdong by 2.66%, while a one percent faster real growth rate raises it by 2.31%. For Henan and Inner Mongolia, where real incomes are lower and skilled labor is relatively scarce, these elasticities are larger. These comparatively large elasticities might reflect the greater specialization of non-ECE investors in high-skill-intensive goods, and their orientation toward the domestic market.

6. Conclusion

Because it is host to the largest share of FDI to the developing world and because environmental stringency varies among its provinces, China is an excellent setting for an investigation of the pollution haven effect. We have created and analyzed a new compilation of foreign EJVs into China during 1993–1996, categorized by industry, source country, and province. These data exhibit wide dispersion in FDI across industries and provinces. Our evidence from conditional and nested logit analysis indicates that ECE-sourced FDI in highly polluting industries is significantly deterred from provinces with relatively stringent pollution regulation. In contrast, FDI from non-ECE countries is not deterred, regardless of pollution intensity. These findings suggest that there are important links between the investor's source country, the pollution intensity of the industry, and PH behavior. While we find evidence of PH behavior by foreign investors in China, it is not by investors from high income countries and it is only in industries that are highly polluting.

One explanation for these findings may be technology differences. Profit-maximizing behavior implies that PH behavior is conditioned by technology. As Bhagwati (2004) has argued, richer countries have higher environmental standards, which have induced innovation and production of environment-friendly technology (Lanjouw and Mody, 1996), so that FDI from these countries often employs newer, cleaner technology even in locations where standards are relatively weak.[43] In contrast, entrepreneurs in poorer countries with lower standards typically use older, less "green" technologies and may import them as second-hand machinery.[44] If regulatory costs are non-negligible, we might expect them to affect decisions of investors from poorer rather than richer countries.

We do not have any direct evidence on the levels of technology used by investors in our sample. However, the non-ECE group is dominated by investors from the US, EU, and Japan, while the ECE group is

---

[42] Wald tests showed no significant difference between the coefficients for low and medium polluters, but significant differences between high polluters and the other two groups.

[43] Empirical evidence supports this claim (Pearson 2000 pp. 319–320). Firms may do this because dirtier techniques: are costly (older less efficient equipment); reduce the ability to export if goods do not meet the latest quality/environmental standards; increase financial risk from publicity of poor environmental performance.

[44] See a number of papers in Blackman (2006).

12   J.M. Dean et al. / Journal of Development Economics 90 (2009) 1–13

dominated by investors from Hong Kong, Taiwan, and Macao. To the extent that these developing economies are characterized by relatively weak environmental standards or relatively limited access to green technologies, our results would be consistent with alternative technology-based explanations of PH behavior. Concern should then be focused on expanding access to abatement technology and lowering the cost of its adoption in developing countries.

Given recent advances in the incorporation of firm heterogeneity into models of offshore production, it seems particularly promising to explore the possibility that firm TFP is correlated with abatement efficiency. If so, and if the lowest productivity level needed to become a multinational varies by source country, due to differences in distance or other cost factors, then these costs factors may provide a partial explanation for the differential behavior we uncover in our sample. Understanding the nature and strength of these and other differences is for future research.

Appendix A. Data definitions and sources

Variable	Definition	Source
EJV project data	Province, value $10,000 (1990), source, industry	*Almanac of China's Foreign Economic Relations and Trade*, various years
EJV source classification	ECE = Macao, Taiwan, Hong Kong, S. Asian countries Non-ECE = all other countries	Coded by authors
EJV industry classification	ISIC revision 2, 3-digit industries	Coded by authors
Average levy	Total collected water pollution levies/wastewater (yuan/ton)	World Bank dataset compiled from *Chinese Environmental Yearbook*, various years
Average effluent intensity	COD (kg)/000 tons wastewater	World Bank dataset compiled from *Chinese Environmental Yearbook*, various years
Industry pollution intensity	COD (kg)/output (thousand 1990 RMB yuan), by ISIC classification	World Bank dataset compiled from *Chinese Environmental Yearbook*, various years
Skilled labor	Percent of population who have a senior secondary school education level or above	*China Statistical Yearbook*, various years, and calculations by authors
Unskilled labor	Percent of population who are either illiterate or have less than primarily level education	*China Statistical Yearbook*, various years, and calculations by authors
Semi-skilled labor	Percent of population who have primary or junior secondary education level	*China Statistical Yearbook*, various years, and calculations by authors
Cumulative FDI value	Cumulative value of real contracted FDI, from 1983 until $t − 1$ (in 1980 prices), $million	Coughlin and Segev (2000)
Number of domestic enterprises	[Number of industrial enterprises − (number of non-ECE industrial enterprises) − (number of ECE industrial enterprises)], township level and above. (000s)	*China Statistical Yearbook*, various years, and calculations by authors.
Telephones	Number of year-end urban subscribers/population, lagged one year	*China Statistical Yearbook*, various years
Incentive	Dummy variable for a province with either SEZ or Open Coastal City (as of 1996)	Constructed by authors.

Appendix A (continued)

Variable	Definition	Source
Roads	Highways (km)/land area (km^2)	*China Statistical Yearbook*, various years
Railroads	Railway (km)/land area (km^2)	*China Statistical Yearbook*, various years
Consumption p.c.	Consumption (1000 yuan)/population	*China Statistical Yearbook*, various years
Growth rate of real GDP	Percentage change in annual real industrial output (1990 yuan), lagged one year	World Bank dataset compiled from *China Statistical Yearbook*, various years
Change in state ownership	Difference between share of industrial output from SOEs in year t and $t − 1$.	World Bank dataset compiled from *China Statistical Yearbook*, various years, and author calculations.

References

Amiti, M., Javorcik, B.S., 2008. Trade costs and the location of foreign firms in China. Journal of Development Economics 85, 129–149.
Bhagwati, J., 2004. In Defense of Globalization. Oxford University Press, New York.
Blackman, A. (Ed.), 2006. Small Firms and the Environment in Developing Countries: Collective Impacts, Collective Action. Resources for the Future, Washington, DC.
Blonigen, B.A., Wang, M.G., 2005. Inappropriate pooling of wealthy and poor countries in empirical FDI studies. In: Moran, T., Graham, E., Blomstrom, M. (Eds.), Does Foreign Direct Investment Promote Development? Institute for International Economics, Washington, D.C., pp. 221–243.
Brandt, L., Zhu, S., undated. FDI, technology transfer and absorption in Shanghai. Department of Economics, University of Toronto, manuscript.
Broadman, H., Sun, X., 1997. The distribution of foreign investment in China. World Economy 20, 339–361.
Cheng, L.K., Kwan, Y.K., 2000. What are the determinants of the location of foreign direct investment? The Chinese experience. Journal of International Economics 51, 370–400.
Copeland, B.R., Taylor, M.S., 1994. North–South trade and the environment. Quarterly Journal of Economics 109, 755–787.
Copeland, B.R., Taylor, M.S., 2003. Trade and the Environment: Theory No. and Evidence. Princeton University Press, Princeton.
Copeland, B.R., Taylor, M.S., 2004. Trade, growth and the environment. Journal of Economic Literature 42, 7–71.
Coughlin, C., Segev, E., 2000. Foreign direct investment in China: a spatial analysis. World Economy 23, 1–23.
Dasgupta, S., Huq, M., Wheeler, D., 1997. Bending the rules: discretionary pollution controls in China. World Bank Policy Research Working Paper No. 1761.
Dean, J.M., 1992. Trade and the environment: a survey of the literature. In: Low, P. (Ed.), International trade and the environment. World Bank Discussion Paper No. 159.
Dean, J.M., 2001. International Trade and Environment. Ashgate Publishers, U.K.
Dean, J.M., 2002. Does trade liberalization harm the environment? A new test. Canadian Journal of Economics 35, 819–842.
Dean, J.M., Lovely, M.E., 2004. Trade growth, production fragmentation, and China's environment. NBER Working Paper No. 13860.
Dean, J.M., Lovely, M.E., Wang, H., 2002a. Foreign direct investment and pollution havens. Research Proposal to the World Bank. manuscript.
Dean, J.M., Lovely, M.E., Wang, H., 2002b. Foreign direct investment and pollution havens: evaluating the evidence from China. manuscript.
Dean, J.M., Lovely, M.E., Wang, H., 2004. Foreign direct investment and pollution havens: evaluating the evidence from China. U.S. International Trade Commission Working Paper 2004-01-B, Washington, D.C.
Dean, J.M., Lovely, M.E., Wang, H., 2005. Are foreign investors attracted to weak environmental regulations? Evaluating the evidence from China. World Bank Working Paper No. 3505.
Demurger, S., Sachs, J., Woo, W.T., Bao, S., Chang, G., 2002. The relative contributions of location and preferential policies in China's regional development. China Economic Review 13, 444–465.
Di, W., 2007. Pollution abatement cost savings and FDI inflows to polluting sectors in China. Environment and Development Economics 12, 775–798.
Eskeland, G.S., Harrison, A.E., 2003. Moving to greener pastures? Multinationals and the pollution haven hypothesis. Journal of Development Economics 70, 1–23.
Fredriksson, P., List, J.A., Millimet, D.L., 2003. Bureaucratic corruption, environmental policy, and inbound US FDI: theory and evidence. Journal of Public Economics 87, 1407–1430.
Fung, K.C., 1997. Trade and Investment: Mainland China, Hong Kong, and Taiwan. City University of Hong Kong Press, Hong Kong.
Head, K., Ries, J., 1996. Inter-city competition for foreign investment: static and dynamic effects of China's incentive areas. Journal of Urban Economics 40, 38–60.
Head, K., Mayer, T., 2004. Market potential and the location of Japanese investment in Europe. Review of Economics and Statistics 86, 959–972.

J.M. Dean et al. / Journal of Development Economics 90 (2009) 1–13 13

Henley, J., Kirkpatrick, C., Wilde, G., 1999. Foreign direct investment in China: recent trends and current policy issues. World Economy 22, 223–243.

Hettige, H., Mani, M., Wheeler, D., 2000. Industrial pollution in economic development: the environmental Kuznets curve revisited. Journal of Development Economics 62, 445–476.

Hettige, H., Martin, P., Singh, M., Wheeler, D., 1995. The industrial pollution projection system. World Bank Working Paper No. 1431.

Huang, Y., 2003. Selling China: Foreign Direct Investment During the Reform Period. Cambridge University Press, Cambridge, MA.

Javorcik, B.S., Wei, S.-J., 2004. Pollution havens and foreign direct investment: dirty secret or popular myth? Contributions to Economic Analysis and Policy 3 (2) (Article 8).

Keller, W., Levinson, A., 2002. Pollution abatement costs and foreign direct investment inflows to the U.S. states. Review of Economics and Statistics 84, 691–703.

Kling, C.L., Herriges, J.A., 1995. An empirical investigation of the consistency of nested logit models with utility maximization. American Journal of Agricultural Economics 77, 875–884.

Lanjouw, J.O., Mody, A., 1996. Innovation and the international diffusion of environmentally responsive technology. Research Policy 25, 549–571.

Lardy, N.R., 1994. China in the World Economy. Institute for International Economics, Washington, D.C.

List, J.A., Co, C.Y., 2000. The effects of environmental regulations on foreign direct investment. Journal of Environmental Economics and Management 40, 1–20.

List, J.A., McHone, W.W., Millimet, D.L., 2004. Effects of environmental regulation on foreign and domestic plant births: is there a home field advantage? Journal of Urban Economics 56, 303–326.

Ministry of Foreign Trade and Economic Cooperation (various years). Almanac of China's Foreign Economic Relations and Trade. Beijing.

OECD, 2005. Governance in China. OECD, Paris, France.

Ondrich, J., Wasylenko, M., 1993. Foreign Direct Investment in the United States. W.E. Upjohn Institute for Employment Research, Kalamazoo, MI.

Pearson, C., 2000. Economics and the Global Environment. Cambridge University Press, Cambridge, U.K.

Popp, D., 2006. International innovation and diffusion of air pollution control technologies: the effects of NO_x and SO_2 regulation in the U.S., Japan, and Germany. Journal of Environmental Economics and Management 51, 46–71.

SEPA, 2007. Report on the State of the Environment. http://english.sepa.gov.cn/standards_reports/soe/SOE2006/.

Shuguang, Z., Yansheng, Z., Zhongxin, W., 1998. Measuring the Cost of Protection in China. Institute for International Economics, Washington, D.C.

Taylor, M.S., 2004. Unbundling the pollution haven hypothesis. Advances in Economic Analysis and Policy 4 (2) (Article 8).

Tseng, W., Zebregs, H., 2002. Foreign direct investment in China: some lessons for other countries. IMF Policy Discussion Paper PDP/02/3.

UNCTAD, 1996. World Investment Report 1996. United Nations Publications, New York, N.Y.

Varian, H.R., 1992. Microeconomic Analysis. W.W. Norton and Company, New York, N.Y.

Wang, H., Wheeler, D., 2003. Equilibrium pollution and economic development in China. Environment and Development Economics 8, 451–466.

Wang, H., Wheeler, D., 2005. Financial incentives and endogenous enforcement in China's pollution levy system. Journal of Environmental Economics and Management 49, 174–196.

Wang, H., Jin, Y., 2002. Industrial ownership and environmental performance: evidence from China. Environmental and Resource Economics 36, 255–273.

Wang, H., Mamingi, N., LaPlante, B., Dasgupta, S., 2003. Incomplete enforcement of pollution regulation: bargaining power in Chinese factories. Environmental and Resource Economics 24, 245–262.

Trade, technology, and the environment: Does access to technology promote environmental regulation?

Mary Lovely [a], David Popp [b,c,*]

[a] Department of Economics, The Maxwell School, Syracuse University, 110 Eggers Hall, Syracuse, NY 13244-1020, USA
[b] Department of Public Administration, Center for Policy Research, The Maxwell School, Syracuse University, 426 Eggers Hall, Syracuse, NY 13244-1020, USA
[c] National Bureau of Economic Research, USA

ARTICLE INFO

ABSTRACT

Article history:
Received 29 April 2009
Available online 15 December 2010

Keywords:
Technology transfer
Patents
Air pollution
Political economy
Regulation

Focusing specifically on regulation of coal-fired power plants, we examine how technological innovation by early adopters influences the timing of new environmental regulation in non-innovating countries. We build a general equilibrium model of an open economy to identify the political-economy determinants of regulation. With a newly created dataset of SO_2 and NO_x regulations for coal-fired power plants and a patent-based measure of the technology frontier, we estimate the determinants of environmental regulation diffusion. Our findings support the hypothesis that international economic integration eases access to environmentally friendly technologies and leads to earlier adoption, ceteris paribus, of regulation in non-innovating countries. However, we also find evidence that domestic trade protection promotes earlier adoption allowing shifts of regulatory costs to domestic consumers. Furthermore, international market power permits large countries to shift costs to foreign consumers. Other political economy factors, such as the quality of domestic coal, are also important determinants.

© 2010 Elsevier Inc. All rights reserved.

1. Introduction

With mounting environmental costs of economic growth, the world looks to technology for an exit ramp from what seems to be a crash course to ecological disaster. Indeed, China, a prominent example of breakneck growth amid rising domestic damage, recently held its first national conference on technology and the environment, declaring scientific innovation the key to "historic transformation of environmental protection" and "leap-frog development."[1,2] For China and other rapidly growing countries, technology seems to offer a panacea for the environmental problems accompanying their economic development.

If technology is a panacea, it is not a costless one. Installation and use of pollution-control technologies are costly and these technologies are rarely acquired without regulatory stimulus.[3] Thus, to understand the diffusion of costly pollution-control technologies, we need to understand the diffusion of regulation. Regulations enacted by advanced economies induce *new*

---

* Corresponding author at: Center for Policy Research, The Maxwell School, Syracuse University, 426 Eggers Hall, Syracuse, NY 13244-1020, USA. Fax: +1 315 443 1075.
E-mail addresses: melovely@maxwell.syr.edu (M. Lovely), dcpopp@maxwell.syr.edu (D. Popp).
URL: http://faculty.maxwell.syr.edu/dcpopp/index.html (D. Popp).
[1] For a description of the environmental costs of growth in China, see [50].
[2] For a brief overview of the National Conference on Environmental Science and Technology, held August on 18–19, 2006, see [44].
[3] Studies supporting the importance of regulation for diffusion of environmental technologies include Gray and Shadbegian [19], Kerr and Newell [28], Snyder et al. [47], and Popp [38].

0095-0696/$ - see front matter © 2010 Elsevier Inc. All rights reserved.
doi:10.1016/j.jeem.2010.08.003

M. Lovely, D. Popp / Journal of Environmental Economics and Management 61 (2011) 16–35   17

innovations needed to comply with regulation. However, for countries making environmental policy after these pioneers, the technologies needed for compliance already exist when the decision to regulate is made. Thus, in this paper, rather than asking to what extent environmental regulation induces new innovation, as in studies of early adopters, we instead ask how the availability of technology influences the regulation decisions of non-innovating countries.[4]

We focus directly on the decision to regulate emissions from coal-fired power plants, using a newly constructed database of sulfur dioxide (SO_2) and nitrogen oxide (NO_x) regulation across 45 countries. The timing of these particular regulations allows us to identify political economy concerns more precisely than if a broad index of regulation was used. Narrowing our study to a specific set of regulations also allows us to more precisely define the relevant technological frontier. We measure innovation using patents specific to the reduction of SO_2 and NO_x emissions. Our study illuminates the determinants of regulation adoption and thus offers useful lessons for promoting diffusion of other emission-control technologies.

Our research is motivated by the observation that countries regulating coal-fired power plants after 1980 generally did so at a lower level of per-capita income than did early adopters. Fig. 1 is a scatter plot of per capita GDP, in 1995 US dollars, in the year of adoption of regulations for SO_2 and NO_x. The figure includes all countries included in our final dataset, which focuses on the years 1980–2000, as described in Section 3. For both SO_2 and NO_x, we see a strong trend of adoption at lower income over time. Also, except for Australia and New Zealand, where coal stocks are naturally low in sulfur [35,46], the countries yet to adopt regulations are all low income countries.[5] Similar trends hold for NO_x, as shown in panel B. This phenomenon suggests that factors other than income drive the regulatory decision and that early adopters may offer an advantage to countries adopting later, presumably through advances in technology that significantly lower the cost of regulation.

Our approach carefully incorporates the role of international markets and trade policies in transmitting both knowledge and cost shocks across economies. Previous studies suggest that access to international markets influences firms' ability to use new technology. Reppelin-Hill [42] finds that adoption of new technology in the steel industry is positively correlated with trade openness. Acharya and Keller [1] estimate that the contribution of international technology transfer to productivity growth exceeds that of domestic R&D and that imports are a major channel for these spillovers. Consequently, we investigate the possibility that low trade barriers ease access to new technology and, thus, increase the likelihood of domestic regulation.[6]

We acknowledge the double-edged nature of openness, however, in that the global market constrains domestic firms' ability to pass along higher abatement costs. To the extent that local firms are protected from such competition through trade restrictions, their ability to shift the regulatory burden to domestic consumers may be larger and their opposition to regulation lessened. We also consider the size of the domestic economy relative to the world market, reflecting the ability of local producers to pass costs through to foreign consumers.

We begin with a political economy model of regulation. This framework guides our thinking about how international economic integration influences the costs and benefits of regulation. Environmentalists often oppose globalization because of concerns over a race-to-the-bottom, where countries compete for industry lowering environmental standards. While there is little evidence of countries weakening existing standards, Esty [13] notes that countries foregoing opportunities to strengthen environmental standards over concerns of international competitiveness is a real concern. Levinson [34] provides several examples of U.S. policymakers raising concerns about the competitiveness effects of environmental regulations. To address competitiveness, our model indicates the need to distinguish between domestic trade policy, such as tariffs and quotas, and international market power, which depends on economic size and affects the ability of local firms to pass the costs of regulation on to consumers. This perspective has a useful message for empirical work – one should include controls for both domestic trade policy and international market size in estimation – and both channels of influence are significant in our hazard regressions. This model consequently guides our empirical work; Section 3.1 of the paper presents comparative-static analysis that offers several empirical predictions that we test using our panel of regulation data. Our findings support the hypothesis that international economic integration eases access to environmentally friendly technologies and leads to earlier adoption, *ceteris paribus*, of regulation in developing countries. Our results are also consistent with the view that domestic trade protection allows costs to be shifted to domestic consumers while large countries can shift costs to foreign consumers, raising the likelihood of adoption.

2. Theoretical framework

To derive testable hypotheses for our empirical analysis, we consider a general equilibrium model of an economy that uses electricity to produce a tradable good. Electricity is generated burning domestically mined coal. Domestic consumers benefit from consumption but experience disutility from emissions from coal-fired power plants. The allowable level of such emissions is endogenously determined by a government that maximizes a weighted sum of social welfare and contributions

---

[4] In recent years, several papers have studied the potential for environmental policy to induce environmentally friendly innovation. Nearly all of these studies have focused on highly developed economies. This is not surprising, as these countries were the first to enact environmental protections and most R&D expenditures occur in these countries. In 2000, global R&D expenditures were at least $729 billion; 82% of this was done in the OECD and half was performed by the United States and Japan alone [36].

[5] Australia and New Zealand do adopt NO_x regulations, but not SO_2, given the low sulfur content of coal in their countries.

[6] Keller and Yeaple [27] suggest productivity spillovers through foreign investment are stronger than those from imports. However, there is very little foreign investment in coal-fired power plants. For example, Fisher-Vanden et al. [14] report that only 1.9% of capital in China's electric power sector is foreign capital.

18   *M. Lovely, D. Popp / Journal of Environmental Economics and Management 61 (2011) 16–35*

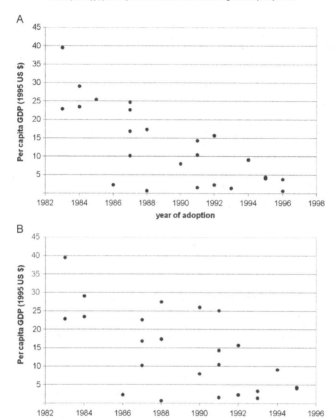

Fig. 1. Per capita GDP in the year of adoption: (A) sulfur dioxide (SO₂) and (B) nitrogen oxide (NOₓ).

from organized interest groups. The country does not engage in pollution control R&D, instead in purchasing abatement services from international suppliers.

2.1. Production

To capture the importance of coal to downstream sectors, we posit a model with four production sectors: agriculture, which serves as numeraire, coal mining, electricity generation, and manufacturing. Each sector uses intersectorally mobile labor as a factor of production while coal, electricity, and manufacturing production also require the use of sector-specific capital. The owners of these sector-specific factors engage in lobbying to influence the level of pollution regulation chosen by the government.[7]

---

[7] Specific-factor models are used frequently in endogenous policy analyses. Because these models imply the existence of factor rents, they provide a mechanism by which agents have resources to expend in an attempt to influence government policy. Hillman [23] provides a useful overview in the context of trade policy.

M. Lovely, D. Popp / Journal of Environmental Economics and Management 61 (2011) 16–35   19

The economy contains L workers, each of which inelastically supplies one unit of labor. We have normalized the number of workers to unity, without loss of generality. Agriculture serves as numeraire and is modeled as a tradable sector with a constant-returns technology. We choose units so that one unit of output requires one unit of labor input, tying the wage at unity. We assume that aggregate labor supply is large enough so that there is always a positive supply of locally produced agricultural products.

Electricity, E, from coal-fired plants is produced with sector-specific capital, labor, and coal, using the technology $E = \min[f_E(K_E, L_E), C_E]$, where C_E is the quantity of coal used in electricity generation. The function $f_E(K_E, L_E)$ exhibits constant returns. Electricity is not traded, so its price is determined on the domestic market. Each unit of coal burned generates one unit of emissions and plants may be required to abate these emissions. A regulatory standard requires electricity plants to apply A units of abatement services per unit of coal burned, resulting in an $A\%$ reduction in the volume of emissions. These services can be obtained only from the installation of imported pollution abatement equipment. The domestic price of abatement services, which reflects the lease price of imported abatement equipment, is $P_A(T)$. We posit that the price of abatement is driven by the level of technology, T, and that innovation reduces the price of abatement: $\partial P_A / \partial T < 0$.

The return to owners of coal-fired power plants is

$$\pi_E = P_E E - (P_C + P_A A) C_E - w L_E = P_E^N E - w L_E, \tag{1}$$

where P_E is the price of electricity and P_C is the price of coal. To obtain the last term, note that one unit of electricity requires one unit of coal and defines the net price of electricity as $P_E^N = P_E - P_C - P_A A$. We assume that coal is not traded, its price is endogenously determined.[8]

Coal, C, is mined by the application of labor to coal reserves. The technology for coal production, $C = f_C(K_C, L_C)$, exhibits constant returns. The return to owners of coal reserves is

$$\pi_c = P_C C - w L_C. \tag{2}$$

Manufactures, M, are internationally traded. The production technology for manufactures is $M = \min[f_M(K_M, L_M), E_M]$, where E_M is the quantity of electricity used in manufacturing and the function $f_M(K_M, L_M)$ exhibits constant returns. Letting P_M denote the domestic price of manufactures, earnings of manufacturing capital owners are

$$\pi_M = P_M M - P_E E - w L_M = P_M^N M - w L_M, \tag{3}$$

where we use the requirement for one unit of electricity per unit of manufactures and define the net price of manufactures as $P_M^N = P_M - P_E$.

Equilibrium in the production sector is defined as a vector of domestic product prices, factor rewards, and output levels for which the value marginal product of labor is equal across all sectors; the domestic supply of electricity and coal equals the domestic demand for electricity and coal, respectively; and labor demanded equals labor supplied, given world prices and the emissions abatement level chosen by the government.[9]

2.2. How are profits affected by a stricter abatement standard?

Profits of specific factor owners are affected by the abatement level chosen by the government. The extent to which profits fall when standards are tightened depends on the ability of firms to pass these costs through to consumers, which is determined by both international and domestic market conditions. Consider first a country pursuing free trade. Firms may pass through some cost increases to foreign consumers if local supply changes influence the world price—that is, if the country is large enough to influence its terms of trade. The ability of local producers to pass through regulatory costs depends on the elasticity of the excess demand for manufactures facing the home country. If the country is small on world markets, it faces an infinitely elastic excess demand curve and it has no pass-through ability.

Even in small countries with no international market power, however, restrictive trade policies may confer on producers an ability to pass through costs to consumers.[10] Consider a small economy with a binding import quota. Domestic demand beyond the quota amount is met by domestic producers, whose ability to pass regulatory costs to consumers depends on the local excess demand elasticity. This elasticity may reasonably be considered a function of the quota level: the more restrictive the quota, the more distorted the consumption compared to the free-trade level and the less elastic the residual demand curve. If this relationship holds, producers in countries with more restrictive trade policies will be able to pass through a larger share of the regulatory burden to consumers.

We denote excess demand by $X_M(P_M)$ and interpret this as excess world or excess (above quota) domestic demand, depending on the case. In equilibrium, domestic supply must equal excess demand, $M = X_M(P_M)$. Using this condition, changes

---

[8] An alternative specification, allowing the price of coal to be exogenously determined, yields the same empirical predictions, with the exception of the effect of larger coal reserves on the political equilibrium.

[9] Details can be found in Appendix A, which is available at JEEM's online archive of supplementary materials. This can be accessed at http://aere.org/journals/.

[10] As in Damania et al. [10], we take trade policy as independent of regulatory policy as the former is constrained by multilateral agreement.

in domestic supply affect price to the extent permitted by the slope of the excess demand curve:

$$\frac{dP_M}{dM} = \frac{1}{\partial X_M / \partial P_M} \equiv -\chi_{MM}.$$

Total profits for specific-capital owners are $\pi_M + \pi_E + \pi_C$. Noting that the price of labor is not affected by regulation and using (1)–(3), the change in profits from stricter regulation is

$$\frac{\partial \pi}{\partial A} = \frac{\partial \pi_M}{\partial A} + \frac{\partial \pi_E}{\partial A} + \frac{\partial \pi_C}{\partial A} = -[P_A E + M \chi_{MM} M_A] < 0. \tag{4}$$

The first term in brackets is the direct cost of the additional regulation. The second term is the addition to profits from a higher equilibrium price when the local supply curve shifts. Appendix A shows that in general equilibrium $M_A \equiv \partial M / \partial A < 0$ and that $\partial \pi / \partial A < 0$.

Result 1. *Effect of a Stricter Abatement Standard on Profits.* The incomes of specific-factor owners are decreasing in the level of the abatement standard. Specific factor owners bear a larger regulatory burden the more limited their ability to pass costs through to consumers.

2.3. How are consumers affected by a stricter abatement standard?

We assume consumers care about the environment as well as consumption and have quasi-linear preferences of the form $U = D_A + u(D_M) - \varphi(1-A)E$, where D_A is agricultural good consumption, and D_M is manufactures consumption.[11] Damage from emissions is proportional to unabated coal burning for electricity generation, $(1-A)E$. Marginal damage φ is assumed to be a function of exogenous country characteristics, such as population density. Consumers earn income from labor and an income of w. Consumers include both workers and capital owners, whom we assume supply one unit of labor in addition to receiving the profits from production. Because we have already considered the effect of regulation on profits, here we consider factory owners only as workers and consumers.[12]

This utility function implies that the marginal utility of income is unity, given the positive consumption of the agricultural good. Consequently, each consumer's demand for the manufactured good, denoted by $D_M(P_M)$, is the inverse of $\delta u(D_M)/\delta D_M$. Consumer surplus is given by $S(P_M) = u(D_M(P_M)) - P_M D_M(P_M)$. Indirect utility, our measure of consumer welfare, is $V(P_M, A, E) = w + S(P_M) - \varphi(1-A)E$. The effect of a stricter standard on consumer welfare is

$$\frac{dV}{dA} = \frac{\partial V}{\partial P_M} \frac{\partial P_M}{\partial A} + \frac{\partial V}{\partial A} + \frac{\partial V}{\partial E} \frac{\partial E}{\partial A} = \varphi E - \varphi(1-A)E_A + D_M(P_M) \chi_{MM} M_A. \tag{5}$$

Appendix A shows that $E_A \equiv \partial E / \partial A < 0$. The environmental effect of regulation, the first two terms on the right-most side of (5), unambiguously raises consumers' welfare directly reducing emissions through tighter standards and reducing emissions indirectly through less electricity generation. The last term in (5) indicates that consumers' welfare is influenced by regulation's impact on P_M. Because a stricter abatement standard leads to a backward shift in the local supply curve, P_M rises and consumer surplus falls if firms have any pass-through ability. In sum, a stricter abatement standard has benefits and possible costs for consumers: it reduces emissions but it also may raise the price of consumption.

Result 2. *Effect of a Stricter Abatement Standard on Consumers.* A stricter standard increases consumers' welfare by reducing damage from emissions. There is a consumer surplus loss from stricter regulation, however, if it raises the relative price of manufactures. Consumer surplus loss is larger the greater firms' ability to pass through compliance costs to consumers.

2.4. Political economy

Because specific-factor owners bear some burden of regulation, they will expend real resources lobbying the government to avoid it. We assume capital owners in the coal mining, electricity, and manufacturing sectors solve the collective action problem and form an organized "coal lobby," which distributes the costs of organized action among its members. The abatement standard is set by a government that values social welfare and contributions (or bribes) from this coal lobby. The government and the organized lobby play a non-cooperative, sequential, complete-information game. In the first stage, the lobby chooses a contribution schedule, $B(A)$, that maximizes its members' net welfare contingent on the abatement standard chosen by the government. In the second stage of the game, the government chooses an abatement standard to maximize a weighted sum of contributions and aggregate social welfare. Denoting social welfare by $W(A)$, the government's objective function is $G(A) = \alpha W(A) + (1-\alpha)B(A)$, where α, $0 \le \alpha \le 1$, is the weight placed by the government on social welfare.

---

[11] Quasi-linear preferences simplify treatment of the political equilibrium and are used by Grossman and Helpman [21] and Damania et al. [10]. Dixit et al. [11] discuss the drawbacks of the method and develop a model with general preferences and nontransferable utility.

[12] Because quasi-linear preferences imply that the marginal utility of income is constant, we are able to distinguish, for analytical purposes, a capital owner as a worker/consumer and as a receiver of profits. The total effect on capitalists is the sum of these two effects and both are included in the welfare expression in Eq. (7).

M. Lovely, D. Popp / Journal of Environmental Economics and Management 61 (2011) 16–35   21

An equilibrium of the game is a subgame-perfect Nash equilibrium consisting of a contribution schedule and an abatement standard. We confine ourselves to equilibria in truthful contribution schedules, which take the form:

$$B(A) = \max\{\pi(A) - b, 0\},\tag{6}$$

where b is a constant. Bernheim and Whinston [4] argue that a truthful Nash equilibrium is among the equilibria of the game.[13]

The coal lobby ignores consumer surplus and environmental damage and, thus, the preferences of the lobby are given by $\pi(A) = \pi_M(A) + \pi_E(A) + \pi_C(A)$. Substituting (6) into the government's objective function and noting that social welfare gross-of-contributions is the sum of profits, labor income, and consumer surplus, minus the damage from coal burning, yields

$$G(A) = \alpha[w + S(P_M(A)) - \varphi(1-A)E(A)] + \pi(A) - b.\tag{7}$$

Using Results 1 and 2, the first-order condition for maximizing the government's objective, allowing for complementary slackness, is

$$\alpha[\varphi E - \varphi(1-A^*)E_A + D_M\chi_{MM}M_A] - [P_A E + M\chi_{MM}M_A] \leq 0; if < 0, A^* = 0.\tag{8}$$

This expression characterizes the political-equilibrium abatement standard. The first term on the left-hand side of (8) gives the (weighted) marginal benefit of regulation. This marginal benefit is the sum of three impacts: the direct effect on emissions, the indirect benefit from reduced coal-fired electricity use, and the possible reduction in consumer surplus. The second term gives the marginal cost for the government, in terms of reduced contributions from the coal lobby.

When a non-negative standard is chosen, the marginal benefit of regulation to the government equals its marginal cost. If firms have no ability to pass through cost increases, from (8) the political-equilibrium level of abatement is $A^* = 1 + (E/\alpha\varphi E_A)(P_A - \alpha\varphi)$. If the government chooses an abatement standard that does not require the complete abatement of emissions ($A^* < 1$), it must be that $P_A - \alpha\varphi > 0$. Thus, the politically chosen abatement standard is weaker, the larger the cost of abatement relative to the value of cleaner air to the government.[14]

When firms do face an elastic excess demand curve, either because of international market power or domestic trade protection, the politically optimal abatement level is

$$A^* = 1 + \frac{1}{\alpha\varphi E_A}\{(P_A - \alpha\varphi)E + \alpha(M - D_M)\chi_{MM}M_A + (1-\alpha)M\chi_{MM}M_A\}.\tag{9}$$

The first term in brackets reflects the balance between the direct regulatory costs and the value to consumers of lower emissions. The second and third terms in brackets reflect the consequences of firms' ability to shift costs forward to consumers. As measured by the second term in brackets, producer revenue gained through the price rise is offset by lost consumer surplus. If the country is a net exporter of manufactures and can influence its terms of trade, the gain to producers must exceed lost domestic consumer surplus as foreign consumers bear some of the burden. If the country is a net importer but imports are relatively small, perhaps as a consequence of trade restriction, this term will also be relatively small. The last term in brackets gives the extra weight placed on producer revenue gains, indicating that a producer price increase, whether from international or domestic market power, reduces the government's regulatory cost in terms of lost contributions and leads to adoption of a stricter standard.

Finally, note that the government may choose not to regulate. The government will not enact an abatement standard if the benefits of abatement are not large enough to offset the cost of lost contributions, either because the relative marginal disutility of emissions (φ) is small or the cost of abatement is high.

3. Empirical strategy

We use our theoretical framework to understand the determinants of a country's initial decision to adopt emissions regulations for coal-fired power plants, as well as how long it takes to adopt regulations above a certain threshold. Thus, the dependent variable is a binary variable indicating whether a country has enacted emission standards (for a specific pollutant) as of year t. A country drops out of the sample the year after adoption. We begin discussion of our empirical strategy by deriving predictions about the relationship between adoption and the determinants identified by our theory. Next, we discuss construction of the dependent variable and our key explanatory variables. Table 1 describes the variables and their sources in greater detail. The final sample includes data from 1980–2000 on 39 countries.[15] Table 2 provides descriptive data for each of these variables for the 39 countries used in the empirical analysis.

---

[13] A locally truthful contribution schedule has the property that $\partial B(A)/\partial A = \partial\pi(A)/\partial A$ at the equilibrium point. Grossman and Helpman [19] provide an application to trade policy, Damania et al. [10] an application to environmental policy and Fredriksson and Wollscheid [17] an application to abatement technology investment.

[14] The abatement rate that maximizes social welfare for a small country is given by (8) when $\alpha = 1$. It is readily seen that the socially optimal level exceeds the politically optimal level when a non-zero standard is chosen.

[15] The countries with missing data are Vietnam (no data in WDI), Poland, Czech Republic (no data in WDI until after the country adopts regulation), Hong Kong (no political data), and Ukraine (no data on merchandise exports). In addition, we do not have trade data for Romania until 1990, and so deleted Romanian observations earlier than 1990. This is consistent with our treatment of other Eastern European countries, where we only consider adoption

22   *M. Lovely, D. Popp / Journal of Environmental Economics and Management 61 (2011) 16–35*

Table 1
Data definitions and sources. Sources: WDI: *World Development Indicators*;EIA/WDI: Coal data from Energy Information Administration *International Energy Annual 2003*, available at http://www.eia.doe.gov/iea. Population data from WDI; FH: Index produced by Freedom House (http://www.freedomhouse.org); DPI: Database of Political Institutions [26]; HK: Hiscox and Kastner [24].

Variable	Description	Source
Openness		
Trade Policy Orientation Index	Index created by fixed country-year effects in a gravity model of bilateral trade	HK
Import share	(Imports)/GDP	WDI
International market position		
World export share	Merchandise exports as share of world merchandise exports	WDI
Political economy—marginal benefit of abatement		
GDP per capita[a]	Per capita GDP in constant 1995 US $	WDI
Population density[a]	People per square km	WDI
Political economy—importance of coal		
% Electricity from coal[a]	% of electricity production from coal sources	WDI
Coal production per capita[a]	Total coal production, in quadrillion BTU, per person	EIA/WDI
Lignite production per capita[a]	Production of lignite coal, in million short tons, per person	EIA/WDI
Political economy—other		
Election year	Dummy=1, if executive branch election held that year	DPI
Political rights	Index of political rights, ranging from 1 (free) to 7 (not free)	FH
Liberal	Dummy=1 if country led by a liberal party	DPI
Conservative	Dummy=1 if country led by a conservative party	DPI

    [a] These variables are scaled in the regression so that a one-unit change represents a 10% deviation from the mean.

Table 2
Descriptive data.

Variable	N	Mean	Std. Dev.	min	Median	max
Import shares	771	30.574	14.410	6.855	27.873	84.398
Import shares from top countries	771	11.765	6.308	0.000	10.623	30.890
Trade policy orientation index	672	−31.454	14.861	−77.978	−27.471	−1.970
World export share	771	2.120	2.890	0.030	0.924	12.775
GDP per capita	771	13724.48	12146.67	166.75	11179.19	46815.50
Population density	771	123.121	114.878	1.912	93.345	476.127
% Electricity from coal	771	33.354	25.811	0	27.263	99.474
Coal production per capita	771	2.17E−08	4.47E−08	0	5.19E−09	3.47E−07
Lignite production per capita	771	0.001	0.001	0	5.55E−08	0.007
Election year	771	0.057	0.232	0	0	1
Political rights	771	2.258	1.784	1	1	7
Liberal	771	0.379	0.485	0	0	1
Conservative	771	0.431	0.495	0	0	1
Eastern Europe dummy	771	0.101	0.302	0	0	1

3.1. Empirical predictions

    Changes in the exogenous factors: the price of abatement services, the country's pass-through ability, domestic coal reserves, the value consumers place on clean air, and the weight placed by the government on social welfare, affect the politically determined abatement standard. We consider a country for which the first-order condition (8) and the second-order condition, $G_{AA} < 0$, hold at a non-negative level of A^*.[16]

Prediction 1. A reduction in the price of abatement services tightens the political equilibrium abatement standard when there is no abatement.

(footnote continued)
decisions made in the post-Communist era. This is due both to data availability and because under the Communist regime, many of these countries had stringent environmental laws on the books that were not enforced.
    [16] We follow the literature and ignore effects that involve third derivatives of production functions as we have no economic interpretation for these effects and because the specific factor model does not place restrictions on them.

M. Lovely, D. Popp / Journal of Environmental Economics and Management 61 (2011) 16–35   23

Proof. Total differentiation of (8), evaluated at $A^* = 0$, yields

$$\frac{dA^*}{dP_A} = \frac{E}{G_{AA}} < 0. \tag{10}$$

The sign follows from the assumption that the second-order condition holds. □

Because most pollution control technologies are developed in just a few countries, international trade increases access to new technologies, effectively reducing the user cost of advanced abatement equipment and making adoption more likely.[17] Therefore, in our hazard analysis we interact the knowledge stock (defined in Section 3.3), representing the available new technologies, with alternative measures of openness. The idea is that the global knowledge stock represents technology *potentially* available to each country. The level of access to this technology depends on a country's openness. Eq. (10) suggests that the sign of the estimated coefficient for this interaction will reflect a higher adoption probability in more open economies when the knowledge stock grows. Support for this form of "access effect" is consistent with technology embodied in imported goods or imports-related learning.

We employ two alternative measures of trade openness for our estimation. First is the ratio of the total value of imports to GDP.[18] To assess access to abatement technology, we use the total value of imports from six countries: US, Japan, Germany, Sweden, Switzerland, and Finland. These six countries are responsible for 85% of the patents on the technologies studied, and are the only countries responsible for 5% or more of the patents for at least one of the technologies.[19] Import shares have been used in many prior studies on technological diffusion and it has the distinct advantage of being available for all countries in our sample for most years. However, this ratio is also influenced by factors other than trade policy, most notably country size, limiting our ability to isolate an "access effect" of openness from the ability to pass-through regulatory costs to foreign consumers.[20] Consequently, we employ an alternative measure that controls for country characteristics, including the size of the economy, the Hiscox–Kastner trade policy orientation index (TPOI). This index is constructed from the residuals of a gravity model of bilateral trade flows, expressed relative to the sample maximum intercept. The numbers represent the percentage reduction in imports in each year due to deviations of trade policy from a free-trade benchmark. TPOI calculates "missing trade" and thus, measures a country's barriers to trade not accounted for by distance, remoteness, and other controls used in the gravity estimation.[21] In our empirical work, we multiply this missing trade by negative 1, so that increases in our TPOI variable can be interpreted as more open trade, just as higher import shares indicate greater openness.

Prediction 2. In the political equilibrium, greater ability by producers to pass compliance costs through to consumers leads to a stricter standard.

Proof. Totally differentiating (8) and rearranging yields

$$\frac{dA^*}{d\chi_{MM}} = \frac{[\alpha(M - D_M) + (1 - \alpha)M]}{G_{AA}} M_A. \quad \square \tag{11}$$

We consider the effect of international market power, conveyed by country size relative to the world economy, separately from the market power conveyed on domestic producers from trade restrictions. First, if the country has some ability to influence the international terms of trade and it is a net exporter of manufactures, the term in brackets is positive and the total derivative is positive. In this case, greater pass-through of compliance costs unambiguously increases the politically determined standard as the weight on producers' contributions exceeds the weight given to that on consumer surplus. Moreover, if the country is a net importer of manufactures but these are relatively small, defined as $(D_M - M)/M < (1 - \alpha)/\alpha$, the term in brackets is positive and the total derivative is positive. These considerations imply that our empirical analysis of the adoption decision should control for the size of the domestic economy relative to the world economy, which we measure as merchandise exports as a share of world merchandise exports. Data for this measure is drawn from the World Development Indicators (WDI).

Even in a country too small to influence its terms of trade, producers may be able to pass regulatory costs along to consumers if trade policy is sufficiently restrictive. For this reason we also include the direct effect of our two alternative openness measures defined above: the total value of imports relative to GDP and the Hiscox–Kastner trade policy orientation index. Unlike the interaction with knowledge, here we use imports from all countries, rather than just producers of pollution

---

[17] The producers of nearly all the SO₂ scrubbers listed in the IEA's CoalPower 4 database [6] are headquartered in the U.S., Japan, Germany, or Switzerland, making international trade important for access to these technologies. For instance, all of the listed FGD units installed in China come from foreign suppliers.

[18] We use import share to measure openness because most countries in our sample are abatement equipment importers. The most commonly used measure of openness is exports plus imports as a share of GDP. This alternative measure is highly correlated with the imports-to-GDP ratio.

[19] Our results are similar if we choose a subset of these countries to construct the import shares. However, adding additional, less relevant countries reduces the significance of the interaction.

[20] Using direct policy measures is also problematic. Average tariff rates underestimate the level of protection as the weights used reflect distorted trade flows and do not measure non-tariff barriers. Non-tariff barriers are available for only isolated years. Commonly used alternatives, such as tariff revenue as a share of total imports, have disadvantages shared by average tariff rates.

[21] Hiscox and Kastner [24] describe the gravity model used to estimate the residuals and the index as well as provide a discussion of the advantages and disadvantages of the index. The Hiscox-Kastner index is available for most countries in our sample, with the exception of Eastern European countries and Zimbabwe, for all years in the sample. We thank Scott Kastner for providing updated data. The correlation between the Hiscox-Kastner index and import shares is -0.4383, suggesting that the two measures pick up different characteristics.

24   *M. Lovely, D. Popp / Journal of Environmental Economics and Management 61 (2011) 16–35*

abatement equipment, to provide a general measure of trade openness. This allows better separation of the access to technology (which depends on trade with countries providing the technology) and protection of manufacturing (which depends on trade with all countries) effects.

Prediction 3. Holding the world price of manufactures and all other factor endowments fixed, larger coal reserves weaken the political equilibrium abatement standard.

Proof. Totally differentiate (8) to obtain

$$\frac{dA^*}{dK_C} = \frac{(P_A - \alpha\varphi)}{G_{AA}} \frac{\partial E}{\partial K_C} < 0. \qquad \square \tag{12}$$

As shown in Appendix A, a larger coal sector reduces the domestic price of coal and increases coal-fired electricity generation: $\partial E/\partial K_C > 0$. The term in brackets is positive if the government chooses a standard that is less than full abatement, as discussed for the small-country case.[22]

In our empirical work, we capture the size of specific investments in coal using coal production per capita and the share of electricity produced with coal.[23] We expect larger coal production to be associated with a lower probability of regulating emissions from coal-fired plants. We also control for lignite production per capita. Lignite coal is the lowest quality coal and is dirtier than other types of coal. We expect countries with more lignite to be more likely to adopt regulation, as the marginal benefit of abatement is higher.

Prediction 4. An increase in the disutility consumers experience from coal burning leads to a stricter abatement standard in the political equilibrium.

Proof. Totally differentiate (8) to obtain

$$\frac{dA^*}{d\varphi} = \frac{[(1-A)E_A - \alpha E]}{G_{AA}} > 0. \tag{13}$$

The sign of the numerator is negative and, thus, the derivative is positive. $\square$

In our analysis, we include several measures that capture the marginal benefit of a cleaner environment, φ. The first measure is GDP per capita. If environmental quality is a normal good, richer consumers will place greater weight on environmental quality and should regulate sooner. The second measure is population density. We expect that more densely populated countries will regulate sooner, all else equal, because of the proximity of residences to power plants.

Prediction 5. An increase in the weight placed on social welfare relative to contributions leads to a stricter political equilibrium abatement standard.

Proof. Totally differentiate (8) to obtain

$$\frac{dA^*}{d\alpha} = -\frac{[\varphi E - \varphi(1-A)E_A + D_M \chi_{MM} M_A]}{G_{AA}} > 0. \tag{14}$$

The sign of the term in brackets, which captures the marginal benefit of abatement, is positive if A^* is non-negative. The denominator is negative by assumption, so the derivative is positive. $\square$

To capture the α term in the government's objective function, we include measures of the country's political conditions. The first measure is the Freedom House political rights index, reasoning that more democratic governments place a higher weight on social welfare. The second measure is whether or not it is an election year, as incumbents may place a higher weight on political contributions when an election is near. We also control for whether the government is liberal or conservative, as opposed to centrist.[24]

3.2. Regulations

No single source of information on coal-fired power plant regulations exists. Using a series of publications by the International Energy Agency (IEA) Clean Coal Centre [35,45,46,49], we collected detailed information on coal-fired power plant regulations in most developed countries, as well as some developing countries, primarily in Southeast Asia and Eastern Europe. We supplemented this information with country-specific sources where necessary.[25] To narrow the task, we searched for additional regulatory information only for countries that get at least 10% of their electric power from coal.[26] In some cases we were unable to identify when, or if, regulations were put in place, leaving us with regulatory data for 45 of the

---

[22] If we amend the model so that coal is freely traded, policy does not depend on the size of domestic coal reserves.
[23] Data on coal production comes from http://www.eia.doe.gov/emeu/international/coal.html.
[24] If the country has a chief executive, we use his or her party. If not, the majority party in the legislature is used.
[25] These sources are listed in Appendix B in the online archive.
[26] These countries get at least 10% of power from coal in at least one year between 1980 and 2001. We also include Sweden, an environmental technology source, even though it does not generate much power from coal.

M. Lovely, D. Popp / Journal of Environmental Economics and Management 61 (2011) 16–35   25

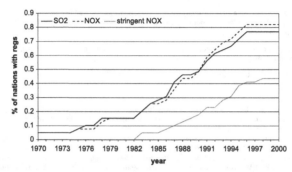

Fig. 2. Adoption of environmental regulations over time. The figure shows the cumulative percentage of countries that have adopted each regulation by the year on the x-axis. In each case, note the S-shaped diffusion pattern that is typical for studies of technology adoption. Note also that adoption of stringent NOₓ regulations has, to date, leveled off with fewer countries adopting than for the other regulations.

50 countries that get at least 10% of electricity from coal.[27] For each, we identify the year in which emissions restrictions on coal-fired power plants were enacted for both SO_2 and NO_x.[28] Additionally, for NO_x we identify both the initial regulation and the adoption of rules stringent enough to necessitate the use of the more expensive post-combustion abatement techniques described in the next section.[29]

Looking at the adoption data supports the notion that adoption of *regulation*, rather than adoption of the technology itself, is the first step in studying the diffusion of environmental technologies. Fig. 2 shows, by year, the percentage of countries that have adopted a regulation.[30] Note the S-shaped pattern that is typical of traditional studies on adoption of technology. Each regulation has a few early adopters, who are typically the technology leaders (e.g. Japan and the U.S.). This is followed by a period of more rapid adoption which, for these policies, occurs in the mid-1980s. A period of slower adoption among the remaining countries follows. As plants will not typically adopt the control technologies used to reduce SO_2 and NO_x without regulatory incentive, understanding the pattern of adoption of these regulations is the first step towards understanding the international diffusion of these environmental technologies.

3.3. Knowledge stocks

A key goal of this paper is to estimate the extent to which access to technological advances increases the likelihood of adopting environmental regulation. For this, we use pollution-control device patents as a measure of innovation. We accumulate these patents over time in a knowledge stock designed to capture the level of technology in any given year.[31]

Patents are granted by national patent offices in individual countries and protection is only valid in the country that grants the patent. An inventor must file for protection in each nation in which protection is desired. Nearly all patent applications are first filed in the home country of the inventor. The date of the initial application is referred to as the *priority date*. If the patent is granted, protection begins from the priority date. If the inventor files abroad within one year, the inventor will have priority over any patent applications received in those countries since the priority date that describe similar inventions.

These additional filings of the same patent application in different countries are known as *patent families*. Because of the costs of filing abroad, along with the one-year waiting period that gives inventors additional time to gage their invention's value, only the most valuable inventions are filed in several countries. Moreover, filing a patent application is a signal that the inventor expects the invention to be profitable *in that country*. Because of this, researchers such as Lanjouw and Schankerman [32] have used data on patent families as proxies for the quality of individual patents. Lanjouw and Mody [31] use such data to

---

[27] The five missing countries are Luxembourg, Russia, North Korea, Dominican Republic, and Moldova.

[28] Our goal was to find regulations that provide incentives to install pollution control devices, such as flue gas desulfurization (FGD) units to remove SO_2 emissions. Thus, we sought the enactment of specific emissions regulations for power plants. Israel never adopts specific regulations, using licenses negotiated with plants on an individual basis, and we drop it from our sample. Mexico enacted an SO_2 standard in 1993, but the allowable level of emissions is so high that plants do not install FGD equipment [2].

[29] We define stringent regulations as those restricting NO_x emissions to 410 mg/m³ or less, which is the regulation introduced in Japan when they tightened NO_x emission limits in 1986.

[30] The figure only includes the 39 countries that remain in our sample after merging with other data sources.

[31] Popp [40] discusses the advantages and disadvantages of using patent data when studying environmental technologies. Among the disadvantages, not all successful innovations are patented, as inventors may choose to forgo patent protection to avoid disclosing proprietary information. Levin et al. [33] report significant differences in the propensity to patent across industries. Fortunately, this is less problematic when studying the development of a single technology than when using patents to study inventive activity across technologies.

26   *M. Lovely, D. Popp / Journal of Environmental Economics and Management 61 (2011) 16–35*

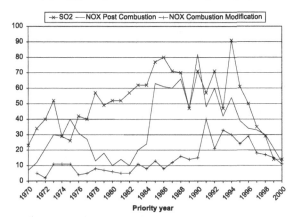

Fig. 3. U.S. pollution control patents. The figure shows patents granted in the U.S. with at least one foreign patent family member for each of three pollution control technologies.

show that environmental technologies patented by developed country firms are more general than similar inventions from developing countries, as the developed country inventions have larger patent families.

To use patents to identify the technological frontier, we take advantage of patent families to find the most important inventions. We begin by selecting all relevant patents granted in the United States since 1969. We choose the U.S. because it is a major supplier of pollution control equipment and, because of the importance of the U.S. market, many foreign companies choose to patent in the U.S.[32] Relevant technologies include those that reduce SO_2 or NO_x emissions. These include flue gas desulfurization (FGD) units to remove SO_2 emissions, combustion modification techniques, such as low NO_x burners, designed to reduce the formation of NO_x in the combustion process, and equipment such as selective catalytic reduction (SCR) units designed to remove NO_x emissions from a plant's exhaust (post-combustion treatment). SCR equipment is more expensive than combustion modification techniques, but also reduces more NO_x emissions. Thus, it is used in cases where regulation requires significant NO_x reductions. We keep only patents with at least one foreign patent family member.

We use the European Classification System (ECLA) to identify relevant patents, as it provides details necessary to distinguish between the types of pollution controlled by various technologies.[33] Appendix C in the online archive lists the relevant ECLA codes for these technologies. Using the European Patent Office's on-line database, esp@cenet, we downloaded a list of patent numbers for documents published in the US.[34,35] We obtained additional descriptive information on these patents from Delphion, an on-line database of patents, including the application, priority, and issue date, the home country of the inventor, and data on patent families, which we use to identify patents with multiple family members.[36] These patents were sorted by priority year, as this date corresponds most closely with the actual inventive activity.[37] Fig. 3 shows the number of U.S. patents with multiple family members for each of three technologies: SO_2, NO_x combustion modification techniques, and NO_x post-combustion treatment. Note that the number of SO_2 patents progresses rather smoothly through time until passage of the 1990 Clean Air Act in the U.S., whereas both NO_x technologies experience periods of growth after major environmental regulations.[38] For example, both Germany and Japan passed stringent NO_x regulations in the 1980s that led to the development of new SCR technologies [39].

---

[32] As a robustness check, we constructed a similar stock using patents granted in Germany. See Appendix E in the online archive.

[33] ECLA classifications are assigned by patent examiners at the European Patent Office. Traditional patent classification systems, such as the International Patent Classification system and the US patent system, do not provide enough detail to distinguish among technologies at the level needed for this paper.

[34] The database can be found at http://ep.espacenet.com/.

[35] These data are also used in Popp [39], and are described in more detail there.

[36] This database is available at http://www.delphion.com.

[37] In addition, using priority dates, rather than the date of grant, removes noise introduced by variations in length of the patent application process. Because only granted patents were published in the U.S. until 2001, the data only includes patent applications that were subsequently granted.

[38] Regarding SO_2, prior to 1990, new utilities in the U.S. were required to install scrubbers. The permit trading regime enacted in the 1990 Clean Air Act gave firms additional flexibility for pollution control, such as the option to switch to low-sulfur coal. However, as noted by Popp [41], while the level of patenting on FGD units fell after 1990, its focus changed from cost-saving innovation designed to help firms comply with the scrubber mandate at low cost to innovations designed to enhance the removal efficiency of scrubbers.

M. Lovely, D. Popp / Journal of Environmental Economics and Management 61 (2011) 16–35   27

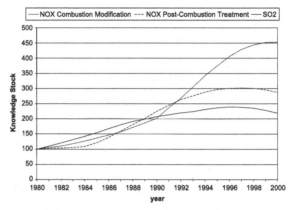

Fig. 4. Knowledge stocks. The figure shows the value of the knowledge stocks constructed for this paper for each of the three technologies. Note that the value of the stock for SO₂ progresses rather smoothly through time, whereas both NOₓ technologies experience periods of growth after major environmental regulations.

Table 3
Knowledge stock descriptive statistics.

Variable	N	Mean	Std. Dev.	min	p25	Median	p75	max
Foreign knowledge stock: SO₂	771	192.35	47.89	48.40	146.55	210.15	233.32	246.51
Foreign knowledge stock: NOₓ pre	771	258.40	132.47	52.48	138.02	208.86	386.26	467.22
Foreign knowledge stock: NOₓ post	771	213.80	81.99	39.95	124.82	231.51	296.85	310.50
Domestic knowledge stock: SO₂	771	181.36	550.03	0.00	0.00	0.00	67.16	3936.80
Domestic knowledge stock: NOₓ pre	771	237.79	918.98	0.00	0.00	0.00	68.44	8784.47
Domestic knowledge stock: NOₓ post	771	199.93	648.83	0.00	0.00	0.00	62.70	4095.79
Stocks without US, Japan, & Germany								
Foreign Knowledge Stock: SO₂	708	196.12	45.93	93.78	159.20	213.39	235.00	246.51
Foreign knowledge stock: NOₓ pre	708	264.42	132.40	91.85	141.87	231.19	409.99	467.22
Foreign knowledge stock: NOₓ post	708	219.15	81.40	99.11	125.27	246.36	297.35	310.50
Domestic knowledge stock: SO₂	708	56.34	130.96	0.00	0.00	0.00	33.04	701.22
Domestic knowledge stock: NOₓ pre	708	52.34	130.80	0.00	0.00	0.00	42.37	956.15
Domestic knowledge stock: NOₓ post	708	27.77	58.40	0.00	0.00	0.00	25.90	355.42
Domestic knowledge stocks & regulation								
SO²: no regulation	366	17.45	63.28	0.00	0.00	0.00	0.00	465.51
SO²: with regulation	405	329.49	725.71	0.00	0.00	33.90	311.88	3936.80
NOₓ pre: no regulation	354	19.58	58.67	0.00	0.00	0.00	0.00	377.25
NOₓ pre: with regulation	417	423.04	1218.75	0.00	0.00	0.00	287.36	8784.47
NOₓ post: no regulation	601	109.18	495.97	0.00	0.00	0.00	12.14	4095.79
NOₓ post: with regulation	170	520.76	954.94	0.00	0.00	89.02	149.04	4047.62

We use these patents to construct a stock of knowledge for each year and country. Because we are focusing on access to technology via trade, we exclude patents assigned to domestic inventors from the stock.[39,40] Using β_1, the rate of decay, to capture the obsolescence of older patent and β_2, the rate of diffusion, to capture delays in the flow of knowledge, we write the stock of knowledge at time t for technology j in country i as

$$K_{i,j,t} = \sum_{s=0}^{\infty} e^{-\beta_1(s)}(1-e^{-\beta_2(s+1)})PAT_{i,j,t-s} \qquad (15)$$

---

[39] For example, the knowledge stock for Germany does not include patents with German inventors, and the stock for the U.S. does not include patents with U.S. inventors.
[40] 76% of all patents come from the U.S., Japan, and Germany, and 85% of all patents come from the top 6 countries used as equipment exporters, so that this adjustment is small for most countries. Moreover, in most cases, patenting activity occurs as a response to regulation, so this adjustment results in few patents being omitted from each country's knowledge stock.

28 M. Lovely, D. Popp / Journal of Environmental Economics and Management 61 (2011) 16–35

The rate of diffusion is multiplied by $s+1$ so that diffusion is not constrained to be zero in the current period. The base results presented below use a decay rate of 0.1, and a rate of diffusion of 0.25 for each stock calculation.[41] For each technology, the stocks are normalized so that the average value across all countries in 1980 equals 100.

Fig. 4 illustrates these stocks and Table 3 provides descriptive data. Fig. 4 shows the global knowledge stock for a country with no domestic patents. Appendix D in the online archive illustrates both foreign and domestic stocks for selected countries. Except for the U.S. and, to a lesser extent, Japan, these foreign stocks closely follow the global knowledge stock. This can be seen in the descriptive data, where we see that the median value for domestic stocks is 0. Moreover, while the mean value of domestic stocks is comparable to the foreign stock, the mean is approximately one-quarter as large if we remove the U.S., Japan, and Germany from the data. This is important, as it illustrates that most of the variation in the data comes from time series variation in the stocks, rather than cross-country variation. Rather, the cross-country variation allowing us to identify the access effect of new knowledge comes from differences in openness.

Finally, Table 3 also includes separate descriptive statistics for domestic knowledge stocks of countries with and without regulation. For each technology, we see little domestic innovation prior to innovation. The mean values of knowledge in unregulated countries are roughly 5% those of regulated countries for SO_2 and NO_x pre-combustion technologies, and 20% of regulated countries for NO_x post-combustion. Moreover, for SO_2 and NO_x pre-combustion technologies, even the 75th percentile of domestic knowledge is 0 for countries without regulation. Thus, while foreign knowledge can be seen as globally available technologies waiting to be acted upon, domestic knowledge is best seen as a reaction to regulation, and thus a reaction to the same forces that drive the regulatory process.

4. Regressions

Following the approach used by economists studying technology adoption, we use a duration model that captures both a baseline hazard and country-specific effects on the adoption of environmental regulation.[42] These models separate the hazard function into two parts, allowing for a baseline hazard, $h_0(t)$, that does not vary by country. Letting X_t represent a vector of explanatory variables, β represent the vector of parameters to be estimated, and t represent time yields a hazard function is to be estimated of the form:

$$h(t, X_t, \beta) = h_0(t)\exp(X'_t\beta). \tag{16}$$

To estimate Eq. (16), the baseline hazard h_0 must be specified. We present results using three specifications common to the adoption literature: the exponential, Weibull, and Gompertz distributions. The exponential distribution assumes the baseline hazard is constant over time, whereas the others assume that the baseline hazard is a function of time. As a further robustness check, we estimate a Cox [8] proportional hazards model, which uses semi-parametric estimation instead of specifying the baseline hazard.[43] Once the baseline hazard is specified, we estimate Eq. (16) using maximum likelihood estimation, calculating robust standard errors because we have multiple observations per country.[44] In the hazard model, $\exp(\beta)$ gives the change in the probability of adoption for each variable. To aid interpretation, we normalize all non-interacted continuous variables so that a one unit change in the normalized variable is equivalent to a 10% change from its mean value.[45] We present results for the adoption of SO_2 regulation, of NO_x regulation, and of stringent NO_x regulations that require the use of post-combustion control techniques.

4.1. SO_2 results

In the case of SO_2, our data include six countries that adopt prior to 1980, which is the first year in our dataset. We drop these six countries from the regression analysis.[46] Table 4 presents results for each possible baseline hazard. For each baseline hazard, the first column uses the Hiscox–Kastner trade policy orientation index (TPOI) to measure trade policy, and the second column uses import shares. While TPOI is our preferred policy measure, as import shares may be complicated by scale effects, TPOI is available neither for the Eastern European countries in our sample nor for Zimbabwe. Note that we are only

---

[41] These rates are consistent with others used in the R&D literature. For example, discussing the literature on an appropriate lag structure for R&D capital, Griliches [20] notes that previous studies suggest a structure peaking between 3 and 5 years. The rates of decay and diffusion used in this paper provide a lag peaking after 4 years. Appendix F in the online archive presents sensitivity analysis with respect to the rates of decay and diffusion.

[42] See, for example, Hannan and McDowell [22], Rose and Joskow [43], Karshenas and Stoneman [25], Kerr and Newell [28], Snyder et al. [47], and Popp [38].

[43] A concern with parameterizing the baseline hazard is that if the parameterization is incorrect, the estimated coefficients will be biased. The Cox model avoids this issue, but has other disadvantages. One is that it is less efficient [5]. In addition, because no country adopts regulation in an election year, the Cox model is unable to estimate a coefficient for the election year variable. The similar results between the Cox model and those that parameterize the baseline hazard suggest that biased estimates are not a concern here. Thus, we focus primarily on the results from the parameterized baseline hazard models. Note also that we cannot directly compare the log-likelihood from the Cox model and the parameterized models, as the Cox model maximizes a partial log-likelihood function.

[44] For an introduction to duration data, see Cox and Oakes [9], Kiefer [29], and Lancaster [30].

[45] The normalization first divides each continuous variable by its mean, multiplies by 10, and then takes deviations from the mean by subtracting 10. This procedure is introduced in Kerr and Newell [28], and results in normalized variables that have a mean of 0. Table 1 indicates the variables that are normalized.

[46] An alternative is to add a term to the likelihood function to account for the six early adopters (see, for example, Popp [38]). One drawback of such an approach is that it assumes that early adopters are influenced by the same forces as later adopters. This seems unlikely, as early adopters tend to be innovators of environmental technology.

M. Lovely, D. Popp / Journal of Environmental Economics and Management 61 (2011) 16–35   29

Table 4
SO$_2$ regression results for alternative baseline hazards.

Variable	Exponential		Weibull		Gompertz		Cox	
Knowledge stock	0.0742***	0.0364***						
	(0.0162)	(0.0126)						
Knowledge × Trade Policy Orientation Index	0.0012***		0.0012***		0.00001		0.0011***	
	(0.0003)		(0.0003)		(0.0002)		(0.0004)	
Trade Policy Orientation Index	−0.2565***		−0.2724***		−0.0275		−0.2226**	
	(0.0618)		(0.0751)		(0.0509)		(0.0898)	
Knowledge × Import share		0.0004		0.0003		0.0004		0.0003
		(0.0003)		(0.0003)		(0.0003)		(0.0003)
Import share		−0.0580**		−0.0436*		−0.0511**		−0.0375
		(0.0235)		(0.0256)		(0.0250)		(0.0236)
World export share	0.3584**	0.2702*	0.3222**	0.2931*	0.2677	0.2219	0.1885**	0.2132
	(0.1513)	(0.1455)	(0.1538)	(0.1769)	(0.1899)	(0.1548)	(0.0906)	(0.1322)
GDP per capita	0.2885***	0.2515***	0.3136***	0.3036***	0.1943***	0.2201***	0.2928***	0.2497***
	(0.0534)	(0.0593)	(0.0714)	(0.0801)	(0.0421)	(0.0453)	(0.0680)	(0.0666)
Population density	0.0282	0.0193	0.0391	0.0227	0.0056	0.0268	0.0364	0.0263
	(0.0327)	(0.0290)	(0.0322)	(0.0331)	(0.0344)	(0.0333)	(0.0297)	(0.0324)
% Electricity from coal	0.0667**	0.0596**	0.0581*	0.0622*	0.0384	0.0552**	0.0394	0.0432
	(0.0285)	(0.0254)	(0.0315)	(0.0330)	(0.0231)	(0.0272)	(0.0268)	(0.0309)
Coal production per capita	−0.1109	−0.1511*	−0.1175	−0.1526*	−0.1164	−0.1445	−0.0631***	−0.0954
	(0.0732)	(0.0831)	(0.0746)	(0.0889)	(0.0852)	(0.0944)	(0.0189)	(0.0591)
Lignite production per capita	0.0425**	0.0499**	0.0455**	0.0519**	0.0329	0.0458	0.0404***	0.0419***
	(0.0174)	(0.0216)	(0.0191)	(0.0237)	(0.0281)	(0.0294)	(0.0118)	(0.0157)
Election year	−14.2866**	−18.1875***	−16.8082***	−16.5412***	−15.3833***	−16.7915***		
	(0.6231)	(1.0146)	(0.6327)	(0.6201)	(0.5052)	(0.4899)		
Political rights	0.2607	0.0221	0.2489	0.0467	0.0254	−0.0818	0.4308**	−0.0125
	(0.1849)	(0.1577)	(0.2176)	(0.1701)	(0.2216)	(0.1751)	(0.1880)	(0.1429)
Liberal	−0.2862	−0.8945	−0.4737	−0.6520	−0.6571	−1.1181*	−0.0829	−0.5996
	(0.7028)	(0.6454)	(0.7395)	(0.6955)	(0.7094)	(0.6658)	(0.6029)	(0.4592)
Conservative	−0.2688	−0.5865	−0.7427	−0.7325	−0.2437	−0.9805	−0.3539	−0.7565
	(0.8767)	(0.6364)	(0.8677)	(0.7032)	(0.7591)	(0.6590)	(0.8434)	(0.7110)
Eastern Europe		1.2240**		1.7468**		1.8535**		1.0749*
		(0.5910)		(0.7749)		(0.7450)		(0.6311)
Constant	−18.4664***	−8.9950***	−17.2630***	−11.0198***	−5.7656***	−4.3280***		
	(3.8916)	(3.2503)	(3.7928)	(3.8404)		(1.6698)		
Duration dependence			1.8262***	1.4706***	0.2054***	0.2483***		
			(0.1773)	(0.2624)	(0.0650)	(0.0717)		
Number of obs.	327	390	327	390	327	390	327	390
log-likelihood	−10.496	−13.227	−5.536	−5.959	−15.280	−11.939	−33.745	−50.711
chi-squared	1558.276	985.886	1501.088	1496.860	1301.366	2010.031	80.077	62.341
AIC	48.991	56.455	39.073	41.918	58.560	53.879	89.489	125.421

The table presents regression results using alternative baseline hazards; standard errors in parentheses. As noted in the text, we are only able to estimate the direct effect of knowledge when using the exponential baseline hazard. In other cases, the knowledge stock is collinear with the baseline hazard trend.
* $p < 0.1$.
** $p < 0.05$.
*** $p < 0.01$.

able to estimate the direct effect of knowledge when using the exponential baseline hazard. In other cases, the knowledge stock is collinear with the baseline hazard trend, as nearly all the variation in the knowledge stocks occurs over time, rather than across countries. In the exponential model, the direct effect of knowledge is positive and significant. For other baseline hazards, the duration dependence parameter is positive, so that the likelihood of adoption increases over time. These results are suggestive of a positive effect for knowledge, but we cannot rule out the possibility that there are other time-varying factors positively correlated with knowledge influencing adoption, such as increasing global awareness of the hazards of air pollution. Of the three parameterized baseline hazards, Aikike's information criterion shows the Weibull to be the best fit, followed by the exponential and Gompertz models.

Our main interest is the interaction of knowledge and trade policy, which describes the effect of access to advanced technologies. Using TPOI, the interaction between policy and the knowledge stock is generally significant, indicating that more open economies are better able to take advantage of foreign knowledge.[47] While the interacted coefficients appear small, recall that the base level of knowledge for a country without domestic patents by 1980 is 100. Thus, for the base level of technology, a one percentage point more open trade policy increases the likelihood of adoption by 12–13% when the coefficient is statistically significant, as calculated using exp(β) from the coefficients in

---

[47] The one exception is the Gompertz model. However, Aikike's information criterion shows this to be the worst fit among the parameterized baseline hazards. Moreover, it is significant using the non-parametric Cox estimation.

30 M. Lovely, D. Popp / Journal of Environmental Economics and Management 61 (2011) 16–35

Table 4.[48] This is the access effect described in Section 3. In contrast, the direct effect of trade openness, which measures the ability of producers to pass cost increases on to domestic consumers, reduces the probability of adopting a regulation, with a one percentage point increase in openness reducing the likelihood of adoption by 20–24%. Using import shares, the interaction is insignificant, and the magnitudes are smaller, with one percentage point more imports per GDP increasing the likelihood of adoption by 3–4%.[49] The direct effect of import shares is statistically significant, but only reduces adoption by about 5%.

These results suggest two competing effects. First, greater openness provides easier access to technology, making countries more willing and able to adopt environmental regulation. At the same time, increased openness raises domestic firms' need to compete with foreign firms, making it harder to pass cost increases to consumers. While the magnitude of the individual effects may seem large, given that the standard deviation of TPOI is nearly 15, it is the net effect that matters. In each case, the access effect dominates when the knowledge stock is just over double its 1980 value.[50] Using TPOI, this occurs between 1992 (exponential) and 1994 (Weibull). Note that most low income countries adopt SO_2 regulations after these dates. Further emphasizing the role of openness, of the nine countries in our sample that never adopt SO_2 regulations, the average level of import shares for each of these countries across the 1980–2000 period is eight percentage points below the average of the sample as a whole and the average TPOI index is 12 percentage points less open than average. Of these nine countries, only New Zealand, Morocco, and Mexico have above average levels of import shares by 2000, and only Australia, New Zealand, Chile, and South Africa have an above average TPOI by 2001.[51]

Our third trade-related measure, world export share, captures the ability of a country to pass cost increases on to foreign consumers through a favorable terms-of-trade effect. This effect is positive (except, again, in the Gompertz model), suggesting that larger countries with greater market power are more likely to regulate, as regulatory cost increases can be at least partially passed on to foreign consumers. While significant using the TPOI, it is only significant at the 10% level for the Weibull and exponential models when using import shares. One drawback of using import shares as a measure of trade policy is that collinearity between import shares and world export share makes separately identifying these two trade effects difficult. When significant, the magnitude of the effect is large, with a one percentage point increase in world export share increasing the likelihood of adoption by 21–43%.

Turning to other variables, we again note that there are no significant differences across the various specifications. A 10% increase in per capita income increases adoption rates by about 36%, supporting the notion that environmental quality is a normal good. As expected, more densely populated countries adopt more quickly, as pollution problems are likely be more severe when population is concentrated and more people are exposed to pollution. However, this is never statistically significant for SO_2.

Our next set of variables describes the coal sector. As expected, regulation is less likely when the coal sector is important. Coal production per capita has a negative, although not always statistically significant, effect on adoption. When significant, a country producing 10% more coal per capita than average is about 11% less likely to adopt SO_2 regulations for coal-fired power plants. However, if a country has a greater share of dirty coal, they are more likely to adopt, as the pollution problems will be greater. Countries producing 10% more lignite coal than average are 5% more likely to adopt. Note that the net effect of the two coal variables remains negative. While countries with dirtier coal are more likely to adopt than a country producing a similar amount of cleaner coal, they remain less likely to adopt than the typical country. Finally, we find that the percentage of electricity from coal is positive, although only significant at the 10% level in the Weibull model. Here there are two competing effects. Having more power come from coal makes the need to regulate more, but it also raises the cost of regulation.

Our more general set of political variables yields mixed results, as most are insignificant. One striking finding is the strong negative effect of an executive branch election year. No country enacted SO_2 regulations in an executive branch election year. Political rights, measured using the Freedom House index, only have a significant positive effect using TPOI and the Cox non-parametric model. The effect of political parties is always insignificant. Although this may be a surprise given that liberal governments are typically seen as environmentally friendly, this is less likely the case in lower income countries, where liberal governments may resist regulation in order to protect the interests of low-income consumers.[52]

4.2. NO_x regulation results

Table 5 compares the results across pollutants, using the Weibull model.[53] For NO_x, we distinguish between two classes of regulation. In most cases, initial regulation levels are weak enough that pre-combustion modifications are sufficient to comply with

---

[48] To interpret TPOI, recall that each percentage point represents one percentage point of missing trade from the free trade benchmark. Note that New Zealand, the most open country in 2000, has a TPOI of −16.9. The least open country in 2000, India, has a TPOI of −48.4. Country pairs with one percentage point difference in TPOI in 2000 include Great Britain and South Africa, Japan and Spain, and Morocco and Greece.

[49] This is not merely a result of the additional countries included in the import shares sample, as the results hold even if we restrict the import shares regression to those countries that have TPOI data available.

[50] The access effect dominates when $\exp(\beta_{open} + \beta_{interact}K) > 1$, so that $\beta_{open} + \beta_{interact}K > 0$. This holds when $K > -\beta_{open}/\beta_{interact}$.

[51] Recall that New Zealand and Australia do not adopt SO_2 regulations because domestic coal supplies are naturally low in sulfur. Only 2 of the 7 remaining non-adopting countries are more open than average.

[52] Dutt and Mitra [12] find empirical support for the proposition that the ideology of the government in power influences the restrictiveness of trade policy, but that the direction of this effect depends on country GDP.

[53] As with SO_2, there is little variation when using baseline hazard parameterizations and the Weibull model provides the best fit of the baseline hazard parameterizations. Other results are available from the authors by request. Also, as with SO_2, countries that adopt NO_x regulations before 1980 are omitted from our sample.

M. Lovely, D. Popp / Journal of Environmental Economics and Management 61 (2011) 16–35   31

Table 5
Regression results: Weibull results for alternative technologies.

Variable	SO$_2$		NO$_x$ Any reg		NO$_x$ Stringent	
Knowledge × Trade Policy Orientation Index	0.0012***		0.0004*		0.0002	
	(0.0003)		(0.0002)		(0.0002)	
Trade Policy Orientation Index	−0.2724***		−0.0641		−0.0969***	
	(0.0751)		(0.0410)		(0.0357)	
Knowledge × Import share		0.0003		0.0007**		0.00003
		(0.0003)		(0.0003)		(0.0002)
Import share		−0.0436*		−0.0590**		−0.0342
		(0.0256)		(0.0263)		(0.0257)
World export share	0.3222**	0.2931	0.0759	0.2702**	0.0704	−0.0118
	(0.1538)	(0.1769)	(0.1477)	(0.1318)	(0.0770)	(0.1207)
GDP per capita	0.3136***	0.3036***	0.2234***	0.2102***	0.3483**	0.2957***
	(0.0714)	(0.0801)	(0.0734)	(0.0605)	(0.0657)	(0.0650)
Population density	0.0391	0.0227	0.0729**	0.0601***	0.0578*	0.0552
	(0.0322)	(0.0331)	(0.0307)	(0.0273)	(0.0336)	(0.0335)
% Electricity from coal	0.0581*	0.0622*	0.0599	0.0561	−0.0340	−0.0293
	(0.0315)	(0.0330)	(0.0506)	(0.0356)	(0.0259)	(0.0294)
Coal production per capita	−0.1175	−0.1526*	−0.0424	−0.1765**	−0.0156	−0.0148
	(0.0746)	(0.0889)	(0.0420)	(0.0880)	(0.0102)	(0.0113)
Lignite production per capita	0.0455**	0.0519**	0.0408***	0.0634***	0.0410**	0.0242
	(0.0191)	(0.0237)	(0.013)	(0.0242)	(0.0164)	(0.0211)
Election year	−16.8082***	−16.5412***	−17.2357***	−16.8967***	−15.9936***	−16.6331***
	(0.6327)	(0.6201)	(0.5646)	(0.6202)	(0.5586)	(0.8444)
Political rights	0.2489	0.0467	0.4100*	0.0953	0.6645	0.0806
	(0.2176)	(0.1701)	(0.2170)	(0.1675)	(0.5500)	(0.2448)
Liberal	−0.4737	−0.6520	−0.7376	−0.8768*	−2.2153**	−2.1105***
	(0.7395)	(0.6955)	(0.5560)	(0.4863)	(1.1054)	(0.7160)
Conservative	−0.7427	−0.7325	−1.1680	−1.0982*	−1.8800**	−1.9325***
	(0.8677)	(0.7032)	(0.8739)	(0.5942)	(0.8962)	(0.6384)
Eastern Europe		1.7468**		0.7484		4.0993***
		(0.7749)		(0.7300)		(1.2740)
Constant	−17.2630***	−11.0198***	−13.2190***	−8.7278***	−10.9210***	−6.7441***
	(3.7928)	(3.8404)	(2.6552)	(1.8390)	(2.0994)	(1.8296)
Duration dependence	1.8262***	1.4706***	1.6886***	1.1270***	1.0175***	0.9078***
	(0.1773)	(0.2624)	(0.1970)	(0.1757)	(0.2146)	(0.2522)
Number of obs.	327	390	317	380	542	618
log-likelihood	−5.536	−5.959	−4.446	−5.141	−10.250	−12.948
chi-squared	1501.088	1496.860	4218.605	3112.505	1242.355	649.266
AIC	39.073	41.918	36.892	40.282	48.500	55.896

The table presents regression results for alternative regulations, using the Weibull baseline hazard; standard errors in parentheses.
* $p < 0.1$.
** $p < 0.05$.
*** $p < 0.01$.

the regulations. The middle columns of Table 5 look at the adoption of these regulations. To consider stringency, we also look at adoption of NO$_x$ regulations stringent enough to require post-combustion treatment of the flue gas. Such treatment requires expensive capital equipment (typically a selective catalytic reduction unit, or SCR), making such regulations less prevalent, particularly among developing countries. Most countries adopting stringent NO$_x$ regulations are rich countries. Exceptions are Indonesia and several Eastern European countries. The last two columns of Table 5 focus on the adoption of these more stringent regulations.

Looking first at the adoption of any NO$_x$ regulation, we see that the interaction between knowledge and TPOI is positive, but that the magnitude is smaller than before. Because the costs of boiler modifications necessary to meet weaker NO$_x$ regulations are lower than the costs of SO$_2$ controls, technological advances and the ability to pass along cost increases appear less important here than for sulfur dioxide. This smaller magnitude is partially offset by greater variation in the knowledge stock for NO$_x$ technologies. Still, at the average value of knowledge, the effect of a 1% change of TPOI is about one-third smaller than for SO$_2$. The direct effect of TPOI is insignificant. Using import shares, both the access and the direct effect of trade policy are significant, with the access effect always dominating. The ability to pass costs on to foreign consumers, measured using world export shares, is only significant using import shares.[54]

As for other variables, the results are very similar to SO$_2$. GDP and population density increase adoption rates, and population density is now significant. The political influences of the coal industry are similar to before, except that the percentage of electricity from coal is insignificant.

---

[54] The differences in results using TPOI versus import shares are due to the smaller sample of countries with TPOI data. If we restrict the import shares regression to countries in the TPOI sample, the trade variables and interaction are also insignificant.

32   *M. Lovely, D. Popp / Journal of Environmental Economics and Management 61 (2011) 16-35*

Finally, the last two columns of Table 5 examine the adoption of stringent NO_x regulations. Unlike the initial adoption of SO_2 or NO_x regulations, availability of knowledge is insignificant. Because it is mainly leading economies that are adopting stringent NO_x regulations and making use of SCR technology, access to technology from abroad appears less important—countries adopting stringent regulations are generally those capable of producing and improving SCR technology on their own. However, complying with stringent NO_x regulations requires the installation of expensive post-combustion emissions treatment equipment. Thus, the ability (or lack thereof) to pass along these higher costs to consumers is important. As with SO_2, more liberal trade policy makes adoption less likely when using TPOI, while having a greater share of world exports makes adoption of stringent regulation more likely.

Among other variables, GDP is still important—richer countries are more likely to increase the stringency of NO_x regulations. Population density also increases adoption, although this effect is only significant at the 10% level. Unlike previous results, political parties appear important, as middle-of-the-road governments are more likely to tighten regulations than either liberal or conservative governments. Finally, the most notable difference is that, controlling for other country characteristics, the Eastern European countries are much more likely to pass stringent NO_x regulations than other countries. Here, the influence of the European Union (EU) is important, as countries wishing to join the EU must comply with EU environmental standards. Desire to join the EU pushes these Eastern European countries to enact regulations more stringent than would otherwise be chosen for their level of development.[55]

4.3. Is it trade?

Finally, we consider the possibility that our trade variables are picking up the effect of other factors also changing over time and across countries. We consider several possible omitted variables, showing that (a) these variables have no impact on the adoption of regulation and (b) including these variables does not change the results for the access and direct effects of trade. Table 6 presents the results for SO_2 using the TPOI. To conserve space, we only present results for the knowledge and trade variables, as other results are consistent across the specifications.[56] Column 1 includes the base model previously discussed.

First, we consider the role of foreign direct investment (FDI). As global FDI has been growing over time, one may be concerned that our knowledge variables pick up increases in FDI, rather than increased knowledge. To alleviate this concern, column 2 of Table 6 includes a regression with both FDI inflows as a percentage of GDP and an interaction of these inflows with the knowledge stock.[57] Note that both are insignificant. More importantly, adding FDI to the model does not change the results for either the direct or the access effect of trade, confirming that it is through trade, rather than FDI, that technology affects regulation of electric utilities.[58]

Column 3 considers the role of education, measured as the percentage of the population completing post-secondary degrees. The data come from Barro and Lee [3]. Unfortunately, the data are only available in five year increments, so that we must interpolate for missing years. Higher education levels provide human capital necessary to work with advanced pollution abatement equipment, and may also increase political demand for regulation. However, the direct effect of education is insignificant, and the interaction with knowledge is only significant at the 10% level. The direct and access effects of trade become even more pronounced. However, because the data must be interpolated, we put less faith in this higher magnitude compared to the base results.

Column 4 includes an index of intellectual property rights (IPR) taken from Park [37]. The index ranges from 1 to 5, with higher numbers representing stronger IPR. As with education, the index is available in five-year increments, leaving us to interpolate for missing years. Once again, we see that the variables have no effect on adoption, and do not change the results for any of our other variable.

Column 5 considers the role of information and communications technology (ICT). Freund and Weinhold [18] find that Internet access, measured as the number of web hosts in each country, increases trade. Unfortunately, these data are only available from 1995 onward, and only for 35 of the 44 countries in our sample. As an alternative measure of ICT, we use the number of fixed and mobile telephones per 100 people, taken from the World Development Indicators, and once again find no change in the access effect. However, we do note that the competition effect becomes insignificant in this specification.

In column 6 we ask whether neighboring countries affect regulation. We use a dummy variable equal to one if a country with a land border regulated SO_2 in the previous year. While Fredriksson et al. [15] and Fredriksson and Millimet [16] both find evidence of such effects for individual states within the U.S., we find no evidence of such effects across international borders.

Finally, column 7 adds domestic knowledge, which is also insignificant. However, the magnitude of the world export share falls by half, and is now insignificant. Domestic knowledge and the world export share are highly correlated, making it difficult to successfully identify both effects.[59] Moreover, while we lag domestic knowledge one period to help deal with

---

[55] See, for example, "Eastern Europe's environment: Clean up or clear out," *The Economist*, December 11, 1999, p. 47.
[56] The only other change is that, in some cases, the percentage of electricity from coal is significant, while in others it is coal production per capita that is significant. Lignite production per capita retains its significance throughout.
[57] FDI inflow data come from the World Development Indicators.
[58] We also ran a model including FDI, but omitting TPOI and its interaction with knowledge. The FDI variables remain insignificant.
[59] For instance, the correlation between world export share and domestic SO_2 stocks is 0.75. The correlation between these stocks and TPOI is just 0.23. It is only large rich economies that have active domestic patenting before a regulation is in place. These are also the countries that dominate world exports. While not reported here, the world export share remains significant for the NO_x regression using import shares.

M. Lovely, D. Popp / Journal of Environmental Economics and Management 61 (2011) 16–35   33

Table 6
Is it trade?

Variable	Base	FDI	Education	IPR	ICT	Neighbor	Domestic
Knowledge × Trade Policy	0.0012***	0.0012***	0.0028***	0.0018***	0.0017**	0.0012***	0.0012***
Orientation Index	(0.0003)	(0.0003)	(0.0009)	(0.0006)	(0.0007)	(0.0003)	(0.0003)
Trade Policy Orientation Index	−0.2724***	−0.2632***	−0.4675***	−0.3326***	−0.3397***	−0.2720***	−0.2547***
	(0.0751)	(0.0708)	(0.1694)	(0.1083)	(0.1222)	(0.0751)	(0.0753)
Domestic knowledge (t − 1)							0.0047
							(0.0035)
World export share	0.3222**	0.2902*	−0.0579	0.5289*	0.2098	0.3320*	0.1422
	(0.1538)	(0.1686)	(0.1162)	(0.2745)	(0.1688)	(0.1712)	(0.2403)
Knowledge × FDI inflows		0.0004					
		(0.0107)					
FDI inflows, % GDP		−0.1709					
		(2.4191)					
Knowledge × post-second ed			−0.0062*				
			(0.0034)				
Post-secondary ed			0.7565				
			(0.6704)				
Knowledge × IPR				−0.0037			
				(0.0075)			
IPR index				−0.7673			
				(1.4165)			
Knowledge × phones					−0.0004		
					(0.0003)		
Phones per 1000					0.0397		
					(0.0608)		
Neighbor has reg						−0.0706	
						(0.7107)	
% Electricity from coal	0.0581*	0.0511	0.0543	0.0569	0.0369	0.0589*	0.0489
	(0.0315)	(0.0361)	(0.0390)	(0.0355)	(0.0382)	(0.0316)	(0.0322)
Coal production per capita	−0.1175	−0.1054	−0.0627**	−0.1436	−0.0727**	−0.1207	−0.1269**
	(0.0746)	(0.0707)	(0.0231)	(0.1229)	(0.0345)	(0.0772)	(0.0633)
Lignite production per capita	0.0455**	0.0440**	0.0645***	0.0449	0.0408**	0.0460**	0.0469***
	(0.0191)	(0.0210)	(0.0166)	(0.0359)	(0.0160)	(0.0193)	(0.0153)
Number of obs.	327	324	306	327	326	327	327
log-likelihood	−5.536	−5.177	5.317	−2.433	−4.014	−5.532	−5.064
chi-squared	1501.088	1720.717	847.418	856.671	1348.295	1745.057	1474.911
AIC	39.073	42.355	21.367	36.866	40.027	41.065	40.129

The table presents regression results for alternative specifications, using the Weibull baseline hazard; standard errors in parentheses. Explanatory variables with no changes are omitted.
* $p < 0.1$
** $p < 0.05$
*** $p < 0.01$.

endogeneity, it is still possible that domestic knowledge is endogenous. As shown in Section 3, domestic knowledge reacts to the same forces driving regulation, as most domestic patents occur after regulations are in place. To the extent that inventors anticipate regulatory changes, even lagged domestic knowledge may be endogenous. Taylor et al. [48] provide evidence of such anticipatory effects before passage of the 1990 Clean Air Act in the U.S. We thus consider the models without domestic knowledge to be our preferred specification.

5. Conclusions

In debates on the effect of globalization and the environment, commonly cited effects are scale effects (more production leads to more pollution), composition effects (a change in the mix of economic activity can improve or exacerbate emissions), and technique effects (cleaner technologies are used as countries grow).[60] One challenge in empirically studying these effects is separately identifying the role of each. Using the adoption of environmental regulations, rather than a generic measure of environmental quality, as our dependent variable, we provide new evidence on the technique effect, showing that increased access to technology via trade increases the likelihood that a country will adopt environmental regulation. While we do find that richer countries adopt regulation first, developing countries adopt environmental regulation at earlier stages of development than did developed countries, as they can take advantage of off-the-shelf technologies to carry out emission reductions. Relating this to the environmental Kuznets curve (EKC) literature, which posits an inverted-U shape relationship

---

[60] Esty [13] provides a review of this literature. Copeland and Taylor [7] provide a rigorous theoretical analysis of these effects in the context of an open economy.

34 *M. Lovely, D. Popp / Journal of Environmental Economics and Management 61 (2011) 16–35*

between economic growth and environmental quality, this result is consistent with the notion of the peak of the EKC falling and shifting to the left over time, as countries gain access to more advanced technologies.

Our results provide new evidence on the role of economic openness in allowing these spillovers to spread across country borders. We posit that openness both eases access to technology and limits domestic firms' ability to pass regulatory costs to consumers. Our findings support the view that small, open economies are least able to transfer these costs away from firms and, thus, are less likely to regulate, *ceteris paribus*. They suggest that international burden shifting is an important factor in the political economy of environmental regulation.

In addition to the links between trade and technology, we find that other political economy forces are important. Factors affecting the value placed on abatement, such as population density and income level, increase the likelihood of regulation. Moreover, regulations that negatively affect the coal sector are less likely in countries with large coal reserves, but more likely with the larger reserves of dirty coal. Finally, the politics of globalization appear important, as Eastern European countries have passed more stringent regulations than other countries at similar levels of development in their progress toward joining the EU.

Studying the adoption of environmental regulation is an important step in understanding the diffusion of environmental technologies. Regulation is particularly important for end-of-the-pipe technologies like those studied in this paper, as these technologies impose costs on firms while only providing the benefit of compliance.[61] Our work suggests that free trade can enhance the diffusion of these technologies, but that this diffusion comes indirectly, with the decision to regulate preceding a plant's decision to adopt clean technology. Given these links, green development efforts might usefully be focused on easing access to technology in ways that promote environmental regulation.

Acknowledgments

We thank Neelakshi Medhi and Tara Holmes for their excellent research assistance. We gratefully acknowledge comments on earlier versions received from Derek Kellenberg, Devashish Mitra, David Sonnenfeld and the seminar participants at Sustainable Resource Use and Economic Dynamics: SURED 2006, the International Monetary Fund, the London School of Economics, the Association for Public Policy Analysis and Management, the ERB Institute at the University of Michigan and Northwestern University's Searle Center on Law, Regulation, and Economic Growth. We thank two anonymous referees and the editor for helpful suggestions. As usual, any remaining errors are the responsibility of the authors.

References

[1] R.C. Acharya, W. Keller, Technology Transfer Through Imports, NBER Working Paper #13086, NBER, Cambridge, MA, 2007.
[2] Asia-Pacific Economic Cooperation, Study on atmospheric emissions regulations in APEC economies, APEC #97-RE-01.7, 1997.
[3] R.J. Barro, J.W. Lee, International data on educational attainment: updates and implications, CID Working Paper No. 42, 2000.
[4] B. Bernheim, D. Whinston, M.D. Whinston, Menu auctions, resource allocation, and economic influence, Quarterly Journal of Economics 101 (1986) 1–31.
[5] M.A. Cleves, W.W. Gould, R.G. Gutierrez, An Introduction to Survival Analysis Using Stata: Revised Edition, Stata Corporation, College Station, TX, 2004.
[6] CoalPower4, CD-ROM database available from the International Energy Agency Clean Coal Centre, 2001.
[7] B.R. Copeland, M.S. Taylor, Trade and the Environment: Theory and Evidence, Princeton University Press, Princeton, NJ, 2003.
[8] D.R. Cox, Regression models and life-tables (with discussion), Journal of the Royal Statistical Society, Series B 34 (1972) 187–220.
[9] D.R. Cox, D. Oakes, Analysis of Survival Data, Chapman and Hall, London, UK, 1985.
[10] R. Damania, P.G. Fredriksson, J.A. List, Trade liberalization, corruption, and environmental policy formation: theory and evidence, Journal of Environmental Economics and Management 46 (2003) 490–512.
[11] A. Dixit, G.M. Grossman, E. Helpman, Common agency and coordination: general theory and application to government policy making, Journal of Political Economy 105 (1997) 752–769.
[12] P. Dutt, D. Mitra, Political ideology and endogenous trade policy: an empirical investigation, Review of Economics and Statistics 87 (1) (2005) 59–72.
[13] D.C. Esty, Bridging the trade-environment divide, Journal of Economic Perspectives 15 (3) (2001) 113–130.
[14] K. Fisher-Vanden, G. Jefferson, Y. Liu, J. Qian, Open economy impacts on energy consumption: technology transfer and FDI spillovers in China's industrial economy, Mimeo, December 12, 2008.
[15] P.G. Fredriksson, J.A. List, D.L. Millimet, Chasing the smokestack: strategic policymaking with multiple instruments, Regional Science & Urban Economics 34 (2004) 387–410.
[16] P.G. Fredriksson, D.L. Millimet, Strategic interaction and the determination of environmental policy across U.S. states, Journal of Urban Economics 51 (2002) 101–122.
[17] P.G. Fredriksson, J.R. Wollscheid, The political economy of investment: the case of pollution control technology, European Journal of Political Economy 24 (1) (2008) 53–72.
[18] C.L. Freund, D. Weinhold, The effect of the Internet on international trade, Journal of International Economics 62 (1) (2004) 171–189.
[19] W.B. Gray, R.J. Shadbegian, Environmental regulation, investment timing, and technology choice, The Journal of Industrial Economics 46 (2) (1998) 235–256.
[20] Z. Griliches, R&D and Productivity: Econometric Results and Measurement Issues, in: P.L. Stoneman (Ed.), Handbook of the Economics of Innovation and Technological Change, Blackwell Publishers, Cambridge, MA, 1995.
[21] G.M. Grossman, E. Helpman, Protection for sale, American Economic Review 84 (1994) 833–850.
[22] T.H. Hannan, J.M. McDowell, The determinants of technology adoption: the case of the banking firm, RAND Journal of Economics 15 (3) (1984) 328–335.
[23] A.L. Hillman, The Political Economy of Protectionism, Harwood Academic Publishers, Chur, London, UK; New York, NY, 1989.

---

[61] While some green technologies may diffuse without regulation, environmental policy will be needed to encourage socially optimal adoption levels. For example, while technologies that increase fuel efficiency, potentially reducing fossil fuel consumption and the associated carbon emissions, could diffuse without regulation; adopters will consider the private gains from lower fuel costs, but not the social benefits of reduced emissions.

[24] M.J. Hiscox, S.L. Kastner, A General Measure of Trade Policy Orientations: Gravity-Model-Based Estimates for 82 Nations, 1960–1992, Harvard University, Department of Political Science, Mimeo, 2002.

[25] M. Karshenas, P.L. Stoneman, Rank, stock, order, and epidemic effects in the diffusion of new process technologies: an empirical model, RAND Journal of Economics 24 (4) (1993) 503–528.

[26] P. Keefer, DPI2004 Database of Political Institutions: Changes and Variable Definitions, Development Research Group, The World Bank, 2005.

[27] W. Keller, S. Yeaple, Multinational enterprises, international trade, and productivity growth: firm-level evidence from the United States, Review of Economics and Statistics (2009).

[28] S. Kerr, R.G. Newell, Policy-induced technology adoption: evidence from the U.S. lead phasedown, Journal of Industrial Economics 51 (3) (2003) 317–343.

[29] N. Kiefer, Economic duration data and hazard functions, Journal of Economic Literature 26 (1988) 646–679.

[30] T. Lancaster, The Econometric Analysis of Transition Data, Cambridge University Press, Cambridge, UK, 1990.

[31] J.O. Lanjouw, A. Mody, Innovation and the international diffusion of environmentally responsive technology, Research Policy 25 (1996) 549–571.

[32] J.O. Lanjouw, M. Shankerman, The quality of ideas: measuring innovation with multiple indicators, Economic Journal 114 (495) (2004) 441–465.

[33] R.C. Levin, A.K. Klevorick, R.R. Nelson, S.G. Winter, Appropriating the returns from industrial research and development, Brookings Papers on Economic Activity 3 (1987) 783–820.

[34] A. Levinson, Offshoring pollution: is the United States increasingly importing polluting goods? Review of Environmental Economics and Policy 4 (1) (2010) 63–83.

[35] A. McConville, Emission Standards Handbook, IEA Coal Research, London, UK, 1997.

[36] National Science Board, Science and Engineering Indicators—2006, National Science Foundation, Arlington, VA (NSB-06-01), 2006.

[37] W.G. Park, Intellectual patent protection: 1960–2005, Research Policy 37 (2008) 761–766.

[38] D. Popp, Exploring links between innovation and diffusion: adoption of NOₓ control technologies at U.S. coal-fired power plants, Environmental and Resource Economics 45 (3) (2010) 319–352.

[39] D. Popp, International innovation and diffusion of air pollution control technologies: the effects of NOₓ and SO₂ regulation in the U.S., Japan, and Germany, Journal of Environmental Economics and Management 51 (1) (2006) 46–71.

[40] D. Popp, Lessons from patents: using patents to measure technological change in environmental models, Ecological Economics 54 (2-3) (2005) 209–226.

[41] D. Popp, Pollution control innovations and the Clean Air Act of 1990, Journal of Policy Analysis and Management 22 (4) (2003) 641–660.

[42] V. Reppelin-Hill, Trade and the environment: an empirical analysis of the technology effect in the steel industry, Journal of Environmental Economics and Management 38 (1999) 283–301.

[43] N.L. Rose, P.L. Joskow, The diffusion of new technologies: evidence from the electric utility industry, RAND Journal of Economics 21 (3) (1990) 354–373.

[44] SEPA, Report on the State of the Environment in China 2006, State Council of the People's Republic of China, Beijing, 2007. ⟨www.english.sepa.gov.cn/standards_report/soe/SOE2006⟩, downloaded February 2008.

[45] L. Sloss, Trends in Emission Standards, IEA Coal Research, London, UK, 2003.

[46] H.N. Soud, Emission Standards Handbook: Air Pollutant Standards for Coal-Fired Power Plants, IEA Coal Research, London, UK, 1991.

[47] L.D. Snyder, N.H. Miller, R.N. Stavins, The effects of environmental regulation on diffusion: the case of chlorine manufacturing, American Economic Review 93 (2) (2003) 431–435.

[48] M.R. Taylor, E.S. Rubin, D.H. Hounshell, Effect of government actions on technological innovation for SO₂ control, Environmental Science & Technology 37 (2003) 4527–4534.

[49] J.L. Vernon, Emission Standards for Coal-Fired Plants: Air Pollutant Control Policies, IEA Coal Research, London, UK, 1988.

[50] World Bank, China: Air, Land, and Water, World Bank, Washington, D.C., 2001.

PART IV

INTERNATIONAL ECONOMIC INTEGRATION AND WAGES

THE LOCATION DECISIONS OF FOREIGN INVESTORS IN CHINA: UNTANGLING THE EFFECT OF WAGES USING A CONTROL FUNCTION APPROACH

Xuepeng Liu, Mary E. Lovely, and Jan Ondrich

Abstract—There is almost no support for the proposition that capital is attracted to low wages from firm-level studies. We examine the location choices of 2,884 firms investing in China between 1993 and 1996 to offer two main contributions. First, we find that the location of labor-intensive activities is highly elastic to provincial wage differences. Generally, investors' wage sensitivity declines as the skill intensity of the industry increases. Second, we find that unobserved location-specific attributes exert a downward bias on estimated wage sensitivity. Using a control function approach, we estimate a downward bias of 50% to 90% in wage coefficients estimated with standard techniques.

I. Introduction

COMPETITION for capital in labor-intensive activities with low entry barriers occurs largely among and within developing countries. This paper uses the location choices of foreign investors in China to estimate the response of capital to regional wage differentials. China is conducive to such a study because large capital inflows have been attracted in part by low wages and because there are substantial intracountry wage differences. During the period of substantial Chinese liberalization, 1992 to 1996, foreign-invested enterprises (FIEs) contributed 32% of fixed asset investment by all nonstate firms and over half of Chinese manufactured exports.[1] During the same period, average real wages of Chinese industrial workers rose 7.2%.[2] There was substantial variation in wage growth across provinces: real wages rose an average of 12.6% in Beijing but by only 0.7% in Hainan. Some observers claim that local governments prevented further wage gains in an effort to maintain flows of foreign capital.[3]

Despite the importance of foreign capital to developing economies, our understanding of the extent to which investors are attracted to low-wage locations is surprisingly incomplete. Studies of aggregate investment flows provide consistent evidence that capital is attracted to low wages, but there is little support for this proposition from studies that use microdata. Such data are prized because aggregate data often are not rich enough to explore key questions such as how production technology influences firms' wage sensitivity.

This study offers two main contributions. First, using information on 2,884 manufacturing equity joint ventures (EJV) in China between 1993 and 1996, we find that low-wage locations are more attractive to unskilled-labor-intensive activities than to skill-intensive activities. These results suggest that rising wages most strongly influence inves-

tors engaged in the least complex production activities. Second, we use a control function approach to conditional logit analysis discussed in Petrin and Train (2005) and estimate a downward bias of 50% to 90% in the wage coefficients estimated with standard techniques. Overall, firms are more responsive to wages than previous estimates indicate.

II. Wages, Firm Location Choice, and Omitted Variable Bias

Because the literature on FDI flows is large, our review of previous studies of wages and firm location choice is necessarily targeted. From all studies using aggregate FDI flows, we discuss only results obtained in studies of investment into Chinese provinces.[4] Among project-level studies, we examine results using data from foreign investment into the United States, the EU, and China. These regions receive the largest shares of foreign investment and permit study of location choice in the context of centralized labor market regulation.

Recent studies of the distribution of aggregate FDI flows among Chinese provinces or regions include Coughlin and Segev (2000), Wei et al., (1999), Cheng and Kwan (2000), Fung, Iizaka, and Parker (2002), Gao (2002), and Fung, Iizaka, and Siu (2003). In all these studies, wages are found to be a statistically significant, negative determinant of FDI flowing into a Chinese province or region. This result is robust to the choice of method and the inclusion of controls for skill level or skill availability.[5] Thus, aggregate studies strongly support the view that firms seek locations with low wages, ceteris paribus.

Given the uniformity of results from aggregate flows, it is surprising that studies using microdata do not typically find wages to be a significant determinant of location choice. An insignificant wage coefficient has been estimated in studies using foreign plant locations in the United States (Ondrich & Wasylenko, 1993; Head, Ries, & Swenson, 1999; List & Co, 2000; Keller & Levinson, 2002), Europe (Devereux & Griffith, 1998; Head & Mayer, 2004), and China (Head & Ries, 1996). Indeed, in some specifications, the estimated wage coefficient is positive.[6] One possible explanation for these results may be that foreign investors invest in these locations for market access rather than cost reductions. However, within a common market, such as the United States or Europe, there remains a presumption that higher wages should influence the state or region that investors choose. Thus, the inability to estimate a significant, negative wage coefficient frustrates many researchers.

A common concern in location choice studies is the possibility that wages and unobserved location characteristics are not independent, so that standard econometric techniques that require exogenous covariates produce biased estimates. As exposited by Berry (1994) to explain low estimated price elasticities in differentiated product stud-

Received for publication October 4, 2006. Revision accepted for publication April 9, 2008.

Liu: Kennesaw State University; Lovely: Syracuse University; Ondrich: Syracuse University.

We have benefited from discussions with Amil Petrin and Ken Train. We acknowledge helpful suggestions from Lee Branstetter, Judith Dean, Devashish Mitra, and seminar participants at the NBER China Working Group and the University of Nottingham. We are grateful to Gary Jefferson for providing Chinese industrial factor intensities.

[1] Investment percentage calculated by authors from Huang (2003, table 1.1). Export share taken from Huang (2003).

[2] Percentage calculated by authors based on the wage data from Branstetter and Feenstra (2002).

[3] Ross and Chan (2002) forcefully articulate this view. Bhagwati (2004) provides a response.

[4] We also note studies that use cross-country variation in wages, such as Wheeler and Mody (1992) and Wei (2000).

[5] The only study that does not find a significant coefficient for wage, Gao (2002), divides the value of investment among fourteen source countries.

[6] A recent exception to this pattern is Amiti and Javorcik (2008), who relate changes in the number of foreign-invested firms in Chinese provinces to changes in the average wage.

The Review of Economics and Statistics, February 2010, 92(1): 160–166

ies, sellers typically receive higher prices when their product has more desirable omitted characteristics.[7] When this logic is applied to the FDI context, omitted location characteristics that influence productivity may lead to biased estimates of the wage sensitivity of investors. If the unobserved factors are otherwise mean independent of observed factors, there is unambiguously a downward bias in standard estimates: firms look less sensitive to the wage than they really are.

The need to control for unobserved location-specific attributes is widely recognized in studies using repeated cross-sections. One approach to spatially correlated errors is to estimate a nested logit model (e.g., Head & Mayer, 2004).[8] A second approach, which is used in both conditional logit estimation and count data methods, is to control for time-invariant unobserved spatial characteristics with fixed effects (e.g., Head & Mayer, 2004; Keller & Levinson, 2002).[9] All of the studies listed include spatial fixed effects or use a nested logit procedure yet still find that the wage is not a significant determinant of location choice.

It is difficult to control for unobserved location-specific attributes for several reasons. First, there may be insufficient variation over time or too many empty cells to use fixed effects defined over the same geographic unit as the choice set. For this reason, Keller and Levinson (2002), in their study of foreign factory openings in U.S. states; Head and Mayer (2004), in their study of Japanese factory openings in regions within European countries; and Head and Ries (1996), in their study of FIE locations in Chinese provinces, use fixed effects defined over a geographic area larger than the unit of location choice.[10]

A second reason that it is difficult to control for unobserved location-specific attributes is that these unobservables may vary with time. This concern is particularly relevant in the Chinese case, where liberalization advanced at a varied pace, beginning in the coastal provinces but then pushing westward and increasing in speed, causing the productivity of local factors to change over time. For example, in 1992, the Chinese government significantly liberalized its FDI regime and decentralized approval from the central government to local governments (Huang, 2003). How quickly this regulatory change resulted in a liberalized investment environment varied from province to province. One way to capture such time-varying unobservables is to introduce time-province fixed effects to the conditional logit. This approach typically is problematic, however, as it would introduce more than 100 additional parameters to the conditional logit.

As an alternative, Berry, Levinsohn, and Pakes (1995) offer the product-market control approach, which has been widely used in estimating differentiated product models. It involves estimation of a set of controls that match observed to predicted market shares. Petrin and Train (2006) identify a number of advantages of this approach but note that unless sampling error in the market shares is minimal, the estimator is not consistent and is not asymptotically normal. Because the sampling error is unknown for the data we employ in this study, we choose not to use the product-market control method.

Another method for estimation of conditional logit models is proposed by Petrin (2005) and Petrin and Train (2005, 2006) based on control functions. A control function is a term added to an econometric specification to capture the effect of unobserved local characteristics, thereby breaking the correlation of the wage with the error term of the location-specific profit function. James Heckman (1976, 1979) pioneered the use of control functions to correct selectivity bias in normal linear regression models. The approach was used in the analysis of the Tobit model by Smith and Blundell (1986) and of the binary probit model by Rivers and Vuong (1988).

Typically the control function approach uses a two-step estimation. In the first step, OLS regression is used to estimate the variables that enter the control function. In our application, this first step requires the construction of an expected wage for each province in each year, with the residual used to specify a control function. In the second step, the likelihood function is maximized with the control function as additional explanatory variables. We find substantial differences between uncorrected estimates and those derived using the control function approach.[11]

III. The Location Choice Model

A. The Profit Function

We use a familiar model in which a firm chooses to locate where profits are maximized.[12] A multinational firm seeks to invest somewhere in China. The firm produces with a generalized Cobb-Douglas technology, using variable inputs of labor, imported inputs, and a vector of locally provided services. Log profits for firm i in province j can be written as

$$\ln \pi_{ij} = \alpha + \ln(1 - \tau_j) - \theta_L \ln w_j - \theta_m \ln p_{mj} - \theta_S \ln p_{Sj} - e_{ij}, \quad (1)$$

where θ_k denotes a cost share, τ_j reflects the tax rate on foreign investment in province j, w_j is the wage, p_{mj} is the price of imported inputs, p_{sj} is a price index for locally provided inputs, and e_{ij} is an idiosyncratic cost shock. The intercept, α, contains all terms that do not vary by province. Our empirical concern is with the estimation of the coefficient on the provincial wage, which depends on θ_L, the labor cost share. It is clear from equation (1) that the effect on profits of a higher wage is larger for firms in labor-intensive industries.

B. Benchmark Estimating Strategy

Our basic estimating strategy is similar to conditional logit procedures in previous studies. We treat these conditional logit results as a benchmark for comparison to results obtained using the control function method. The profit function (1) yields a linear function for log profits with arguments given by the vector

$$\mathbf{X} = [\ln(1 - \tau), \ln w, \ln p_m, \ln p_S]. \quad (2)$$

Using (1), we obtain $\Pi = \mathbf{X}\beta + e$, where β is the vector of parameters to be estimated. Our estimation strategy depends on the distribution of the unobserved idiosyncratic terms, e_{ij}. If these features are distributed independently according to an extreme value distribution,

---

[7] Petrin and Train (2006) provide many examples from studies of differentiated product models, including the well-known study by Berry et al. (1995).

[8] Discussion of the application of these methods to modeling firm location decisions can be found in Ondrich and Wasylenko (1993).

[9] As Head et al. (1999) note, this provides a convenient way to capture common attributes. Many studies observe fewer than 1,000 investments, and there are few observations in many year-location cells. Consequently, parsimony is necessary.

[10] Keller and Levinson (2002) control for time-invariant state characteristics in their analysis of the value of foreign-owned gross property, plant, and equipment but are limited to the use of regional fixed effects in their analysis of planned new foreign-owned factory openings.

[11] Petrin and Train (2006) find that estimated elasticities are similar across the control function and product-market approaches, but they both differ significantly from the uncorrected estimates.

[12] We condition on the decision to produce in China. We also use a static model of the investment decision, as is common in the literature.

then the probability, P_k, that province k is chosen, where k is a member of choice set J, is given by

$$P_k = \frac{\exp(x_k\beta)}{\sum_{j\in J}\exp(x_j\beta)}. \tag{3}$$

This conditional logit is well suited to the location choice problem since it exploits information on alternatives, accounts for match-specific details, and allows multiple alternatives.

C. Control Function Approach

The possible endogeneity of the wage in estimation of (1) can be illustrated by specifying the error in the profit function as a two-component error:[13]

$$e_{ij} = \beta_\xi \xi_j + \varepsilon_{ij}, \tag{4}$$

where ξ_j is location specific, observed by workers and firms but not by the researcher. ε_{ij} is an idiosyncratic error, assumed to be independent across firms and locations. Defining $\mathbf{X}_j$ as in (2) and letting Z_j be a variable not in $\mathbf{X}_j$, under certain regularity conditions the log wage can be expressed as an implicit function of all factors taken as given at the time of the decision:

$$\ln w_j = \ln w_j(\mathbf{X}_j, Z_j, \xi_j). \tag{5}$$

Because wages will be higher in locations with more desirable omitted characteristics, e_{ij} and $\ln w_j$ will be correlated even after conditioning on $\mathbf{X}_j$, violating the weak-exogeneity requirement for conditional logit covariates and leading to inconsistent parameter estimates.

Petrin and Train (2005, 2006) illustrate how a control function can be used to test for and correct the omitted variables problem. The method proceeds in two steps. The first step is a linear regression of log wages ($\ln w_j$) on exogenous variables $\mathbf{X}_j$ and Z_j using provincial-level data across years. We use this regression to construct the expected wage for each province in each year. The residual is used to estimate the control function, $f(\mu_j, \lambda)$, where μ_j is the disturbance from the first-stage regression and λ is a vector of estimated parameters. The profit function for firm i locating in province j can now be written as

$$\ln \pi_{ij} = \alpha + \mathbf{X}_{ij}\beta + f(\mu_j, \lambda) + (\beta_\xi \xi_j - f(\mu_j, \lambda)) + \varepsilon_{ij}. \tag{6}$$

The new error, $\eta_{ij} = \beta_\xi \xi_j - f(\mu_j, \lambda) + \varepsilon_{ij}$, includes the difference between the actual province-specific error $\beta_\xi \xi_j$ and the control function, plus the idiosyncratic error.

Therefore, we assume that at location j, the log wage, $\ln w_j$, can be expressed as

$$\ln w_j = E(\ln w_j | \mathbf{X}_j, Z_j) + \mu_j(\xi_j), \tag{7}$$

where $\mu_j(\xi_j)$ is one-to-one in ξ_j. Including $f(\mu_j, \lambda)$ in the conditional logit specification holds constant the variation in the error term of the location-specific profit function that is not independent of the wage. The equation for $\ln w_j$ above implies that $\hat{\mu}_j$ can be constructed as the residual from a first-stage regression of $\ln w_j$ on $\mathbf{X}_j$ and Z_j. Because the residual $\hat{\mu}_j$ replaces the disturbance μ_j in the control function when estimation is performed, the usual standard errors are incorrect.

---

[13] This discussion adapts the discussion of consumers' choice among differentiated products in Petrin and Train (2006) to the location choice context.

As described in the appendix, we use bootstrapping methods to correct the standard errors.

This approach requires a regressor for the first-stage wage regression that is correlated with the wage paid by EJVs but uncorrelated with foreign firms' location choices, conditional on other covariates. Identifying a suitable choice requires characterization of the wage-setting process in China. As discussed in Chan (2003), although local governments set minimum wages, private firms are otherwise free to set wage levels. Given this, our first-stage regression is a reduced-form wage equation with controls for labor supply (e.g., the share of the labor force with secondary education) and for labor demand (e.g., the rate at which output of state-owned enterprises is falling).

We use the log of the average industrial wage paid by SOEs as Z_j in our first-stage regression. Both state-owned enterprises (SOEs) and EJVs hire labor that is relatively skilled. Our choice is valid if private sector wages are influenced by some provincial characteristics that drive multifactor productivity, while SOE wages are not. We rely on the nature of the SOE wage-setting process and SOE productivity-wage gaps to argue for the independence of SOE wages from unobserved factors that drive foreign-firm productivity. In China, SOE wages prior to 1996 were largely determined by the central government, despite several rounds of wage reforms. Starting in 1985, the Ministry of Labor (MOL) provided some profit-oriented incentives to SOEs, but to a very limited extent.[14] Deeper reforms of China's SOE wage structure were not implemented until the Ninth Five Year Plan (1996–2000). Therefore, during the time frame of our sample, SOE wages were largely set by central government guidelines and were largely unresponsive to changes in private sector productivity.[15]

IV. Data Description and Sources

The sample of equity joint venture investments was constructed by Dean, Lovely, and Wang (2009), who provide details of the construction. The sample contains EJVs undertaken between 1993 and 1996 using project descriptions available from the Chinese Ministry of Foreign Trade and Economic Cooperation (MOFTEC).[16] We add regional fixed effects to capture regional correlation in supply and demand shocks. Complete descriptions and sources for all variables are provided in table 1.

The wage measure is the average annual wage paid by private and foreign enterprises in the province, drawn from Branstetter and Feenstra (2002), who also provide the average annual wage paid by SOEs, which we use in the first-stage wage regression. Average wages do not control for provincial variation in labor quality, so we include the share of the provincial labor force that has completed senior secondary school or above.

---

[14] For example, as Yueh (2004) showed, the State Council in 1992 permitted SOEs to set wages within the confines of a budget established by the government. However, if a wage bill exceeded the MOL standard, the enterprise paid a wage adjustment tax of 33%. Alternatively, the enterprise could propose a wage budget and then submit it for approval.

[15] Evidence from SOE productivity-wage gaps also supports the view that SOE wages do not reflect local attributes that influence foreign firms' productivity. Parker (1995) finds that "in 1992, state industrial wages were 43 percent higher than those available in urban collectives, and only 22 percent below those of the other ownership forms; these workers in other ownership forms, however, were 130 percent (in 1990 prices) to 200 percent (in 1980 prices) more productive than those under state-ownership."

[16] Equity joint ventures are limited liability companies incorporated in China, in which foreign and Mainland Chinese investors hold equity. For further details, see Fung (1997).

TABLE 1.—DATA DEFINITIONS AND SOURCES

Variable	Definition	Source	Mean[a]	s.d.[a]
EJV project		*Almanac of China's Foreign Economic Relations*		
Location	Province	*and Trade*, various years, Dean, Lovely, and		
Industry	3-digit ISIC Rev. 2 classification	Wang (2009)		
SOE wage	Average annual wage for industrial workers in state-owned enterprises, in 1990 yuan	Branstetter and Feenstra (2002), from *China Statistical Yearbook*, various years	2,837	656
Private wage	Average annual wage for industrial workers in other enterprises (private, foreign), in 1990 yuan	Branstetter and Feenstra (2002), from *China Statistical Yearbook*, various years	3,254	951
Agglomeration	Cumulative value of real contracted FDI, from 1983 until $t - 1$, in millions of 1980 U.S. dollars	Coughlin and Segev (2000)	1,536	3,023
Local firms	SOE and collective enterprises at the township level and above	*China Statistical Yearbook*, various years, Dean, Lovely, and Wang (2009)	16,061	10,871
Population	Province population, in millions	*China Statistical Yearbook*, various years	41	27
Skilled labor ratio	Share of population who have a senior secondary school education level or above, in percentage points	*China Statistical Yearbook*, various years and calculations by authors	12.08	6.19
Telephone density	Number of urban telephone subscribers per million persons	*China Statistical Yearbook*, various years	29,266	29,382
Road density	Road (km) per thousand km² of land area	*China Statistical Yearbook*, various years	248	147
Private market size	Real provincial GDP × (1 − SOE share), where SOE share is the production share of SOEs; GDP is value in billions of 1990 yuan	*China Statistical Yearbook*, various years, and calculations by authors	57	56
Change in state ownership	Difference in shares of industrial output from SOEs in year t and $t - 1$	*China Statistical Yearbook*, various years, Dean, Lovely, and Wang (2009)	−0.04	0.05
SEZ or OCC	Dummy variable for a province with SEZ or open coastal city	Dean, Lovely, and Wang (2009)	0.43	0.50
Capital stock	Capital stock, in 100 million 1978 yuan	Kui-Wai Li (2003)	1,784	1,610
S&T Intensity	Science and Technology expenditure as share of value-added × 10, by ISIC 3-digit classification (concordance by authors)	NBS Large and Medium Enterprise Survey, 1995, calculated by Gary Jefferson	0.50	0.30

[a]Descriptive statistics for provincial characteristics calculated from pooled data for 1993–1996 (excluding Tibet and Gansu).

We do not have direct measures of the cost of imported inputs (p_m) or the corporate tax rate (τ). To control for provincial variation in these factors, we include an incentive dummy that takes a value of 1 if there is a special economic zone (SEZ) or open coastal city (OCC) in the province. We also include two measures of provincial infrastructure: length of roads adjusted for provincial size and number of urban telephone subscribers relative to population.

To account for provincial variation in the price of local intermediate services (p_s), we follow Head and Ries (1996) and include two determinants of this price: the number of foreign firms and the number of potential local suppliers.[17] The number of foreign firms is measured as the real value of cumulative FDI, which we refer to as agglomeration, for the period 1983 to the year before the project is undertaken. Availability of potential suppliers of intermediate goods is measured by the number of domestic enterprises at the township level and above. To control for local market demand, we include population size and provincial private GDP and its square. Sales may also be affected by the extent to which a province is liberalizing, so we include change in the share of industrial output produced by SOEs.

V. Results

Theory suggests that wages have a larger effect on profits in labor-intensive industries, and so we expect these industries to be more responsive to provincial variations in labor costs when choosing an investment location. To allow for this differential response, we

characterize industries using Chinese industrial data on skill intensity, expecting a more elastic response in industries that are less skill intensive. Each industry's skill intensity is based on data from the Chinese National Bureau of Statistics' Large-and-Medium Enterprise (LME) Survey; it is calculated as total science and technology expenditures, including personnel, as a share of value added.[18] We predict that the estimated coefficient for the interaction of the private wage and skill intensity will be positive: wage sensitivity should be lower for more skill-intensive ventures.

A. Standard Estimation Results

The first two panels of table 2 report results estimated using standard techniques, without the inclusion of a control function. All covariates are lagged one year. The overall fit of the equation is comparable to other studies using similar procedures (e.g., Head & Ries, 1996; Head & Mayer, 2004). All coefficients have their expected signs, except provincial capital stock in the model without regional fixed effects, and are all statistically significant.

For both specifications, we estimate a negative and highly significant coefficient for the private wage. In comparing results in the first and second models, we see that the estimated value of the wage coefficient drops by 35% when regional fixed effects are included. Evidently controlling for time-invariant regional characteristics that may be correlated with the wage reduces the estimated attraction of low wages.

---

[17] Head and Ries (1996) develop a model of self-reinforcing FDI in which the equilibrium number of intermediate suppliers depends on the final-good price, the number of foreign firms to which domestic suppliers may sell and the number of domestic firms that may undertake the costly upgrading necessary to serve foreign firms.

[18] The LME survey is the most comprehensive firm-level data set available for Chinese industrial firms. Access to the LME is restricted. Results obtained using U.S. data to characterize skill intensity produce similar results.

TABLE 2.—CONDITIONAL LOGIT ANALYSIS OF EJV PROVINCIAL LOCATION

	Without Control Function				With Control Function			
	Coefficient	s.e.	Coefficient	s.e.	Coefficient	s.e.	Coefficient	s.e.
Log private wage	−2.40***	0.24	−1.55***	0.25	−3.75***	0.50	−2.93***	0.57
Log wage × S&T intensity	1.04***	0.26	1.06***	0.26	1.25***	0.30	1.33***	0.30
Log agglomeration	0.22***	0.05	0.33***	0.05	0.35***	0.07	0.48***	0.08
Log local firms	0.82***	0.11	1.04***	0.12	0.67***	0.14	0.95***	0.13
Log population	0.99***	0.15	1.97***	0.18	0.79***	0.18	1.80***	0.22
Skilled labor ratio	0.09***	0.01	0.09***	0.01	0.09***	0.01	0.07***	0.01
Log telephone density	0.53***	0.10	0.49***	0.13	0.61***	0.12	0.69***	0.17
Log road density	0.41***	0.08	0.10	0.10	0.50***	0.09	0.11	0.11
Log private market size	−1.85***	0.24	−3.13***	0.27	−1.80***	0.26	−3.12***	0.30
Squared log private market								
size	0.21***	0.02	0.16***	0.03	0.22***	0.02	0.16***	0.03
Change in state ownership	−2.91***	0.78	−6.06***	0.84	−3.66***	1.12	−6.65***	1.12
SEZ or OCC	0.86***	0.10	1.05***	0.17	0.72***	0.12	0.88***	0.19
Log capital stock	−0.15***	0.06	0.41***	0.14	−0.24***	0.08	0.45***	0.15
Regional fixed effects								
Central			1.42***	0.17			1.41***	0.17
Coastal			2.01***	0.20			1.96***	0.22
Northeast			0.69***	0.20			0.38	0.25
Northwest			0.06	0.24			−0.10	0.27
Residual					2.82***	0.85	2.79***	0.91
Residual × S&T intensity					−1.18	0.95	−1.62	0.92
Number of observations	2,884		2,884		2,884		2,884	
LR test	3,358		3,522		3,384		3,542	
Log likelihood	−7,931		−7,849		−7,918		−7,839	
Pseudo-R^2	0.175		0.183		0.176		0.184	
Schwarz criterion	−7,983		−7,917		−7,978		−7,915	
CF Wald statistic					11.74***		9.38***	
(*p*-value)					(0.003)		(0.009)	

Notes: *significant at 10%; **significant at 5%; ***significant at 1%. Variables are lagged by one year. Gansu and Tibet excluded.

In both models, the interaction of wage and industrial skill intensity is positive and highly significant, as expected. The estimated coefficient for this interaction is very similar across the two models. Because the maximum value of the skill intensity measure is 1.13, either model suggests that higher wages make a province a less attractive site for investment, ceteris paribus, for every industry. However, the reduction in the wage coefficient caused by inclusion of regional fixed effects, as in standard estimating strategy, leads to a wage coefficient for firms with the mean level of skill intensity (0.54) of −0.98.

Coefficients for other covariates also change in value when regional fixed effects are added, but only the capital stock coefficient changes sign. The regional coefficients indicate that EJVs are more likely to locate in any region other than the Southwest, although the difference is not significant for the Northwest region. As expected, these coefficients are largest for the central and coastal zones, which have the longest history of market liberalization.

B. Control Function Results

The third and fourth models in table 2 provide results estimated using the control function approach. Specifically, we include the residual from the first-stage wage regression and the interaction of this residual and industry skill intensity in the conditional logit estimation. The third model omits regional fixed effects, while the fourth model includes them. The reported standard errors (as well as variance matrices used in the testing of joint hypotheses) are corrected using a bootstrapping technique described in the appendix. The first-stage regression explains 86% of the variation in the private wage, and the coefficient of the log of the SOE wage is highly significant, with a

t-statistic of 8.76. Adding the log of the SOE wage to the first stage explains an additional 5% of the variation in private wages.[19]

When the control function is added, the wage coefficient remains negative and highly significant. However, it increases in absolute value, providing an estimate of the downward bias in the standard method. Comparing the first and third equations, those estimated without regional effects, we find that the coefficient of −3.75 estimated with the control function is 56% larger than the coefficient of −2.40 estimated without the control function. Again, the coefficient for the interaction of wage and industry skill intensity is highly significant. This estimated coefficient is only slightly affected by inclusion of the control function. The estimates obtained from the third model indicate a wage coefficient of −3.10 for firms with average skill intensity.

When we include regional fixed effects as well as the control function, the estimated coefficient is reduced somewhat, from −3.75 to −2.93 but remains larger than either model estimated without the control function. Indeed, in comparison to the standard estimating strategy using regional fixed effects, the wage coefficient is 89% larger. Again we find that skill intensity significantly influences firms' wage sensitivity. The wage response for all firms is negative, and the estimated wage coefficient for firms with average skill intensity is −2.21. Coefficient estimates on other variables are similar to those estimated in the second model, with regional fixed effects.

We use theoretical concerns, knowledge of the Chinese context, and diagnostic statistics to set criteria for choosing a preferred spec-

---

[19] First-stage wage regression results are available from the authors by request. We include regional fixed effects in the wage regression when they are included in the conditional logit.

ification among these four models. From theory, we expect that unobserved location advantages will be reflected in equilibrium wages, leading us to suspect that omitted variables may be present in the standard estimating strategy. From the Chinese context, we understand that liberalization proceeded rapidly but not uniformly between 1993 and 1996, implying that the investment environment in all provinces evolved during the period.

For diagnostics, Petrin and Train (2006) suggest the use of a joint significance test for the control function coefficients as a test of the exogeneity of the log wage. In the two models estimated with the control function, the values of the control function (CF) Wald statistic reject exogeneity. We use the Schwarz criterion to assess which of the four models performs best. The Schwarz criterion selects a model from a set of proposed models of different dimensions by finding its Bayes solution and evaluating the first terms of the asymptotic expansion, which do not depend on the prior distribution. It penalizes the log likelihood of each model by subtracting half of the product of the number of parameters and log sample size. Heckman and Walker (1987) include the Schwarz criterion in their set of criteria to choose among competing duration models. Mills and Prasad (1992) find that the Schwarz criterion consistently outperforms other model selection criteria in a Monte Carlo analysis. In our case, the Schwarz criterion favors the model in which both the control function and regional fixed effects are included.

Based on these criteria, we use the model that includes the control function and regional fixed effects to illustrate the varying response of industries to wage differentials. For this purpose, we calculate the elasticity with respect to the wage of the probability that a particular province is chosen by a particular industry. This elasticity measure is directly relevant to the policy concerns of local officials, who are interested in the extent to which wage growth reduces the likelihood that their province will be selected. As these elasticity calculations depend on provincial characteristics, we illustrate our results using Jiangsu, the province that received the largest number of projects in our sample. We also calculate the associated standard error for this estimate, using the delta method, and we test whether the elasticity estimate is significantly different from unity.

Our estimates suggest that location choices of labor-intensive industries are quite elastic with respect to wage increases. Foreign-invested enterprises account for a large share of export production in these industries. The least skill-intensive industry, wood products, has a skill measure of 0.17 and an estimated own-wage elasticity in Jiangsu of −2.15 (standard error of 0.32). The two industries that accounted for the largest shares of Chinese exports in 1995 are also highly sensitive to local wage differences: the estimated own-wage elasticity for the textile industry is −1.77 (0.38) and for apparel, −2.12 (0.31). Footwear, another industry that accounts for a large share of exports, also has a high own-wage elasticity: −2.11 (0.31). Each of these elasticities is significantly different from unity. For comparison, the most skill-intensive industry, the manufacture of professional, scientific, and controlling equipment, received little foreign investment during this time period. This industry has a skill measure of 1.13 and an estimated own-wage elasticity of −1.13 (0.25). We cannot reject the hypothesis of unitary elasticity for this industry or for other highly skill-intensive industries.

VI. Conclusion

Previous microdata studies of firm location choice provide little support for the standard theoretical prediction that firms are sensitive to local wages in choosing a location for foreign investment. Using

data from equity-joint-venture projects in China, we explore the possibility that unobserved location-specific attributes exert a downward bias on estimates of investors' response to wage differentials. We introduce to the location-choice context a control function approach applied by Petrin and Train (2005, 2006). Our results indicate that standard conditional logit techniques underestimate the sensitivity of investors to local wages and that coefficient estimates using the control function are 50% to 90% larger in absolute value.

A second contribution of the paper is new evidence on the nature of firms' attraction to low wages. Firms' responses to wages vary systematically with the skill intensity of production. Investors in the least skill-intensive industries exhibit the largest wage sensitivity in choosing a host. Textiles, apparel, and footwear constituted large shares of China's overall manufacturing exports in 1995 and exhibited highly elastic responses to local wage differences. In recent years, exports of more skill-intensive products, such as office and computing machinery and communications equipment, have grown rapidly. Our results indicate that investors in skill-intensive industries are less sensitive to local wages. Together these results suggest that wage pressures on local hosts change as the development process matures.

REFERENCES

Amiti, Mary, and Beata Smarzynska Javorcki, "Trade Costs and the Location of Foreign Firms in China," *Journal of Development Economics* 85 (2008), 129–149.

Berry, Steven, "Estimating Discrete Choice Models of Product Differentiation," *RAND Journal of Economics* 25 (1994), 242–262.

Berry, Steven, James Levinsohn, and Ariel Pakes, "Automobile Prices in Market Equilibrium," *Econometrica* 63 (1995), 841–890.

Bhagwati, Jagdish, *In Defense of Globalization* (New York: Oxford University Press, 2004).

Branstetter, Lee, and Robert C. Feenstra, "Trade and Foreign Direct Investment in China: A Political Economy Approach," *Journal of International Economics* 57 (2002), 335–358.

Chan, Anita, "A Race to the Bottom," *China Perspective* 46 (2003), 41–49.

Cheng, Leonard K., and Yum K. Kwan, "What Are the Determinants of the Location of Foreign Direct Investment? The Chinese Experience," *Journal of International Economics* 51 (2000), 370–400.

Coughlin, Cletus C., and Eran Segev, "Foreign Direct Investment in China: A Spatial Econometric Study," *World Economy* 23 (2000), 1–23.

Dean, Judith M., Mary E. Lovely, and Hua Wang, "Are Foreign Investors Attracted to Weak Environmental Regulations? Evaluating the Evidence from China," *Journal of Development Economics* 90 (2009), 1–13.

Devereux, Michael, and Rachel Griffith, "Taxes and the Location of Production: Evidence from a Panel of U.S. Multinationals," *Journal of Public Economics* 68 (1998), 1–23.

Fung, Kwok-Chiu, *Trade and Investment: Mainland China, Hong Kong, and Taiwan* (Hong Kong: City University of Hong Kong Press, 1997).

Fung, Kwok-Chiu, Hitomi Iizaka, and Stephen Parker, "Determinants of U.S. and Japanese Direct Investment in China," *Journal of Comparative Economics* 30 (2002), 567–578.

Fung, Kwok-Chiu, Hitomi Iizaka, and Alan Siu, "Japanese Direct Investment in China," *China Economic Review* 14 (2003), 304–315.

Gao, Ting, "Labor Quality and the Location of Foreign Direct Investment: Evidence from FDI in China by Investing Country," University of Missouri mimeograph (2002).

Head, Keith, and Thierry Mayer, "Market Potential and the Location of Japanese Investment in the European Union," this REVIEW 86 (2004), 959–972.

Head, Keith, and John Ries, "Inter-City Competition for Foreign Investment: Static and Dynamic Effects of China's Incentive Areas," *Journal of Urban Economics* 40 (1996), 38–60.

Head, Keith, John Ries, and Deborah Swenson, "Attracting Foreign Manufacturing: Investment Promotion and Agglomeration," *Regional Science and Urban Economics* 29 (1999), 197–218.

Heckman, James, "The Common Structure of Statistical Models of Truncation, Sample Selection and Limited Dependent Variables and a Simple Estimator for Such Models," *Annals of Economic and Social Measurement* 5 (1976), 475–492.

——— "Sample Selection Bias as a Specification Error," *Econometrica* 47 (1979), 153–162.

Heckman, James J., and James R. Walker, "Using Goodness of Fit and Other Criteria to Choose among Competing Duration Models: A Case Study of Hutterite Data," *Sociological Methodology* 17 (1987), 247–307.

Henley, John, Colin Kirkpatrick, and Georgina Wilde, "Foreign Direct Investment in China: Recent Trends and Current Policy Issues," *World Economy* 22 (1999), 223–243.

Huang, Yasheng, *Selling China: Foreign Investment during the Reform Era* (Cambridge: Cambridge University Press, 2003).

Karaca-Mandic, Pinar, and Kenneth Train, "Standard Error Correction in Two-Stage Estimation with Nested Samples," *Econometrics Journal* 62 (2003), 401–407.

Keller, Wolfgang, and Arik Levinson, "Pollution Abatement Costs and Foreign Direct Investment Inflows to the United States," this REVIEW 84 (2002), 691–703.

Li, Kui-Wai, "China's Capital and Productivity Measurement Using Financial Resources," Economic Growth Center, Yale University working paper no. 851 (2003).

List, John A., and Catherine Y. Co, "The Effects of Environmental Regulations on Foreign Direct Investment," *Journal of Environmental Economics and Management* 40 (2000), 1–20.

Mills, Jeffrey, and Kislaya Prasad, "A Comparison of Model Selection Criteria," *Econometric Reviews* 11 (1992), 201–234.

Ondrich, Jan, and Michael Wasylenko, *Foreign Direct Investment in the United States* (Kalamazoo, MI: W. E. Upjohn Institute for Employment Research, 1993).

Parker, Elliott, "Prospects for the State-Owned Enterprise in China's Socialist Market Economy," *Asian Perspective* 19 (1995), 7–35.

Petrin, Amil, "The Use of Control Functions to Identify Demand when Errors are Non-Additive," GSB working paper and University of Chicago mimeograph (2005).

Petrin, Amil, and Kenneth Train, "Tests for Omitted Attributes in Differentiated Product Models," University of Minnesota mimeograph (2005).

——— "Control Function Corrections for Omitted Attributes in Differentiated Product Models," University of Minnesota mimeograph (2006).

Rivers, Douglas, and Quang H. Vuong, "Limited Information Estimators and Exogeneity Tests for Simultaneous Probit Models," *Journal of Econometrics* 39 (1988), 347–366.

Ross, Robert, J. S., and Anita Chan, "From North-South to South-South: The True Face of Global Competition," *Foreign Affairs* 81 (2002), 8–13.

Smith, Richard J., and Richard W. Blundell, "An Exogeneity Test for a Simultaneous Equation Tobit Model with an Application to Labor Supply," *Econometrica* 54 (1986), 679–686.

Wei, Shang-Jin, "How Taxing Is Corruption on International Investors?" this REVIEW 82 (2000), 1–11.

Wei, Yingqi, Xiaming Liu, David Parker, and Kirit Vaidya, "The Regional Distribution of Foreign Direct Investment in China," *Regional Studies* 33 (1999), 857–867.

Wheeler, David, and Ashoka Mody, "International Investment Location Decisions: The Case of U.S. Firms," *Journal of International Economics* 33 (1992), 57–76.

Yueh, Linda Y., "Wage Reforms in China during the 1990s," *Asian Economic Journal* 18 (2004), 149–164.

APPENDIX

First-Stage Results and Bootstrapping Procedures

A maintained primitive of the control function approach is that wages are additively separable in the observed (X_j and Z_j) and the unobserved factors (ξ_j); that is, the unobserved factors are mean independent of the observed factors. This assumption implies uncorrelatedness of unobservables and covariates. It enables use of linear regression in the first stage and ensures the consistent estimation of the residual from the first stage. In the first stage, we regress log private wage on all variables in the conditional logit and log SOE wage, as described in the text.

When a control function that includes predicted values is added to the estimation, the coefficients are consistent, but the standard errors are incorrect. Petrin and Train (2006) use bootstrapping to correct standard errors in their applications. In the first stage, we bootstrap a wage sample and regress the private wage on the exogenous variables and the log of the SOE wage for the years 1990 to 1996.[20] The control function in the second stage is a function of the first-stage residual and the interactions of the residual with industrial skill intensity. We run the conditional logit with this control function and repeat this process 100 times. The variances of these bootstrapped coefficients in the second stage are added to the traditional variance estimates from the conditional logit regression with the control function.[21] We experiment with different orders of the polynomial of the residuals to specify the control function. Typically higher orders are insignificant and have only a small effect; hence they are not included in our regressions.

---

[20] We do not use years after 1996 in the first stage to avoid possible structural changes in wage structure after 1996 due to SOE reforms. We also do not use years before 1990 for similar concerns. Years after 1989 and before 1993 are kept to increase the sample size and the reliability of the estimates. The direction and magnitude of bias are consistent when we experiment with different years in the first stage.

[21] Karaca-Mandic and Train (2003) propose alternative standard error correction procedures, but find results very similar to bootstrapping.

Does Final Market Demand Elasticity Influence the Location of Export Processing? Evidence from Multinational Decisions in China

Xuepeng Liu[1], Mary E. Lovely[2] and Jan Ondrich[3]

[1]*Department of Economics and Finance, Kennesaw State University, Kennesaw, GA, USA,* [2]*Department of Economics, Syracuse University, Syracuse, NY, USA, and* [3]*Department of Economics, Center for Policy Research, Syracuse University, Syracuse, NY, USA*

1. INTRODUCTION

BETTER working conditions and higher wages remain elusive for millions of workers engaged in export processing throughout the developing world. While some argue that multinational firms can afford to pay higher labour costs, others claim that manufacturers at the bottom of the global supply chain compete fiercely to earn small profit margins. These small margins underlie industry claims that higher labour costs force them to shift investment to locations where wages remain low. Companies making goods as different as computers and sporting goods assert that they do not have the 'pricing power' to absorb higher labour costs. They argue that since competition makes it difficult to pass higher costs on to their customers, they are forced to avoid locations with relatively high wages or labour-market regulation.[1] This reasoning places final market demand conditions at the heart of location decisions for export processing. If firms are price takers in international markets, any jurisdiction that experiences increased labour costs must offer a fully offsetting differential in some form or see new investment flow to lower wage locations.

Recent estimates of final market demand elasticities, however, find that these elasticities are substantially less than infinite in many industries, suggesting that some firms' claims of having no 'pricing power' are overstated. Indeed, Broda and Weinstein (2006) estimate the elasticity of substitution across alternative sources of similar goods imported into the United States and find wide variation in the competitive conditions faced by exporters in different industries. Dividing goods into the three Rauch (1999) categories, they find that the average

We thank Amil Petrin and Ken Train for a discussion of the econometric methodology. We have benefited from comments by Devashish Mitra, Judith Dean, an anonymous referee, and seminar participants at the 2010 American Economic Association meetings, at the University of Western Ontario, and at the 2011 Chinese Economic Association Meetings.

[1] Many news articles report company and analysts' perceptions of export processing firms' ability to cope with higher costs. These issues arose, for example, in reports following two highly publicised suicides at export processing factories in Southern China. See 'Supply Chain for iPhone Highlights Costs in China', The New York Times, 5 July 2010. <http://www.nytimes.com/2010/07/06/technology/06iphone.html?pagewanted=1&sq=Foxconn%20Technology&st=cse&scp=2>.

elasticity of substitution is much higher for commodities than it is for reference priced goods and that the average for reference priced goods is higher than that for differentiated goods. These demand differences imply that firms in different industries that produce for the American market face varying degrees of pressure to minimise offshore production costs.

Given the importance many developing countries attach to attracting foreign investors engaged in export-processing activities, surprisingly little is known about the sensitivity of these investors to local wage differences and the role played by final product market conditions. Using project-level data from China, this study offers what we believe are the first estimates of how foreign investor sensitivity to interjurisdictional wage differences depends on final market demand elasticity, in addition to other factors previously identified in the literature. We posit a model in which Chinese-made goods are imperfect substitutes for similar goods exported by other countries to a final (consuming) market. Foreign investors compare profits across alternative provincial locations, taking the behaviour of other firms as given. In this monopolistically competitive framework, firms perceive some ability to pass higher wage costs in any one location on to consumers. Consequently, multinationals operating in industries that are imperfectly competitive need smaller compensating differentials to choose a high-wage location than do those operating in highly competitive markets.

We test the empirical implications of the theory using an approach developed by Petrin and Train (2010) and introduced to the location-choice literature by Liu et al. (2010) to address possible endogeneity of local wages. Unlike earlier contributions, the study focuses not only on testing for potential bias in estimated coefficients, but also on estimating the influence of final market demand conditions on foreign firms' sensitivity to local wage differences. The interplay between host factor markets and foreign final good markets is significantly under-explored in the literature, but the implications of this relationship are increasingly important for development policy in a world with product fragmentation, outsourcing and export-processing trade. Our intent is to highlight the theoretical relevance of final market demand elasticity to firm-location choice and to illustrate its empirical salience using microdata on Chinese FDI inflows.

To measure export-market demand conditions in our empirical work, we employ the Broda and Weinstein (2006) estimates for US elasticities of substitution across similar products imported from different countries. These estimates are well suited to our purpose for several reasons. First, Broda and Weinstein estimate these elasticities using an econometric procedure derived from a model of monopolistic competition that we share and which fits the Chinese setting. In this context, the substitution elasticity determines the firm's markup over marginal cost and, thus, is an appropriate measure of market power. Second, the US market is the largest market for foreign invested enterprise (FIE) exports from China and, thus, American market conditions reflect important constraints on the pricing behaviour of multinational firms exporting from China. Lastly, these estimates are based on thousands of observations and thus are quite precise.

A second feature of our analysis is that we separately analyse the behaviour of foreign investors from Hong Kong, Macao and Taiwan (ethnically Chinese investors) and those from other countries/regions (Foreign). Many earlier studies suggest that the development level as well as previous investment of the source country matters for investor location behaviour. In the Chinese context, another important consideration is the latent traditional customs and rules, including *guanxi* and social networks, shared by mainland business agents and investors from Hong Kong, Macao and Taiwan.

EVIDENCE FROM MULTINATIONAL DECISIONS IN CHINA   511

After deriving an estimating equation from a model of profit-maximising location choice, we apply a control-function estimation technique to data on 2,884 manufacturing equity joint venture (EJV) projects undertaken by foreign investors. China is a suitable setting for studying investors' responsiveness to wages. It is a large country with centralised labour-market regulation but, due in part to limit labour mobility, there is wide geographic variation in wage levels. China also provides a setting to observe variation in behaviour across industries, because foreign investment flows are large and dispersed. As Huang (2003) notes, in comparison with other countries at a similar stage of development, FDI inflows to China during the 1990s are remarkable for their wide distribution among industries and provinces.[2] The time period we study, 1993–96, also fits our purposes well. During this period, most foreign investment entering China was used to produce for export markets, as assumed in our theoretical model. Second, we need an instrument to make use of the control-function technique. The wage for state-owned enterprises (SOEs) forms a good IV for private-firm wages during our sample period, as the former was administratively set during the time period. Deep SOE wage reform was implemented after 1996, during the 9th Five Year Plan.

Results from our conditional logit estimation imply a significant, elastic response of foreign investors to local wages, with investors in the least capital-intensive activities exhibiting the greatest wage sensitivity. Even while controlling for factor intensity, however, we find that location choice is significantly influenced by export market demand conditions. *Ceteris paribus*, investors in those industries where demand for Chinese made goods is most elastic are the most sensitive to wage differences. Sectors with the highest estimated average location-probability elasticity with respect to wages include those producing homogeneous products, such as iron and steel, nonferrous metals, food processing and chemicals. Among the least sensitive sectors are those producing differentiated products, such as electrical machinery (including communication devices), professional and scientific equipment and glass and glass products.

We also find some interesting differences between firms from different sources and offer explanations drawn from previous findings in the literature. We provide detailed analysis of the estimated own-wage elasticity by industry and source as well as the own and crosswage elasticities by province. Finally, we perform some dynamic simulations and show how relative wage changes across provinces are expected to affect the distribution of FDI among Chinese provinces.

The next section discusses the difficulties previous project-level studies of FDI have encountered in estimating investor's location-choice decisions. These studies indicate the need to control for omitted variable bias in estimation. In Section 3, we model the location choice of firms engaged in export processing and we use this model to form our estimation strategy. Section 4 describes the sample of foreign investment projects and measures of industry characteristics. Section 5 presents the results of our econometric analysis, emphasising differences across industries and investor groups. We conclude in Section 6 with a discussion of how awareness of the role of export-demand elasticity in firms' location decisions informs efforts to improve labour-market conditions in developing countries.

---

[2] In the 1995 Industrial Census, no industry received more than 10 per cent of total FDI. The geographic distribution of foreign investment within China is highly uneven, as it is in most host countries. Henley et al. (1999) report that 80 per cent of cumulative FDI inflows is located in one of China's 10 eastern provinces. However, while interior regions received only 13 per cent of cumulative FDI from 1992 to 1998, the quantity exceeded all FDI inflows to India during the same period.

512   X. LIU, M. E. LOVELY AND J. ONDRICH

2. CONTROL-FUNCTION CORRECTIONS FOR OMITTED ATTRIBUTES

Recent studies of the distribution of aggregate FDI flows among Chinese provinces or regions include Cheng and Kwan (2000), Coughlin and Segev (2000), Fung et al. (2002, 2003) and Gao (2005). In all these studies, the wage is found to be a statistically significant, negative determinant of the value of FDI flowing into a Chinese province or region. With the exception of Gao (2005), this result is robust to the choice of method and to the inclusion of controls for regional skill availability. These studies based on aggregated flow data strongly support the view that firms seek locations with low wages, *ceteris paribus*.

Surprisingly, studies using project-level data do not typically find wages to be a significant determinant of location choice. An insignificant wage coefficient has been estimated in studies using foreign plant locations in the United States (Ondrich and Wasylenko, 1993; Head et al., 1999; List and Co, 2000 and Keller and Levinson, 2002); in Europe (Devereux and Griffith, 1998; Head and Mayer, 2004); and in China (Head and Ries, 1996).[3] Indeed, in some specifications, the estimated wage coefficient is positive. An explanation for the failure to precisely estimate a negative wage coefficient is that wages and unobserved location characteristics may not be independent, leading standard econometric techniques that require exogenous covariates to produce biased estimates. To address this issue, Liu et al. (2010) apply a control-function approach to location-choice studies.

As proposed by Berry (1994) to explain low-price elasticity estimates in differentiated product studies, sellers will receive higher prices when their product has more desirable omitted characteristics. These omitted characteristics may include any attribute that affects the true value of the product to the buyer. When independence is maintained, buyers look less price sensitive than they are because they receive more for the price they pay than the econometrician takes into account.[4] Applying this logic to the FDI context, omitted location characteristics that influence worker productivity and wages could lead to biased estimates of the wage sensitivity of investors. If the unobserved factors are otherwise mean independent of observed factors, there is unambiguously a downward bias in standard estimates – firms look less sensitive to the wage than they really are.

One approach to spatially correlated errors is to estimate a nested logit model (e.g. Head and Mayer, 2004).[5] A second approach, which is used in both conditional logit estimation and count data methods, is to control for time invariant unobserved spatial characteristics with fixed effects (e.g. Head and Mayer, 2004; Keller and Levinson, 2002).[6] As demanding of the data as these procedures are, neither approach fully accounts for the omission of location characteristics correlated with the wage. It is difficult to control for unobserved location-specific attributes for several reasons. First, there may be insufficient variation over time or too many empty cells to use fixed effects defined over the same geographic unit as the choice set. Keller and Levinson (2002), in their study of foreign factory openings in US states, Head and

---

[3] A recent exception to this pattern is Amiti and Javorcik (2008), who use a different technique. They relate changes in the number of foreign invested firms in Chinese provinces to changes in the average wage.

[4] Petrin and Train (2010) provide examples from studies of differentiated product models, including the well known study by Berry et al. (1995).

[5] Further discussion of the application of these methods to modelling firm location decisions can be found in Ondrich and Wasylenko (1993).

[6] As Head et al. (1999) note, this provides a convenient way to capture common attributes. Many studies observe fewer than 1,000 investments and as they sometimes span a decade or more, there are few observations in many year-location cells. Consequently, parsimony is necessary given data limitations.

EVIDENCE FROM MULTINATIONAL DECISIONS IN CHINA 513

Mayer (2004), in their study of Japanese factory openings in regions within European countries, and Head and Ries (1996), in their study of FIE locations in Chinese provinces, use fixed effects defined over a geographic area larger than the unit of location choice.[7] A second reason why it is difficult to control for location-specific attributes is that these unobservables may vary with time. In China, where liberalisation advanced at a varied pace, beginning in the coastal provinces but then pushing westwards and increasing in speed, the productivity of local factors changed over time and across provinces. One way to capture such time varying unobservables is to introduce time-province fixed effects to the conditional logit. This approach typically is problematic, however, as it would introduce more than 100 additional parameters to the estimation.

An alternative two-stage method is proposed by Petrin and Train (2010) based on control functions and further developed by Kim and Petrin (2010a). A control function is a factor added to an econometric specification to capture the effect of unobserved characteristics, thereby breaking the correlation of the wage variable with the error term of the location-specific profit function. The use of control functions was pioneered by Heckman (1976, 1979) to correct selectivity bias in linear regression models. The control-function approach was later used in analysis of the Tobit model by Smith and Blundell (1986) and in the analysis of the binary probit model by Rivers and Vuong (1988). Petrin and Train (2010) introduce the use of control functions to the estimation of conditional logit models.

Liu et al. (2010) apply this control-function method to firm-location choice. Their approach proceeds in two steps: in the first step, ordinary least squares (OLS) regression is used to estimate the variables that enter the control function; in the second step, the likelihood function is maximised with the control function added in the form of additional explanatory variables. They find that coefficient estimates differ significantly across the corrected and the uncorrected procedures. Using a control function, they estimate a downward bias of 50 to 90 per cent in wage estimates estimated with standard techniques. We adopt this technique in our estimation procedures, as a parsimonious and powerful way to correct for potential omitted variables bias. Chen and Moore (2010) also adopt a control-function technique in their study of the location decisions of French multinational firms.

3. THE LOCATION CHOICE MODEL

a. The Profit Function

A multinational firm seeks to invest one unit of capital somewhere in China.[8] The new venture will engage in processing of a differentiated good for export.[9] The multinational firm compares potential profits per unit of capital across locations, taking the behaviour of other

---

[7] Keller and Levinson (2002) control for time invariant state characteristics in their analysis of the value of foreign-owned gross property, plant and equipment but are limited to the use of regional fixed effects in their analysis of planned foreign-owned factory openings.
[8] During the span of this study, significant restrictions on wholly owned subsidiaries were in place and EJVs were the dominant mode of entry for foreign investors.
[9] In 1995, FIEs export sales accounted for about 40 per cent of total FIE sales (Huang, 2003, Table 1.4), with wide variation by industry and source. This share is an underestimate of the importance of foreign markets to FIE sales because it does not include sales of goods that are further processed within China and then re-exported.

514   X. LIU, M. E. LOVELY AND J. ONDRICH

firms as given and will locate production in the province that maximises its profit.[10] The firm produces with a generalised Cobb–Douglas technology, using variable inputs of labour, imported intermediates and a vector of locally provided services. Log profits for a firm producing good g if it locates in province j can be written as:

$$\ln \pi_{gj} = \ln(1 - \tau_j) + \ln(p_{gC} - c_{gj}) + \ln D_{gC},   \tag{1}$$

where τ_j reflects the (perhaps concessionary) tax rate on foreign investment in province j, p_{gC} is the price on world markets of the Chinese (C) variety of good g, c_{gj} is the unit cost of producing good g in province j, and D_{gC} is global demand for Chinese exports of good g.

Let E_g denote global expenditure on all varieties of good g. Consumers allocate their expenditure across varieties by maximising an asymmetric constant elasticity of substitution subutility function for each good, as in Broda and Weinstein (2006).[11] Global demand for Chinese varieties of good g, which depends on prices for varieties from all producing countries, $n = 1, \ldots, N$, is:

$$D_{gC} = \frac{d_{gC} p_{gC}^{-\sigma_g}}{\sum\limits_{n=1}^{N} d_{gn} p_{gn}^{1-\sigma_g}} E_g.   \tag{2}$$

The asymmetric subutility function allows for idiosyncratic preference terms, d_{gC}, and resulting demand functions that differ by country of origin.[12] The elasticity of substitution among varieties of good g is assumed to exceed unity: $\sigma_g > 1$.

Whichever location it chooses, the firm will set its product price to maximise profits. Following Dixit and Stiglitz (1977), if the number of firms is large, firms treat the elasticity of substitution across varieties, σ_g, as if it were the price elasticity of demand. The resulting producer prices are markups over marginal costs: $p_{gj} = (\sigma_g/(\sigma_g - 1))c_{gj}$.

To express the potential profitability of locating in province j, we begin by taking the natural log of (2) and substituting the resulting expression for log demand into (1). Note that when firms choose among locations in China, the only relevant information is the ordering of profits across provinces. Factors that do not vary across locations do not affect the ordering of profits and can be omitted. Subtracting these location invariant factors from profits and denoting the resulting variable profits potentially earned in province j as V_{gj}, yields

$$\ln V_{gj} = \ln(1 - \tau_j) - \sigma_g \ln c_{gj}.   \tag{3}$$

Cost is a function of provincial factor prices – the wage, w, the price of imported intermediates, p_m, a price index for locally provided inputs, p_s

---

[10] We condition on the decision to produce in China. We also use a static model of the investment decision, as is common in the literature.

[11] An alternative to the assumption of global market demand is to follow Head et al. (1999) and assume that demand facing the representative firm locating in province j depends on price, local income I_j and an idiosyncratic demand shock: $\ln D_j = \eta_I \ln I_j - \eta_p \ln p_j + e_{ij}^d$. In our empirical work, we test the sensitivity of our results to this alternative form for demand.

[12] As in Romer (1994), Rutherford and Tarr (2002) and Broda and Weinstein (2006), variety is defined by country of origin. See Broda and Weinstein (2006, p. 556–8) for a discussion of the asymmetric CES function and resulting demand functions. Their methodology relies on Feenstra (1994).

EVIDENCE FROM MULTINATIONAL DECISIONS IN CHINA 515

$$\ln c_{gj} = \theta_{gl} \ln w_j + \theta_{gm} \ln p_{mj} + \theta_{gs} \ln p_{sj}, \tag{4}$$

where θ_{gk} ($k = l, m, s$) denotes a variable cost share in industry g. Using (3) and (4), we obtain an expression for variable profits that is decreasing in local factor prices and tax rate:

$$\ln V_{gj} = \ln(1 - \tau_j) - \sigma_g \theta_{gl} \ln w_j - \sigma_g \theta_m \ln p_{mj} - \sigma_g \theta_s \ln p_{sj}. \tag{5}$$

It is clear from (5) that the effect on potential variable profits of a higher provincial wage, *ceteris paribus*: (i) is larger for firms in industries in which labour costs form a larger share of noncapital costs, θ_{gl}; and (ii) is larger for firms in industries facing a higher elasticity of substitution in export markets, σ_g. This observation leads us to predict that both capital intensity and final market demand elasticity will influence investors' response to provincial wage differences, as evidenced by their location decisions.

b. Agglomeration and Local Suppliers

Previous research has shown that foreign firms have a strong tendency to locate in areas where other foreign firms have located. We incorporate agglomeration into our model by adapting the Head and Ries (1996) framework for localisation economies. Head and Ries argue that agglomeration in China is the result of localisation economies from concentrations of intermediate service providers. They assume that the market for local services is monopolistically competitive and that foreign firms use a composite of these services. They show how the equilibrium number of intermediate suppliers depends on the price of the final good, the number of foreign firms, N_j^f, and the number of domestic firms who may undertake the costly upgrading necessary to serve foreign firms, $\bar{N}_j^s$. Assuming log-linear functional forms, this framework allows us to derive an intermediates price index for locally provided service inputs:

$$\ln p_{sj} = \ln A + \mu_L \ln w_j + \mu_p \ln p_j + \mu_f \ln N_j^f + \mu_s \ln \bar{N}_j^s, \tag{6}$$

where A is a constant and the coefficients are functions of the underlying production parameters for final goods and intermediates. Substituting this expression back into the firm's profit function (5) yields an expression that can be used as the basis for estimation.

c. Benchmark Estimating Strategy

Our basic estimating strategy is similar to conditional logit procedures in previous studies. We treat these conditional logit results as a benchmark for comparison with results obtained using the control-function method. The profit function (5) and the price index (6) yield a linear function for log profits with arguments given by the vector

$$\mathbf{X} = [\ln w, \ln p_m, \ln(1 - \tau), \ln N^f, \ln \bar{N}^s]. \tag{7}$$

Adding an error vector e to capture firm-province idiosyncratic cost shocks, we obtain $\Pi = \mathbf{X}\beta + e$, where β is the vector of parameters to be estimated. Our estimation strategy depends on the distribution of the unobserved idiosyncratic terms, e_{ij}. If these features are distributed independently according to an extreme value distribution, then the probability, P_k, that province k is chosen, where k is a member of choice set J, is given by

$$P_k = \frac{\exp(\mathbf{X}_k \beta)}{\sum_{j \in J} \exp(\mathbf{X}_j \beta)}. \tag{8}$$

516   X. LIU, M. E. LOVELY AND J. ONDRICH

This conditional logit is well suited to the location-choice framework since it exploits extensive information on alternatives, can account for match specific details and allows for multiple alternatives.[13] Regional fixed effects are added to the list of regressors to capture regional correlation in supply and demand shocks.

We use information on the location choices of multinational firms investing in China to estimate the sensitivity of foreign investors to wage differences. As suggested by the variable profit function (5), we expect this response to vary across industries by factor intensity and by export-market demand elasticity. To test for varying parameters, we interact the provincial wage with these two characteristics of the industry in which the Chinese-based venture is engaged.

The first industry characteristic we interact with wage is a measure of physical and human capital intensity. The theoretical framework suggests that cross-provincial differences in wages are less important when local labour costs are a small share of variable production costs per unit of capital invested; that is, wage differences are less important to a more capital-intensive industry. We measure capital intensity using the average wage paid by the industry in China. The average wage reflects both physical and human capital intensity of the activity in which workers are engaged. Data on average wages by industry is drawn from the 1995 Third Industrial Census, a complete census of formal economic activity in China. Correlation across industries of the average wage with estimates of the 1995 capital/labour ratio is 0.71. We prefer using the average wage rather than the measured capital/labour ratio because capital is poorly measured in 1995 and the error is likely to be correlated with the extent of state ownership. We expect that firms in industries with high average wages, and thus relatively low unskilled labour cost shares, will be less responsive to provincial wage differentials than are firms with low average wages and high unskilled labour cost shares.

The second industry characteristic we interact with the provincial wage is the elasticity of substitution across imported product varieties, estimated by Broda and Weinstein (2006) using US import data for 3-digit industries over the period 1990–2001.[14] We expect that investors in an industry facing relatively high demand elasticity in export markets will be less able to shift wage costs onto consumers and, thus, will be more sensitive to provincial wage variation.

Finally, to permit responsiveness to vary by source, we estimate conditional logits for each of three samples: the full sample, projects funded from ethnically Chinese economies (ECE) sources of Hong Kong, Macau and Taiwan and projects funded from other, primarily OECD, sources.[15] Previous work suggests that investors from Hong Kong, Macau and Taiwan are less

---

[13] An alternative approach is to use count data with a Poisson or negative binomial specification. These count data approaches are appropriate when there is a preponderance of zeroes and small values for counts (Greene, 2003). US data used by Keller and Levinson (2002) have this characteristic but the Chinese data do not.
[14] US import elasticity estimates were downloaded from files made available at http://faculty.chicago-booth.edu/christian.broda/website/research/unrestricted/TradeElasticities/TradeElasticities.html.
[15] Grouping of projects into ECE and other foreign is described by Dean et al. (2009). The ECE designation includes those with a partner from Hong Kong, Macao, Taiwan, Malaysia, Indonesia and the Philippines, with the first three accounting for 87 per cent of the total identified with these countries. Other foreign partners are those from other sources, primarily OECD countries, with the largest shares from the US and Japan. There is no source for 12 per cent of projects in 1996, 17 per cent in 1995, 10 per cent in 1994 and 3 per cent in 1993. Since most FDI inflows at this time were ECE, these projects were designated ECE. Because Malaysia, Indonesia and the Philippines have large ethnically Chinese populations, the few projects from these countries are also included in the ECE subsample. Our results are not sensitive to either inclusion.

EVIDENCE FROM MULTINATIONAL DECISIONS IN CHINA 517

responsive to wage differences (Fung et al., 2003, 2005), a finding that may reflect technology differences or strong attachment to specific locations. Technological differences between ECE and OECD investors are consistent with the findings of Dean et al. (2009), who find that ECE investors are deterred by pollution taxes while OECD investors are not. Other researchers, such as Wang (2001), emphasise the importance of local connections for the profitability of joint ventures in China, suggesting that ECE investors may be less sensitive to input cost differences across province as they choose investment locations based on geographic or personal proximity. For these reasons, we investigate the extent to which these two types of investors differ in their response to wages.

d. The Control-Function Approach

Despite the inclusion of regional fixed effects, possible endogeneity of the wage remains. This fact can be illustrated by specifying the error in the profit function as a two-component error:[16]

$$\varepsilon_{ij} = \beta_\xi \xi_j + e_{ij}. \tag{9}$$

ξ_j is location specific, observed by workers and firms but not by the researcher. e_{ij} is a firm-specific idiosyncratic error, assumed to be independent across firms and locations. Defining $\mathbf{X}_j$ as in (8) and letting Z_j be the instrumental variable, under certain regularity conditions the log wage can be expressed as an implicit function of all factors taken as given at the time of the decision:

$$\ln w_j = \ln w_j(\mathbf{X}_j, Z_j, \xi_j). \tag{10}$$

Because wages will be higher in locations with more desirable omitted characteristics, ε_{ij} and $\ln w_j$ will be correlated even after conditioning on $\mathbf{X}_j$, violating the weak exogeneity requirement for conditional logit covariates and leading to inconsistent parameter estimates.

Kim and Petrin (2010a, 2010b) illustrate how a control function can be used to test for and correct the omitted variables problem. The method proceeds in two steps. The first step is a linear regression of log wages ($\ln w_j$) on exogenous variables $\mathbf{X}_j$ and Z_j using provincial-level data across years. We use this regression to construct the expected wage for each province in each year. The residual is used to form the control function, $f(\mu_j, \lambda)$, where μ_j is the disturbance from the first-stage regression and λ is a vector of estimated parameters. The variable profit function for firm i locating in province j can now be written as $\ln \pi_{ij} = \alpha + \mathbf{X}_{ij}\beta + f(\mu_j, \lambda) + (\beta_\xi \xi_j - f(\mu_j, \lambda)) + e_{ij}$. The new error, $\eta_{ij} = \beta_\xi \xi_j - f(\mu_j, \lambda) + e_{ij}$, includes the difference between the actual province specific error $\beta_\xi \xi_j$ and the control function, plus the idiosyncratic error. Appendix A explains the bootstrapping methods used to correct the reported errors.

We assume that at location j the log wage, $\ln w_j$, can be expressed as:

$$\ln w_j = E(\ln w_j | \mathbf{X}_j, Z_j) + \mu_j(\xi_j), \tag{11}$$

where $\mu_j(\xi_j)$ is one to one in ξ_j. Including $f(\mu_j, \lambda)$ in the conditional logit specification holds constant the variation in the error term of the location-specific profit function that is not inde-

---

[16] This discussion adapts the discussion of consumers' choice among differentiated products in Petrin and Train (2010) to the location-choice context.

pendent of the wage. The equation for ln w_j above implies that $\hat{\mu}_j$ can be constructed as the residual from a first stage regression of ln w_j on $\mathbf{X}_j$ and Z_j.

This approach requires an instrument for the first-stage wage regression that is correlated with the wage paid by foreign-invested enterprises, which are 'private sector' wages, but uncorrelated with the location choices of foreign firms, conditional on other exogenous variables. As in Liu et al. (2010), our first stage regression is a reduced form wage equation with controls for labour supply (e.g. population, share of labour force with secondary education or more) and for labour demand (e.g. the rate at which output of state owned enterprises is falling, cumulative foreign investment and the number of local enterprises). The log of average industrial wage paid by state owned enterprises in province j is used as Z_j. Liu et al. provide justification for the assumption that private sector wages are influenced by provincial characteristics that drive multifactor productivity, while SOE wages are not. They rely on the administrative SOE wage setting process and SOE productivity-wage gaps to argue for the independence of SOE wages from unobserved factors that drive foreign firm productivity.[17]

Figure 1 illustrates the relationship between the average SOE wage and the private wage during 1992–95. The SOE wage tends to be high where the private wage is high, but the gap between them varies widely across provinces and regions. The figure illustrates gaps that are larger in provinces with the longest tradition of market orientation, as in the central and coastal regions, with smaller and even negative gaps in the remaining areas.

4. DATA DESCRIPTION AND SOURCES

The sample of foreign investments was compiled by Dean et al. (2009).[18] It was compiled from project descriptions available from the Chinese Ministry of Foreign Trade and Economic Cooperation for foreign EJVs undertaken during 1993–96.[19] Provinces are grouped into five

---

[17] In China, SOE wages prior to 1996 were largely determined by the central government, despite several rounds of wage reforms. Starting in 1985, the Ministry of Labour provided some incentives to SOEs, but to a very limited extent. Deeper reforms of China's SOE wage structure were not implemented until the Ninth Five Year Plan (1996–2000). Therefore, during the span of our sample, SOE wages were largely set by central government guidelines and were largely unresponsive to changes in private sector productivity. Evidence from SOE productivity-wage gaps also supports the view that SOE wages do not reflect local attributes that influence firm productivity. Parker (1995, p. 9) finds that, 'In 1992, state industrial wages were 43 per cent higher than those available in urban collectives, and only 22 per cent below those of the other ownership forms; these workers in other ownership forms, however, were 130 per cent (in 1990 prices) to 200 per cent (in 1980 prices) more productive than those under state ownership'.

[18] More recent samples of new foreign investment projects, distinguished by location, industry and source country, do not exist. Amiti and Javorcik (2008) examine the role of trade costs in the location of foreign firms, using data from 1998 to 2001. Their data are drawn from the Annual Survey of Industrial Firms, collected by China's National Bureau of Statistics, for firms with sales above 5 million RMB. They estimate the number of new foreign firms entering each year by comparing year to year foreign firm counts. While this approach has some advantages, including broad coverage, it misses new entrants with sales below the cut-off level, it treats firms moving above scale as new entrants, and it cannot distinguish inflows from net flows.

[19] Equity joint ventures are limited liability companies incorporated in China, in which foreign and Mainland Chinese investors hold equity. For further details, see Fung (1997). Wang (2001) provides additional details on the legal framework for foreign investment.

EVIDENCE FROM MULTINATIONAL DECISIONS IN CHINA   519

FIGURE 1
Average Private Wage and Average SOE Wage, by Province, 1992–95

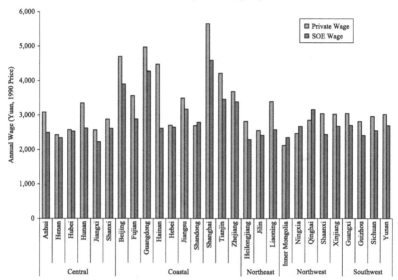

Source: See Table 1.

regions: coastal, north-east, central, south-west and north-west.[20] ECE and OECD partners engage in EJVs in all provinces. Investment into the southern coastal region is predominantly ECE, reflecting the geographic proximity and early opening of these provinces. Investment in the northern coastal region is split more equally between both sources. The most prominent specialisation occurs in the north-west region, where natural resource–dependent activities dominate.

After China reformed its foreign investment regime in 1992, the entry of foreign investment, mostly funnelled into EJVs, fuelled rapid export growth.[21] During the following five years of stable and liberal policy towards FDI, foreign-invested enterprises contributed 32 per cent of fixed asset investment by all non-state firms and accounted for more than half of Chinese-manufactured exports.[22] As reported by Huang (2003), working with data from the 1995 Chinese Industrial Census, foreign enterprises were dominant in export sales in a wide variety of industries, accounting for more than 50 per cent of all exports in garments and footwear,

---

[20] Coastal: Beijing, Fujian, Guangdong, Hainan, Hebei, Jiangsu, Shandong, Shanghai, Tianjin, Zhejiang; Northeast: Heilongjiang, Jilin, Liaoning; Central: Anhui, Henan, Hubei, Hunan, Jiangxi, Shanxi; Northwest: Gansu, Inner Mongolia, Ningxia, Qinghai, Shaanxi, Tibet, Xinjiang; Southwest: Guangxi, Guizhou, Sichuan, Yunnan.
[21] In 1992, China removed many sectoral and regional FDI restrictions (Lardy, 1994).
[22] The investment percentage is calculated by authors from Huang (2003, Table 1.1). The export share is taken from Huang (2003, p. 18).

TABLE 1
Data Definitions and Sources

Variables	Definition	Source	Mean*
Equity joint venture project			
Location	Province	Almanac of China's Foreign Economic Relations and Trade, various years, Dean et al. (2009)	
Source	ECE = Macao, Taiwan, Hong Kong, other South Asian countries, OECD = all other countries		
Industry	3-digit ISIC Rev.2 classification		
SOE wage	Average annual wage for industrial workers in state owned enterprises, in 1990 yuan, by province	Branstetter and Feenstra (2002), from China Statistical Yearbook, various years	2,837
Private wage	Average annual wage for industrial workers in other enterprises (private, foreign, etc.), in 1990 yuan, by province	Branstetter and Feenstra (2002), from China Statistical Yearbook, various years	3,254
Capital intensity	Average annual wage calculated as total industrial wage payment divided by total industrial employment, concorded with ISIC 3-digit classification	China Industrial Census, 1995	6,175
U.S. elasticity of substitution	US elasticity of substitution across import varieties, estimated using 1990–2001 data, concorded by authors from SITC Rev. 3 to ISIC Rev.2 classification	Broda and Weinstein (2006)	3.88
Agglomeration	Cumulative value of real contracted FDI, from 1983 until $t-1$, in millions of 1980 US dollars	Coughlin and Segev (2000)	1,536
Local firms	Number of SOE and collective industrial enterprises at the township level and above, by province	China Statistical Yearbook, various years, Dean et al. (2009)	16,061
Population	Population, in millions, by province	China Statistical Yearbook, various years	41

TABLE 1 *Continued*

Variables	Definition	Source	Mean*
Skilled labour ratio	Share of population who have a senior secondary school education level or above (in percentage points), by province	*China Statistical Yearbook*, various years and calculations by authors	12.08
Telephone density	Number of urban telephone subscribers per million persons, by province	*China Statistical Yearbook*, various years	29,266
Private market size	Real Provincial GDP × (1 − SOE share), where SOE share is the production share of SOEs; GDP is value in billions of 1,990 yuan	*China Statistical Yearbook*, various years, and calculations by authors	57
Change in state ownership	Difference between shares of industrial output from SOEs in year t and $t - 1$, by province	*China Statistical Yearbook*, various years, Dean et al. (2009)	−0.04
Special economic zone (SEZ) or open coastal city (OCC)	Dummy variable for a province with SEZ or OCC	Dean et al. (2009)	0.43

Note:
(i) *Descriptive statistics for provincial characteristics calculated from pooled data for 1993–96 (excluding Tibet and Gansu).

leather products, sporting goods, timber processing and related products, furniture making, electronics and telecommunications, food processing, wood products, paper products, printing and record pressing, electric equipment, plastic products, metal products and instruments.[23]

Our theoretical framework implies the use of the covariate vector X_j given by (7). Complete descriptions and sources for all variables are provided in Table 1. The *Chinese Statistical Yearbook* (various years) was used to compile data on labour supplies, agglomeration, intermediates suppliers, infrastructure and incentives. Summary data for provincial characteristics are provided in Table 2.

The provincial private wage is measured by the average annual wage paid by private and foreign enterprises, drawn from Branstetter and Feenstra (2002). We also draw from Branstetter and Feenstra the average annual wage paid by SOEs in each province, which we use as a first-stage instrument.[24] Wage measures are deflated by a national price deflator to create an average annual real provincial wage. Average wages do not control for provincial variation in labour quality, so we also include in the conditional logit analysis, the share of the provincial labour force that has completed senior secondary school or above.

We do not have direct measures of the cost of imported inputs (p_m) nor the corporate tax rate (τ). To control for provincial variation in these factors, we include an incentive dummy that takes a value of one if there is a special economic zone (SEZ) or open coastal city (OCC) in the province. This variable does not vary during the 1993–96 period. We also include a measure of provincial infrastructure, which influences the local cost of imported inputs. Infrastructure is proxied by the number of urban telephone subscribers relative to population. The number of foreign firms (N^f) is measured as the real value of cumulative FDI, which we refer to as agglomeration, for the period 1983 to the year before the project is undertaken. Availability of potential suppliers of intermediate goods ($\bar{N}_S$) is measured by the number of domestic firms, defined as the total number of domestic enterprises at the township level and above (thereby capturing larger enterprises that may have the capacity to supply a foreign-invested plant).

To control for potential local market demand, we include the population of the province and several measures of provincial income. The income measure is the size of the provincial private market, calculated as the private share of output multiplied by provincial GDP. We use non-state output to gauge the size of the market open to foreign enterprises because domestic sales in a province will be limited if demand is substantially satisfied by the state sector. Additionally, to allow for a flexible form for this market measure, we include the square of this variable. Sales may also be affected by the extent to which a province is liberalising, so we include the change in state ownership, measured as the difference in the share of industrial output produced by SOEs between time $t-1$ and time t.

5. RESULTS

We begin by estimating the conditional logit for the sample of all investors, for ECE investors alone, and for OECD investors alone. Our results support the use of the control function to address endogeneity concerns. They also indicate that ECE and OECD investors place dif-

---

[23] See sales and export shares by industry in Huang (2003, Table 1.4, p. 24).
[24] Banister (2005) discusses problems in Chinese labour statistics of geographic coverage, nonwage compensation, and under-reporting.

TABLE 2
Provincial Characteristics, Period Averages (1993–96)

	Annual Private Wage (1,990 yuan)	Cumulative FDI (Million 1,980 US$)	Number of Local Firms	Population (Millions)	Share of Skilled Workers	Phones per Million Persons	Output Share of SOEs	Private Market Size (Billion 1,990 Yuan)
Anhui	3,083	353	23,000	59	7	13,000	0.41	53
Beijing	4,695	1,981	7,000	11	32	119,000	0.51	34
Fujian	3,561	4,499	12,000	32	8	28,000	0.23	73
Guangdong	4,970	13,876	25,000	67	11	47,000	0.25	192
Guangxi	3,045	933	11,000	45	8	12,000	0.50	37
Guizhou	2,810	87	6,000	34	6	6,000	0.71	10
Hainan	4,476	1,336	1,000	7	12	26,000	0.53	9
Hebei	2,701	566	21,000	64	8	18,000	0.38	82
Heilongjiang	2,819	434	17,000	37	15	30,000	0.72	28
Henan	2,426	450	20,000	90	8	10,000	0.40	83
Hubei	2,574	704	23,000	57	10	17,000	0.49	58
Hunan	3,346	475	23,000	63	9	15,000	0.48	54
Inner Mongolia	2,122	78	9,000	22	13	22,000	0.68	13
Jiangsu	3,489	4,273	39,000	70	12	27,000	0.23	184
Jiangxi	2,565	293	16,000	40	8	12,000	0.50	29
Jilin	2,553	333	13,000	26	17	33,000	0.65	20
Liaoning	3,390	2,064	26,000	41	14	37,000	0.49	75
Ningxia	2,462	11	2,000	5	11	22,000	0.74	2
Qinghai	2,850	5	1,000	5	11	17,000	0.83	1
Shaanxi	3,042	483	13,000	35	12	14,000	0.61	20
Shandong	2,691	2,929	25,000	87	9	16,000	0.30	160
Shanghai	5,654	3,514	9,000	14	29	124,000	0.46	65
Shanxi	2,876	107	11,000	30	12	17,000	0.49	27
Sichuan	2,960	759	37,000	112	7	10,000	0.44	94
Tianjin	4,213	1,039	8,000	9	22	65,000	0.41	26
Xinjiang	3,027	64	6,000	16	14	20,000	0.71	12
Yunnan	3,021	113	7,000	39	5	11,000	0.73	16
Zhejiang	3,684	1,251	36,000	43	9	32,000	0.19	127

524 X. LIU, M. E. LOVELY AND J. ONDRICH

TABLE 3
Multinomial Logit Estimates of Location Choice, by Model and Sample

	With Control Functions			Without Control Functions		
	Full Sample	ECE Subsample	OECD Subsample	Full Sample	ECE Subsample	OECD Subsample
Log private wage	−2.079*** (0.462)	−1.716*** (0.598)	−2.944*** (0.653)	−0.949*** (0.195)	−0.659*** (0.251)	−1.790*** (0.318)
Log Agglomeration	0.459*** (0.075)	0.522*** (0.090)	0.298*** (0.114)	0.323*** (0.050)	0.400*** (0.063)	0.141 (0.086)
Log local firms	0.956*** (0.121)	0.827*** (0.148)	1.173*** (0.194)	1.069*** (0.108)	0.918*** (0.138)	1.319*** (0.177)
Log population	1.675*** (0.185)	1.798*** (0.234)	1.418*** (0.280)	1.757*** (0.163)	1.838*** (0.215)	1.583*** (0.258)
Skilled labour ratio	0.104*** (0.011)	0.074*** (0.013)	0.150*** (0.016)	0.117*** (0.008)	0.087*** (0.010)	0.165*** (0.013)
Log telephone density	0.570*** (0.151)	0.621*** (0.205)	0.572*** (0.200)	0.338*** (0.109)	0.376*** (0.143)	0.399** (0.173)
Log private market size	−2.881*** (0.268)	−2.646*** (0.346)	−3.127*** (0.409)	−2.936*** (0.255)	−2.687*** (0.333)	−3.203*** (0.395)
Squared log private market size	0.193*** (0.026)	0.152*** (0.035)	0.261*** (0.037)	0.204*** (0.024)	0.164*** (0.032)	0.270*** (0.035)
Change in state ownership	−5.908*** (1.033)	−6.387*** (1.285)	−5.853*** (1.381)	−5.383*** (0.823)	−5.881*** (1.112)	−5.370*** (1.251)
Special economic zone or open coastal city	1.195*** (0.168)	0.827*** (0.203)	1.638*** (0.243)	1.344*** (0.139)	0.933*** (0.189)	1.850*** (0.210)
Regional fixed effects						
Central	1.595*** (0.166)	1.632*** (0.198)	1.345*** (0.272)	1.618*** (0.158)	1.645*** (0.194)	1.359*** (0.269)
Coastal	1.687*** (0.186)	1.920*** (0.236)	1.251*** (0.296)	1.723*** (0.174)	1.971*** (0.223)	1.230*** (0.288)
North-east	0.678*** (0.201)	0.616** (0.263)	0.614** (0.304)	0.991*** (0.162)	0.910*** (0.208)	0.906*** (0.265)
North-west	0.163 (0.227)	−0.037 (0.301)	0.257 (0.352)	0.325 (0.213)	0.103 (0.282)	0.435 (0.340)
Residual	1.721*** (0.614)	1.518** (0.763)	1.914** (0.922)			
Number of observations	2,884	1,711	1,173	2,884	1,711	1,173
Pseudo R^2	0.183	0.182	0.203	0.182	0.181	0.202
Log-likelihood	−7,854.583	−4,663.425	−3,115.200	−7,862.422	−4,666.986	−3,118.752

Notes:
(i) All covariates are lagged by one year; Gansu and Tibet are excluded.
(ii) '***' and '**' denote significance levels at 1% and 5%, respectively.

ferent weights on the wage and other provincial characteristics when choosing an investment location. After discussion of these benchmark results, we re-estimate the model, allowing wage sensitivity for each group to vary with industry characteristics.

EVIDENCE FROM MULTINATIONAL DECISIONS IN CHINA 525

a. Investor Group Heterogeneity: Control-function Results

Table 3 reports the results of conditional logit estimation, for the full sample, the ECE subsample, and the OECD subsample. All variables are lagged one year to represent predetermined information, available to investors at the time of the location decision. Models (1), (2) and (3) provide results estimated with inclusion of the control function as well as regional fixed effects for the full sample and both subsamples. The overall fit of the equation is good and comparable with prior studies using similar procedures (e.g. Head and Mayer, 2004). The estimated coefficient for the residual from the first-stage wage regression is positive and significant at the 1 per cent level for the full sample and each subsample. The reported standard errors (as well as variance matrices used in the testing of joint hypotheses) were corrected using a bootstrapping technique described in the Appendix. The Appendix also provides the first-stage regression results. This regression explains 86 per cent of the variation in the private wage and the coefficient of the log of the SOE wage is highly significant, with a *t*-statistic of 9.07. Adding the log of the SOE wage to the first stage explains an additional 5 per cent of the variation in private wages.

Kim and Petrin (2010b) interpret the significance of the control function as a test for omitted variable bias. The significance of the residual, therefore, indicates the presence of omitted variable bias in the uncorrected estimates. The estimated wage coefficient is substantially larger in absolute value when we include the control function than the estimate we obtain without its use, as seen in comparison models (4), (5) and (6) This comparison provides an estimate of the downward bias in the standard method, consistent with findings reported in Liu et al. (2010). The coefficient of -2.079 estimated with the control function for the full sample is more than twice as large in absolute value as the coefficient of -0.949 estimated without the control function. The estimated coefficient for ECE investors increases from -0.66 to -1.72 when the control function is added, while for OECD investors it increases from -1.79 to -2.94. All remaining covariates have the expected signs, are highly significant even in the presence of regional fixed effects and are unchanged by the addition of the control function.[25]

As shown in the second and third models of Table 3, the probability of an ECE or an OECD investor locating in a given province is negatively affected by the provincial wage and this response is highly significant for both groups. The coefficient estimate for the OECD sample, however, is larger than it is for the ECE sample, suggesting that although both types of investors respond to wage differences, the OECD sample appears to be more responsive, *ceteris paribus*. Indeed, the elasticity of the probability of locating in a given province with respect to a unit decrease in its log wage is 72 per cent higher for OECD investors than for ECE investors. OECD investors' lack of family and business ties to specific provinces may allow these investors to be more sensitive to differences in production costs when choosing a location. The clustering of Chinese-funded overseas export activities, rather than being evidence of single minded attraction to low wage havens, as it is often depicted, may instead be explained by an expectation of personal connections to protect and promote business interests.[26]

---

[25] While we expect that a larger local market will attract foreign investors producing for local consumption, in the presence of regional fixed effects we do not have strong priors for the coefficients for log private market size and its square. Estimates suggest a U-shaped relation between log private market size and the probability of its being chosen.
[26] Huang (2003, p. 40, n. 67) documents the greater clustering of ECE funded ventures, which are less evenly distributed across provinces than is investment from Japan and the United States. Expectations of favours based on local business connections of ECE investors are supported by extensive interviews summarised in Wang (2001).

Observed clustering by ECE investors may also reflect a heavy weight placed on proximity to related investments and to the source country. Evidence consistent with either view is the larger weight placed by ECE investors on past investment, indicative of production clusters: the estimating coefficient for the agglomeration measure is 0.522 for ECE investors but less than 60 per cent of that magnitude, 0.298, for OECD investors, both estimates highly significant. The probability of locating in a given province with respect to a one unit increase in log agglomeration is 43 per cent less for OECD investors than for ECE investors. ECE investors also place a lower weight on the presence of local firms who may be potential local suppliers (their elasticity is 42 per cent higher). ECE investors are somewhat more likely than OECD investors to locate in the coastal and central provinces, closer to their sources and less likely to locate in the north-west. They are also less sensitive to the skilled labour share in the province, and designation of the province as an SEZ or OCC, all consistent with the view that these investors have access to networks and local connections perhaps not accessed by OECD investors.

These findings differ from inferences drawn from econometric analyses of regional FDI inflows that distinguish investors by source. Fung et al. (2005), who estimate a random effects model using regional data from 1990 to 1999, find that Hong Kong investment flows are more sensitive to local labour costs than are flows from the United States. The authors ascribe the observed difference in behaviour to clustering by US-owned firms in capital-intensive sectors and to the export-processing focus of Hong Kong owned enterprises. Fung et al. (2003) compare Japanese and Hong Kong flows into Chinese regions and also find that Hong Kong investment is more sensitive to wage differences. Our results, based on project-level data and conditional logit analysis, do not support this characterisation of differences in behaviour. Rather, our findings suggest that OECD investors weight local wages more heavily than do ECE investors, at least at the time that the host province is chosen.

These differences by investor group are consistent with the view of Lu (2012), who argues that a social-network behavioural approach is a useful complement to classic explanations of FDI location. Lu identifies *guanxi*, defined as reciprocal relationships in Chinese culture, as the main form of expression for Chinese social networks. Moreover, he argues that social networks are an endogenous firm-specific asset that influences location choice for those with ethnic ties to local areas, that is for ECE but not for non-ECE investors. Using surveys of ethnically Chinese and other foreign investors, Lu finds that more that more than 70 per cent of the ethnically Chinese investors surveyed agree that *guanxi* with local governments is important for access to land and preferential policies. Given this emphasis on social relationships, these investors are less sensitive to classic determinants of location-specific costs. We now turn to additional analysis that allows for differences along industrial characteristics, including factor intensity, as well as by investor group.

b. Allowing for Differences in Export-market Demand and Factor Intensity

To investigate how wage sensitivity is conditioned by industry characteristics, we interact the provincial wage with measures of factor intensity and export-market conditions. Based on our previous findings supporting its use, we estimate these conditional logits using a control-function approach. Results are shown in Table 4.

We proceed by first introducing an interaction of the provincial wage with a measure of the industry's capital intensity, expecting a less elastic response from investors whose Chinese ventures are more capital intensive. The first three models of Table 4 provide little support

EVIDENCE FROM MULTINATIONAL DECISIONS IN CHINA   527

TABLE 4

Allowing Wage Sensitivity to Vary with Factor Intensity and US Substitution Elasticity, by Model and Sample

	With Control Functions			With Control Functions		
	Full Sample	ECE Subsample	OECD Subsample	Full Sample	ECE Subsample	OECD Subsample
Log private wage	-2.451*** (0.720)	-1.942** (0.880)	-3.772*** (1.114)	-3.185*** (0.726)	-2.793*** (0.915)	-4.345*** (1.157)
Log private wage × capital intensity	0.060 (0.090)	0.037 (0.114)	0.133 (0.143)	0.371*** (0.106)	0.356** (0.141)	0.452*** (0.165)
Log private wage × demand elasticity				-0.368*** (0.069)	-0.339*** (0.091)	-0.431*** (0.107)
Log agglomeration	0.459*** (0.075)	0.522*** (0.088)	0.299*** (0.115)	0.463*** (0.075)	0.525*** (0.087)	0.302*** (0.115)
Log local firms	0.952*** (0.122)	0.824*** (0.147)	1.170*** (0.195)	0.971*** (0.121)	0.836*** (0.150)	1.208*** (0.199)
Log population	1.676*** (0.193)	1.799*** (0.228)	1.423*** (0.280)	1.670*** (0.186)	1.794*** (0.232)	1.422*** (0.283)
Skilled labour ratio	0.103*** (0.011)	0.074*** (0.013)	0.149*** (0.016)	0.104*** (0.011)	0.075*** (0.013)	0.151*** (0.016)
Log telephone density	0.578*** (0.159)	0.626*** (0.197)	0.585*** (0.202)	0.562*** (0.152)	0.618*** (0.190)	0.549*** (0.208)
Log private market size	-2.876*** (0.273)	-2.644*** (0.343)	-3.129*** (0.412)	-2.911*** (0.268)	-2.669*** (0.345)	-3.193*** (0.410)
Squared log private market size	0.193*** (0.027)	0.152*** (0.034)	0.261*** (0.037)	0.196*** (0.026)	0.154*** (0.034)	0.266*** (0.037)
Change in state ownership	-5.915*** (1.066)	-6.383*** (1.271)	-5.906*** (1.396)	-5.991*** (1.044)	-6.437*** (1.270)	-5.980*** (1.427)
Special economic zone or open coastal city	1.190*** (0.170)	0.824*** (0.201)	1.633*** (0.243)	1.197*** (0.169)	0.830*** (0.208)	1.651*** (0.250)

TABLE 4 Continued

	With Control Functions			With Control Functions		
	Full Sample	ECE Subsample	OECD Subsample	Full Sample	ECE Subsample	OECD Subsample
Regional fixed effects						
Central	1.591***	1.630***	1.341***	1.602***	1.637***	1.362***
	(0.167)	(0.199)	(0.272)	(0.167)	(0.201)	(0.275)
Coastal	1.689***	1.920***	1.256***	1.703***	1.928***	1.286***
	(0.190)	(0.233)	(0.297)	(0.187)	(0.240)	(0.299)
North-east	0.673***	0.613**	0.606**	0.680***	0.614**	0.630**
	(0.207)	(0.256)	(0.306)	(0.202)	(0.254)	(0.311)
North-west	0.162	-0.037	0.252	0.162	-0.039	0.258
	(0.232)	(0.297)	(0.353)	(0.229)	(0.292)	(0.353)
Residual	-2.839*	-1.848	-3.718	-1.880	-0.377	-3.055
	(1.634)	(2.057)	(2.672)	(1.669)	(2.198)	(2.722)
Residual × capital intensity	0.768***	0.572*	0.937**	0.398	0.046	0.642
	(0.251)	(0.334)	(0.401)	(0.309)	(0.425)	(0.458)
Residual × import demand				0.411**	0.535**	0.358
				(0.193)	(0.258)	(0.285)
Number of observations	2,884	1,711	1,173	2,884	1,711	1,173
Pseudo R^2	0.183	0.183	0.204	0.185	0.184	0.206
Log-likelihood	-7847.471	-4661.122	-3110.259	-7832.277	-4653.435	-3102.665
CF Wald Statistic (p-value)	16.93*** (0.00021)	6.97** (0.0307)	10.61** (0.00497)	21.91*** (0.000068)	10.73** (0.013)	11.47*** (0.0094)

Notes:
(i) All covariates are lagged by one year; Gansu and Tibet are excluded.
(ii) '***', '**' and '*' denote significance levels at 1%, 5% and 10% levels, respectively.

EVIDENCE FROM MULTINATIONAL DECISIONS IN CHINA   529

for the contention that attraction to low wages is a function of factor intensity. The interaction of log provincial wage and industry capital intensity is positive, as expected, but not significantly significant, for the full sample and for each subsample.[27] Other inferences are not affected by the inclusion of the interaction term.

Because these models include interactions involving wages, we form the control function by including interactions between the first-stage residual and the industry characteristic. Testing whether the related coefficients are all zero requires a joint hypothesis test. We present the value of the Wald χ^2 in the row labelled 'CF Wald Statistic'. The Wald Statistic is significant at the 5 per cent level in all three samples. These results reinforce the indication of omitted variable bias present in the models that omit the control function.

To explore the hypothesis that export-market conditions influence firms' wage sensitivity, we also interact the provincial wage with a measure of demand elasticity, the Broda and Weinstein (2006) elasticities of substitution estimated for the US import market.[28] These demand elasticities are shown in Table 5 for each industry. There is a positive correlation between the capital-intensity measure and the Broda–Weinstein elasticities – more capital-intensive industries face more elastic market conditions, in part because these industries tend to produce homogeneous commodities. Because high capital intensity is predicted to reduce wage sensitivity while elastic market demand raises it, by not accounting explicitly for the demand elasticity, we may incorrectly infer that factor intensity does not matter for wage sensitivity. This correlation may explain why we obtain insignificant coefficients for the wage-interaction terms in the first three columns of Table 4, when demand elasticity is omitted.

Following our theoretical model, we expect the coefficient on an interaction of the wage and the demand elasticity to be negative – a higher price elasticity reduces the ability to shift higher wage costs to consumers and makes investors more sensitive to provincial wage variation. We control for both factor intensity and demand elasticity simultaneously. As shown in the last three columns of Table 4, the wage and both wage-interaction terms have the expected signs and are highly significant for all three samples. Larger demand elasticity is associated with greater aversion to high-wage provinces: for the full sample, the estimated coefficient on the interaction of wage and demand elasticity is −0.368 and highly significant. This result is consistent with the hypothesis that firms facing more competitive conditions in export markets are less able to absorb higher wages by passing them to customers. We also find that more capital-intensive industries are less sensitive to the wage: for the full sample, the estimated coefficient on the wage-factor intensity interaction is 0.371 and highly significant.

When the sample is split into investor groups, as shown in the fifth and sixth models, capital intensity reduces wage sensitivity for both groups, but more so for OECD investors. Export-demand conditions are significant influences on wage sensitivity for both groups but the estimated coefficient for the OECD sample is larger than it is for the ECE sample,

---

[27] One may wonder if the inclusion of the control function leads to the insignificant interaction term. Unreported estimates, performed without inclusion of the control function, produce coefficients for the wage-capital intensity interaction that are significant at the 10 per cent level for the full and OECD samples only. These estimates are available from the authors upon request.

[28] In unreported regressions, we substituted the Broda et al. (2006) estimates of China's import demand elasticity for the US elasticity of substitution. These results indicate no significant relationship between the wage sensitivity of foreign investors and Chinese domestic market conditions. Given that on average foreign invested enterprises export more than half of their output, this result is not surprising.

530   X. LIU, M. E. LOVELY AND J. ONDRICH

TABLE 5
Average Estimated Own Wage Elasticity, by Industry

ISIC	Industry Name	Industry Capital Intensity	Industry Demand Elasticity	Full Sample Elasticity	ECE Sample Elasticity	OECD Sample Elasticity
324	Footwear	4.29	2.41	−1.99	−1.69	−2.70
331	Wood	4.51	1.95	−1.81	−1.52	−2.50
321	Textiles	4.63	2.64	−1.99	−1.68	−2.72
390	Other	4.80	2.27	−1.83	−1.53	−2.52
323	Leather	4.81	1.77	−1.67	−1.39	−2.35
341	Paper	5.22	3.16	−1.94	−1.64	−2.64
311	Food	5.33	3.57	−2.03	−1.72	−2.74
356	Plastic	5.41	1.69	−1.47	−1.19	−2.10
361	Pottery	5.45	1.85	−1.51	−1.23	−2.14
322	Apparel	5.53	3.16	−1.85	−1.55	−2.53
313	Beverages	5.57	2.45	−1.64	−1.35	−2.28
332	Furniture	5.75	2.53	−1.59	−1.31	−2.21
381	Fabricated metal	5.76	3.03	−1.75	−1.45	−2.40
369	Mineral	5.81	1.80	−1.38	−1.11	−1.99
355	Rubber	5.94	2.57	−1.56	−1.28	−2.18
382	Non-electric machinery	6.29	3.06	−1.58	−1.30	−2.19
342	Printing	6.38	3.13	−1.60	−1.31	−2.23
354	Misc. petroleum and coal	6.41	2.51	−1.40	−1.12	−2.00
362	Glass	6.41	1.69	−1.15	−0.89	−1.71
352	Other chemicals	6.43	5.07	−2.12	−1.80	−2.82
351	Industrial chemicals	6.52	4.83	−2.02	−1.70	−2.70
385	Professional	6.57	1.83	−1.16	−0.89	−1.72
383	Electric machinery	6.75	2.02	−1.15	−0.89	−1.71
384	Transport	6.96	3.26	−1.45	−1.17	−2.04
372	Nonferrous metals	7.38	6.64	−2.29	−1.95	−3.01
371	Iron and steel	8.27	8.54	−2.55	−2.18	−3.29
353	Petroleum refineries	9.88	7.16	−1.67	−1.35	−2.24

Notes:
(i) Data sources for capital intensity measure and demand elasticity: see Table 1. (ii) Jiangsu Province is taken as the benchmark province in elasticity calculation. (iii) The last three columns are based on the coefficient estimates in the last three columns of Table 4. (iv) Industries are sorted by capital intensity.

−0.431 vs. −0.339. As in the models without wage-interaction terms, we find that ECE investors place a higher weight on prior investment, but a lower weight on local firms, the skilled labour share, and designation of the province as an SEZ or OCC than do foreign investors.

We find that OECD investors are more responsive to wage differences than ECE investors, controlling for industrial variation in behaviour. At the mean capital intensity and mean demand elasticity, the wage coefficient for OECD investors is −2.01, while for ECE investors it is −0.76. The estimated wage coefficient for OECD investors in footwear, the least capital intensity industry, is −2.46, compared with an estimate of −1.06 for ECE investors. Again, these estimates are precisely estimated. Differences between the two groups widen as the capital intensity of the industry rises. For example, the wage coefficient for the most capital-intensive activity, petroleum refining, is more than four times larger for

EVIDENCE FROM MULTINATIONAL DECISIONS IN CHINA 531

OECD investors (-1.26) than for ECE investors (-0.29). Thus, differences in investor group behaviour do not merely reflect differences in the sectoral composition of their foreign activities.

Foreign investment typically flows into particular sectors, shifting the pattern of production toward these favoured sectors. To consider how shifts in production composition might change the elasticity of demand for domestic labour, we calculate the average estimated own-wage elasticities for each industry, for both the ECE and the OECD samples, as shown in Table 5, using estimated coefficients from Table 4. Comparing the last two columns, we see that the OECD elasticity is larger than the ECE elasticity for every industry, but both subsamples produce a similar ranking across industries. Some interesting comparisons across industries emerge when we look at these rankings. In the mid-1990s, industries with large shares of total exports are among those industries with above average responsiveness to wage differences, a finding consistent with their rapid movement into China after the liberalisation of FDI rules in 1992.[29] These industries include footwear, wood products, textiles and food. However, over the following decade, Chinese exports grew strongly in sectors with below average wage responsiveness, particularly professional, scientific, and controlling equipment, electrical machinery and non-electrical machinery. That China was able to shift its export profile so quickly away from labour-intensive sectors toward sectors that are less responsive to wage differences is worthy of further study.

c. Wage Elasticities, By Province

There is some concern, well expressed by Chan (2003), that coastal provinces maintain low wages for foreign employers to fend off competition for FDI from interior provinces. Our estimates shed some light on how much power an individual province has to engage in this form of 'wage competition'. Table 6 provides estimated own-wage and cross-wage probability elasticities, by province, calculated using the estimates in Table 4. The elasticities of province j are calculated by $\sigma_j^{own} = \beta^w(1 - P_j)$ and $\sigma_j^{cross} = -\beta^w P_j$ where β^w and P_j are the estimated wage coefficient and predicted probability that an investor chooses province j (see Greene, 2003). Looking across locations, the own-wage elasticity is smallest for those provinces with the highest predicted probability of being chosen, including Beijing, Guangdong, Jiangsu and Shandong. These provinces, conversely, have the largest predicted cross-wage effects, implying that a decrease in their wage has a larger effect on other provinces than the effect other provinces have on them. These estimates imply a dynamic that differs somewhat from the view expressed by those who fear interprovincial competition in labour standards. Our estimates indicate that coastal provinces have less incentive to behave in this manner than do interior provinces; coastal provinces are less likely to lose investment to other provinces when their own wages rise (owing to lower own elasticities in coastal provinces) or when inland provinces lower their wages (owing to very low cross-elasticities of inland provinces). However, our estimates also imply that these coastal provinces have the largest effect on other province's chances of attracting investment if they do attempt to keep wages low.

---

[29] Dean and Lovely (2010) provide Chinese export shares for 2005 and 1995.

532   X. LIU, M. E. LOVELY AND J. ONDRICH

TABLE 6
Estimated Own-Wage and Cross-Wage Probability Elasticities, by Province

Provinces	Full Sample		ECE Sample		OECD Sample	
	Own Elasticity	Cross Elasticity	Own Elasticity	Cross Elasticity	Own Elasticity	Cross Elasticity
Anhui	−2.09	0.04	−1.71	0.02	−2.99	0.01
Beijing	−1.96	0.17	−1.67	0.06	−2.87	0.13
Fujian	−2.07	0.06	−1.70	0.04	−2.98	0.02
Guangdong	−1.86	0.27	−1.57	0.17	−2.91	0.10
Guangxi	−2.11	0.02	−1.72	0.01	−2.99	0.01
Guizhou	−2.12	0.00	−1.73	0.00	−3.00	0.00
Hainan	−2.12	0.01	−1.72	0.01	−3.00	0.00
Hebei	−2.00	0.13	−1.67	0.06	−2.93	0.08
Heilongjiang	−2.07	0.06	−1.71	0.03	−2.97	0.03
Henan	−2.08	0.05	−1.71	0.03	−2.98	0.02
Hubei	−2.06	0.07	−1.69	0.04	−2.97	0.03
Hunan	−2.08	0.05	−1.70	0.03	−2.98	0.02
Inner Mongolia	−2.12	0.01	−1.73	0.00	−2.99	0.01
Jiangsu	−1.72	0.41	−1.55	0.18	−2.74	0.26
Jiangxi	−2.10	0.03	−1.72	0.02	−2.99	0.01
Jilin	−2.09	0.04	−1.72	0.02	−2.97	0.03
Liaoning	−2.00	0.13	−1.69	0.04	−2.90	0.11
Ningxia	−2.13	0.00	−1.73	0.00	−3.00	0.00
Qinghai	−2.13	0.00	−1.73	0.00	−3.00	0.00
Shaanxi	−2.11	0.02	−1.73	0.01	−3.00	0.01
Shandong	−1.89	0.24	−1.62	0.12	−2.87	0.14
Shanghai	−2.03	0.10	−1.70	0.04	−2.94	0.07
Shanxi	−2.11	0.02	−1.73	0.01	−3.00	0.01
Sichuan	−2.11	0.02	−1.72	0.01	−2.99	0.01
Tianjin	−2.07	0.06	−1.71	0.02	−2.97	0.04
Xinjiang	−2.13	0.00	−1.73	0.00	−3.00	0.00
Yunnan	−2.13	0.00	−1.73	0.00	−3.00	0.00
Zhejiang	−2.02	0.11	−1.68	0.05	−2.94	0.06

Note:
(i) Elasticities based on the coefficient estimates in the last three columns of Table 4.

6. CONCLUSION

In developing countries, foreign direct investment is desired as a source of new capital, for employment, to increase specialisation and access world markets and for technology transfer.[30] The location choices of foreign investors reflect complex calculations along many dimensions that influence business costs. Using a control-function approach to control for unobserved attributes of potential hosts, we find that local wages do play a significant role in these considerations. There are important differences in firm behaviour, however, consistent with the existence of production networks and connections to particular regions. ECE inves-

---

[30] Muendler and Becker (2010) examine the margins of multinational labour substitution and find that employment adjustments are made primarily at the extensive, rather than intensive, margin in a sample of German firms. This evidence highlights the importance of attracting new investment for employment growth.

EVIDENCE FROM MULTINATIONAL DECISIONS IN CHINA 533

tors, in contrast to OECD investors, are less influenced by wage differences across provinces. They also place greater weight on previous investment, much of it from ECE sources. For both groups, the response to wage differences depends on the factor intensity of the venture.

Recent wage increases in coastal Chinese provinces appear to promise a larger share of FDI for inland provinces. It is often presumed that labour-intensive industries will be attracted to the lower-wage interior.[31] Our estimates provide strong support for the presumption that factor intensity matters, but we do not find that the most labour-intensive industries are the most responsive to relative wage differences. Because final market demand conditions also influence the location of export processing, we find that investors producing homogenous commodities, such as metals, chemicals and food processing, are most likely to be attracted by lower interior wages. These findings enrich our understanding of multinational behaviour by identifying the previously unexamined influence of export-market conditions on FDI-location choice.

To gauge the ability of interior provinces to shift FDI location through regional development policy, we use our estimated coefficients to simulate the effect of a wage subsidy offered only to new firms locating in inland provinces. Following the simulation procedure of Head and Ries (1996), we permit endogenous investment changes to alter the stock of foreign firms and, thus, the agglomeration effect in subsequent years. Provinces in the coastal region, which we assume receive no subsidy, lose investment. However, for a 10 per cent wage subsidy in the interior, the flow to each coastal province is diminished by only 6 per cent. For inland provinces, a 10 per cent wage subsidy increases the flow of foreign investment by 16 to 17 per cent. These impacts indicate that regional development policies could lead to substantially larger accumulations of foreign capital in inland provinces, perhaps contrary to the view that these areas are unattractive to many industries.

Export-processing FDI integrates the host country more deeply into world markets. The ability of firms to pass forward labour cost increases, such as those resulting from enforcement of minimum wages or maximum work hours, shapes the policy space available to local communities seeking better wages and working conditions. Even the perception that labour-market regulation will deter foreign investors may lead to weak enforcement by governments and muffled calls for reform from labour organisers. Such a chain of responses fuels fears of a 'race to the bottom' in labour standards.[32]

Progress in measuring the response of international investment flows to rising wages in China and other locations is important in addressing these fears. We find separate roles for factor intensity and host country endowments, on the one hand, and export-market demand elasticity, on the other. Explicit acknowledgment of market conditions can also inform analyses of policies that seek to improve labour conditions by altering consumer demand, such as 'fair trade' labelling, or the sourcing patterns of producers of final goods, such as 'no sweatshop' campaigns.[33] At a minimum, a focus on export-market conditions helps identify those industries in which such efforts may be useful. Given the large flows of direct investment predicted in the wake of the recent global recession, additional research on the links between developed country export markets and developing country labour markets seems warranted.

---

[31] This logic appears in numerous articles in the business press, including *The Economist*, Economic Focus, June 12, 2010, p. 86.

[32] The case for a 'race to the bottom' in labour standards is developed by Chan (2003).

[33] Harrison and Scorse (2010) find that antisweatshop activity targeted at specific final goods producers led to large wage gains and limited job losses at Indonesian contract manufacturers in the textile, footwear and apparel sectors.

534   X. LIU, M. E. LOVELY AND J. ONDRICH

TABLE A1
First-Stage OLS Regression: Dependent Variable is Log Private Wage

Variables	Coefficient	Robust SE
Constant	0.788	0.862
Log agglomeration	0.101***	0.011
Log local firms	−0.020	0.029
Log population	−0.121***	0.044
Skilled labour ratio	−0.008***	0.002
Log telephone density	−0.014	0.031
Log private market size	0.111**	0.052
Squared log private market size	−0.022***	0.006
Change in state ownership	−0.284	0.279
Special economic zone or OCC	−0.077	0.043
Regional fixed effects		
Central	0.059	0.043
Coastal	0.042	0.045
North-east	−0.000	0.041
North-west	−0.032	0.036
Log SOE wage	0.846***	0.093
Number of observations	196	
R^2	0.86	

Notes:
(i) '***' and '**' denote significance levels at 1% and 5% respectively. (ii) variables are lagged by one year. (iii) Gansu and Tibet excluded.

APPENDIX A

a First Stage Results and Bootstrapping Procedures

A maintained primitive of the control-function approach is that wages are additively separable in the observed (X_j and Z_j) and the unobserved factors (ξ_j); the unobserved factors are mean independent of the observed factors. This assumption implies uncorrelatedness of unobservables and covariates. It enables use of linear regression in the first stage and ensures the consistent estimation of the residual in the first stage. First stage results are shown in Table A1.

When a control function that includes predicted values is added to the estimation, the coefficients are consistent but the standard errors are incorrect. Petrin and Train (2010) use bootstrapping to correct standard errors in their applications. In the first stage, we bootstrap a wage sample and regress the private wage on the exogenous variables and the instrumental variable, the log of the SOE wage, for years 1990–96.[34] The control function in the second stage is a function of the first stage residual (and the interactions of the residual with other covariates when we use interactions of these covariates with wages). We run the conditional logit with this control function and repeat this process 100 times. The variances of these bootstrapped coefficients in the second stage are added to the traditional variance estimates from

---

[34] We do not use years after 1996 in the first stage to avoid possible structural changes in wage structure after 1996 due to SOE reforms. We also do not use years before 1990 for similar concerns. Years after 1989 and before 1993 are kept to increase the sample size and the reliability of bootstrapping. However, the direction and magnitude of bias is consistent when we experiment with different years in the first stage.

EVIDENCE FROM MULTINATIONAL DECISIONS IN CHINA 535

the conditional logit regression with the control function.[35] We experiment with different orders of the polynomial of the residuals to specify the control function, but typically, higher orders are insignificant and have only a small effect.

REFERENCES

Amiti, M. and B. S. Javorcik (2008), 'Trade Costs and Location of Foreign Firms in China', *Journal of Development Economics*, **85**, 1–2, 129–49.

Banister, J. (2005), '*Manufacturing Employment and Compensation in China*', Working Paper (Beijing: Javelin Investment Consulting Company).

Berry, S. (1994), 'Estimating Discrete Choice Models of Product Differentiation', *RAND Journal of Economics*, **25**, 2, 242–62.

Berry, S., J. Levinsohn and A. Pakes (1995), Automobile Prices in Market Equilibrium', *Econometrica*, **63**, 4, 841–90.

Branstetter, L. and R. C. Feenstra (2002), 'Trade and Foreign Direct Investment in China: A Political Economy Approach', *Journal of International Economics*, **58**, 2, 335–58.

Broda, C. and D. E. Weinstein (2006), 'Globalization and the Gains from Variety', *Quarterly Journal of Economics*, **121**, 2, 541–85.

Broda, C., J. Greenfield and D. E. Weinstein (2006), 'From Groundnuts to Globalization: A Structural Estimate of Trade and Growth', Working Paper No. 12512, (Washington, DC: NBER).

Chan, A. (2003), 'A Race to the Bottom', *China Perspective*, **46**, March–April, 41–9.

Chen, M. X. and M. O. Moore (2010), 'Location Decision of Heterogeneous Multinational Firms', *Journal of International Economics*, **80**, 2, 188–99.

Cheng, L. K. and Y. K. Kwan (2000), 'What are the Determinants of the Location of Foreign Direct Investment? The Chinese Experience', *Journal of International Economics*, **51**(2), 379–400.

Coughlin, C. C. and E. Segev (2000), 'Foreign Direct Investment in China: A Spatial Econometric Study', *The World Economy*, **23**, 1, 1–23.

Dean, J. M. and M. E. Lovely (2010), 'Trade Growth, Production Fragmentation, and China's Environment', in R. C. Feenstra and S.-J. Wei (eds.), *China's Growing Role in World Trade* (Chicago: University of Chicago Press), 429–69.

Dean, J. M., M. E. Lovely and H. Wang (2009), 'Are Foreign Investors Attracted to Weak Environmental Regulations? Evaluating the Evidence from China', *Journal of Development Economics*, **90**, 1, 1–13.

Devereux, M. and R. Griffith (1998), 'Taxes and the Location of Production: Evidence from a Panel of US Multinationals', *Journal of Public Economics*, **68**, 3, 335–67.

Dixit, A. and J. Stiglitz (1977), 'Monopolistic Competition and Optimum Product Diversity', *American Economic Review*, **67**, 3, 297–308.

Feenstra, R. C. (1994), 'New Product Varieties and the Measurement of International Prices', *American Economic Review*, **84**, 1, 157–77.

Fung, K. C. (1997), *Trade and Investment: Mainland China. Hong Kong, and Taiwan* (Hong Kong: City University of Hong Kong Press).

Fung, K. C., H. Iizaka and S. Parker (2002), 'Determinants of U.S. and Japanese Direct Investment in China', *Journal of Comparative Economics*, **30**, 3, 567–78.

Fung, K. C., H. Iizaka and A. Siu (2003), 'Japanese Direct Investment in China', *China Economic Review*, **14**, 3, 304–15.

Fung, K. C., H. Iizaka, C. Lin and A. Siu (2005), 'An Econometric Estimation of Locational Choices of Foreign Direct Investment: The Case of Hong Kong and U.S. Firms in China, ' in Y. K. Kwan and E. S. H. Yu (eds.), *Critical Issues in Chinese Growth and Development*, Conference Volume in Honor of Gregory Chow (Basingstoke: Ashgate Publishing).

Gao, T. (2005), 'Labor Quality and the Location of Foreign Direct Investment: Evidence from FDI in China by Investing Country', *China Economic Review*, **16**, 274–92.

---

[35] Karaca-Mandic and Train (2003) propose alternative standard error correction procedures, but find results very similar to bootstrapping.

536   X. LIU, M. E. LOVELY AND J. ONDRICH

Greene, W. H. (2003), *Econometric Analysis* (Upper Saddle River, NJ: Prentice Hall).
Harrison, A. and J. Scorse (2010), 'Multinationals and Anti-sweatshop Activism', *American Economic Review*, **100**, 1, 247–73.
Head, K. and T. Mayer (2004), 'Market Potential and the Location of Japanese Investment in the European Union', *The Review of Economics and Statistics*, **86**, 4, 959–72.
Head, K. and J. Ries (1996), 'Inter-city Competition for Foreign Investment: Static and Dynamic Effects of China's Incentive Areas', *Journal of Urban Economics*, **40**, 1, 38–60.
Head, K., J. Ries and D. Swenson (1999), 'Attracting Foreign Manufacturing: Investment Promotion and Agglomeration', *Regional Science and Urban Economics*, **29**, 2, 197–218.
Heckman, J. (1976), 'The Common Structure of Statistical Models of Truncation, Sample Selection and Limited Dependent Variables and a Simple Estimator for Such Models', *Annals of Economic and Social Measurement*, **5**, 4, 475–92.
Heckman, J. (1979), 'Sample Selection Bias as a Specification Error', *Econometrica*, **47**, 2, 153–61.
Henley, J., C. Kirkpatrick and G. Wilde (1999), 'Foreign Direct Investment in China: Recent Trends and Current Policy Issues', *World Economy*, **22**, 2, 223–43.
Huang, Y. (2003), *Selling China: Foreign Investment during the Reform Era* (Cambridge: Cambridge University Press).
Karaca-Mandic, P. and K. Train (2003), 'Standard Error Correction in Two-Stage Estimation with Nested Samples', *Econometrics Journal*, **6**, 2, 401–7.
Keller, W. and A. Levinson (2002), 'Pollution Abatement Costs and Foreign Direct Investment Inflows to the United States', *Review of Economics and Statistic*, **84**, 4, 691–703.
Kim, K. and A. Petrin (2010a), *Control Function Corrections for Unobserved Factors in Differentiated Product Models*, University of Minnesota, mimeograph.
Kim, K. and A. Petrin (2010b), *Tests for Price Endogeneity in Differentiated Product Models*, University of Minnesota, mimeograph.
Lardy, N. R. (1994), *China in the World Economy* (Washington, DC: Institute for International Economics).
List, J. A. and C. Y. Co (2000), 'The Effects of Environmental Regulations on Foreign Direct Investment', *Journal of Environmental Economics and Management*, **40**, 1, 1–20.
Liu, X., M. E. Lovely and J. Ondrich (2010), 'The Location Decisions of Foreign Investors in China: Untangling the Effect of Wages Using a Control Function Approach', *The Review of Economics and Statistics*, **92**, 1, 160–66.
Lu, J. (2012), 'A Social-network Behavioural Approach to Overseas Chinese and Overseas Non-Chinese Investments in China', *Journal of Economic and Social Geography*, **103**, 4, 426–42.
Muendler, M.-A. and S. O. Becker (2010), 'Margins of Multinational Labor Substitution', *American Economic Review*, **100**, 5, 1999–2030.
Ondrich, J. and M. Wasylenko (1993), *Foreign Direct Investment in the United States* (Kalamazoo, MI: W.E. Upjohn Institute for Employment Research).
Parker, E. (1995), 'Prospects for the State-owned Enterprise in China's Socialist Market Economy', *Asian Perspective*, **19**, 1, 7–35.
Petrin, A. and K. Train (2010), 'A Control Function Approach to Endogeneity in Consumer Choice Models', *Journal of Marketing Research*, **47**, 1, 3–13.
Rauch, J. (1999), 'Networks versus Markets in International Trade', *Journal of International Economics*, **48**, 1, 7–35.
Rivers, D. and Q. H. Vuong (1988), 'Limited Information Estimators and Exogeneity Tests for Simultaneous Probit Models', *Journal of Econometrics*, **39**, 3, 347–66.
Romer, P. (1994), 'New Goods, Old Theory, and the Welfare Costs of Trade Restrictions', *Journal of Development Economics*, **43**, 1, 5–38.
Rutherford, T. and D. Tarr (2002), 'Trade Liberalization, Product Variety and Growth in a Small Open Economy: A Quantitative Assessment', *Journal of International Economics*, **56**, 2, 247–72.
Smith, R. J. and R. W. Blundell (1986), 'An Exogeneity Test for a Simultaneous Equation Tobit Model with an Application to Labor Supply', *Econometrica*, **54**, 3, 679–85.
Wang, H. (2001), *Weak State, Strong Networks* (New York: Oxford University Press).

Labor Allocation in China: Implicit Taxation of the Heterogeneous Non-State Sector

Fariha Kamal*,[†] and Mary E. Lovely**

*Center for Economic Studies, U.S. Census Bureau, Washington, DC 20233, USA.
e-mail: fariha.kamal@census.gov
**Department of Economics, Maxwell School of Citizenship and Public Affairs,
Syracuse University, Syracuse, NY 13244, USA. e-mail: melovely@maxwell.syr.edu

Abstract

Using China's Annual Survey of Industrial Production, we estimate the marginal revenue product of labor (MRPL) for all state-owned and above-scale non-state manufacturing firms for 2001–2004 and 2004–2007. We find that labor productivity varies systematically within industries by ownership type and that non-state firms face implicit labor taxation relative to state-owned enterprises (SOEs). We also find that, in keeping with ongoing reforms of the state sector, ownership differentials fall over time, with gaps between non-state enterprises and SOEs falling by about half over time. Within the non-state sector, enterprises registered as legal persons have higher MRPL, on average, than do firms registered as collective or private enterprises. Disaggregating this group using information on equity shares reveals that firms registered as legal persons and majority owned by legal persons have the highest MRPL relative to SOEs. Indeed, these enterprises show significantly higher MRPL than those firms directly controlled by the state. Legal-person firms with majority state ownership have MRPL differentials similar to those for legal-person firms with majority private or majority collective ownership. This evidence is consistent with continuing, albeit diminishing, implicit labor subsidies for directly SOEs but not for firms whose shares are owned by the state, even if those shares are registered to legal persons. (JEL codes: L16, O53, P23, P31)

Keywords: labor allocation, privatization, labor subsidies

1 Introduction

Low aggregate productivity in the developing world is, in part, the result of micro-level resource misallocation. Structural accounting exercises indicate that barriers to sectoral reallocation, particularly out of agriculture, are a quantitatively important explanation for income differences across countries (Restuccia et al. 2008; Gancia and Zilibotti 2009; Duarte and Restuccia 2010). An emerging and growing body of research focuses on misallocation of resources within, rather than between, sectors and

---

[†] The research in this article was undertaken while the author was at Syracuse University. Any opinions and conclusions expressed herein are those of the author and do not necessarily represent the views of the U.S. Census Bureau. The research in this article does not use any confidential Census Bureau information.

F. Kamal and M. E. Lovely

calibrations by Restuccia and Rogerson (2008), Bartelsman et al. (2008) and Alfaro et al. (2009) suggest that misallocation of resources across heterogeneous firms can explain much of the total factor productivity (TFP) gap across countries. For China, Hsieh and Klenow (2009) estimate that if capital and labor were reallocated across firms to equalize marginal products to the extent observed in the United States, manufacturing productivity could rise by 30–50%. Looking at a longer time period, 1985–2007, and across provinces and sectors, Brandt and Zhu (2010) estimate that factor misallocations have reduced aggregate Chinese TFP by ~30%.

Banerjee and Moll (2009) argue that a natural explanation for so much misallocation is asset market inefficiencies, which make it difficult for successful firms to expand and simultaneously allow failed firms to survive.[1] In China, the prominence of state-controlled financial institutions has focused attention on differential access to capital by state-owned enterprises (SOEs) relative to non-state firms. Using data from China's Annual Survey of Industrial Production (ASIP), Brandt and Zhu (2010) provide evidence that outside of agriculture, non-state firms have higher TFP and higher returns to capital, yet lower capital–labor ratios, than do state firms.[2] Poncet et al. (2010) also use data from the ASIP and conclude that private Chinese firms are credit constrained while state-owned firms and foreign-owned firms are not.

In addition to substantial capital market distortions, however, China remains plagued by labor market distortions arising from a wide variety of policies that favor the state sector. The reward for state-sector employment includes differential access to social services, preferential treatment for urban 'hukou', even proximity to opportunities for corruption and side payments. Among college graduates, state employment remains a desired goal. Despite these non-wage factors, which suggest that state firms should be able to pay lower money wages, numerous studies find a state-sector money-wage premium. Brandt and Zhu (2010) report that non-state-sector wages in 2007 were only 66% of those inside the state sector. Mincerian wage regressions based on urban household surveys also consistently find a state-sector premium (Knight and Song 2008).[3]

---

[1] Given the high rates of return to investment in firms that are capital starved, the question arises as to why such misallocations are not corrected. Banerjee and Moll (2009) build a simple model with credit constraints to explain how such inefficiencies could persist.

[2] The Annual Surveys of Industrial Production includes all non-state-owned firms whose annual sales exceed five million yuan (referred to as 'above-scale' industrial firms) and all SOEs.

[3] Existing data make it difficult to control for unobservable individual characteristics of workers, and positive selection by state employers may explain some of the wage premium.

Labor Allocation in China

High non-wage compensation and a money wage premium, coupled with high capital–labor ratios relative to the non-state sector, should be matched by high labor productivity in the state sector. It is puzzling, therefore, that state firms have lower labor productivity than do non-state firms. Jefferson and Su (2006) find that the largest Chinese state-owned industrial enterprises have the lowest labor and capital productivity compared to other ownership types, controlling for industry and year.[4] Fleisher et al. (2011) estimate production functions by sector and find that the marginal product of labor in state-owned manufacturing enterprises is about half that of private enterprises for both highly educated and less educated workers. These systematic gaps between labor productivity and labor costs suggest implicit subsidies to the state sector to maintain employment, perhaps to promote social stability.

This article contributes to our understanding of factor misallocation in China by estimating labor productivity by ownership status and then using these estimates to characterize implicit taxation of labor in the non-state sector. Like Fleisher et al. (2011) we use production function estimation to calculate labor's marginal product for China's state-owned and above-scale domestic enterprises, but unlike previous studies we allow production functions to vary by ownership status. We also control for variation across ownership classes in industry composition and geographic location before measuring the gap between the state and non-state sectors. We calculate relative labor productivities for two recent periods, 2001–2004 and 2004–2007. We also provide estimates of implicit tax rates on non-state labor by industry.

Our second contribution is to decompose the non-state sector into its member components. The non-state domestic sector encompasses a wide variety of organizational types, including private enterprises, collectives, and firms registered as legal persons. Although Naughton (2007: p. 325) notes, '...we do not have a very detailed understanding of Chinese privatization', the non-state sector is often termed the 'private sector' and thus implicitly associated with private ownership, profit maximization, market input and output prices, and a hard budget constraint.[5] Strong growth in TFP in the non-sector sector supports a maintained

---

[4] Jefferson and Su (2006) measure labor productivity as value added per worker and capital productivity as value added divided by the net value of fixed assets.
[5] For example, Song et al. (2011) include a wide range of organizational forms under the category 'domestic private enterprises' to show rapid growth in China's private sector. In their modeling, they equate growth of the private sector with a reallocation of resources from low productivity firms to high productivity firms in their model of the Chinese economy.

F. Kamal and M. E. Lovely

assumption of productive efficiency, but the sector encompasses many different organizational forms, about which we know relatively little.

The spectacular growth in China's non-state GDP has been widely noted, but a large share of non-state value added is produced by enterprises whose ownership and control structures are only vaguely understood. One group of enterprises, those registered as legal persons, is particularly shrouded. These enterprises are mostly shareholding firms, an organization form integral to reform of China's SOEs (Jefferson et al. 2005). Shareholding firms are primarily not publicly traded companies, and they may operate under state control, may be privately controlled, or may simply be an unknown 'hybrid ownership'. Particular concern about the classification of these firms is raised by Huang (2008), who argues that these firms, especially the largest ones, remain state-controlled and that they should be considered part of the state sector, not part of the non-state sector. As we show below: (i) the extent to which many of these firms are state owned cannot be determined from available information and (ii) these firms account for a large share of value added in the manufacturing sector. Their size and veiled ownership structure require us to consider their performance in isolation from either SOEs or privately owned enterprises. Therefore, we estimate differences in labor productivity between SOEs and private enterprises, collective-owned enterprise (COE), and legal-person enterprises and we then further disaggregate our results using information on equity ownership. To our knowledge, we are the first to examine the comparative performance of legal person enterprises.

We begin by reviewing briefly the unique role of shareholding firms in the restructuring of Chinese enterprises. We show that whether these firms, many of which are registered as legal person firms, are considered private or state enterprises affects how one views the extent to which Chinese manufacturing is 'privatized'. Next, we explain how labor misallocation can be inferred from residuals in first-order conditions for profit maximization. We describe how we use the ASIP to estimate the marginal revenue product of labor (MRPL) for each enterprise and then employ regression analysis to measure the difference between the marginal product of SOEs and other firm types. We present these results as the MRPL of each non-state enterprise relative to state-owned firms, showing this ratio for two time periods, for the full sample and for incumbents, and for groups of legal-person enterprises reclassified using equity shares. This method also allows us to estimate the implied tax on labor, relative to its use in the state sector, for each industry and non-state-owned ownership type. We provide summary measures of the dispersion of MRPL across firms. We conclude by discussing the implications of our findings for Chinese restructuring and reform.

Labor Allocation in China

2 Ownership restructuring, enterprise classification, and the size of the private sector

The largest group of firms registered as legal persons are those organized as shareholding enterprises. According to Jefferson et al. (2005), the emergence of Chinese shareholding enterprises stems from policy changes of the 1980s and early 1990s, which allowed new firm entry, strengthened managerial incentives, and permitted accumulation of non-state assets in the state sector. Formal conversion of SOEs to joint stock companies was introduced in 1993, but shareholding conversion became a broad-based initiative involving large numbers of SOEs and COEs only after 1997 when the Chinese Communist Party's 15th Party Congress elevated the shareholding system as a vehicle for enterprise restructuring. From 1997 to 2001, Jefferson et al. find that the number of large and medium-size SOEs declined by over 40%, and the number of large and medium-size COEs declined by 35%, while the number of shareholding firms soared.

Since 2001, the evolution of the Chinese industrial sector has continued, but tracking the extent to which shareholding firms are state controlled is difficult. China's National Bureau of Statistics assigns each firm an ownership classification, known as its 'registration status'. Table A1 provides a disaggregation of the ownership forms included under each registration code. SOEs include those that are majority owned by the central government or a local government, those registered to the state but jointly operated with a non-state entity, and those wholly state owned. Private-owned firms, by registration status, include those registered to natural persons, whether solely, in partnership, as limited liability enterprises, or shareholding firms. Distinctions between ownership types become blurred in the fourth type of domestic registration status, legal person. Firms registered as legal persons include limited liability and shareholding limited liability firms. Their relationship to the state is not indicated by their registration status, unlike other classes.[6]

Some progress in relating firms classified as legal persons to either state, collective or private ownership status can be made by reference to information on equity shares. The ASIP includes information on the origin of the various sources of capital in the firm—state-owned, collective-owned, legal person, private-owned, and foreign-owned.[7] This information on equity shares can be used to reclassify legal person firms based on majority ownership. If 50% or more of equity originates from

---

[6] The number of firm registered in a final category, 'other', accounts for < 1% of firms in the ASIP.

[7] Foreign-owned includes capital from Hong Kong, Macao, Taiwan, and all other foreign sources.

F. Kamal and M. E. Lovely

state, collective, private, or foreign sources, the enterprise can be reclassified accordingly. However, for many firms, legal person is a significant source of capital, making it impossible to reclassify these firms without arbitrarily treating this share as state or private. Indeed, of the 54 320 firms officially registered as legal person, 21 910 enterprises cannot be reclassified using equity information because the majority of their capital originates from a legal person. In other words, equity shares do not allow us to completely peer around the veil of legal-person status.

Other researchers have faced this problem. Dollar and Wei (2007) add legal-person capital to private capital before calculating majority ownership. While subsequent researchers have followed the same procedure, this method ignores Huang's (2008) observation that categorizing legal person firms as private can be misleading because '(e)ven a casual glance at the data reveals that many of these legal-person shareholding firms are among the best-known and quintessential SOEs in China' (p. 16). He concludes that '(t)he majority of the shareholding firms, especially the large ones, are still state-controlled' (p. 46). Huang's observation suggests that an alternative grouping of firms, in which legal person capital is treated as state-owned capital before calculating majority ownership, is also reasonable.[8]

When ownership is defined using NBS registration status, Table 1 shows that the number of SOEs fell by 93% between 1998 and 2007 (Panel A), accounting for only 2.22% of all above-scale firms by 2007 (Panel B). COEs also declined sharply in number, falling 86% over the period and accounting for only 5.14% of firms by 2007. In contrast, firms registered as private enterprises rose sharply, with the number of private firms growing by a 670%, and constituting 53.6% of all above-scale firms by 2007. The number of firms registered as legal persons, the majority of which are shareholding enterprises, rose 160% and accounting for 17.4% of firms by 2007.

Using information in the ASIP on equity shares to define ownership allows us to reclassify 59% of legal-person firms to other ownership categories, with only 3.9% reclassified as state and another 4.9% reclassified as collective. The remainder, 51% of enterprises registered as legal-persons, is privately owned. However, that leaves 41% of legal-person enterprises with an unknown relationship to the state.

As seen in Table 1, adding legal-person capital to private capital before reclassifying enterprises reduces the calculated growth in the number of private enterprises, but increases the share of firms classified as private

---

[8] Other methods for classifying firms have also been used. For example, Brandt et al. (2011) look at registered capital and use equity shares to classify firms as state, private, or 'hybrid'.

Labor Allocation in China

Table 1 Distribution of firms by various ownership classification schemes, selected years

	Panel A. Number of firms in sample				Panel B. Percent share in sample			
	1998	2001	2004	2007	1998	2001	2004	2007
Registration status								
State owned	46 916	27 664	17 994	6962	31.55	17.76	7.00	2.22
Collective owned	53 705	38 861	23 328	16 079	36.12	24.95	9.08	5.14
Foreign owned	26 047	30 903	56 412	66 490	17.52	19.84	21.95	21.24
Private owned	10 348	35 182	114 838	167 716	6.96	22.59	44.68	53.58
Legal person	9923	21 673	43 357	54 320	6.67	13.92	16.87	17.35
Others	1746	1448	1070	1479	1.17	0.93	0.42	0.47
Classifying legal person equity as state								
State owned	68 776	60 150	78 920	93 655	46.26	38.62	30.71	29.92
Collective owned	42 951	29 101	19 231	12 857	28.89	18.69	7.48	4.11
Foreign owned	17 172	21 484	41 322	49 611	11.55	13.80	16.08	15.85
Private owned	19 786	44 996	117 526	156 923	13.31	28.89	45.73	50.13
Classifying legal person equity as private								
State owned	48 923	30 565	20 048	8526	32.90	19.63	7.80	2.72
Collective owned	42 416	28 709	19 100	12 756	28.53	18.43	7.43	4.07
Foreign owned	17 186	21 455	41 240	49 503	11.56	13.78	16.05	15.81
Private owned	40 160	75 002	176 611	242 261	27.01	48.16	68.72	77.39
Total	148 685	155 731	256 999	313 046				

Note: The table displays the number of manufacturing firms only from the raw data prior to performing data cleaning. Definitions of ownership: 'Registration Status' refers to the codes provided by China's National Bureau of Statistics (see Table A1 for the list); 'classifying legal person equity as state equity' categorizes ownership based on equity shares of the firm and legal person equity in treated as state owned; 'classifying legal person equity as private equity' categorizes ownership based on equity shares and legal person equity in treated as private owned. See text for details.

Source: Authors' calculations from Annual Surveys of Industrial Production, selected years.

from 27% in 1998 to 77.4% in 2007. Using this classification system, then, one would characterize the Chinese economy as largely 'privatized'. When one chooses an alternative attribution method instead, and includes legal-person capital with state capital before reclassifying enterprises, the private sector share of enterprises in 2007 is lower—50% of all firms rather than 77.4% of all firms.

While these differences due to reclassification may seem trivial, it is important to recognize that firms officially registered as legal-person

F. Kamal and M. E. Lovely

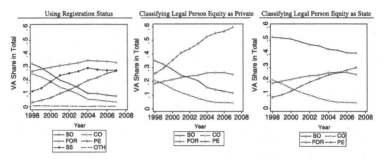

Figure 1 Value-added shares by various ownership classification schemes, 1998–2007. *Notes*: The values are expressed as shares in the industrial total. Definitions of ownership: 'Registration Status' refers to the codes provided by China's National Bureau of Statistics; 'classifying legal person equity as state' categorizes ownership based on equity shares of the firm and legal person equity in treated as state owned; 'classifying legal person as private equity' categorizes ownership based on equity shares and legal person equity in treated as private owned. See text for details. SO refers to state-owned enterprises, CO refers to collective-owned enterprises, FOR refers to foreign-owned enterprises, PE refers to private enterprises, SS refers to legal person (shareholding) enterprises.
Source: Authors' calculations from Annual Surveys of Industrial Production, selected years.

enterprises are larger than average when measured by value added. Figure 1 shows that reclassification can lead to quite different conclusions about the extent of 'privatization' when we consider contributions to industrial value added. The first panel shows trends in value-added shares when firms are classified by registration status. We see a dramatic decline over the 10-year period in the value-added shares of SOEs and COEs, and increases in both the private enterprise share and the legal person share, both of which contribute about one-fourth of value added by 2007. Because of their large value-added share, when legal-person enterprises are grouped with private enterprises, as shown in the middle panel, the private share of industrial value-added skyrockets, with 60% contributed by domestic private enterprises and another 22% contributed by foreign-invested enterprises in 2007. Alternatively, if we group legal-person enterprises with SOEs, as in the rightmost panel of Figure 1, growth in the private share of value-added stalls after 2004 as the state share flattens out at 40%. When measured in this way, privatization appears to have stopped with less than half of value added from domestic enterprises privately produced. These trends clearly indicate the need to better understand the performance of the Chinese 'private' sector, particularly those firms registered as legal persons.

Labor Allocation in China

3 Using first-order conditions to infer implicit labor subsidies

Our empirical method infers labor misallocation from the residuals in first-order conditions for profit maximization.[9] Deviations between factor cost and marginal product inform the business cycle accounting of Chari et al. (2007) as well as the measurement of potential Chinese manufacturing TFP gains by Hsieh and Klenow (2009). Unlike these two contributions, which seek to measure aggregate losses from factor misallocation, our objective is to characterize deviations across the state and non-state sector, and estimate implicit non-state labor tax-cum-subsidy rates by industry. We measure these distortions as the extent to which labor's marginal revenue product differs by ownership.

Our approach recognizes the distinction, emphasized by Hsieh and Klenow (2009) and Foster et al. (2008), between a firm's physical productivity and its revenue productivity. It is common in the productivity literature to have industry deflators, but not plant-specific or firm-specific deflators, making accurate calculation of physical product difficult at the plant or firm level. Calculation of revenue product, however, does not require the missing deflators and, thus, matches well the data available to us through China's ASIP.

We maintain the hypothesis that all firms profit maximize and face market input and output prices. The allocation of resources across firms depends on the output and factor distortions they face. Let τ_{Lot} be the labor tax and τ_{Yit} the output tax facing a firm in industry I with ownership type o at time t. Regardless of the implicit capital tax or subsidy a firm faces, profit maximization requires that the firm choose its labor optimally; this implies that firms will equate the MRPL with the after-tax cost of labor. For firm j at time t, operating in industry i with ownership class o, the first-order condition for labor input is:

$$\text{MRPL}_{jt}(o, i) = w(1 + \tau_{Lot})/(1 - \tau_{Yit}). \tag{1}$$

If firms face the same market wage, w, after-tax marginal revenue products will be equalized and before-tax MRPL must be higher in firms that face disincentives relative to those that do not.

Our objective is to estimate the implicit labor distortion, τ_{Lot}, facing non-state firms operating in each Chinese industry. To do this, we first estimate the marginal revenue product for each firm, allowing for differences in productivity by industry and ownership type. Next, we use

---

[9] We follow the literature and use the term 'misallocation' to refer to residuals in first-order conditions for profit maximization. However, welfare maximization may require deviations between labor cost and marginal revenue product across industry, space, or time. Our method controls for these factors and estimates deviations by ownership status.

F. Kamal and M. E. Lovely

regression analysis to estimate the relative labor productivity for each ownership type, controlling for the enterprise's geographic location and industry. Such controls are needed given previous evidence of robust differences in wages for similar workers across Chinese cities (e.g. Hering and Poncet 2010; Kamal et al. 2012), and of compensating differentials across Chinese industries (e.g. Knight and Song 2008).

We estimate labor productivity differentials for each non-state ownership class (defined using registration type) and SOEs. We do so for two periods, 2001–2004 and 2004–2007, in an attempt to see if continuing economic restructuring of the state sector has reduced the misallocation of labor. Data needs limit us to these two periods, as our production function estimation makes use of firm fixed effects.

Previous research has found that entry and exit accounts for a large share of Chinese TFP growth (Brandt et al. 2010). Therefore, we recognize that changes over time in labor productivity differences may be driven by exit from the state sector and entry in the non-state sector. To avoid confounding entry and exit effects with reductions in distortions over time, we also analyze a panel of incumbent firms, defined as enterprises that operate for the entire length of the time period.

As discussed above, firms owned by a legal person have an unknown relation to the state and so we disaggregate our data to focus on these firms. Specifically, we isolate those firms with official registration status as legal persons and we re-classify them on the basis of equity shares. About 60% of legal-person firms can be assigned to the state, collective, or private sector based on majority equity ownership. The remainder, however, remain behind a veil and we compare their labor productivity to that of reclassified legal-person firms. We ask whether firms that cannot be reclassified using equity shares perform differently than legal-person firms that have majority non-state ownership.

We also use regressions to estimate the implicit labor tax-cum-subsidy for each non-state ownership type by industry. Finally, we decompose the overall dispersion of MRPL in each time period, assessing the extent to which observed heterogeneity within industries can be explained by ownership patterns, geographic clustering, and firm size, and seeing if dispersion decreases over time.

4 Estimating the MRPL

4.1 Data

To estimate marginal revenue products, we use the Annual Surveys of Industrial Production conducted by the Chinese government's National Bureau of Statistics (NBS) between 2001 and 2007. We divide the data into

Labor Allocation in China

two time periods—the first period spanning 2001–2004 and the second spanning 2004–2007. The data set contains detailed information on about 100 variables, including firm identification code, four-digit industry code, six-digit geographic code, ownership classification, gross industrial output value, value added, export value, total employment, capital stock, and intermediate inputs.

We impose several restrictions on the raw data to generate our analysis data set. We filter the raw data to exclude observations with missing information and improbable values for certain variables. Since we utilize the equity share information to classify ownership of a firm, we are forced to exclude firms from our analysis that do not have information on total capital. To correct for improbable values we exclude those firms that employ eight or fewer workers since most improbable values are associated with smaller firms.[10] We further restrict the sample to include firms that have non-negative values for value added and capital.

4.2 Production function estimation

Each firm in the data set belongs to a two-digit Chinese Industrial Classification (CIC) code.[11] We estimate production functions for every two-digit industry and ownership type combination. There are 28 two-digit industries and 5 ownership types based on the registration status codes.[12] In total, we compute 140 sets of factor coefficients. The input coefficients, β_L and β_K are first determined by estimating a Cobb–Douglas production function,

$$\ln(\text{value added}_{it}) = \beta_L \ln(\text{labor}_{it}) + \beta_K \ln(\text{capital}_{it}) + \omega_{it} + \varepsilon_{it} \qquad (2)$$

---

[10] Individual businesses, known as *getihu*, are owned by private individuals or households and not legally considered enterprises. These businesses are officially limited to member of a family and up to seven non-family employees. See Song (2004) for a history of the development of small private enterprises in China.

[11] Prior to 2003, NBS followed GB/T 4754—1994 industry classification system and while from 2003 onwards used GB/T 4754—2002. Two changes were made in the two-digit divisions: (i) the 1994 division 39 ('Arms and Ammunition Manufacturing') was added to 2002 division 36 ('Special Equipment Manufacturing'). Then the remaining 2002 division codes were renumbered accordingly, i.e. 1994 division 40 corresponds to 2002 division 39, 1994 division 41 corresponds to 2002 division 40, 1994 division 42 corresponds to 2002 division 41, and 1994 division 43 corresponds to 2002 division 42. (ii) 2002 division 43 ('Waste Resources and Old Material Recycling and Processing') was added which was not part of manufacturing in the previous period. Consequently, we recoded firms in years prior to 2003 ensuring that all codes are comparable across the sample period.

[12] There are a total of 30 2-digit manufacturing industries under CIC. However, Industry 16 ('Tobacco Products Processing') and Industry 43 ('Waste Resources and Old Material Recycling and Processing') were excluded. Almost 100% of firms in the former are state-owned and data is not available for the latter prior to 2003. We also exclude about 1500 firms with the industry code 'other' from our estimations.

F. Kamal and M. E. Lovely

where ω_{it} represents the part of productivity shock that is observed by firm i at time t, but unobserved by the econometrician and ε_{it} represents an error term uncorrelated with the other inputs. Since the firm observes the unobserved component of productivity, ω_{it}, it will be correlated with input choices, implying that OLS yields inconsistent estimates of β_L and β_K (Marschak and Andrews 1944).

To address this potential simultaneity bias, we employ the semi-parametric method proposed by Levinsohn and Petrin (2003) (hereafter LP). This procedure uses intermediate inputs to proxy for the unobservable productivity shock, ω_{it}.[13] Production function estimation using the LP method requires information on firm value-added, labor, capital, and intermediate inputs. The data set provides information on nominal values of firm value-added, capital, and intermediate inputs. These are converted to real terms using the output, investment, and input deflators, respectively, in Brandt et al. (2011).[14]

All regressions control for firm, year, and city fixed effects. Comparing the parameter estimates from OLS and LP, we see that on an average, the OLS labor coefficient estimates exceed the LP estimates.[15] This is in keeping with both the theoretical and empirical results discussed in Levinsohn and Petrin (2003). We tested the Cobb–Douglas estimates against the more general translog specification and we were able to reject translog for about half of our samples.

4.3 Calculating MRPL estimates

Once we obtain production function coefficients for labor, we use these to construct the MRPL for every firm in every sample year.[16] The marginal revenue product (MRPL) for each firm i is constructed as follows:

$$\text{MRPL}_i = \beta_L(\text{VA}_i/L_i), \tag{3}$$

---

[13]   The production function coefficients are estimated in two stages. First, the labor coefficient is consistently identified from a regression of value added on an intercept term, labor, and unobserved productivity modeled as a function of capital and intermediate inputs. The second stage identifies the capital coefficient assuming productivity innovation is orthogonal to current capital input and lagged intermediate inputs.

[14]   The deflators are available at http://www.econ.kuleuven.be/public/N07057/CHINA/appendix/. The output and input deflators are at the four-digit CIC level of disaggregation, while we use a national investment deflator.

[15]   Labor coefficients based on OLS, LP, and a translog production function can be obtained from the authors on request. We obtain two (five) negative labor coefficients in period 1 (2) for state-owned firms using the LP method. These are in industries 18 and 28 in period 1 and industries 15, 27, 28, 29, and 42 in period 2. We code these coefficients to be zero for the marginal revenue product calculations.

[16]   See Fleisher et al. (2011) for a derivation of the marginal revenue products assuming production functions are Cobb–Douglas and firms are price takers in output and input markets.

Labor Allocation in China

where β_L is an estimate of the labor coefficient in (2) for the relevant industry and ownership class, L_i indicates total employment at firm i and VA_i is the value added of the firm.

5 Estimates of labor productivity differentials

5.1 Using regression analysis to estimate MRPL differentials

We use residuals from first-order conditions to characterize the implicit tax-cum-subsidy embedded in our marginal revenue product estimates. Recalling equation (1), τ_{Lot}, gives the relevant wedge for ownership type o at time t. Taking the log of (1) yields a linear expression,

$$\ln MRPL_{jt} = \ln w_{ict} - \ln(1 - \tau_{Yit}) + \ln(1 + \tau_{Lot}), \qquad (4)$$

where $MRPL_{jt}$ is the MRPL for firm j, and where i and c denote industry and city, respectively. Our goal is to understand how the MRPL varies by firm ownership type. We employ a regression framework to control for possible differences in the MRPL because firms must pay different wages in different industries, years, or cities.[17] In some regressions, we also allow for a wage premium by firm size. These regressions take the form:

$$\ln MRPL_{jt} = \alpha + \chi_c + \beta_i + \eta_o + \gamma_t + \mu \ln(S_{jt}) + \varepsilon_{jt}, \qquad (5)$$

where α is a constant, χ_c is a city fixed effect, β_i is an industry fixed effect, η_o is an ownership fixed effect, γ_t is a year fixed effect, S_{jt} is employment of firm j at time t, and μ is an estimated coefficient, and ε_{jt} is an iid error term.

Ownership is defined by registration status—state, collective, private, and legal person—unless otherwise specified, and we estimate (5) treating state ownership as the left-out ownership category. The coefficient for ownership type, η_o, can be used to measure the wage distortion for ownership type o relative to state ownership, holding two-digit industry, year, and firm size constant. In our tables, we report average MRPL by ownership type relative to the average MRPL for SOEs.[18]

---

[17] China is divided into 27 provinces plus four province-status municipalities of Beijing, Chongqing, Shanghai, and Tianjin. The provinces are further divided into prefectures and prefecture level cities which can be further subdivided into counties and districts. The term 'city' in this article is used to refer to prefectures, prefecture level cities and the four municipalities.

[18] This is computed as $\exp \eta_o$.

F. Kamal and M. E. Lovely

Table 2 Marginal revenue product of labor relative to state-owned enterprises, by registration status, controlling for industry and year

	2001–2004	2004–2007
(a) All firms		
Ownership categories		
Collective owned	3.216 (0.005)	1.747.007)
Private owned	3.528 (0.005)	1.665.006)
Legal person	4.055 (0.005)	1.893 (0.006)
Total number of firms	712 823	1 054 340
Adjusted R^2	0.20	0.12
(b) Balanced panel		
Ownership categories		
Collective owned	2.843 (0.007)	1.306 (0.009)
Private owned	3.068 (0.007)	1.251 (0.008)
Legal person	3.604 (0.008)	1.433 (0.008)
Total number of firms	285 593	651 745
Adjusted R^2	0.23	0.13

Notes: Ownership defined as 'Registration Status'. This table reports the ratio of average marginal revenue product of labor by firm type relative to state-owned enterprises, controlling for year and two-digit industry fixed effects. All estimated MRPL differentials are statistically significant at the 1% level.

5.2 Labor productivity differences using registration status

Table 2 provides estimates of the MRPL for various non-state ownership categories, relative to the MRPL for state-owned firms, controlling for industry and year. Here, enterprises are classified using their official registration status. Looking first at the estimates for the period 2001–2004, we find very large gaps between non-state enterprises and state enterprises. Collective-owned firms have marginal revenue products of labor that are estimated to be 3.22 times that of state-owned firms. Private enterprises have marginal labor productivity that is 3.53 times that of state-owned firms. Firms registered as legal-person enterprises have the highest estimated MRPL of all ownership types and thus the largest gap: legal-person enterprises on an average have marginal labor productivity that is 4.06 times that of SOEs.

When we estimate MRPL for the second time period, 2004–2007, we find that the gaps have decreased for all ownership types relative to SOEs. As shown in the rightmost columns of panel (a), collective firms are estimated to have average marginal labor productivity 1.7 times that of SOEs, while the differential falls to 1.67 for private firms and 1.89 for

Labor Allocation in China

legal-person enterprises. Thus, our estimates suggest a dramatic narrowing of the implicit labor subsidy for state enterprises over time.[19]

As shown in panel (b) of Table 2, we estimate (5) again with industry and year controls, using a sample that includes only firms present in every year of each period. There is active churning of firms, in and out of the ASIP and across ownership categories, and we estimate the differential for incumbent firms only to avoid confounding ownership changes with allocative reforms.[20] Restricting our sample to incumbent firms reduces the size of estimated productivity gaps, but not the ordering across ownership types. In the first time period, 2001–2004, incumbent legal-person enterprises have the highest marginal labor productivity, with an estimated MRPL 3.60 times that of SOEs. Interestingly, the gaps we estimate for the later period, 2004–2007, are substantially smaller. Incumbent collective enterprises have an estimated marginal labor productivity 1.31 times that of the state sector, labor in incumbent private enterprises is 1.25 times as productive at the margin, and labor in incumbent legal-person firms is 1.43 times as productive. Differences between the full sample and the incumbent sample are consistent with the finding of Brandt et al. (2011), who show that exit and entry has substantial impacts on productivity growth during this period. Our results suggest that new entrants face implicitly higher labor costs.

Table 3 uses additional controls to isolate differences in factor productivity across similar firms with different organizational forms. As seen by a comparison of the estimates from regression (1) to those in Table 2, controlling for the city in which an enterprise is located tends to reduce the differentials we find between the non-state sector and the state sector. The marginal labor productivity of collectives falls from 3.22 times that of SOEs to 2.87, the differential for private firms falls from 3.53 to 3.15 and the differential for legal-person firms falls from 4.06 to 3.76. Therefore, the slight tendency of SOEs to be located in higher wage cities explains a bit of the observed productivity differentials, but very large productivity differentials remain. When we also control for firm size, as measured by firm employment, we find no significant differences from those productivity gaps estimated without accounting for size, as seen by regression (2) in Table 3.

---

[19] Estimates for MRPL differences using labor coefficients estimated from a translog function or by OLS show the same qualitative patterns across ownership but magnitudes that are smaller by ~25%. The decline in productivity gaps is also smaller, with estimated differentials falling ~10% between the two periods. Because non-state firms are free to adjust labor input in response to shocks, we prefer the LP estimates.

[20] This churning is well documented in Brandt et al. (2011).

F. Kamal and M. E. Lovely

Table 3 Marginal revenue product of labor relative to state-owned enterprises, by registration status, with additional controls

	2001–2004		2004–2007	
	(1)	(2)	(3)	(4)
Ownership categories				
Collective owned	2.872 (0.005)	2.875 (0.005)	1.608 (0.007)	1.597 (0.007)
Private owned	3.149 (0.005)	3.152 (0.005)	1.570 (0.006)	1.560 (0.006)
Legal person	3.762 (0.005)	3.766 (0.005)	1.820 (0.006)	1.813 (0.006)
Firm employment?	N	Y	N	Y
Year dummies?	Y	Y	Y	Y
City dummies?	Y	Y	Y	Y
Industry dummies?	Y	Y	Y	Y
Total number of firms	712 823		1 054 340	
Adjusted R^2	0.25		0.18	

Notes: Ownership defined as 'Registration Status'. This table reports the ratio of the average marginal revenue product of labor by firm type relative to state-owned enterprises, controlling for the indicated effects. All estimated MRPL differentials are statistically significant at the 1% level.

Looking at estimates for the later period, 2004–2007 regressions (3) and (4) in Table 3, we find similar results: controlling for the city in which the enterprise is located reduces the estimated productivity differentials only slightly and controlling for firm size has virtually no effect. Additional controls also do not change our finding that productivity differentials between non-state enterprises and state enterprises clearly fall over time.

5.3 Labor productivity differences for reclassified legal-person enterprises

Table 4 provides greater detail on the performance of firms that are registered as legal persons. We use equity share information to reclassify these domestic firms as majority-owned state, collective, or private, to the extent possible. When the majority of equity is contributed by legal persons, reclassification is not possible and we continue to classify them as legal person enterprises and we compare their performance to other reclassified groups.

Looking first at the top panel, which provides results for the full sample, we see that there are significant differences by ownership within the group of firms registered as legal persons.[21] For the period 2001–2004, among

---

[21] While we do not indicate the significance of differences among members of the non-state sector in Table 4, separate significance tests show that all differences are significant, with the exceptions noted in the text.

Labor Allocation in China

Table 4 Marginal revenue product of labor relative to state-owned enterprises, firms registered as legal persons disaggregated and reclassified, controlling for industry and year

	All firms		Balanced panel	
	2001–2004	2004–2007	2001–2004	2004–2007
Ownership categories				
Collective owned	3.216 (0.017)	1.747 (0.012)	2.841 (0.021)	1.305 (0.012)
Private owned	3.534 (0.017)	1.665 (0.010)	3.066 (0.022)	1.250 (0.010)
Legal person reclassified as:				
State owned	2.999 (0.034)	1.750 (0.022)	2.863 (0.045)	1.320 (0.020)
Collective owned	4.006 (0.046)	1.758 (0.021)	3.581 (0.056)	1.343 (0.019)
Private owned	3.967 (0.026)	1.801 (0.012)	3.469 (0.031)	1.349 (0.012)
Legal person	4.497 (0.031)	2.041 (0.014)	4.026 (0.039)	1.565 (0.014)
Total number of firms	712 823	1 054 340	285 475	651 608
Adjusted R^2	0.21	0.12	0.23	0.13

Notes: This table reports the ratio of the average marginal revenue product of labor by firm type relative to state-owned enterprises, controlling for year, and two-digit industry fixed effects. All estimated MRPL differentials are statistically significant at the 1% level. Firms registered as legal persons have been reclassified as state, private, collective, foreign, or legal person using equity shares.

legal person enterprises reclassified by equity ownership, all groups show labor productivity that, on average, exceeds that of collective or private enterprises that are not registered as legal persons, with the exception of those with majority state ownership. However, it is interesting and important that the majority state-owned shareholding firms have labor productivity that is three times larger than state-owned firms that are directly controlled by the state. This category of firms is the category that best matches those firms identified by Huang (2008) and we find that they perform more like private firms than state-owned firms. Firms that we cannot further classify, those shareholding firms with majority equity held by legal persons (and which therefore may also be owned by the state) also have labor productivities that far exceed state-owned non-shareholding firms: the estimated MRPL for these legal-person majority owned firms is 4.5 times higher than traditional state-owned firms. These results suggest a connection between how state firms were restructured and their subsequent treatment. To the extent that we can identify majority state-owned legal person firms as formerly directly state-owned firms, our findings suggest that those firms 'let go' by the state now face labor costs similar to non-state firms.

F. Kamal and M. E. Lovely

When we consider the second period, 2004–2007, in the second column in the top panel of Table 4, we see that the labor productivity differential between state-owned firms and all firms registered as legal persons fell over time. For example, the differential between enterprises registered as legal person with majority legal-person ownership falls from 4.5 to 2.04.

Gaps across ownership types are also reduced in the second period. Indeed, we find there is no significant difference between the relative MRPL of collective firms and those firms registered as legal persons but majority collective owned. There is also no statistically significant difference between collective firms and those firms registered as legal persons but majority state owned. Firms registered as private are now estimated to have a lower MRPL differential than any reclassified group of legal person firms and these differences are statistically significant. Legal person firms with majority ownership by legal persons remain the category of enterprises with the larger relative MRPL.

The bottom panel of Table 4 provides the same analysis using only incumbent firms. As before, we see that accounting for entry and exit reduces somewhat the estimated MRPL differences for all firm types compared to state-owned firms. However, as before, the ranking of firms is unchanged within each time period and differentials are smaller later in the decade.

Table 5 re-estimates the regressions with additional controls. Accounting for spatial differences in labor costs reduces our estimated differentials by ~10%, while controlling for firm size, as measured by employment, makes virtually no difference.

5.4 Implicit labor taxes by industry

We calculate the implicit labor tax-cum-subsidy for collective, private, and legal person ownership types in each two-digit industry and time period. The ownership fixed effect, η_o, can be used to obtain an estimate of the implicit labor tax. We recover these tax rates using (4) and (5) and assuming that wages and output taxes do not vary by ownership type:

$$\eta_o = \ln(1 + \tau_{\text{Lot}})$$
$$\tau_{\text{Lot}} = \exp(\eta_o) - 1. \tag{6}$$

In our estimations, the state-owned group and food processing industry are the left out categories. Our estimates of implied labor taxes by industry are displayed in Table 6. The left panel shows the results for 2001–2004 and the right panel for 2004–2007.

Looking at the first time period, several features of the table emerge. First, with the exception of food manufacturing, in every industry labor employed by the non-state sector is implicitly taxed relative to the state

Labor Allocation in China

Table 5 Marginal revenue product of labor relative to state-owned enterprises, firms registered as legal persons disaggregated and reclassified, additional controls

	2001–2004		2004–2007	
	(1)	(2)	(3)	(4)
Ownership categories				
Collective owned	2.873 (0.015)	2.877 (0.015)	1.606 (0.011)	1.596 (0.011)
Private owned	3.157 (0.016)	3.161 (0.016)	1.570 (0.009)	1.558 (0.009)
Legal person reclassified as				
State owned	3.005 (0.033)	3.003 (0.033)	1.697 (0.020)	1.701 (0.020)
Collective owned	3.609 (0.041)	3.612 (0.041)	1.663 (0.019)	1.656 (0.019)
Private owned	3.667 (0.024)	3.672 (0.024)	1.740 (0.012)	1.731 (0.012)
Legal person	4.149 (0.028)	4.152 (0.028)	1.950 (0.013)	1.942 (0.013)
Firm employment?	N	Y	N	Y
Year dummies?	Y	Y	Y	Y
City dummies?	Y	Y	Y	Y
Industry dummies?	Y	Y	Y	Y
Total number of firms	712 823		1 054 340	
Adjusted R^2	0.25		0.18	

Notes: This table reports the ratio of the average marginal revenue product of labor by firm type relative to state-owned enterprises, controlling for the indicated effects, using the full sample. All estimated MRPL differentials are statistically significant at the 1% level. Firms registered as legal persons were reclassified as state, private, collective, foreign, or legal person using equity shares.

sector. Secondly, implicit tax rates on labor employed by private firms or legal-person firms typically exceed those for collective enterprises. Lastly, private enterprises face the highest labor tax rates overall.

The estimated implicit tax rates on non-state employment in the second period, 2004–2007, indicate that the non-state sector continued to face adverse factor market conditions. However, the implied tax rates are substantially and generally lower than in the earlier period. Indeed, for six industries we estimate that state-owned firms are taxed relative to the non-state sector: textiles, wood production, rubber, plastics, special machinery, and communication equipment. These industries are quite diverse in terms of skill intensity, but many contribute a significant share of China's overall exports.[22] While textiles form a declining share

---

[22] Matching CIC industries to trade flows requires the use of several concordances, but Dean and Lovely (2010) provide trade shares using ISIC Rev.3 that suggest these patterns.

F. Kamal and M. E. Lovely

Table 6 Implicit subsidy/tax rates relative to state-owned enterprises in food processing, by industry and time period

Industry	2001–2004			2004–2007		
	Collective owned	Private owned	Legal person	Collective owned	Private owned	Legal person
Food manufacturing	−0.38	−0.20	−0.34	0.51	0.22	0.32
Beverages	0.17	0.50	0.23	1.33	0.88	1.04
Textiles	0.76	1.25	0.85	−0.28	−0.42	−0.37
Apparel	0.35	0.73	0.42	0.36	0.10	0.19
Leather	0.48	0.89	0.55	0.44	0.17	0.26
Wood production	1.43	2.10	1.54	0.28	0.03	0.11
Furniture	0.88	1.40	0.97	−0.02	−0.21	−0.14
Paper	0.59	1.03	0.66	1.32	0.87	1.03
Printing	1.21	1.83	1.32	1.15	0.73	0.88
Culture art	0.89	1.42	0.98	0.69	0.36	0.48
Petroleum Processing	1.71	2.47	1.84	1.53	1.04	1.21
Chemicals	2.57	3.56	2.74	0.47	0.19	0.29
Medicine	0.84	1.35	0.93	2.82	2.08	2.34
Chemical fibers	4.59	6.15	4.87	6.35	4.93	5.42
Rubber	0.27	0.62	0.33	−0.07	−0.25	−0.19
Plastics	1.34	1.99	1.45	−0.09	−0.26	−0.20
Mineral	0.38	0.77	0.45	0.43	0.16	0.25
Smelting ferrous	1.72	2.48	1.85	0.71	0.38	0.49
Smelting non-ferrous	2.77	3.82	2.95	2.44	1.78	2.01
Metal prod.	0.94	1.49	1.04	0.71	0.38	0.50
General machinery	1.66	2.41	1.80	1.12	0.71	0.85
Special machinery	1.26	1.89	1.37	0.11	−0.10	−0.03
Transport	1.79	2.57	1.93	0.29	0.04	0.13
Electrical machinery	1.68	2.43	1.81	0.57	0.27	0.37
Communication equipment	1.25	1.88	1.36	−0.83	−0.87	−0.85
Instruments	0.95	1.50	1.05	3.70	2.80	3.11
Artwork	0.44	0.84	0.51	0.57	0.27	0.38

Notes: Ownership defined as 'Registration Status'. A positive value is an implicit labor tax.

of total exports, the industry still provides a large share of export-based employment. Furniture, communication equipment, and special machinery are sectors that had growing shares in the manufacturing export bundle during the decade. Non-state employment in three industries that use relatively high shares of skilled labor—chemical fibers, medicines, and instruments—face higher taxes relative to state employment in the second period.

Labor Allocation in China

The implied tax rates in Table 6 suggest that legal-person firms face labor costs that are broadly similar to those faced by other non-state firms. Interesting, the big change over time seems to be in the treatment of private enterprises. On an industry-by-industry basis, private enterprises face higher tax rates than other non-state types in 2001–2004, but they tend to face lower rates than do collectives or legal person firms in the 2004–2007 period.

Overall, these implicit tax rates suggest that, like credit policies, labor policies are a tool for state restructuring and overall industrial policy. Our results are consistent with continuing structural forces in labor markets, such as better access to non-wage benefits or services, which reduce the relative cost of labor for SOEs. These factors lead to relatively smaller non-state enterprises in a given industry, perhaps diminishing the competition faced by the state sector. The evidence suggests that these policies affect individual industries and ownership types in different ways, even as overall implied labor tax rates have fallen.

5.5 Labor productivity dispersion across the manufacturing sector

Our last exercises examine the dispersion of labor productivity across manufacturing, recognizing that there will be differences across industries due to differences in average skill attainment and compensating wage differentials. We follow Hsieh and Klenow (2009) and measure the dispersion of MRPL across firms using deviations from industry means. Table 7 provides several measures of this dispersion in each time period. While we find a small decline in the SD across firms in the industry-adjusted labor productivities, we actually find a slight increase in the 90–10 difference.[23]

Table 7 Dispersion of MRPL

	2001–2004	2004–2007
Standard deviation	1.09	1.07
75–25	1.29	1.32
90–10	2.56	2.58
Number of firms	712 823	1 054 340

Notes: Statistics are for deviations of log(MRPL) from industry and year means. S.D. = standard deviation, 75–25 is the difference between the 75th and 25th percentiles, and 90–10 the 90th versus 10th percentiles.

---

[23] Hsieh and Klenow (2009) find only small reductions in the dispersion of TFP in China between 2001 and 2005. See their Tables I and II (p. 1418).

F. Kamal and M. E. Lovely

Table 8 Sources of MRPL variation within industries

	Ownership	City	Employment
2001–2004	13.68	18.22	18.22
2004–2007	4.05	10.76	10.77

Notes: Ownership defined as 'Registration Status'. This table displays the cumulative percent of within industry-year MRPL variance explained by dummies for ownership, city, and firm employment. The results are cumulative in that 'City' includes dummies for both ownership and city, and so on.

Table 8 provides additional detail about the forces that drive this dispersion across enterprises. In the first time period, we find that variation across ownership type accounts for 13.68% of the variation within industries. When we also consider variation in location (city), we are able to account for 18.22% of overall variation. Differences in firm size, as measured by employment, explain none of the cross-firm variation in labor productivity. Overall, in 2001–2004, ownership type was the most important source of productivity dispersion, among those factors considered.

In the later period, 2004–2007, in keeping with our previously shown finding that implicit tax rates fell, the share of variation within industries that is explained by ownership falls to only 4.05%. The share explained by location (city) rises, with 10.76% of variation explained by both ownership and city. Firm size again explains virtually none of the variation in labor productivity.

Figure 2 displays the kernel density of the dispersion of MRPL for all firms and two time periods. We include only domestic firms and we exclude firms with MRPL below the 10th and above the 90th percentile. We consider deviations from industry and year means. The graph shows that the density has shifted to the left between the two periods. There are more firms with relatively low labor productivity, suggesting that firms with low labor productivity, mainly in the state sector, did not exit. This shift occurred even as overall labor productivity has increased and as gaps between state and non-state firms generally have narrowed.

6 Conclusion

By estimating the MRPL for all state-owned and all above-scale non-state sector manufacturing firms over two periods, we find that labor productivity varies systematically within industries by ownership type. Despite previous studies that show that non-state firms have lower capital–labor

Labor Allocation in China

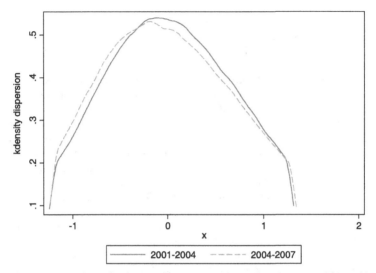

Figure 2 Dispersion of MRPL, 2001–2004 and 2004–2007. *Notes*: This table displays the kernel density of the dispersion of MRPL by time period. Measures below the 10th and above the 90th percentiles have been excluded. All foreign firms have been excluded. Graphs are for derivatives of ln(MRPL) from industry and year means.

ratios than state-owned firms, we find that non-state firms, on average, have higher marginal revenue products of labor than do SOEs. Analysis of incumbent enterprises suggests that exit and entry explain only a small part of the observed differences across ownership types. We also find that, in keeping with ongoing reforms of the state sector, labor productivity differentials associated with ownership fall over time, with the gap in MRPL between each segment of the non-state sector and SOEs falling by about half between the two periods analyzed.

While the non-state sector as a whole has a higher average MRPL than state-owned firms, we do find significant differences across the ownership types that comprise the non-state sector. Enterprises registered as legal persons have higher MRPL, on average, than do either those firms registered as collective enterprises or those registered as private enterprises. This ranking appears in both time periods and for the balanced and unbalanced panels. When we estimate the labor tax implied by these observed productivity differentials separately for each industry, we find that differences in the distribution across industries by ownership type hide underlying patterns in the treatment of private

F. Kamal and M. E. Lovely

enterprise. On an industry-by-industry basis, private enterprises face higher tax rates than other non-state types in 2001–2004, but they tend to face lower rates than do collectives or legal person firms in the second period.

Disaggregating the group of firms registered as legal persons on the basis of equity ownership reveals interesting patterns in labor productivity. In 2001–2004, all segments of the legal-person-registered group exhibit relatively high MRPLs, with the differential ranging from 200% to 350% larger than that estimated for the registered state-owned sector. A particular surprise is that legal person firms with majority state ownership also show much higher MRPL than those firms directly controlled by the state. For 2004–2007, MRPL differentials for all firm types are substantially smaller, ranging from 25% to 57% above the registered state-owned sector. In this period, legal-person firms with majority state ownership have MRPL differentials that are very similar to those for legal-person firms with majority private or majority collective ownership. In both time periods, legal-person firms with majority ownership by legal persons have the highest MRPL relative to state-owned firms.

This evidence is consistent with continuing but reduced implicit labor subsidies for directly SOEs but not for firms whose shares are owned by the state, even if those shares are registered to legal persons. In this sense, the shareholding conversions of the late 1990s, which Li et al. (2000) claim were covert forms of privatization, appear to have created a class of enterprises that function more like private enterprises than like SOEs, even when their shares are majority state owned.

Our findings also suggest that continued development of labor markets, as well as capital markets, will produce improvements in allocative efficiency. Labor market reform is inherently far-reaching as it is interwoven with social security, health care, housing policy, and the household registration system. As China tackles these issues, successful reform will produce direct dividends in enhanced and more accessible public services. Our findings suggest it will also produce an efficiency dividend as it reduces the dispersion across firms in the value of labor.

Acknowledgements

We thank Peter Egger, Shang-Jin Wei, Gary Jefferson, and participants at CESifo Summer Workshop for helpful comments. We also thank seminar participants at Nankai University's Institute for International Economics for insights and suggestions.

Labor Allocation in China

References

Alfaro, L., A. Charlton and F. Kanczuk (2009), "Firm-Size Distribution and Cross-Country Income Differences", NBER International Seminar on Macroeconomics 2008 (J. Frankel and C. Pissarides eds.). University of Chicago Press, pp. 243–272.

Banerjee, A. and B. Moll (2010), "Why Does Misallocation Persist?", *American Economic Journal: Macroeconomics* **2**, 189–206.

Bartelsman, E., J. Haltiwanger and S. Scarpetta (2012), "Cross Country Differences in Productivity: The Role of Allocative Efficiency", *American Economic Review* (forthcoming).

Brandt, L., J. V. Biesebroeck and Y. Zhang (2011), "Creative Accounting or Creative Destruction? Firm-level Productivity Growth in Chinese Manufacturing", *Journal of Development Economics* **97**, 339–351.

Brandt, L., T. Tombe and X. Zhu (2010), *Factor Market Distortions Across Time, Space and Sectors in China*, University of Toronto, MS.

Brandt, L. and X. Zhu (2010), *Accounting for China's Growth*, University of Toronto, MS.

Chari, V. V., P. J. Kehoe and E. C. McGrattan (2007), "Business Cycle Accounting", *Econometrica* **75**, 781–836.

Dean, J. M. and M. E. Lovely (2010), "Trade Growth, Production Fragmentation, and China's Environment", in R. C. Feenstra and S.-J. Wei, eds., *China's Growing Role in World Trade*, University of Chicago Press, Chicago, IL.

Dollar, D. and S.-J. Wei (2007), "Das (Wasted) Kapital: Firm Ownership and Investment Efficiency in China", NBER Working Paper No 13103, National Bureau of Economic Research, Cambridge, MA.

Duarte, M. and D. Restuccia (2010), "The Role of Structural Transformation in Aggregate Productivity", *Quarterly Journal of Economics* **125**, 129–174.

Fleisher, B. M., Y. Hu, H. Li and S. Kim (2011), "Economic Transition, Higher Education, and Worker Productivity in China", *Journal of Development Economics* **94**, 86–94.

Foster, L., J. Haltiwanger and C. Syverson (2008), "Reallocation, Firm Turnover, and Efficiency: Selection on Productivity or Profitability?", *American Economic Review* **98**, 394–425.

Gancia, G. and F. Zilibotti (2009), "Technological Change and the Wealth of Nations", *Annual Review of Economics* **1**, 93–120.

F. Kamal and M. E. Lovely

Hering, L. and S. Poncet (2010), "Market Access and Individual Wages: Evidence from China", *The Review of Economics and Statistics* **92**, 145–159.

Hsieh, C.-T. and P. Klenow (2009), "Misallocation and Manufacturing TFP in China and India", *Quarterly Journal of Economics* **124**, 1403–1448.

Huang, Y. (2008), *Capitalism with Chinese Characteristics*, Cambridge University Press, New York, NY.

Jefferson, G. H. and J. Su (2006), "Privatization and Restructuring in China: Evidence from Shareholding Ownership, 1995–2001", *Journal of Comparative Economics* **34**, 146–166.

Jefferson, G. H., J. Su, Y. Jiang and X. Yu (2005), "China's Shareholding Reform: Effects on Enterprise Performance", in J. Nellis and N. Birdsall, eds., *Reality Check: The Distributional Impact of Privatization in Developing Countries*, Center for Global Development, Washington, DC.

Kamal, F., M. E. Lovely and P. Ouyang (2012), "Does Deeper Integration Enhance Spatial Advantages? Market Access and Wage Growth in China", *International Review of Economics and Finance* **23**, 59–74.

Knight, J. and L. Song (2008), "China's Emerging Urban Wage Structure", in B. A. Gustafsson, L. Shi and T. Sicular, eds., *Inequality and Public Policy in China*, Cambridge University Press, New York, NY, pp. 221–242.

Levinsohn, J. and A. Petrin (2003), "Estimating Production Functions Using Inputs to Control for Unobservables", *Review of Economic Studies* **70**, 317–342.

Li, S., S. Li and W. Zhang (2000), "Competition and Institutional Change in China", *Journal of Comparative Economics* **23**, 269–292.

Marschak, J. and W. H. Andrews (1944), "Random Simultaneous Equations and the Theory of Production", *Econometrica* **12**, 143–205.

Naughton, B. (2007), *The Chinese Economy: Transitions and Growth*, MIT Press, Cambridge, MA.

Poncet, S., W. Steingress and H. Vandenbussche (2010), "Financial Constraints in China: Firm-level Evidence", *China Economic Review* **21**, 411–422.

Restuccia, D. and R. Rogerson (2008), "Policy Distortions and Aggregate Productivity with Heterogeneous Establishments", *Review of Economic Dynamics* **11**, 707–720.

Labor Allocation in China

Restuccia, D., D. Yang and X. Zhu (2008), "Agriculture and Aggregate Productivity: A Quantitative Cross-Country Analysis", *Journal of Monetary Economics* **52**, 234–250.

Song, L. (2004), "Emerging Private Enterprise in China: Transitional Paths and Implications", in R. Garnaut and L. Song, eds., *China's Third Economic Transformation: The Rise of the Private Economy*, RoutledgeCurzon, New York, pp. 29–47.

Song, Z., K. Storesletten and F. Zilibotti (2011), "Growing Like China", *American Economic Review* **101**, 196–233.

F. Kamal and M. E. Lovely

Appendix

Table A1 Registration status codes

Registration code	Description
State owned	
110	State-owned enterprises
141	State-owned jointly operated enterprises
151	Wholly state-owned companies
Collective owned	
120	Collective-owned enterprises
130	Shareholding cooperatives
142	Collective jointly operated enterprises
Foreign owned	
210	Overseas joint ventures
220	Overseas cooperatives
230	Overseas wholly owned enterprises
240	Overseas shareholding limited companies
310	Foreign joint ventures
320	Foreign cooperatives
330	Foreign wholly owned enterprises
340	Foreign shareholding limited companies
Private owned	
170	Private
172	Private Partners
173	Private Limited
174	Private Share Holding
Legal person	
159	Other limited liability companies
160	Shareholding limited companies
Other	
143	State-collective jointly operated enterprises
149	Other jointly operated enterprises
190	Other enterprises

Note: Overseas refers to Hong Kong, Macao, and Taiwan; Foreign refers to all other countries.

Source: National Bureau of Statistics.

Does deeper integration enhance spatial advantages? Market access and wage growth in China [☆]

Fariha Kamal [a], Mary E. Lovely [a,*], Puman Ouyang [b]

[a] Syracuse University, Syracuse, New York 13244, United States
[b] Southwestern University of Finance and Economics, Chengdu, Sichuan, PR China

ARTICLE INFO

Available online 8 October 2011

JEL classification:
F15
F16

Keywords:
Market access
Wages
New economic geography

ABSTRACT

New economic geography models predict that costly transport and the spatial distribution of demand affect the profits firms can earn in different locations, leading to higher wages for workers employed in cities with better geographic access to markets. In light of the dramatic embrace of globalization and labor market reforms that occurred in China after 1995, we measure the extent to which the influence of market access on wages strengthened and influenced wage growth over the subsequent period. Using survey data from two waves of the Chinese Household Income Project, we find that urban wages became more strongly influenced by access to markets, including domestic markets, between 1995 and 2002. The estimated elasticity of the wage with respect to market access of the worker's location more than doubles over the period. We also find that market access influences wages paid to both skilled and unskilled workers. Within provinces, we find no significant relationship between market access and either group's wages when adjusted for living costs, as expected in the context of internal labor migration. However, across provinces wages net of living costs are positively correlated with the market access of the worker's location. Consistent with deregulation of wage setting in state enterprises, the influence of market access on wages strengthened most for state-owned firms. A decomposition of the change in the mean wage indicates that market access is an economically important factor explaining the growth in average wages between 1995 and 2002.

© 2011 Elsevier Inc. All rights reserved.

1. Introduction

China's rapid integration into the global economy has reordered the international division of labor. Within China, it has helped to raise wages, while also increasing domestic income inequality. Over the past 25 years, China's real gross domestic product has expanded at an average rate of 9% per year. Much of this income growth has been driven by export production, with the growth in foreign trade averaging 15% annually since 1978. Early in the reform period, China integrated with the world economy only at its margins, allowing market sales of goods produced in excess of those meeting the planning quota, opening specific cities and zones to foreign trade and investment, and authorizing only a limited number of firms to engage in foreign trade. After 1992, China's international engagement broadened, as it permitted a surge in foreign investment, reduced tariffs, and expanded the number of authorized trading companies. As Branstetter and Lardy (2008, p. 633) stress, however, China's drive to liberalize trade and foreign direct investment dramatically accelerated in the late 1990s. Paving the way for eventual accession to the World Trade Organization in 2001, China unilaterally reduced tariffs on imports, dramatically cut quantitative restrictions on imports, eliminated many restrictions on foreign direct investment, and expanded public investment in roads, ports, airports and communications capacity.

[☆] We thank Laura Hering and Sandra Poncet for making available to us the 1995 CHIPS data used in their 2010 study. We are indebted to Devashish Mitra, Jeffrey Kubik, Lourenço Paz, and an anonymous referee for helpful comments and suggestions.
* Corresponding author.
E-mail addresses: fkamal@maxwell.syr.edu (F. Kamal), melovely@maxwell.syr.edu (M.E. Lovely), ouyangpm@swufe.edu.cn (P. Ouyang).

1059-0560/$ – see front matter © 2011 Elsevier Inc. All rights reserved.
doi:10.1016/j.iref.2011.10.006

60   F. Kamal et al. / International Review of Economics and Finance 23 (2012) 59–74

Perhaps not as well recognized as China's accelerated integration into global markets is the depth of its labor market reforms during the same period. In 1994, China passed the Labor Law, which took effect in 1995.[1] This law established the legal framework for worker–employer relations in the context of expanded employment flexibility. In addition to providing a framework for safeguarding workers' rights, the Law calls for equal treatment of workers across ownership sectors and permits no-fault dismissal of workers. Toward the end of the decade and in recognition of the employment mobility unleashed by the Labor Law, the Chinese government began strengthening social insurance programs and improving conditions for the increasingly large number of migrant workers. Although far from fully realized, these regulatory and policy changes represent significant steps toward market-mediated labor relations.

The combination of deeper international economic integration and labor market liberalization undertaken by China in the second half of the 1990s clearly influenced domestic wages and employment. Cai, Park, and Zhao (2008) report that mean annual real wages increased at an annual rate of 14% from 1997 to 2003.[2] Freeing firms to set wages according to market forces also led to increased spatial wage dispersion. Knight and Song (2008, p. 236), through an analysis of data from household surveys, find that about 11% of urban wage inequality is explained by the province in which the worker is employed.[3]

This paper investigates the spatial dimension of urban wages in China, adopting the new economic geography (NEG) approach taken by Hering and Poncet (2010). Our goal is to link cross-city variation in wages to spatial differences in access to markets. NEG models predict that costly transport and the spatial distribution of demand affect the prospective profits firms can earn in alternative locations, leading to the concentration of production in cities with better access to markets. If factor supplies are sufficiently different across locations so that factor prices are not equalized, workers in cities that offer firms higher potential profits, because of better "market access," will receive higher wages, specifically higher wages before adjustment for spatial cost-of-living differences. Hering and Poncet estimate Mincer (1974) equations using household data from 1995 and find that Chinese inter-city differences in individual wages can be partly explained by variation in the market access of the worker's location. They also find that the relationship is stronger for skilled workers and those employed by foreign-invested firms.

In light of the dramatic embrace of globalization and labor market liberalization that occurred in China after 1995, we revisit and extend the work of Hering and Poncet (2010). First, using household survey data from the 1995 and 2002 waves of the Chinese Household Income Project (CHIP), we measure the extent to which the influence of market access on wages changed over this period of intense domestic labor market liberalization and international integration. We measure changes in the influence of market access on wages of different types of workers and for different types of firms. Secondly, we examine the relationship between market access and real wages, defined as market wages adjusted for the local cost of living, seeking to find evidence of the extent to which internal migration offset the spatial advantages. Lastly, we decompose the change in mean wages and estimate the extent to which income growth between 1995 and 2002 was related to stronger spatial advantages made possible by continuing integration into global markets.

We find that urban wages did become strongly influenced by access to markets, including domestic markets, between 1995 and 2002. The estimated elasticity of the wage with respect to market access of the worker's location more than doubles over the period. We also find that market access influences wages paid to both skilled and unskilled urban workers but that this relationship is significantly stronger by 2002 only for skilled workers. We use quantile regressions to explore the possibility that more able workers migrate to central locations and find that market access is a significant determinant of wages for all quantiles. Consistent with a reduction in barriers to within-province migration, we find no significant relationship between market access and worker's wages when we adjust them for cost-of-living differences and include provincial fixed effects in our estimating equation. These results suggest that, within provinces, higher nominal wages made possible by the cost advantages of central locations attract workers from other areas, transferring spatial advantages to fixed local factors such as land and fixed housing stock. When we exclude provincial fixed effects from the Mincerian wage regressions, however, we find that workers in cities with better market access earn higher real wages. While we are unable to rule out the possibly confounding influence of unobserved provincial characteristics, this result suggests that inter-provincial migration is not sufficient to equalize workers' real rewards and that the growing importance of spatial advantages in factor rewards is another source of coastal-inland wage inequality.

We also find that the responsiveness of wages to market access depends on the employer's ownership type. While the estimated wage elasticity is lower for state-owned enterprises than for private or foreign firms, the relationship between market access and wages grew most quickly for state-owned firms, in keeping with the deregulation of wage setting in this sector. A decomposition of the change in the mean wage indicates that market access is an economically important factor explaining growth in average wages between 1995 and 2002. At least 7% of the difference over time is due to the growing wealth of markets close to Chinese producers, especially those within China itself. At least another 13% of wage growth is due to the stronger influence over time of market access on wages.

2. Theoretical framework and its application to China

2.1. Theoretical framework

NEG models emphasize the interplay of transport costs and plant-level increasing returns to scale. Beginning with Helpman and Krugman (1985) and Krugman (1991), the Dixit–Stiglitz model of monopolistic competition has been used to derive a

---

[1] Gallagher and Jiang (2002) provide an overview and analysis of the Labor Law of the People's Republic of China.
[2] Cai, Park, and Zhao (2008, p. 184) provide a time series for 1978 through 2003.
[3] Income inequality, as well as wage inequality, has a spatial dimension. Gustafsson et al. (2008, p. 54) report that in 2002 19% of urban income inequality can be attributed to provincial differences in mean incomes.

F. Kamal et al. / International Review of Economics and Finance 23 (2012) 59–74   61

relationship between the distribution of expenditure across trading economies and the distribution of production. Plant-level scale economies imply that firms find it most profitable to concentrate production at one location, with that location chosen to minimize transportation costs to the firm's geographically dispersed markets. Redding and Venables (2004) show that the potential net profits earned in each location are a linear function of the location's "market access," which is essentially a discounted sum of local and foreign expenditures available to the firm.

Predictions of the model for production and factor prices depend on the full general equilibrium. If factor price equalization (FPE) obtains in equilibrium, Behrens, Lamorgese, Ottaviano and Tabuchi (2004) provide tests of the model appropriate for a multi-country world.[4] The model predicts that larger and more centrally located countries attract a disproportionate share of firms and account for a disproportionate share of production. Their approach has been applied to data from 57 European regions over the period 1985–2000 by Head and Mayer (2006), who find little support for the model characterized by FPE. More recently, Niepmann and Felbermayr (2010) investigate the implications of the Behrens et al. model for the response of production shares to decreasing trade costs. Using data from 20 OECD countries for 1980 to 1999, they find that the distribution of firms across countries becomes increasingly skewed as trade becomes freer, a finding consistent with the model's theoretical predictions.

Because these approaches rely on FPE, they are not appropriate for a study focused on regional disparities in China. As noted above, wages are not equalized across Chinese regions; studies using individual level data have found a strong relationship between a worker's location and his or her wage. An alternative approach is provided by Redding and Venables (2004), who focus on how market access influences wages in a world in which FPE does not obtain. Taking the size of markets and the number of competitors serving those markets as exogenous, the theory relates a location's market access to the wages manufacturing firms are able to pay there. In equilibrium, wages in places with better market access are higher so that profits are equalized across locations and firms have no unilateral incentive to move.

The Redding and Venables (2004) framework leads to a log–linear relationship between the wage paid in a given location and a discounted sum of the economic activities in all relevant regions accessible from this location.[5] The NEG prediction is that wages will be higher in locations with better market access, or that the estimated coefficient for a market access measure in a wage regression will be positive and statistically significant. Redding and Venables apply this approach to an analysis of variation in GDP per capita across 110 countries, from 1992 to 1996, and find evidence consistent with the theory. Similarly, Head and Mayer (2006) investigate the dispersion of average wages across European regions and obtain results consistent with the NEG prediction.

A significant innovation in Redding and Venables (2004) is the use of a gravity model to measure "real market potential," as Head and Mayer (2006) term the Redding–Venables market access term, and also to estimate the effect of physical distance on trade. The NEG model provides for a formal definition of real market potential, showing its dependence on expenditures in each potential market, but also on the capabilities of potential competitors at these locations. This real market potential measure is often distinguished from the Harris (1954) market potential measure, which implicitly treats competitor capabilities as constant across all location and, thus, is often considered a "nominal market potential" measure. Redding and Venables show how exporter fixed effects recovered from a gravity model of international trade can be used to measure real market potential.

In their analysis of 1995 Chinese urban wages, Hering and Poncet (2010) make an important technical contribution by combining an analysis of individual, rather than average, wage levels with the Redding–Venables measure of market access.[6] To create this measure, they use geographically detailed Chinese trade data to estimate a gravity model and recover the importer and exporter fixed effects. Their procedure entails the use of bilateral trade data at the provincial level merged with trade flows from other countries in the world trading system. Further disaggregation of market potential to the city level requires an allocation of provincial market access among cities based on city shares of provincial GDP. Their procedure requires use of restricted China Customs data recording import and export values to or from each province to all international partners. Controlling for individual characteristics, province and sector of employment, they estimate a positive and statistically significant relationship between a city's market access and Chinese urban workers' wages.

2.2. Liberalization and the strength of the market access effect, 1995 to 2002

While Hering and Poncet (2010) provide evidence that the size of foreign markets influenced Chinese wages as early as 1995, the purpose of this paper is to measure the extent to which wages reflect market access in 2002, and also the contribution of market access to growth in average urban wages between 1995 and 2002. Given extensive changes in Chinese commercial policy and labor market regulation over the period, we predict that market access has become a more important determinant of spatial wage inequality. Our prediction rests on two observations about policy changes in China occurring over this horizon. First, liberalization of China's commercial policy and expansions in domestic infrastructure substantially reduced trade frictions, strengthening the relationship between domestic prices and foreign markets. Secondly, even if no changes to commercial policy had been made over the period, changes in Chinese labor market regulation allowed wages to increasingly reflect market determinants. We briefly review changes in Chinese commercial policy and labor market regulation between 1995 and 2002 to support these claims.

---

[4] Behrens, Lamorgese, Ottaviano and Tabuchi (2009) provide predictions for the case in which FPE does not hold.

[5] Fujita, Krugman, and Venables (1999) provide a fully specified general equilibrium model in which this relationship between market access and wages is identified.

[6] In a recent paper, Fally, Paillacar, and Terra (2010) also estimate the impact of market access on wages controlling for individual worker characteristics. Their study uses Brazilian microdata and also controls for supplier access and firm productivity. They find a positive and significant effect of market access on measured differences in wages across Brazilian states and industries.

62   *F. Kamal et al. / International Review of Economics and Finance 23 (2012) 59–74*

Branstetter and Lardy (2008) describe in detail China's changing commercial policy in the second half of the 1990s. As noted above, China undertook significant unilateral trade liberalization in anticipation of WTO accession (p. 634–9). The government also made far reaching changes to its FDI regime that greatly expanded the freedom with which foreign firms could operate in China (p. 645). Branstetter and Lardy conclude that "the view of the export sector as an enclave with little connection to the local economy became increasingly out of date by the eve of China's accession to the WTO (p. 638)".

Branstetter and Lardy (2008) also question the depiction of China's internal markets as deeply fragmented. While a number of studies document the extent of interprovincial protectionism and market fragmentation (Poncet 2003, Poncet, 2005, Wedeman, 2003, Young, 2000), other research suggests that internal markets are substantially integrated. Bai, et al. (2004) and Holz (2009) provide extensive analysis of industrial specialization, interprovincial trade, and inter-city price dispersion to contradict this characterization. Branstetter and Lardy weigh the conflicting evidence and conclude that "international integration appears to be proceeding along with intranational integration." With this view, access to domestic, as well as foreign, markets could be viewed as an increasingly important determinant of urban wage levels.

While adjusting to the extensive commercial policy reforms undertaken after 1995, the Chinese labor market also was subject to seismic changes unleashed by regulatory reform. As noted by Cai, Park, and Zhao (2008), the 1994 Labor Law facilitated the massive restructuring of state-owned enterprises, which led to layoffs of at least 10 million workers by 1997 and 27 million more from 1998 to 2004.[7] Giles, Park, and Zhang (2005) estimate that the unemployment rate for all urban residents rose from 6.8% in 1996 to 11.1% in 2002. Workers remaining in the state sector were subject to removal of most administrative controls on the determination of wages and benefits. Thus, over the period, wages were largely freed to adjust to market-determined levels.

Hering and Poncet (2010) characterize 1995 as a time in which internal migration was unlikely to affect urban wages.[8] Between 1995 and 2002, however, central and local governments loosened controls on domestic migration, including migration without formal changes in household registration (non-*hukou* migration). Cai, Park, and Zhao use the 2000 census to calculate the stock of migrants, defined as the share of persons residing in a location for more than six months in the prior year whose *hukou* is from outside the city or county. By this definition, they estimate that by the turn of the century migrants comprised 14.6% of the population and 19.6% of the employment in China's cities (p. 191). Therefore, by 2002 labor markets, as well as product markets, were significantly freer and more open than they had been in 1995.

To summarize, we test the NEG model prediction that variation in wages reflects variation in access to domestic and foreign markets. We adapt the approach taken by Hering and Poncet (2010) for 1995 and extend it to an analysis of individual urban wages in 2002, and compare across the two sample years. We predict that (a) wages in both periods are positively and significantly related to the market access of the city in which the worker is employed; and (b) this relationship became significantly larger by 2002. We estimate the relationship for all urban workers, for skilled urban workers and for unskilled urban workers. We also test for differences in the strength of the effect by firm ownership type, state-owned, private-owned, and foreign-owned.

3. Econometric specification, data, and measurement

3.1. Econometric specification

To test our predictions, we specify augmented Mincer equations for 1995 and 2002, estimating the influence of market access on wages in each location. We then test whether the strength of this relationship is statistically different across the two years. We apply this relationship to data on the hourly wages, w, of individual Chinese urban workers, taking the market access (MA) of region j as exogenous. In its simplest form, letting X_i be a vector of personal characteristics of worker i who is employed in region j, this relationship can be expressed as:

$$\ln w_{ij} = a + b \ln MA_j + \gamma X_i + \varepsilon_{ij}, \qquad (1)$$

where a and b are (scalar) coefficients to be estimated, γ is a vector of coefficients to be estimated, and ε_{ij} is an error term assumed to be identically and independently distributed. We estimate Eq. (1) using OLS, allowing for constants specific to province and sector of employment, and in other specification, for constant specific to each province-sector. Observable and unobservable characteristics of workers in the same location may be correlated, causing OLS measure to understate true standard errors. We correct for this problem by clustering errors at the sector-province level and report only robust standard errors.

To see if differences in the market access effect are stronger in 2002 than in 1995, we estimate (1), pooling the data across years and interacting all terms with a year indicator variable. This method allows us to test whether cross-year differences in the estimated coefficients are statistically significant. Next, separating the sample into skilled and unskilled workers on the basis of their educational attainment, we see if our findings hold for both groups of workers. We also interact the market access measure with the employer's ownership type and test whether market access is a significant determinant of wages for state-owned firms as well as private sector employers.

Our data also allow us to explore whether real wages are related to spatial characteristics of the worker's location. When workers are free to migrate from one location to another, spatial equilibrium requires that workers as well as firms have no unilateral incentive

---

[7] See Cai, Park, and Zhao (2008) for details of SOE restructuring and analysis of labor market responses.

[8] See Hering and Poncet (2010), footnote 7, where they argue that the impact of migrants on urban wages is negligible since urban labor markets are strictly segmented. Our point is that this segmentation deteriorated between 1995 and 2002 due to a relaxation of formal controls.

F. Kamal et al. / International Review of Economics and Finance 23 (2012) 59–74   63

to change location. Hanson (2005) follows Helpman (1998) and posits that areas with high market access will have high nominal wages to keep firms in equilibrium while prices for local nontradeables, such as housing, will rise to equalize real wages. We test this prediction by replacing the market wage on the left-hand side of Eq. (1) with the real wage, defined as the market wage adjusted for living costs. If migration is sufficient to equalize real wages across locations, there should be no statistically significant relationship between market access, MA, and the real wage. We can also test whether this relationship was the same in 1995 and 2002.

Lastly, we test whether the relationship between measured market access and wages is robust to the inclusion of controls for local agglomeration of economic activity. We note that NEG theory predicts that spatial differences in market access will lead to industrial concentration, and thus agglomeration can be viewed as an outcome of the same process that leads to higher wages in spatially advantaged cities. However, agglomeration can be the outcome of other processes that also raise wages and so we test whether the market access effect is robust to the inclusion of these controls.

3.2. Data description

To estimate the Mincer equations, we use data drawn from individual surveys of the Chinese Household Income Project (CHIP) for the years 1995 and 2002.[9] The 1995 surveys cover 6931 households and 21,698 individuals across 11 provinces; the 2002 surveys cover 6835 households and 20,632 individuals in 12 provinces.[10] The surveys do not follow the same individuals over time so CHIP is not an individual panel dataset. We restrict our attention to the sample of the urban population employed in nonagricultural tradable good sectors.[11] We further restrict the sample to only include workers who are between the ages of sixteen and sixty, not self-employed in their primary job and not missing information for years of schooling and years of work experience.[12] To control for the influence of extreme observations of our dependent variable, log hourly wage, we exclude outlier observations identified using Hadi's (1994) method.[13]

The dependent variable, log hourly wage, is constructed from annual deflated labor income and total annual work hours information. Nominal annual income in 2002 is converted to real 1995 yuan using province level Consumer Price Index (CPI) obtained from various issues of the China Statistical Yearbook.[14] Annual total labor income in 2002 is calculated as the sum of basic salary, bonus, allowances and subsidies, and living expenses for the laid-off.[15] Annual work hours are calculated by multiplying average work hours per day by average work days per month and finally by months worked. The reported average work time excludes periods of unemployment as well as days worked in informal activity while unemployed.

The CHIP data allows us to control for a wide set of individual characteristics, including gender, years of schooling, experience, age, communist party membership. These characteristics have been shown to be significant determinants of urban wages by Knight and Song (2008) in both 1995 and 2002.[16] We also control for the ownership type of the worker's employer, private enterprise, state enterprise, or foreign-invested enterprise. Table 1 contains a complete list of variables used and summary statistics for the sample of individuals included in our analysis.

3.3. Measuring market access

While we would prefer to measure market access using the Redding–Venables method, we do not have access to the proprietary China Customs data used by Hering and Poncet (2010) for their application of the method to Chinese provincial trade. As an alternative, we use a measure of market access that is similar to the Harris (1954) nominal market potential measure, with the distance discount factor drawn from Hering and Poncet's gravity model. In other words, we implicitly assume that the competitive conditions China faces in each potential market is constant across destinations. We do not consider our use of nominal market potential, rather than the Redding–Venables real market potential, to be a major drawback to our analysis for several reasons. First, our study concerns variation across Chinese cities. It is clear that the only difference in access to foreign markets between any two Chinese cities is the distance to the nearest port. It is these differences, rather than the market size or competitive

---

[9] 1995 surveys accessed at http://www.icpsr.umich.edu/icpsrweb/ICPSR/studies/03012; 2002 surveys accessed at http://www.icpsr.umich.edu/icpsrweb/ICPSR/studies/21741. We thank Laura Hering and Sandra Poncet for sharing the final sample of the 1995 CHIP that was used in Hering and Poncet (2010).

[10] The data appendix identifies the cities included in both the 1995 and the 2002 CHIP urban surveys.

[11] Hukou status is provided for the 2002 sample only and in that sample 99% of respondents have urban hukou in the resident city.

[12] The questionnaires ask for employment information in the primary and any secondary jobs. Workers are classified based on their primary job situations since most people do not report having second jobs.

[13] See Hering and Poncet (2010) for details on the construction of the final 1995 sample. Of the 6079 individuals in the final sample, we could not construct the market access variable for 555 individuals due to missing information on GDP or land area for seven cities of Fenyang, Bozhou, Tianmen, Geiju, Dali, Wuwei, and Pingliang. Therefore, the final 1995 sample consists of 5555 individuals. In the original 2002 sample 4609 individuals work in the three nonagricultural tradable sectors. Of these, we could not identify the exact location of 76 individuals, 629 are self-employed and 27 are not between the ages of sixteen and sixty. A further 74 are identified as outliers via Hadi's (1994) method. Of the 3803 remaining individuals, 10 have missing wage information. The market access variable could not be constructed for four cities of Fenyang, Geiju, Pu'er Hani-Yi and Dali due to missing information on GDP or land area which led to a further reduction of 135 individuals living in these cities. Therefore, the final 2002 sample consists of 3658 individuals.

[14] The China Statistical Yearbooks report province level CPI with the base year set to the preceding year. The CPI was re-indexed setting 1995 as the base year.

[15] We exclude income not directly from the primary employer, subsidy for minimum living standard, living hardship subsidies from work unit, the second job and sideline income and monetary value of income in kind. We recalculate hourly wage based on all the above sources of income and find the estimation results to be qualitatively unchanged.

[16] Knight and Song (2008) use a slightly different set of individual characteristics to explain the variation in urban wages. We follow the specification used by Hering and Poncet (2010) to facilitate comparison with their results. We note that the exact set of individual controls included in the estimation does not affect our qualitative results.

64   *F. Kamal et al. / International Review of Economics and Finance 23 (2012) 59–74*

Table 1
Variable definitions, sources, and summary statistics.

Variable	Definition	Source	1995		2002	
			Mean	St. Dev.	Mean	St. Dev
Log hourly wage	Annual labor income divided by the total annual work hours, in 1995 yuan	Urban Individual Data, 1995 and 2002	0.88	0.66	2.03	0.82
Female	Categorical variable equal to 1 if individual is female	Urban Individual Data, 1995 and 2002	0.50	0.50	0.43	0.49
Years of schooling	Number of years of education	Urban Individual Data, 1995 and 2002	10.06	2.81	10.77	2.68
Experience	Number of years of work experience	Urban Individual Data, 1995 and 2002	19.91	9.64	20.82	9.35
Age	Age of individual	Urban Individual Data, 1995 and 2002	39.14	9.99	40.54	8.85
Age^2	Age squared	Urban Individual Data, 1995 and 2002	1631.71	787.55	1721.41	702.92
Communist	Categorical variable equal to 1 if individual is a communist party member	Urban Individual Data, 1995 and 2002	0.19	0.39	0.24	0.42
Log minimum living cost	The average household expenses per month needed to maintain a minimum living standard in the city where the worker resides, in 1995 yuan	Urban Household Data, 1995 and 2002	6.65	0.30	7.70	0.35
Log market access (MA)	Sum of international and domestic market access, in billion 1995 yuan[a]	China Statistical Yearbook, 1998 and 2003; Urban Statistical Yearbook, 1998 and 2003	0.38	0.40	0.67	0.46
Log employment density	Total employment in a city, per km^2	1998 and 2002 Annual Surveys of Industrial Production	3.42	1.08	2.97	1.22
Log firm density	Total number of firms in a city, per km^2	1998 and 2002 Annual Surveys of Industrial Production	−2.57	1.07	−2.77	1.26
Log population	Total population in a city, in ten thousand people	Urban Statistical Yearbook, 1998 and 2003	6.16	0.51	6.33	0.61

Notes: The table reports the sample means. There are 44 and 56 cities in 1995 and 2002 respectively. Domestic market access is the city-specific, distance-weighted sum of Chinese city 1997 and 2002 GDP, in billion 1995 yuan.
[a] International market access is the city-specific, distance-weighted sum of export partner 1997 and 2002 GDP, in billion 1995 yuan.

conditions of foreign markets that drive the cross-city variation in market access that we use to identify the market access effect. Secondly, a direct comparison of estimation results using the Redding–Venables measure and the Harris measure is provided by Head and Mayer (2006). They report that while the Harris measure yields a larger estimated market access coefficient, the root mean squared error of the regressions are virtually identical. Either measure, as well as other alternatives, produces a significant market access coefficient.

To create our market access measure, we decompose total market access of a city into domestic and international market access:

$$MA_c = MA_c(D) + MA_c(I), \hspace{3cm} (2)$$

where c, D, I denote city, domestic, and international respectively. Each component is a distance weighted sum of real GDP as described below.

3.4. Domestic market access

Domestic market access measures the potential demand faced by city c firms from other cities within China. It can be thought of as the sum of demand from within the city itself, from other cities within the province it resides in, and from all other cities in China.

$$MA_c(D) = GDP_c/dist_{cc}^\delta + \sum_{k \in Province} GDP_{c_k}/dist_{cc_k}^\delta + \sum_{l \in China} GDP_{c_l}/dist_{cc_l}^\delta \hspace{1cm} (3)$$

where the first term is the city's own GDP weighted by $dist_{cc}^\delta$, the distance between city c and itself, and δ is a discount factor.[17] We assume the discount factor to be 1.5 in all our regressions, drawing this from the gravity estimates for Chinese provinces in Hering and Poncet (2010).[18] The second term is the sum of GDP of all other cities, c_k, in province k where city c is located but excluding city c, weighted by the sum of distance between city c and all other cities within province k. The final term is the sum of GDP of all other cities, c_l, in provinces excluding province k, weighted by the sum of distance between city c and these cities. We use city level GDP data in 1997 and 2002 to construct (3).[19] City level GDP is converted to real values using the national GDP deflator.[20] Distance, in kilometers, is calculated as the arc distance between the geographic centroid of each city using ArcGIS software.

[17] The distance between a city and itself is calculated as the average distance between a producer and consumer in a circular country as $\left(\frac{2}{3}\sqrt{area_c/\pi}\right)^\delta$ following Amiti and Javorcik (2008), Head and Mayer (2004), Hering and Poncet (2010), and Redding and Venables (2004).
[18] We carried out robustness checks using a range of values between 1 and 2 and we find our benchmark results to remain qualitatively unchanged.
[19] City level GDP data is unavailable prior to 1996. We follow Hering and Poncet (2010) who construct their market access variable using information as of 1997.
[20] We also deflate city GDP using province level CPI and the results are qualitatively unchanged.

F. Kamal et al. / International Review of Economics and Finance 23 (2012) 59–74 65

3.5. International market access

International market access measures the potential demand faced by city c firms from the rest of the world:

$$MA_c(I) = \sum_{j \, Export \, Partners} GDP_j / \left(dist_{cp} + dist_{pj} \right)^\delta, \tag{4}$$

where j and p denote export partner and port city respectively. International market access is calculated as the sum of GDP of China's 40 major export destinations weighted by the sum of the distance between city c and the nearest port city p and the distance between the port city and the capital city of the partner country, j.[21] Export partner GDP is drawn from the World Bank's World Development Indicators.[22] There are three major port cities in China – Guangzhou, Shanghai, and Tianjin. We assume that goods are first delivered from a city to a port prior to being exported out of China (Lin, 2005). Therefore, we first determine which of these three port cities is closest to city c and then calculate the arc distance between the two cities and finally the arc distance between the closest port city and the capital city of China's export destinations.[23]

Fig. 1 shows total market access and its constituent parts for all cities that appear in both waves of the CHIP. It is interesting to note that there is very little growth in the average distance weighted foreign real market access, MA(I), as shown by the first column for each year. In contrast, due to the rapid growth of real GDP within China, the average distance-weighted domestic market access, MA(D), almost doubles, as shown by the second columns in Fig. 1. It is domestic market growth that drives the 75% increase in the value of the average market access measures for cities in our sample.

4. Estimation results

4.1. Market access and individual wages, 1995 and 2002

Results of estimating the augmented Mincer Eq. (1) for the full sample of urban workers are shown in Table 2. The first panel provides wage regressions for 1995 and 2002 estimated without including the market access measure. These equations also contain occupation controls and sector-province fixed effects. We cluster errors at the sector-province level. As expected from previous research, all of the individual worker characteristics, as well as indicators for employer ownership type, are highly statistically significant and have the expected sign. Overall, the included variables explain 52% of the variance in wages. The third column of the panel provides the difference in the coefficient estimate for 2002, relative to that estimated for 1995. We find that the penalty for being female is somewhat higher in 2002, experience is somewhat less valued, and the return to education has doubled. Knight and Song (2008) use the same dataset to provide an extensive discussion and analysis of changes over time in urban wage determinants.

Our focus here is on the influence of market access on urban wages and coefficient estimates for 1995 and 2002 can be found in panels (2) and (3) in Table 2. Panel (2), estimated with sector fixed effects and province fixed effects, and panel (3), estimated with sector-province fixed effects, tell the same story. The estimated elasticity of wages with respect to the market access of the worker's location is 0.28 for the 1995 sample and 0.67 for the 2002 sample, and both are highly statistically significant. As predicted from our consideration of commercial and labor market policy changes, wages are more responsive to spatial differences in potential profits by 2002. The estimated elasticity for 2002 is 2.4 times the elasticity estimated for 1995 and this difference is highly significant. Perhaps surprisingly, the fit of the equation is not noticeably improved by the inclusion of our market access measure, which may be due to the inclusion of province fixed effects in all equations as these control for a large share of the variation in access to coastal ports and domestic markets.[24]

4.2. Quantile regression

In our basic estimations, shown in Table 2, we achieved an R-squared value of 0.52, indicating that the explanatory variables in the base model explain only about 50% of the variation in individual hourly wages. Although we control for an individual worker's years of schooling, we do not have an individual level panel and, therefore, cannot include individual fixed effects to control for individual unobservables. A particular concern is that more able workers have a higher likelihood of migrating to larger cities.[25]

---

[21] The countries considered are Argentina, Australia, Austria, Belgium, Brazil, Brunei, Cambodia, Canada, Chile, South Korea, Denmark, Egypt, Finland, France, Germany, Hong Kong, India, Indonesia, Italy, Japan, Laos, Macao, Malaysia, Mexico, Netherlands, New Zealand, Philippines, Poland, Russia, Saudi Arabia, Singapore, South Africa, Spain, Switzerland, Taiwan, Thailand, U.A.E., U.K., U.S.A., and Vietnam. These countries together represented approximately 92% and 90% of China's total exports in 1997 and 2002 respectively.

[22] GDP in constant 2000 USD was converted to 1995 USD using the implicit GDP price deflator in Table B-3, *Economic Report of the President*, U.S. Government Printing Office, 2006. It was converted to Chinese RMB by applying the 1995 official exchange rate, 8.3514, published in the IMF's 2006 *International Financial Statistics*.

[23] To calculate the distance between a port city and capital city of China's export partners we first obtain the latitude and longitude points for each location at http://www.mashupsoft.com/maps/latlonlocator. We input this information into the arc distance formula provided at www.nau.edu/~cvm/latlongdist.html to obtain the arc distance between any pair of locations.

[24] While it would be desirable to decompose the market access measure and allow separate coefficients for domestic and international market access, the two measures have a very high cross-sectional correlation (0.83) and this makes identification of the separate influences difficult. Unreported regression results suggest that the influence of domestic MA has risen over time, consistent with decreased interprovincial trade barriers.

[25] A higher migration probability has been estimated for more highly educated workers by Knight and Song (1999) using a rural household survey and logistic regression.

66   F. Kamal et al. / International Review of Economics and Finance 23 (2012) 59–74

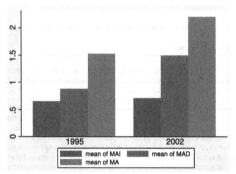

Notes: MA refers to total market access, MAI refers to international market access, and
MAD refers to domestic market access, as defined in the text. The graph shows the mean
value of each measure for the sample of cities that appears in both the 1995 and 2002
waves of the Chinese Household Income Project.

Fig. 1. Composition of the market access measure (in 1995 billion yuan), 1995 and 2002.

Table 2
Market access and wages, 1995 and 2002.

Dependent variable: log hourly wage									
	(1)			(2)			(3)		
	1995	2002	Difference	1995	2002	Difference	1995	2002	Difference
Market access									
Log MA	–	–	–	0.281***	0.666***	0.385***	0.286***	0.668***	0.382***
				(0.034)	(0.067)	(0.067)	(0.041)	(0.065)	(0.069)
Individual characteristics									
Female	−0.100***	−0.149***	−0.049**	−0.098***	−0.141***	−0.042	−0.099***	−0.138***	−0.040*
	(0.017)	(0.019)	(0.023)	(0.021)	(0.019)	(0.034)	(0.018)	(0.020)	(0.023)
Years of schooling	0.023***	0.046***	0.023***	0.023***	0.043***	0.021***	0.022***	0.042***	0.020***
	(0.004)	(0.005)	(0.006)	(0.002)	(0.004)	(0.003)	(0.004)	(0.005)	(0.006)
Experience	0.017***	0.005*	−0.012***	0.017***	0.004	−0.013***	0.017***	0.004	−0.013***
	(0.002)	(0.003)	(0.004)	(0.002)	(0.005)	(0.004)	(0.003)	(0.003)	(0.004)
Age	0.068***	0.062***	−0.006	0.067***	0.070***	0.004	0.067***	0.068***	0.001***
	(0.011)	(0.013)	(0.015)	(0.007)	(0.013)	(0.006)	(0.011)	(0.013)	(0.000)
Age²	−0.001***	−0.001***	0.000	−0.001***	−0.001***	0.000	−0.001***	−0.001***	0.000
	(0.000)	(0.000)	(0.000)	(0.000)	(0.000)	(0.000)	(0.000)	(0.000)	(0.000)
Communist	0.073***	0.079**	0.006	0.077***	0.092**	0.016	0.075***	0.086**	0.011
	(0.024)	(0.029)	(0.036)	(0.016)	(0.034)	(0.032)	(0.024)	(0.029)	(0.036)
Ownership dummies									
State-owned	0.156***	0.143***	−0.013	0.158***	0.148***	−0.011	0.158***	0.141***	−0.017
	(0.025)	(0.039)	(0.034)	(0.011)	(0.023)	(0.034)	(0.024)	(0.037)	(0.034)
Foreign-owned	0.326***	0.356***	0.030	0.316***	0.331***	0.015	0.316***	0.331***	0.015
	(0.031)	(0.086)	(0.101)	(0.011)	(0.034)	(0.038)	(0.011)	(0.084)	(0.103)
Occupation dummies	Yes	Yes	Yes	Yes	Yes	Yes	Yes	Yes	Yes
Sector and province									
Fixed effects	No	No	No	Yes	Yes	Yes	No	No	No
Sector-province fixed effects	Yes	Yes	Yes	No	No	No	Yes	Yes	Yes
Observations		9213			9213			9213	
R²		0.52			0.52			0.53	

Notes: Robust standard errors in parentheses. Private-owned is the left out category.
  * 10% significance.
  ** 5% significance.
  *** 1% significance.

F. Kamal et al. / International Review of Economics and Finance 23 (2012) 59–74   67

Table 3
Market access and wages, quantile regression, 1995 and 2002.

Dependent variable: log hourly wage												
Quantile	0.125				0.375			0.625			0.875		
	1995	2002	Difference	1995	2002	Difference	1995	2002	Difference	1995	2002	Difference
Market access												
Log MA	0.355***	0.677***	0.324***	0.309***	0.622***	0.313***	0.221***	0.616***	0.395***	0.160**	0.568***	0.408***
	(0.061)	(0.070)	(0.093)	(0.045)	(0.048)	(0.066)	(0.048)	(0.052)	(0.071)	(0.060)	(0.068)	(0.091)*
Occupation dummies	Yes	Yes	Yes	Yes	Yes	Yes	Yes	Yes	Yes	Yes	Yes	Yes
Sector-province fixed effects	Yes	Yes	Yes	Yes	Yes	Yes	Yes	Yes	Yes	Yes	Yes	Yes
Observations	9213				9213			9213			9213		
Pseudo R²	0.33				0.39			0.43			0.43		

Notes: Private-owned is the left out category. The specification is the same as in Table 2, panel 3; only the market access coefficients are reported.
  * 10% significance.
  ** 5% significance.
  *** 1% significance.

Because we cannot control for heterogeneous worker ability, we may erroneously attribute higher observed wages to greater local market access rather than to ability. To shed some light on what type of unobservable factors might be at play, we follow Knight and Song (2008) and estimate quantile regressions.

Quantile regression, introduced by Koenker and Bassett (1978), models the relationship between a set of explanatory variables, X, and the conditional quantiles of the outcome variable, Y given $X=x$ in contrast to ordinary least-squares regression which models the relationship between X and the conditional mean of Y given $X=x$.[26] In the context of this study, this allows us to compare the wage equation across different points in the conditional wage distribution. Differences in the coefficients on an explanatory variable of interest across various quantiles could reveal a relationship between itself and the unobserved variables. We carry out quantile regressions for values of the quantile $q = 0.125, 0.375, 0.625$, and 0.875 and the results are reported in Table 3.

The specification is identical to that in Table 2, but our focus is on the market access variable. We observe that in each year and at each quantile, the coefficient on market access is highly significant and similar across each of our four chosen quantiles. This is in contrast to what we would expect under our hypothesis that higher ability individuals tend to migrate to larger cities. Assuming that the conditional wages represent unobserved ability, we would expect the effect of market access to be lower for higher ability individuals and therefore decrease as we move up the quantiles. However, the estimated market access coefficient remains positive and highly significant and is not significantly different across the quantiles for each of the years, lending confidence that the coefficient on market access is not contaminated by the effect of unobserved worker ability.

4.3. Differences across education groups

Table 4 presents Mincer regressions including the market access measure, with the full sample split into two subgroups based on educational attainment. Skilled workers are defined as those who have completed at least nine years of schooling, while those with fewer years of schooling are classified as unskilled workers. For skilled workers, we see that market access is a significant determinant of the wage in both 1995 and 2002. As estimated using the full sample, the strength of the market access effect increased over the period and this difference is highly statistically significant. Surprisingly, perhaps, we estimate very similar wage elasticities for the unskilled worker sample, with the estimate for 2002 very close to that found for the skilled worker sample. However, there is more variation within this smaller subsample and the difference in the estimated coefficients across the years is not significant. Thus, while we estimate a larger elasticity for low skilled wages in 2002 than in 1995, we cannot reject the hypothesis that wage responsiveness to spatial advantages has not increased over the period for unskilled workers. One possibility is that unskilled migration has accelerated over the period due to policy changes discussed above and that this internal labor reallocation has dampened the response of wages for low-skilled workers to enhanced export opportunities.[27]

---

[26] Estimates from quantile regression models are solutions to the problem of minimizing the sum of absolute residuals. (Koenker and Bassett, 1978; Koenker and Hallock, 2001).

[27] Although a Heckscher–Ohlin framework suggests that capital inflows for export processing in China raise the relative price of skilled workers if such processing is skill intensive, such a result need not hold in other settings. Chakrabarti and Mitra (2010), in a model with asymmetric capital adjustment costs and four goods, show that offshoring-induced capital inflow will not raise the skilled wage premium. Thus, inferences about how deeper economic integration influences domestic skilled and unskilled wages depend on the assumed input–output structure.

68   F. Kamal et al. / International Review of Economics and Finance 23 (2012) 59–74

Table 4
Market access and wages, by education group, 1995 and 2002.

Dependent variable: log hourly wage	Skilled			Unskilled		
	1995	2002	Difference	1995	2002	Difference
Market access						
Log MA	0.270***	0.683***	0.414***	0.313*	0.653***	0.340
	(0.045)	(0.069)	(0.096)	(0.158)	(0.164)	(0.265)
Individual characteristics						
Female	−0.074***	−0.121***	−0.050*	−0.179***	−0.263**	−0.084
	(0.017)	(0.020)	(0.027)	(0.039)	(0.092)	(0.075)
Years of schooling	0.022***	0.046***	0.024**	0.013	0.014	0.002
	(0.003)	(0.008)	(0.008)	(0.011)	(0.012)	(0.018)
Experience	0.013***	0.004	−0.008**	0.023***	0.002	−0.021**
	(0.003)	(0.003)	(0.004)	(0.004)	(0.007)	(0.007)
Age	0.064***	0.066***	0.003	0.083**	0.085**	0.002
	(0.010)	(0.013)	(0.016)	(0.028)	(0.041)	(0.027)
Age^2	−0.001***	−0.001***	0.000	−0.001***	−0.001***	0.000
	(0.000)	(0.000)	(0.000)	(0.000)	(0.000)	(0.000)
Communist	0.089***	0.084**	−0.005	0.016	0.089	0.073
	(0.024)	(0.032)	(0.041)	(0.068)	(0.054)	(0.082)
Ownership dummies						
State-owned	0.155***	0.152***	−0.003	0.167***	0.016	−0.151
	(0.031)	(0.038)	(0.035)	(0.042)	(0.090)	(0.091)
Foreign-owned	0.307***	0.341***	0.034	0.371***	0.233	−0.138
	(0.046)	(0.088)	(0.092)	(0.104)	(0.143)	(0.151)
Occupation dummies	Yes	Yes	Yes	Yes	Yes	Yes
Sector-province fixed effects	Yes	Yes	Yes	Yes	Yes	Yes
Observations		7382			1831	
R^2		0.54			0.47	

Notes: Robust standard errors in parentheses; Private-owned is the left out category.
 * 10% significance.
 ** 5% significance.
 *** 1% significance.

4.4. Real wages and market access

Consideration of internal labor migration leads us to estimate the relationship between spatial advantages and real wages. We define the real wage as the market wage divided by the minimum expense needed to reside in the city where the worker lives. [28] NEG theory predicts that if workers are sufficiently mobile across cities, spatial advantages will be shifted away from workers to the owners of fixed factors, through higher land prices and higher rents for housing and other land improvements.

Table 5a provides the results of regressing market access and individual characteristics on this measure of the real wage, including in the estimating equation provincial fixed effects. The first panel shows coefficient estimates for the full sample. Market access is found to be an insignificant determinant of real wages in both years, with the point estimate actually negative for 1995. The estimated coefficient for 2002 is positive, however, and the difference in the coefficients across the two years is significant. This evidence suggests that intra-provincial migration is sufficiently large in both periods for fixed factors to gain the within-province advantages created by market access. Looking at panel (2) and panel (3) in Table 5a, we see that market access is not a significant determinant of within-province real wages differences for skilled workers or unskilled workers. Mobility of both types of workers appears to be sufficient to shift rents forward to other factor owners.

Table 5b shows coefficient estimates for the same regression, but omitting provincial fixed effects in the estimation. In contrast to the results obtained looking within provinces, we find that workers in provinces with better market access receive higher wages net of living costs than those in less advantageous locations. The first panel provides results for the full sample and we

[28] Average monthly minimum living cost for each city in the sample is calculated as follows. The CHIP surveys report the monthly minimum living expenses for each individual's household. The survey in 1995 asks: "According to actual conditions in your household, please estimate the monthly cost of maintaining a minimum standard of living for the whole family in 1995 (Yuan)". The survey question in 2002 asks: "According to your actual situation, please estimate how much household living expenses per month are needed to maintain a minimum living standard in 2002? (Yuan)". The monthly minimum household living expenses are averaged for every city in each sample to arrive at the average monthly minimum living cost. Nominal monthly living cost in 2002 is converted to 1995 yuan using province level Consumer Price Index (CPI) obtained from various issues of the China Statistical Yearbook. The monthly minimum living cost is converted to hourly terms using the total number of hours worked per month.

F. Kamal et al. / International Review of Economics and Finance 23 (2012) 59–74

69

Table 5a
Market access and wages net of living costs, 1995 and 2002, including provincial fixed effects.

Dependent variable: (log hourly wage − log hourly living costs)[a]									
	All			Skilled			Unskilled		
	1995	2002	Difference	1995	2002	Difference	1995	2002	Difference
Market access									
Log MA	−0.022	0.147	0.170**	−0.043	0.161	0.204**	0.012	0.143	0.131
	(0.069)	(0.094)	(0.068)	(0.079)	(0.103)	(0.093)	(0.144)	(0.166)	(0.235)
Individual characteristics									
Female	−0.096***	−0.118***	−0.021	−0.076***	−0.103***	−0.027	−0.169***	−0.233**	−0.064
	(0.021)	(0.020)	(0.026)	(0.019)	(0.022)	(0.031)	(0.043)	(0.097)	(0.080)
Years of schooling	0.014***	0.035***	0.021***	0.013***	0.040***	0.027***	0.009	0.007	−0.001
	(0.004)	(0.006)	(0.005)	(0.003)	(0.008)	(0.008)	(0.012)	(0.017)	(0.023)
Experience	0.015***	0.000	−0.015***	0.011***	0.001	−0.010**	0.023***	0.000	−0.023**
	(0.002)	(0.003)	(0.004)	(0.003)	(0.004)	(0.004)	(0.004)	(0.004)	(0.009)
Age	0.067***	0.065***	−0.003	0.066***	0.065***	−0.001	0.083***	0.087**	0.004
	(0.010)	(0.014)	(0.014)	(0.010)	(0.013)	(0.016)	(0.024)	(0.043)	(0.032)
Age²	−0.001***	−0.001***	0.000	−0.001***	−0.001***	0.000	−0.001***	−0.001***	0.000
	(0.000)	(0.000)	(0.000)	(0.000)	(0.000)	(0.000)	(0.000)	(0.000)	(0.000)
Communist	0.074***	0.088***	0.013	0.095***	0.081**	−0.014	−0.013	0.124***	0.137
	(0.023)	(0.032)	(0.037)	(0.022)	(0.035)	(0.041)	(0.058)	(0.059)	(0.082)
Ownership dummies									
State-owned	0.150***	0.143***	−0.007	0.153***	0.144***	−0.009	0.142***	0.053	−0.090
	(0.020)	(0.043)	(0.042)	(0.029)	(0.044)	(0.042)	(0.041)	(0.098)	(0.103)
Foreign-owned	0.269***	0.316***	0.047	0.271***	0.317***	0.046	0.280***	0.253*	−0.027
	(0.040)	(0.083)	(0.096)	(0.045)	(0.085)	(0.086)	(0.087)	(0.136)	(0.150)
Occupation dummies	Yes	Yes	Yes	Yes	Yes	Yes	Yes	Yes	Yes
Sector-province fixed effects	Yes	Yes	Yes	Yes	Yes	Yes	Yes	Yes	Yes
Observations	9213			7382			1831		
R²	0.17			0.16			0.25		

Notes: Robust standard errors in parentheses. Private-owned is the left out category.
[a] Hourly living cost is calculated as monthly minimum living cost divided by the number of hours worked per month.
   * 10% significance.
   ** 5% significance.
   *** 1% significance.

see that the elasticity of the real wage with respect to market access is 0.059 in 1995 and 0.181 in 2002 and that the difference is significant across the two years. Very similar elasticities are estimated for both the sample of skilled workers and the sample of unskilled workers. While we cannot rule out the influence of unobserved provincial characteristics, these results suggest that barriers to cross-provincial migration are sufficiently high for all workers, skilled and unskilled, to deter the real-wage equalizing impact of internal migration. Workers in locations with better market access earn wages that more than compensate for the higher living costs of spatially advantaged cities. These results are consistent with the view that market access is an independent cause of coastal-inland income inequality.

4.5. Heterogeneity by employer type

We are particularly interested in variation in responsiveness to market access in the wages paid by various types of employers. As noted earlier, between 1995 and 2002, state-owned enterprises (SOEs) shed excess labor and were freed of many administrative controls on wage setting. Hering and Poncet (2010) found a significant relationship between market access and the wages of worker employed by SOEs, but also that the estimated elasticity was substantially smaller than that found for private and foreign enterprises. Table 6 shows our estimates of market access elasticities by firm ownership type for 1995 and 2002. Our results for 1995 are qualitatively similar to those obtained by Hering and Poncet – market access is a significant determinant of wages for all firm types, but the responsiveness of wages in SOEs is significantly less than that of private and foreign enterprise.

For all ownership types, the estimated elasticity of the wage with respect to market access was larger in the 2002 sample than in the 1995 sample and the difference across years was statistically significant for both SOEs and private firms. While the estimated coefficient for foreign firms is larger for the 2002 sample than for the 1995 sample, this difference is not statistically significant. Nevertheless, in 2002 wages paid by foreign enterprises are the most responsive to cross-city differences in market access.

As expected given the changes in wage-setting controls, the 2002 sample indicates a much stronger response of SOE wages to market access than does the 1995 sample. The estimated elasticity more than doubles between the two years. This difference is highly significant and is consistent with increasingly market-determined wage levels within the state sector. By 2002, the estimated elasticity for SOEs is two-thirds that estimated for private and foreign firms, compared to an estimated elasticity that is half as large as its private counterparts in 1995.

Table 5b
Market access and wages net of living costs, 1995 and 2002, excluding provincial fixed effects.

Dependent variable: (log hourly wage − log hourly living costs)[a]									
	All			Skilled			Unskilled		
	1995	2002	Difference	1995	2002	Difference	1995	2002	Difference
Market access									
Log MA	0.059***	0.181***	0.122***	0.072***	0.188***	0.116***	0.040	0.161***	0.121***
	(0.019)	(0.043)	(0.025)	(0.010)	(0.043)	(0.033)	(0.051)	(0.025)	(0.030)*
Individual characteristics									
Female	−0.095***	−0.110***	−0.015	−0.073***	−0.096***	−0.023	−0.164***	−0.181***	−0.016
	(0.016)	(0.019)	(0.029)	(0.015)	(0.017)	(0.030)	(0.015)	(0.046)	(0.049)
Years of schooling	0.015	0.035***	0.019***	0.016***	0.043***	0.027**	0.021***	0.004	−0.018
	(0.029)	(0.004)	(0.002)	(0.002)	(0.011)	(0.011)	(0.003)	(0.008)	(0.011)
Experience	0.014***	0.002	−0.013**	0.010***	0.003	−0.007	0.021***	0.001	−0.019***
	(0.001)	(0.005)	(0.004)	(0.001)	(0.004)	(0.004)	(0.003)	(0.010)	(0.007)
Age	0.065***	0.070***	0.005	0.066***	0.071***	0.005	0.072***	0.085***	0.013
	(0.006)	(0.015)	(0.010)	(0.011)	(0.017)	(0.006)	(0.009)	(0.019)	(0.010)
Age²	−0.001***	−0.001***	−0.001***	−0.001***	−0.001***	−0.001***	−0.001***	−0.001***	−0.001***
	(0.000)	(0.000)	(0.000)	(0.000)	(0.000)	(0.000)	(0.000)	(0.000)	(0.000)
Communist	0.078***	0.089***	0.011	0.102***	0.078**	−0.024	−0.026	0.141***	0.167***
	(0.015)	(0.036)	(0.039)	(0.020)	(0.034)	(0.047)	(0.028)	(0.030)	(0.012)
Ownership dummies									
State-owned	0.175***	0.136***	−0.039	0.177***	0.143***	−0.034	0.172***	0.085***	−0.087**
	(0.014)	(0.020)	(0.033)	(0.016)	(0.033)	(0.033)	(0.024)	(0.012)	(0.032)
Foreign-owned	0.245***	0.315***	0.069	0.256***	0.319***	0.063	0.195***	0.238***	0.043
	(0.014)	(0.036)	(0.049)	(0.015)	(0.023)	(0.037)	(0.054)	(0.014)	(0.068)
Occupation dummies	Yes	Yes	Yes	Yes	Yes	Yes	Yes	Yes	Yes
Sector fixed effects	Yes	Yes	Yes	Yes	Yes	Yes	Yes	Yes	Yes
Observations	9213			7382			1831		
R²	0.59			0.60			0.59		

Notes: Robust standard errors in parentheses. Private-owned is the left out category.
[a] Hourly living cost is calculated as monthly minimum living cost divided by the number of hours worked per month.
* 10% significance.
** 5% significance.
*** 1% significance.

4.6. Controlling for agglomeration

NEG theory predicts that freer trade will induce greater concentration of production as firms locate in places with the best access to foreign markets. Thus, increased agglomeration of economic activities may be seen as a by-product of the same forces that relate local wages to foreign market access. However, urban economic theory provides other reasons for firms to cluster spatially and these forces also raise local wages. For example, China's progressive opening to foreign trade led to significant clustering of foreign firms in eastern cities, and these cities are closer to each other than to inland cities. External economies from these foreign firms may have driven wages higher in eastern provinces, even if there is no response of firms to differences across Chinese cities

Table 6
Estimated market access elasticity, by firm ownership type, 1995 and 2002.

Dependent variable: log hourly wage			
	1995	2002	Difference
Market access			
Log MA × state-owned	0.215***	0.463***	0.248***
	(0.053)	(0.070)	(0.074)*
Log MA × private-owned	0.409***	0.610***	0.201**
	(0.043)	(0.095)	(0.090)
Log MA × foreign-owned	0.423***	0.624***	0.200
	(0.080)	(0.143)	(0.173)
Observations		9213	
R²		0.53	

Notes: Robust standard errors in parentheses. Regressions include individual characteristics, ownership, occupation, and province-sector dummies.
* 10% significance.
** 5% significance.
*** 1% significance.

F. Kamal et al. / International Review of Economics and Finance 23 (2012) 59–74   71

in access to markets. If such a mechanism is at work, we may inappropriately attribute the effect of external economies to market access.

To the extent that these agglomerative factors occur at the provincial and sector level, we have controlled for them by our inclusion of province and sector fixed effects. These fixed effects, however, cannot capture the wage effect of spillovers created by the density of economic activity at the city level. Therefore, we include in our wage regressions a number of alternative measures of city-level economic activity. The first measure is employment density, which we create using firm level data from China's Annual Survey of Industrial Production (ASIP). It is defined as total employment in the city per square kilometer. The second measure is firm density, also created using ASIP data, and defined as the number of industrial firms located in the city per square kilometer. Our last measure is city population, a measure of city size.

Results of our wage regressions including these agglomeration measures are shown in Table 7. Panel (1) provides estimated coefficients when we include log employment density, panel (2) provides results when we include firm density, and panel (3) when we include population. In all cases, market access remains a significant determinant of urban wages in both sample years. Interestingly, the agglomeration measures are negatively and insignificantly related to wages in 1995. By 2002, however, a positive relationship between economic density and wages appears and this relationship is significant for employment density, as seen in panel (1). The estimated elasticity of wages with respect to employment density and firm density become significantly larger between 1995 and 2002 and inclusion of either measure reduces the estimated coefficient for market access in 2002. As noted above, a city with market access advantages may be predicted to experience both rising wages and greater firm or employment density in response to liberalization, so these results could indicate this process at work in China. Nevertheless, we cannot rule out the possibility that agglomerative forces other than market access are driving the increased spatial component of urban wage inequality, even as market access remains a significant determinant of wages. Finally, we note that the impact of market access on wages is unchanged by inclusion of a control for

Table 7
Market access and wages, controlling for agglomeration, 1995 and 2002.

Dependent variable: log hourly wage	(1)			(2)			(3)		
	1995	2002	Difference	1995	2002	Difference	1995	2002	Difference
Market access									
Log MA	0.396***	0.422***	0.025	0.525**	0.446***	−0.080	0.288***	0.651***	0.362***
	(0.103)	(0.119)	(0.175)	(0.184)	(0.130)	(0.239)	(0.046)	(0.057)	(0.060)
Agglomeration variables									
Log employment density	−0.031	0.066*	0.098*	–	–	–	–	–	–
	(0.027)	(0.036)	(0.053)						
Log firm density	–	–	–	−0.070	0.061	0.130*	–	–	–
				(0.048)	(0.039)	(0.070)			
Log population	–	–	–	–	–	–	0.011	0.045	0.034
							(0.059)	(0.072)	(0.082)
Individual characteristics									
Female	−0.098***	−0.137***	−0.039	−0.100***	−0.137***	−0.038	−0.099***	−0.138***	−0.039
	(0.018)	(0.024)	(0.024)	(0.018)	(0.020)	(0.024)	(0.018)	(0.020)	(0.024)
Years of schooling	0.022***	0.041***	0.019***	0.023***	0.041***	0.019***	0.022***	0.042***	0.020***
	(0.004)	(0.005)	(0.006)	(0.004)	(0.005)	(0.005)	(0.003)	(0.005)	(0.006)
Experience	0.016***	0.003	−0.013***	0.017***	0.003	−0.013***	0.017***	0.003	−0.013***
	(0.002)	(0.003)	(0.004)	(0.002)	(0.003)	(0.004)	(0.002)	(0.003)	(0.004)
Age	0.068***	0.068***	0.000	0.067***	0.068***	0.000	0.067***	0.068***	0.001
	(0.011)	(0.013)	(0.014)	(0.011)	(0.013)	(0.015)	(0.011)	(0.013)	(0.015)
Age^2	−0.001***	−0.001***	0.000	−0.001***	−0.001***	0.000	−0.001***	−0.001***	0.000
	(0.000)	(0.000)	(0.000)	(0.000)	(0.000)	(0.000)	(0.000)	(0.000)	(0.000)
Communist	0.076***	0.087**	0.011	0.074***	0.087***	0.014	0.075***	0.086***	0.011
	(0.025)	(0.029)	(0.036)	(0.024)	(0.029)	(0.036)	(0.024)	(0.029)	(0.036)
Ownership dummies									
State-owned	0.154***	0.137***	−0.017	0.155***	0.140***	−0.015	0.158***	0.140***	−0.018
	(0.024)	(0.037)	(0.035)	(0.023)	(0.036)	(0.034)	(0.024)	(0.037)	(0.033)
Foreign-owned	0.318***	0.323***	0.005	0.316***	0.326***	0.010	0.316***	0.327***	0.011
	(0.036)	(0.083)	(0.010)	(0.039)	(0.084)	(0.102)	(0.037)	(0.081)	(0.099)
Occupation dummies	Yes	Yes	Yes	Yes	Yes	Yes	Yes	Yes	Yes
Sector-province fixed effects	Yes	Yes	Yes	Yes	Yes	Yes	Yes	Yes	Yes
Observations	9078				9213			9213	
R^2	0.53				0.53			0.53	

Notes: Robust standard errors in parentheses. Private-owned is the omitted category.
* 10% significance.
** 5% significance.
*** 1% significance.

city size. Panel 3 shows that the estimated market access elasticity remains essentially unchanged from that estimated without including population and the increase in the elasticity across the two samples is statistically significant.

4.7. Decomposing the change in mean wages

A decomposition of the change in the mean wage indicates that location is an economically important factor explaining the growth in average wages between 1995 and 2002. The Mincer wage equations take the form $y = f(x)$ where y is the logarithm of individual hourly wages in 1995 yuan and x is the vector of explanatory variables. Using the wage equations, displayed in Table 2, the growth of wages between 1995 and 2002 can be decomposed as,

$$\bar{y}_{2002} - \bar{y}_{1995} = f_{2002}(\bar{x}_{2002} - \bar{x}_{1995}) + (f_{2002} - f_{1995})\bar{x}_{1995},$$

where the first term reflects the effect of differences in the characteristics and the second the effect of differences in the coefficients between 2002 and 1995. We also carry out the alternative decomposition as,

$$\bar{y}_{2002} - \bar{y}_{1995} = f_{1995}(\bar{x}_{2002} - \bar{x}_{1995}) + (f_{2002} - f_{1995})\bar{x}_{2002},$$

Results of this Oaxaca–Blinder decomposition are shown in Table 8.

This decomposition allows us to measure the percentage change in mean wages that is due to the growth in the size of distance-weighted markets access (mean characteristics) and the percentage due to increased importance of market access as a determinant of wages (coefficient estimates). Looking first at the top half of Table 8, we see that between 7.5% (using 2000 as the base year) and 17.5% (using 1995 as the base year) of the difference in mean wages can be explained by the growth in the size of potential markets. As seen in Table 1, the size of markets accessible to workers in the sample grew by 76% between 1995 and 2002. By either decomposition method, changes in accessible market size are the largest determinant of the change in mean wages attributable to changes in worker characteristics.

Mean wages also changed because of differences across the two years in the market value of given worker characteristics. Looking at the bottom half of Table 8, we see that between 22.7% (using 1995 as the base year) and 12.8% (using 2002 as the base year) of the change in mean wages is due to the heightened responsiveness of wages to market access. The increased importance of market access explains as much of the growth in mean wages as does the increased importance of education. Thus, access to richer markets and heightened importance of that market access for factor prices are important explanations for the growth in average urban wages over the period.

Table 8
Blinder–Oaxaca decomposition of the increase in mean wages, 1995–2002.

Percentage due to:	(1)	(2)
Mean characteristics		
Total	10.67	25.93
Market access	7.51	17.52
Female	0.43	0.60
Communist party membership	0.29	0.34
Education	0.99	1.89
Experience	2.51	0.53
Occupation	0.01	0.32
Age	0.19	2.16
Ownership	−2.16	−1.84
Sector-province	0.90	4.41
Coefficients		
Total	89.33	74.07
Market access	22.76	12.75
Female	−1.50	−1.67
Communist party membership	0.23	0.19
Education	19.17	18.27
Experience	−24.59	−22.61
Occupation	−19.68	−19.99
Age	19.04	17.07
Ownership	−0.79	−1.11
Sector-province	−7.09	−10.60

Notes: The explained variable is the difference in mean wages, expressed in 1995 yuan, between 1995 and 2002; Decompositions based on results from Table 2, column 3; column 1 shows the differences in the predictors between 1995 and 2002 weighted by the coefficients and predictor levels in 1995, and column 2 shows the differences in the predictors between 1995 and 2002 weighted by the coefficients and predictor levels in 2002.

F. Kamal et al. / International Review of Economics and Finance 23 (2012) 59–74   73

5. Conclusion

Motivated by the far-reaching liberalization of trade and labor markets undertaken by China after 1995, we measure the extent to which the influence of market access on wages strengthened and influenced wage growth over the subsequent period. We find that the strength of this city characteristic on urban wages did increase and that it contributed in an economically significant way to the growth in average wages between 1995 and 2002. Our estimates indicate that market access influenced wages of both skilled and unskilled workers, with the estimated elasticity almost identical for the two groups. Therefore, while a stronger market access effect is associated with higher average wages, this spatial factor does not seem to be an explanation for a rising skill premium within cities.

Our results for differences in wages adjusted for cost of living indicate the need for further research on how migration influences spatial wage differences. We find no empirical support for the existence of within-province differences in net-of-living-cost wages caused by market access. Thus, our results are suggestive of sufficient within-province labor migration and sufficiently low segmentation between markets for resident and migrant workers to eliminate difference across cities in the same province. When we omit provincial fixed effects from the Mincerian wage regressions, however, our estimates open the possibility of other inferences. Coefficient estimates suggest that barriers to inter-provincial migration are large enough to prevent cross-province labor flows from eliminating the advantages to workers of coastal locations. These findings point to the relevance of further study of cross-province income differences and shifts between owners of mobile and fixed factors.

We also find that while the wages of workers employed by state-owned enterprises had the lowest responsiveness to intercity differences in market access, it is this group of workers for whom the market access effect increased the most. The evidence is consistent with other measures of increasingly market-driven behavior by state enterprises. Overall, our study provides evidence directly from the wages of urban workers that the structure of Chinese product and labor markets has been significantly influenced by ongoing commercial and regulatory policy changes.

Data Appendix

Province	Cities in 1995 CHIP	Cities in 2002 CHIP
Beijing	Beijing	Beijing
Shanxi	Changzhi, Datong, Fenyang, Taiyuan, Yangquan	Changzhi, Datong, Fenyang, Hunyuan, Taiyuan, Yuncheng, Xing
Liaoning	Dalian, Jinzhou, Shenyang	Changtu, Dalian, Jinzhou, Shenyang, Wafangdian
Jiangsu	Changzhou, Dafeng, Nanjing, Nantong, Suqian, Taixing, Wuxi, Xuzhou, Yixing	Dafeng, Nanjing, Nantong, Taixing, Suqian, Wuxi, Xuzhou, Yangzhou, Yixing
Anhui	Bengbu, Bozhou, Hefei, Huainan, Tongcheng, Wuhu	Bengbu, Bozhou, Hefei, Huainan, She, Wuhu
Henan	Huixian, Kaifeng, Pingdingshan, Xiangcheng, Xinxiang, Zhengzhou	Gushi, Hua, Huixian, Kaifeng, Pingdingshan, Xiangcheng, Xinxiang, Zhengzhou
Hubei	Honghu, Huangshi, Macheng, Tianmen, Wuhan, Xiangfan	Honghu, Jingzhou, Wuhan, Xiangfan, Xianning, Xishui, Yichang
Guangdong	Foshan, Guangzhou, Huizhou, Puning, Shenzhen, Shunde, Zhanjiang, Zhaoqing	Foshan, Guangzhou, Huizhou, Puning, Shaoguan, Shunde, Zhanjiang, Zhaoqing
Chongqing	Chongqing	Chongqing
Sichuan	Chengdu, Guangyuan, Leshan, Luzhou, Zigong	Chengdu, Emeishan, Guanguyuan, Luzhou, Nanchong, Neijiang
Yunnan	Dali, Geiju, Kunming, Xuanwei	Dali, Geiju, Kunming, Lijiang Naxi, Pu'er Hani-Yi, Xuanwei
Gansu	Lanzhou, Pingliang, Wuwei	Lanzhou, Pingliang, Wuwei

Note: These are cities in the final samples.

Sectors included in 1995: (i) industry; (ii) transportation, communications, posts and telecommunications; and (iii) commerce and trade, restaurants and catering, materials supply, marketing and warehousing.

Sectors included in 2002: (i) manufacturing; (ii) transportation, storage, post office and communication; and (iii) wholesale, retail and food services.

Ownership categories in 1995: state-owned enterprises at the central or provincial level (central SOEs), local publicly owned enterprises (local SOEs), urban collective enterprises, private enterprises, foreign-invested enterprises, Sino-foreign joint ventures, and others which includes township and village enterprises.

Ownership categories in 2002: state-owned enterprises at the central or provincial level (central SOEs), local publicly owned enterprises (local SOEs), urban collective enterprises, private enterprises, foreign-invested enterprises, Sino-foreign joint ventures, and others which includes rural private and rural individual enterprises and other share-holding companies. An additional category, state share-holding company, appears in the 2002 individual survey. We experimented including this category with central SOEs and local SOEs.[29] Our benchmark results are invariant to the alternative categorizations. Therefore, we chose to display results which include this category with central SOEs to minimize the number of tables.

[29] Huang (2008) provides evidence that share-holding companies are mostly privatized state-owned firms at local levels of government. Levels of local government in China include the province, prefecture, county, township and village.

74   *F. Kamal et al. / International Review of Economics and Finance 23 (2012) 59–74*

We collapse the various ownership categories in each of the survey years into three broad types — state-owned, private-owned, and foreign-owned enterprises. State-owned includes central and local SOEs; private-owned includes urban collective enterprises, private enterprises, and other enterprises; and foreign-owned includes foreign-invested enterprises, and Sino-foreign joint ventures.

References

Amiti, M., & Javorcik, B. S. (2008). Trade costs and location of foreign firms in China. *Journal of Development Economics, 85*(1–2), 194–217.
Bai, C. E., Du, Y., Tao, Z., & Tong, S. (2004). Local protectionism and regional specialization: Evidence from China's industries. *Journal of International Economics, 63*, 397–418.
Behrens, K., Lamorgese, A. R., Ottaviano, G. I. P., & Tabuchi, T. (2004). Testing the home market effect in a multi-country world: The theory. *CEPR Discussion Paper No. 4468*.
Behrens, K., Lamorgese, A. R., Ottaviano, G. I. P., & Tabuchi, T. (2009). Beyond the home market effect: Market size and specialization in a multi-country world. *Journal of International Economics, 79*, 259–265.
Branstetter, L., & Lardy, N. (2008). China's embrace of globalization. In L. Brandt, & T. G. Rawski (Eds.), *China's great economic transformation*. New York, NY: Cambridge University Press.
Cai, F., Park, A., & Zhao, Y. (2008). The Chinese labor market in the reform era. In L. Brandt, & T. G. Rawski (Eds.), *China's great economic transformation*. New York, NY: Cambridge University Press.
Chakrabarti, A., & Mitra, R. (2010). Skilled–unskilled wage inequality and offshore outsourcing with asymmetric adjustment costs. *International Review of Economics and Finance, 19*(2), 340–345.
Fally, T., Paillacar, R., & Terra, C. (2010). Economic geography and wages in Brazil: Evidence from micro-data. *Journal of Development Economics, 91*, 155–168.
Fujita, M., Krugman, P., & Venables, A. J. (1999). *The spatial economy: Cities, regions and international trade*. Cambridge, MA: MIT Press.
Gallagher, M. E., & Jiang, J. (2002). China's national labor law: Introduction and analysis. *Chinese Law and Government, 35*, 3–15.
Giles, J., Park, A., & Zhang, J. (2005). What is China's true unemployment rate? *China Economic Review, 16*, 149–170.
Gustafsson, B., Shi, L., Sicular, T., & Ximing, Y. (2008). Income inequality and spatial differences. In B. A. Gustafsson, L. Shi, & T. Sicular (Eds.), *Inequality and public policy in China*. New York, NY: Cambridge University Press.
Hadi, A. S. (1994). A modification of a method for the detection of outliers in multivariate samples. *Journal of the Royal Statistics Society, 56*(B), 393–396.
Hanson, G. (2005). Market potential, increasing returns, and geographic concentration. *Journal of International Economics, 67*, 1–24.
Harris, C. D. (1954). The market as a factor in the localization of industry in the United States. *Annals of the Association of American Geographers, 64*, 315–348.
Head, K., & Mayer, T. (2004). The empirics of agglomeration and trade. In V. Henderson, & J. F. Thisse (Eds.), *Handbook of regional and urban economics, Volume 4*. Amsterdam: Elsevier.
Head, K., & Mayer, T. (2006). Regional wage and employment responses to market potential in the EU. *Regional Science and Urban Economics, 36*, 573–594.
Helpman, E. (1998). The size of regions. In D. Pines, E. Sadka, & Y. Zilcha (Eds.), *Topics in public economics: Theoretical and applied analysis*. Cambridge, UK: Cambridge University Press.
Helpman, E., & Krugman, P. (1985). *Market structure and foreign trade*. Cambridge, MA: MIT Press.
Hering, L., & Poncet, S. (2010). Market access and individual wages: Evidence from China. *The Review of Economics and Statistics, 92*(1), 145–159.
Holz, C. (2009). No razor's edge: Reexamining Alwyn Young's evidence for increasing interprovincial trade barriers in China. *The Review of Economics and Statistics, 91*(3), 599–616.
Huang, Y. (2008). *Capitalism with Chinese characteristics*. New York, NY: Cambridge University Press.
Knight, J., & Song, L. (1999). *The rural–urban divide: Economic disparities and interactions in China*. Oxford, U.K: Oxford University Press.
Knight, J., & Song, L. (2008). China's emerging urban wage structure. In B. A. Gustafsson, L. Shi, & T. Sicular (Eds.), *Inequality and public policy in China* (pp. 1995–2002). New York, NY: Cambridge University Press.
Koenker, R., & Bassett, G. W. (1978). Regression quantiles. *Econometrica, 46*, 33–50.
Koenker, R., & Hallock, K. F. (2001). Quantile regression. *Journal of Economic Perspectives, 15*(4), 143–156.
Krugman, P. (1991). Increasing returns and economic geography. *Journal of Political Economy, 99*, 483–499.
Lin, S. (2005). International trade, location and wage inequality in China. In R. Kanbur, & A. J. Venables (Eds.), *Spatial inequality and development*. New York, NY: Oxford University Press.
Mincer, J. (1974). *Schooling, experience, and earnings*. New York: Columbia University Press.
Niepmann, F., & Felbermayr, G. (2010). Globalisation and the spatial concentration of production. *The World Economy, 33*, 680–709.
Poncet, S. (2003). Measuring Chinese domestic and international integration. *China Economic Review, 14*, 1–21.
Poncet, S. (2005). A fragmented China: Measure and determinants of Chinese domestic market disintegration. *Review of International Economics, 13*(3), 409–430.
Redding, S., & Venables, A. (2004). Economic geography and international inequality. *Journal of International Statistics, 62*, 53–82.
Wedeman, A. H. (2003). *From Mao to market: Rent seeking, local protectionism, and marketization in China*. Cambridge, UK: Cambridge University Press.
Young, A. (2000). The razor's edge: Distortions and incremental reform in the People's Republic of China. *Quarterly Journal of Economics, 115*, 1091–1135.

Printed in the United States
By Bookmasters